The Prosperous Years:
The Economic History of Ontario,
1939–1975

THE ONTARIO HISTORICAL STUDIES SERIES

The Ontario Historical Studies Series is a comprehensive history of Ontario from 1791 to the present, which will include several biographies of former premiers, numerous volumes on the economic, social, political, and cultural development of the province, and a general history incorporating the insights and conclusions of the other works in the series. The purpose of the series is to enable general readers and scholars to understand better the distinctive features of Ontario as one of the principal regions within Canada.

BOARD OF TRUSTEES

Margaret Angus, Kingston
J.M.S. Careless, Toronto
David Coombs, Burlington
R.E.G. Davis, Toronto
Edith Firth, Toronto

Gaetan Gervais, Sudbury
Jacqueline Neatby, Ottawa
James J. Talman, London
Charles Taylor, Toronto

PUBLISHED

J.M.S. Careless, ed *The Pre-Confederation Premiers: Ontario Government Leaders, 1841–1867* (1980)
Charles W. Humphries *'Honest Enough to Be Bold': The Life and Times of Sir James Pliny Whitney* (1985)
Peter Oliver *G. Howard Ferguson: Ontario Tory* (1977)

Christopher Armstrong *The Politics of Federalism: Ontario's Relations with the Federal Government, 1867–1942* (1981)
David Gagan *Hopeful Travellers: Families, Land and Social Change in Mid-Victorian Peel County, Canada West* (1981)
Robert M. Stamp *The Schools of Ontario, 1876–1976* (1982)
K.J. Rea *The Prosperous Years: The Economic History of Ontario, 1939–1975* (1985)

Olga B. Bishop, Barbara I. Irwin, Clara G. Miller, eds *Bibliography of Ontario History, 1867–1976: Cultural, Economic, Political, Social* 2 volumes (1980)
R. Louis Gentilcore and C. Grant Head *Ontario's History in Maps* (1984)
Joseph Schull *Ontario since 1867* (McClelland and Stewart 1978)

K.J. REA

The Prosperous Years:
The Economic History of Ontario
1939–1975

A PROJECT OF THE
ONTARIO HISTORICAL STUDIES SERIES
FOR THE GOVERNMENT OF ONTARIO
PUBLISHED BY UNIVERSITY OF TORONTO PRESS
TORONTO   BUFFALO   LONDON

© Her Majesty the Queen in right of the Province of Ontario 1985
Printed in Canada

ISBN 0-8020-2576-5

Canadian Cataloguing in Publication Data

Rea, K.J. (Kenneth John), 1932-
   The prosperous years

   (Ontario historical studies series, ISSN 0380-9188)
   Includes bibliographical references and index.
   ISBN 0-8020-2576-5

   1. Ontario – Economic conditions – 1918 – 1945.*
   2. Ontario – Economic conditions – 1945–*
   3. Ontario – Economic policy. I. Title. II. Series.

   HC117.O5R4 1985   330.9713'04   c85-099860-3

This book has been published with the assistance of funds provided by the Government of Ontario through the Ministry of Citizenship and Culture.

Contents

The Ontario Historical Studies Series
  Goldwin French, Peter Oliver, Jeanne Beck, and Maurice Careless *vii*

General Preface
  Ian Drummond *ix*

Preface *xi*

Tables *xiii*

Introduction *3*

1 War, Recovery, and Management of the Provincial Economy *14*

2 Population and Labour Force *26*

3 Land and Capital Resources *39*

4 Transportation and Communications *56*

5 The Services Sector, Trade, and Finance *82*

6 Education, Health, and Welfare *101*

7 Agriculture, Fishing, Fur Production, and Tourism *134*

8 Mines and Forests *162*

9 Manufacturing *193*

10 The Economic Role of the Provincial Government *223*

11 Conclusion *239*

Notes *257*

Index *279*

The Ontario Historical Studies Series

For many years the principal theme in English-Canadian historical writing has been the emergence and the consolidation of the Canadian nation. This theme has been developed in uneasy awareness of the persistence and importance of regional interests and identities, but because of the central role of Ontario in the growth of Canada, Ontario has not been seen as a region. Almost unconsciously, historians have equated the history of the province with that of the nation and have depicted the interests of other regions as obstacles to the unity and welfare of Canada.

The creation of the province of Ontario in 1867 was the visible embodiment of a formidable reality, the existence at the core of the new nation of a powerful if disjointed society whose traditions and characteristics differed in many respects from those of the other British North American colonies. The intervening century has not witnessed the assimilation of Ontario to the other regions in Canada; on the contrary it has become a more clearly articulated entity. Within the formal geographical and institutional framework defined so assiduously by Ontario's political leaders, an increasingly intricate web of economic and social interests has been woven and shaped by the dynamic interplay between Toronto and its hinterland. The character of this regional community has been formed in the tension between a rapid adaptation to the processes of modernization and industrialization in modern Western society and a reluctance to modify or discard traditional attitudes and values. Not surprisingly, the Ontario outlook is a compound of aggressiveness, conservatism, and the conviction that its values should be the model for the rest of Canada.

From the outset the objective of the Board of Trustees of the series has been to describe and analyse the historical development of Ontario as a distinct region within Canada. The series as planned will include some thirty-two volumes covering many aspects of the life and work of the province from its original establishment in 1791 as Upper Canada to our own time. Among these will be biographies of several premiers, numerous works on the growth of the provincial economy, educational institutions, minority groups, and the arts, and a synthesis of the history of Ontario, based upon the contributions of the biographies and thematic studies.

In planning this project, the editors and the board have endeavoured to maintain a reasonable balance between different kinds and areas of historical research and to appoint authors ready to ask new questions about the past and to answer them in accordance with the canons of contemporary scholarship. *The Prosperous Years: The Economic History of Ontario, 1939–1975* is the fourth theme study to be published and the third volume in a projected three-volume economic history of Ontario. It is a comprehensive account of the development of the provincial economy from the outbreak of the Second World War to the mid-1970s. This was a period characterized by steady economic growth, by the increasing importance of the services sector of the economy, and by the rapid expansion of the role of government in economic life. In these years, in Ontario as elsewhere 'people did not look to private interests to solve the problems of the day'; government policy was expected to shape the course of events. Thus, in this work, the author has emphasized 'the way ideas interacted with events, giving rise to outcomes which in the last analysis are not "explained" in the sense that they have been shown to be inevitable.'

Kenneth Rea has given us a very perceptive analysis of a crucial phase in the evolution of the Ontario economy. We hope that it will encourage others to examine closely the distinctive features of our economic history.

The editors and the Board of Trustees are grateful to Dr Rea for undertaking this task.

GOLDWIN FRENCH
PETER OLIVER
JEANNE BECK
MAURICE CARELESS, Chairman of the Board of Trustees

Toronto
3 September 1985

General Preface

The present volume is one of a series of three, which will treat the economic development of Ontario from the late eighteenth century until the middle of the 1970s. The first volume, by Douglas McCalla, will cover the period that ends with Confederation. The second, by Ian Drummond, will deal with the years from Confederation to the Second World War. The present volume surveys what most readers will see as the 'modern period.' Taken together, the three volumes are meant to provide a general narrative account of, as well as an interpretative and analytical comment on economic developments. Because the three authors have naturally chosen to emphasize different elements in their stories, because different sorts of questions properly and naturally emerge as decade follows decade, and partly because there is a parallel evolution in the documentary evidence, both numerical and qualitative, the three volumes will not conform to a single mould. Thus, for instance, McCalla must concern himself with settlement and with the role of agricultural subsistence production and the process of capital formation in early Ontario agriculture, while Rea has to give extensive consideration to questions of economic policy which in earlier decades arose in very different forms, or not at all. Similarly, the economic history of pre-Confederation Ontario can be written, and perhaps must be written, on the basis of archival materials, but no one could treat the modern period on such a basis: for the period since 1940 there is little archival documentation, while government statistics and government reports exist in great profusion. Inevitably, the character of the evidence affects the texture of the narrative. In principle, and to some extent in practice, the existing literature has the same effect. But on most topics in Ontario economic history the scholarly literature is remarkably scant, and the popular literature is strikingly uninformative. Thus none of the three authors could proceed by summarizing and synthesizing what others have written about the Ontario economy.

All three authors have tried to write for a wide audience. They supply the sorts of information that non-specialists would expect to find in a work of reference and avoid certain topics about which only other economists and historians would care. In the space and time available, no one could hope to be comprehensive. The three authors have conferred about coverage and distribution of emphasis, but since each writer has, in the end, made his own choices, the final products must reflect each one's decisions about importance and relevance. Although the three books form part of a single project, and although they will provide a single survey with a considerable unity of content, it is not to be expected that they will be homogeneous.

IAN DRUMMOND

Preface

My purpose in this book has been to provide a straightforward account of the development of the Ontario economy in the period between the beginning of the Second World War and the mid-1970s. The book is written with the general reader in mind. The economic theory employed is kept well in the background, further back than most of my professional colleagues will think appropriate. The underlying model of economic development used is not formally specified and consists of little more than a conventional classification of the components of a market-based economy with the production of goods and services determined by the quantity and quality of the principal inputs of labour, capital, natural resources, and enterprise, and with the structure of demand shaped by tastes and income levels in domestic and external markets. This organizational pattern is reflected in the table of contents.

While the period covered in this volume was notable for the high rates of real economic growth and the prolonged prosperity that followed the Great Depression of the 1930s, it was also characterized by the pervasive expansion of government's role in economic life. Although it is difficult to see why people came to believe that government could exert a significant influence on the course of economic events, it became commonplace during the years following the Depression and the war for governments, including the government of Ontario, to accept such responsibilities. Consequently, I have devoted considerable attention to the matter of economic policy, particularly at the provincial level, and in respect of this must acknowledge the assistance provided by the provincial government during the almost ten years the research for this volume was under way. The office of the premier granted us virtually unrestricted access to departmental files and other collections held by the Archives of Ontario which would not normally have been open to researchers for many years in the future. I must also express my thanks to those in public office for otherwise treating this project with benign neglect.

My other obligations are extensive. The substantial research funding provided by the Ontario Historical Studies Series supported a small but hard-working labour force of graduate and undergraduate students at the University of Toronto for several summers. I am particularly indebted to two senior researchers: Diane Way for her meticulous work in the Ontario Archives; and Cynthia Smith, who worked so effectively on the newspaper sources and a variety of other materials. The manuscript benefited from the criticism of my colleague Ian Drummond and others who read it at various stages. I also wish to thank the editors of the series, Goldwin French, Peter Oliver, and Jeanne Beck, for their generous support, friendly encouragement, and patience.

KENNETH REA
University of Toronto
May 1985

Tables

1 Employment in Service Industries, Canada, 1941 and 1971 *8*
2 Population of Ontario and Canada, Census Years 1941–71 *27*
3 Percentage Growth of the Population of Ontario by Five-Year Periods, 1941–75 *27*
4 Components of Population Growth, Ontario 1941–71 *29*
5 Distribution of Population by Major Age Groups, Ontario, 1941–71 *31*
6 Average Annual Unemployment Rate, Ontario, 1946–75 *34*
7 Private and Public Capital Expenditures on Construction and New Equipment, Ontario, Selected Years 1948–75 *43*
8 Value of Construction, Ontario, 1939–75 *44*
9 Dwelling Starts, Ontario, 1945–75 *50*
10 Engineering Construction by Type, Ontario, 1939–75 *51*
11 Highway and Road Mileage, Ontario, 1939–75 *52*
12 Motor Vehicle Registrations, Ontario, Selected Years 1939–75 *63*
13 Tonnage and Transits, St Lawrence Seaway, 1959–75 *70*
14 Telephones in Ontario *77*
15 Sectoral Composition of Output and Employment, Ontario, Selected Years 1940–75 *83*
16 Personal Income and Personal Income Per Capita, Selected Years 1941–75 *84*
17 Real Per Capita Personal Expenditure on Goods and Services, Ontario, Selected Years 1947–75 *85*
18 Imports and Exports, Ontario, Selected Years 1947–75 *86*
19 Retail Sales, Ontario, 1939–75 *88*
20 Total Enrolment and Teaching Staff, Elementary and Secondary Schools, Ontario, Selected Years 1940–75 *104*
21 Full-Time Non-University Post-Secondary Enrolment, Ontario, Selected Years 1955–75 *105*
22 Total Spending on Elementary and Secondary Education in Ontario by Level of Government, Selected Years 1946–71 *108*

xiv Tables

23 Hospital Bed Capacity, Ontario, Selected Years 1947–75 *116*
24 Patient Days, Public General and Allied Special Hospitals, Ontario, Selected Years 1953–75 *117*
25 Number of Physicians, Ontario, Selected Years 1941–75 *118*
26 Expenditures on Personal Health Care as a Percentage of GPP and Personal Income, Ontario, 1960–75 *119*
27 Per Capita Health Care Expenditures, Ontario, 1960–75 *119*
28 Expenditures on Income Maintenance, Ontario, 1946–71 *130*
29 Trends in Major Social Security Programs, Ontario, Selected Years 1959–75 *131*
30 Index Numbers of Physical Volume of Agricultural Production, Ontario, 1941–75 *135*
31 Census Farms Classified by Size of Farm, Ontario, 1951 and 1975 *136*
32 Quantity of Commercial Fish Landed and Persons Employed in Commercial Fishing, Ontario, 1939–75 *153*
33 Fur Production, Ontario, 1940–75 *156*
34 Volume and Value of Gold Production, Ontario, 1939–75 *165*
35 Volume and Value of Iron Ore Produciton, Ontario, 1939–75 *168*
36 Volume and Value of Uranium Production, Ontario, 1955–75 *172*
37 Volume and Value of Cobalt Production, Ontario, 1939–75 *173*
38 Volume and Value of Silver Production, Ontario, 1939–75 *175*
39 Volume and Value of Nickel Production, Ontario, 1939–75 *176*
40 Volume and Value of Copper Production, Ontario, 1939–75 *178*
41 Volume and Value of Zinc Production, Ontario, 1939–75 *180*
42 Primary Forest Production, Ontario, 1939–75 *185*
43 Value of Manufacturing Production, Ontario, 1939–75 *194*
44 Manufacturing Establishments and Total Employment, Ontario, 1939–75 *196*
45 Ontario's Share of Certain Large, Medium, and Small Manufacturing Industries in Canada, 1957 *198*
46 Position of Ontario's Leading Industries in Canadian Manufacturing, 1960 *199*
47 Twenty Leading Manufacturing Industries, Ontario, 1941 and 1971 *201*
48 Production of Steel Ingots and Castings, Ontario, 1939–75 *211*
49 Production of Wood Pulp, Ontario, 1940–75 *215*
50 Production of Wood Pulp by Process, Ontario, 1946, 1966, 1973 *216*
51 Ratio of Government Spending on Goods and Services and Capital Formation to Gross Provincial Expenditure, Ontario, 1951–75 *225*

The Prosperous Years:
The Economic History of Ontario
1939–1975

Introduction

The economic history of the province of Ontario from the end of the Great Depression to the mid-1970s closely paralleled that of the Canadian economy as a whole. Had the general economic history of Canada been written for this recent period, most of the developments in Ontario could have been derived from it with only a few modifications. But contemporary Canadian economic historians have not been interested in surveying general trends and extending the broad treatment of earlier periods into the recent past. They have concentrated instead on applying the techniques of econometric analysis to a narrow range of earlier topics, producing detailed reinterpretations of the traditional account of the country's past.[1] While this neglect of the larger view of 'recent' Canadian economic development cannot be rectified here, it may be useful by way of introduction to provide a brief overview of the national economic context in which the Ontario economy functioned during this period and to comment on certain problems of interpretation that arise in connection with it.

The National Economic Context: Stability of the System

Although the depths of the great collapse were already several years in the past, the Canadian economy in the late 1930s was still struggling out of the most serious depression in history. Unemployment had peaked in 1933 when 20 per cent of the Canadian labour force had been without work; the price level had fallen slightly in the first few years of the Depression, then increased gradually to become almost stable in 1937 and 1938, and declined slightly again in 1939.[2] More than 11 per cent of the labour force in 1939 remained unemployed.

Recovery from the Depression accelerated remarkably when the war began. As the level of total spending in the economy increased, unemployment declined rapidly, incomes rose, and inflation became a concern. A substantial part of the potential labour force was absorbed into the armed forces: 9,000 in 1939, 107,000 in 1940. The numbers in military service subsequently grew rapidly, reaching 779,000 in 1944. The total civilian labour force remained virtually constant during the war years. The number of persons 'without jobs and seeking work' declined from 529,000 in 1939 to 63,000 in 1944 – an unemployment rate of less than 1.4 per cent.

Price controls and rationing were imposed by the federal government to restrain the inflationary pressures generated by the high levels of government spending on military goods and services, rising levels of private investment, increased consumption, and booming export markets. With the aid of wage and price controls, the overall increase in prices was held reasonably well in check: the GNE price deflator rose from 33.1 in 1940 to 40.8 in 1945.

At the end of the war the expected post-war recession did not materialize. The economy operated at high levels of employment and, even after the removal of controls, without serious inflation through the remainder of the 1940s. So strong were the underlying forces of growth that, despite rapid expansion of the civilian labour force, unemployment remained below 4 per cent until well into the 1950s.

Early in the 1950s heavy military spending in the United States associated with the Korean War and other pressures on aggregate demand spilled over into Canada and caused a sharp increase in the price level. As these pressures subsided, Canadians experienced several years of relative economic stability with the average annual rate of inflation over the 1953–9 period running at about 1.2 per cent. Unemployment averaged 4.7 per cent. There were, however, growing concerns about the performance of the economy. By the late 1950s a recession in the United States, declining investment spending, a growing current account deficit, rising unemployment, and a surprising persistence of inflation led to intense debate over appropriate economic policy measures, particularly with respect to the monetary strategy advocated by James Coyne, governor of the Bank of Canada.[3] The uncertainty surrounding the conduct of the nation's economic affairs was increased when the long period of Liberal government rule in Ottawa was interrupted by the Conservative victory in 1957.

The recession of the late 1950s ended in the early 1960s. Mr Coyne was replaced as governor of the bank in July 1961, monetary policy was loosened, unemployment began to decline, and the value of the Canadian dollar fell on the exchanges. In May 1962 the dollar was pegged at 92.5 cents U.S., well below the values that had prevailed under the floating exchange rate regime adopted in 1950. Fiscal policies in both the United States and Canada were strongly expansionary. The Canadian federal budgets of the years from 1962 to 1965 increased spending and reduced taxation. In the United States spending was encouraged by the Kennedy tax cut of 1964 and subsequently by heavy military outlays related to the war in Viet Nam, outlays that were not offset by increased taxation. Canadian exports to the United States boomed. Aggregate demand in Canada increased faster than output could be expanded, unemployment dropped from 7.1 per cent in 1961 to 3.6 per cent in 1966, and the country experienced another bout of severe inflation. Between the mid-1960s and the end of the decade the average annual rate of increase in the general price level rose from 2.4 to 4.6 per cent.

The high levels of Canadian exports in the late 1960s helped generate large balance of payments surpluses in Canada. In order to maintain the fixed value of the Canadian dollar on the foreign exchanges, the monetary authorities in Canada were forced to buy up large quantities of foreign exchange. The result was to increase the cash reserves of the commercial banks and cause the money supply in Canada to expand faster than was compatible with the central bank's efforts to limit the domestic inflation rate. To break out of this situation, at the end of May 1970 the bank abandoned the fixed exchange rate for the Canadian dollar and again allowed it to float.[4] The currency quickly rose to near parity with the U.S. dollar. But instead of exploiting the possibility this created to pursue a more restrictive monetary policy and possibly to keep the Canadian inflation rate lower than the American, the bank continued to allow the money supply to expand, perhaps because the priority in economic policy was shifting from the control of inflation to the management of unemployment. For whatever reason, the economy was allowed to expand and the inflation rate continued to rise. Despite a recovery in economic activity in 1972 and 1973, the unemployment rate remained high (5.5 per cent), and, to the surprise of policy-makers and most economists, the inflation rate too not only remained high but increased sharply, reaching 7.5 per cent in 1973. Part of the explanation of what was happening must lie in the severe shock given to the international economy by the OPEC oil embargo of 1973 and the ensuing increases in oil prices, although disagreement continues among analysts as to the real impact of these events on the Canadian economy.

The onset of a protracted world depression in the mid-1970s marked the end of a thirty-five-year period of generally strong economic growth during which the main concern with respect to the performance of the economy was its short-term stability as measured by annual fluctuations in national income, price levels, the unemployment rate, and the country's balance of payments position.

By the mid-1970s, however, worries about the short-term performance of the economy – the coexistence of high levels of unemployment, an apparently rising rate of inflation, and very high interest rates – were accompanied by a potentially more sinister and analytically more challenging economic phenomenon: a massive slowing down in the rate of economic growth and a sharp drop in productivity.

In Canada and other industrial countries of the West the recurrence of what threatened to become a major world-wide depression forced policy-makers and their advisers to confront problems that had been largely out of mind since the early 1940s, problems that had almost become 'unthinkable' within the framework of mainstream economic doctrine.

The National Economic Context: Growth and Productivity

The facts of the situation were clear. Since the end of the war the Gross National Product (GNP) had grown rapidly if irregularly. Much of this growth in real output was attributable to increasing supplies of labour, capital, and other productive factors. But about half the 2.7 per cent average annual growth of real GNP in the post-war period to 1973 was due to rising labour productivity.[5]

In the early 1970s this increase in labour productivity decelerated sharply. Whereas productivity per man hour had been growing at about 3.6 per cent annually in the 1950s and 1960s, the rate fell to about 1 per cent in 1973 and remained approximately the same during the rest of the decade.

What caused this break in the post-war trend? At the time of writing, economists had to admit that they did not know. A number of hypotheses were advanced. One was that the environmental protection measures in the 1960s pushed up costs and discouraged investment. Another was that for some reason outlays on research and development fell and caused a decline in the rate of technological improvement. Nearly everyone believed that the enormous increase in energy prices in the mid-1970s must have had something to do with the situation, although it was difficult to show how. It was even suggested that the whole thing was a statistical illusion caused by the difficulties encountered in deflating prices to get output estimates comparable with earlier periods. But even the elementary textbooks, which normally adopt a positive tone in discussing the limitations of economic analysis, accepted the fact that 'we simply do not know with any degree of confidence the reasons for the drastic deterioration in the productivity performance of the Canadian economy during the 1970s.'[6] Similarly, Denny and Fuss, the leading authorities on the productivity of the firm in Canada, wrote in the early 1980s that 'we have no concise explanation of the current slowdown.'[7]

What is known is that the Canadian experience was not unique. Similar decreases in the rate of productivity growth were observed at the same time in other countries, notably in the United States.

While there was obviously an important connection between the short-run, cyclical performance of the national economy in the mid-1970s and the slowdown in growth and productivity, it appeared to many observers that something more was happening than simply another swing in the business cycle which existing tools of economic management were for one reason or another incapable of dealing with effectively; it seemed likely that there were underlying, long-term structural changes taking place as well.

The National Economic Context: Structure and Organization

While the connection between the general structural changes referred to above and the slowing of economic growth in the 1970s (followed by its eventual cessation by the end of the decade) remains tenuous, the experience of the mid-1970s served to redirect attention to aspects of economic performance that had been neglected since the 1930s. The preoccupation with the effect of changes on the demand side of the system associated with the dominant Keynesian school of analysis was modified by renewed interest in forces that might be operating on the supply side of the economy. Interest also revived in the analysis of long-run economic growth, a topic that had begun to claim attention in Canada with the development of nationalistic sentiments in the 1960s and was stimulated by the perception that the Canadian economy was growing more slowly than a number of other industrial economies were. There ensued a flurry of studies and reports by public agencies and numerous books and articles by Canadian academics examining the evolution and performance of the Canadian economy. Many of these studies sought to link the economy's perceived shortcomings to foreign ownership and the country's dependence on the United States.[8]

Much of this concern focused on the characteristics of the Canadian manufacturing industries. Surprisingly little attention was paid to another structural feature of the economy that was equally conspicuous: the growing importance of the service industries as a source of employment and income for Canadian workers relative to manufacturing and other goods-producing activities.

The Services Economy

While the distinction between goods-producing and services-producing industries is rather arbitrary and the interconnections among such activities are strong, it is customary to define the services sector as comprising wholesale and retail trade; finance; insurance and real estate; general government; and the services proper, including professional, personal, business, and repair services. The goods-producing or 'industry' sector may be defined to include agriculture, mining, forestry, trapping and fishing, manufacturing, and construction. Some industries, such as transportation and communications, which literally produce services, are often put in the latter category as well on the grounds that they are large-scale operations that require large amounts of capital equipment.[9]

Nearly all the net increase in new jobs created in Canada during the period of rapid economic expansion between the end of the war and the mid-1970s was attributable to the growth of industries producing services. Although employment also increased in some goods-producing industries, it declined greatly in others: rising employment in manufacturing, for example, was largely offset by declining employment in agriculture and other primary industries.

In 1941 employment in the services sector accounted for 33.5 per cent of total employment in Canada. In 1971 the percentage was 50.9. Of the 4,430,974 new jobs created during these thirty years, 2,975,211, or over 67 per cent, were in services. The 421,278 new jobs created in the health and welfare fields during this period exceeded the total 1971 employment in a number of major goods-

8 The Prosperous Years

TABLE 1
Employment in Service Industries, Canada, 1941 and 1971
(numbers of workers)

	1941*	1971†
Retail and wholesale trade	496,150	1,269,290
Finance, insurance, real estate	89,680	358,060
Education	110,946	569,485
Health and welfare services	91,812	513,090
Food and lodging	120,320	331,500
Personal and recreational	263,395	253,555
Other services	91,315	373,750
Government	139,636	709,705
Total	1,403,254	4,378,435

* 'Gainfully Occupied'
† 'Labour Force'
SOURCE: F.H. Leacy, ed., *Historical Statistics of Canada*, 2nd ed. (Ottawa: Statistics Canada, 1983), D8–85

producing industries, including, for example, the 'wood products, paper and publishing' category.

Part of the explanation for this structural shift lies in the relative rates of productivity increase in the two sectors. While it is very difficult to measure the productivity of labour in the services sector, evidence suggests that it grew more slowly over this period than was the case in many of the goods-producing industries. An expanding output of goods was possible with a relatively slow growth (in the case of agriculture an actual absolute decline) in the number employed. Most of the service industries were different in this respect. The nature of these industries made it difficult to standardize products, to mechanize or automate operations, or to achieve economies of scale. Thus, while the total output of goods and services increased (and the composition of total output probably remained much the same, with goods and services accounting for about the same proportions of total output in the 1970s as in the 1940s), the productivity gains in the goods industries reduced their labour requirements relative to the requirements of the service sector.

The Theoretical Context

The period from 1939 to the mid-1970s was marked by the widespread acceptance of a great new system of economic doctrine, modern 'macro-economics' and, more narrowly, the particular founding version of macro-economic analysis associated with the British economist, John Maynard Keynes. Most of the categories by which we understand the major economic events of the period are defined by this body of ideas. The economic history of the years since the 1930s must consequently be written using concepts that themselves were a product of the period and probably influenced the real-world events taking place during it. This interaction of real-world events and our theoretical understanding of them raise methodological conundrums which cannot be explored here, but two brief digressions appear to be required: one (which may well be ignored by a reader acquainted with elementary economic analysis) is a brief sketch of the main elements of the Keynesian analysis; the other concerns the way considerations of economic theory have affected the form and substance of this particular volume.

The Keynesian Theory

Modern macro-economics has its origins in the efforts of Keynes to explain why, contrary to the accepted doctrine of his time, a capitalist economy could experience prolonged periods of unemployment, operating at levels of total output well below the full capacity of the system, as was the case in the 1930s. His explanation ran in terms of aggregate demand: the level of output and employment in the economy could fall below capacity and remain below capacity if the total amount of spending in the system was less than was required to maintain output at the full-employment level. The expert opinion of the time was that this problem could not persist, because prices would fall, consumers would find themselves better off, and spending would increase; if unemployment existed, money wages would fall and producers would be encouraged to increase employment; if savings were excessive, interest rates would fall and saving would be discouraged – that is, spending would increase. Such automatic mechanisms built into the market system would ensure that the economy would operate near full capacity, with departures from this desired equilibrium instigating self-correcting adjustments. Keynes argued convincingly that such mechanisms were unlikely to operate effectively.

In a closed economy, one without significant foreign trade, total demand would be the sum of all the spending done on consumer goods and services and on capital goods (machinery and equipment, structures, inventories, and other goods used in the production process). There was some reason to believe, based on the evidence then beginning to accumulate through studies of total spending in Britain and the United States, that as the level of national incomes rose, consumption spending would absorb a decreasing share of total output. The deficiency in total spending needed to maintain capacity operation would have to be met by investment spending – spending on capital goods. But because the latter type of spending was strongly influenced by the outlook of businessmen with respect to future profits, it was possible that a shortfall of total spending could become chronic as an economy matured. In the short run, business spending on capital goods could be extremely variable, giving rise to sharp changes in the level of total spending, even if consumption spending remained (as we later learned was likely to be the case) more or less a stable function of the income individuals received. The policy prescription seemed obvious: some way had to be found to stimulate spending during periods of deficient aggregate demand. The possibilities of increasing consumer spending appeared to be distinctly limited. Investment spending was another matter. Private investment spending might be stimulated by using the government's control over the supply of money and credit to reduce interest rates, thereby making it cheaper to borrow and more attractive to invest (to spend on capital goods). Even more direct and, to many early Keynesians, more desirable for other reasons, would be to have the government undertake the necessary spending. From whatever source, increased spending was expected to have an effect on the level of output and employment greater than the amount by which spending was increased initially. The theory of the 'multiplier' showed how an initial increase in spending could give rise to successive 'rounds' of spending as new income received by some people found its way into the hands of others and, as they increased their spending, to others, and so on.

In an open economy – one like Canada's with a large foreign trade sector – this analysis had to be considerably modified. (If the analysis were to be applied to a subnational economy such as that of a Canadian province, the modifications would be even more extensive, but similar in kind.) In such an economy exports would constitute a major component in total spending (in 'aggregate demand'). Sales of goods and services to foreigners would have an effect on the level of employment and output in the country similar to consumption or investment or net government spending. Spending on imports would have an opposite effect, similar to the effect of consumers' not spending on domestic production (i.e., saving). Thus, a depression in the United States, Canada's main trading partner, would reduce demand for Canadian-produced goods and, unless offset by some increase in spending within Canada, would reduce aggregate demand in Canada, thereby causing a drop in output and unemployment.

To the extent that the amount Canadians spent on imports seemed likely to be determined by the level of incomes received by Canadians, any fall in Canadian incomes would result in a fall in imports as well. But again, one could not count on such a reduction in imports being equal in magnitude to the fall in exports. If it were not, the net effect of foreign trade could be to lower output below the full-employment level. A further implication of this analysis was that if consumers in a country had a fairly strong tendency to buy imported goods (a strong 'propensity to import'), this would reduce the size of the multiplier effect. Since any new spending (by governments, for example) would lead to increased incomes some part of which would be spent to buy imports, the net effect of the initial new spending on income in the system would be less than if the propensity to import were low. Under such conditions the effectiveness of efforts to stimulate the economy and to offset a chronic tendency towards inadequate demand could be severely restricted – unless, of course, practical ways could be found to control the volume of trade – by means of exchange-rate manipulation, commercial policies (export subsidies, tariff negotiations, etc.), or direct controls. The general direction suggested by such analysis was, apparently, increased government intervention in the economy.

Two other aspects of the Keynesian system warrant our attention here. One is the fact that the analysis focused attention on relatively short periods of time; as conventionally interpreted, this was a theory designed to explain short-run fluctuations in the level of national income. As already indicated, however, it also had possible long-run implications, both in its early versions, which were influential in North America in the late 1930s and early 1940s and later, in the 1950s, when a number of economists devised Keynesian growth models that emphasized (we would now say exaggerated) the role of capital creation in economic growth. As will be shown in more detail later, the earliest interpreters of Keynes and certainly his principal American popularizer, Alvin Hansen, linked the idea of deficient aggregate demand to the view that the depression of the 1930s was more a secular than a cyclical phenomenon, suggesting that the western industrial world was experiencing the end of a long period of capitalist development, not just another downturn in the business cycle. And this point brings us to how Keynesianism has affected the present study.

It is not uncommon for economic historians to interpret the past using the wisdom, or at least the theoretical dogmas, of the present. Economic history is conventionally written by experts who have confidence in the analytical techniques of their time. This bias is probably unavoidable and it may in many ways be desirable, particularly if the theoretical perspective is clearly defined. The approach used here, however, is different. The emphasis throughout this volume is on the way ideas interacted with events, giving rise to outcomes which in the last analysis are not 'explained,' in the sense that they have been shown to be inevitable. A great deal of attention is given to government policy, not because it can be shown that policy greatly affected the course of events in Ontario during this period, but because so many people apparently expected it to – or at least behaved as though they expected it to. If the activities of the private sector are neglected, it is because they were not the focus of attention; they may have been of overwhelming practical importance, but such was the fashion of thought that people did not look to private interests to solve the problems of the day. Attention rested on the possibilities of control, regulation, manipulation. Keynesianism was part of an intellectual environment, shared with democratic socialism and other anti-individualistic, collectivist movements that had gained strength from the experiences of the inter-war years, which legitimized the abandonment of laissez-faire as the ideal (however infrequently practised) upon which to model the economic role of government in a democratic society. Thus, the beginning of the 1940s was marked by a growing acceptance of government intervention in economic life and intense interest in the mechanics of economic control. Thirty-five years later, in the mid-1970s, confidence in intervention was on the wane and the intellectual systems that had inspired it were under severe attack – if not yet in ruins. This was particularly true of Keynesian economics, whose practitioners, while still powerful and still in command of the introductory textbooks, were devoting much skill and ingenuity to fending off the attacks of resurrected neoclassical economists.

A further limitation on the direct applicability of modern macro-economics to the present study derives from the fact that it relates to a subnational political-economic entity. Just as the 'openness' of the Canadian economy introduces the substantial complexities of international trade and factor movements at the national level, the even greater openness of the provincial economy exacerbates such analytical difficulties. The problem is further aggravated by the relatively primitive state of provincial 'national income' accounting.[10] While much current work is being done to develop formal models that may be used to study the behaviour of the Ontario economy in relation to that of the country as a whole, it has not been possible, given the current state of this activity and the resources available to the present study, to apply such a model in any systematic way.

It seems appropriate, therefore, to acknowledge that the theoretical perspective employed in this study has been less positive than it might have been had modern macro-economics, particularly in its long-term applications, been more securely established. While it is possible to use many of the definitions and relationships embodied in modern short-run economics, both 'micro' and 'macro,' to clarify particular events, the existing body of orthodox economic theory simply does not provide the kind of comprehensive explanation of economic change that could serve as the framework for this kind of study.

If what is needed is a framework within which to organize an account of long-term economic growth in a major subnational economy, what use might be found for the Canadian economic historian's traditional approach, the 'staple theory'? In its most general form, this approach directed attention to a succession of major export-based industries – codfish, fur, eastern wheat and timber, prairie wheat, and then the minerals, pulp and paper, and hydroelectric industries of the Canadian Shield – which earlier Canadian economic historians saw as leading the forces of growth and change in the Canadian economy from the 1500s to perhaps as late as the 1940s. In a more highly specified form (developed in the 1950s and 1960s) the staple theory became a theory of export-led growth in which the national economy grew as a consequence of expanding export trade in such 'staple' goods, whose economic impact was transmitted to the national economy through a network of 'linkages.'[11] In yet another version, the staple approach turned into a theory of economic underdevelopment, highlighting the

Canadian economy's dependence not only on export markets but on another nation's enterprise, capital, and culture as an alternative to developing indigenous economic and cultural forms.[12] While there is much in these various versions of the staple theory that relates to the problem of accounting for the economic development of Ontario – the approach generally is well suited to explaining regional experience in this country – it is perhaps least suited to the particular experience of Ontario, especially after 1940, because of the provincial economy's high degree of internal integration and its substantial manufacturing sector. Relative to the rest of Canada, Ontario in this period functioned more as a centre than as a periphery. It is also difficult to imagine that the province's growth after 1940 was led by the expansion of exports such as minerals, pulp and paper, or agricultural goods, given the relatively small share of the value of total production attributable to these industries. Again, then, the traditional staple approach, like the more modern macro-economic theories of growth and change, may be invoked to explain certain features of Ontario's growth and development in the period but must be rejected as a general theory around which to organize the treatment of the material.

Because of the particular attention paid to the role of government in modern economic life, it must also be acknowledged that the present study lacks the benefit of a theory of government policy. Despite the rise of a new discipline, 'policy science' in the 1960s and 1970s and the efforts of economists to devise theories of public decision-making based on micro-economic models of rational choice, no operational model exists that could be used in this kind of work to predict the behaviour of governments, either in the present or in the past. Considerable attention is given in what follows to the making of public policy, at least to the extent that it has been possible to describe what those involved in the process seemed to think the problems were and the way they might best be addressed. Extensive use has been made of ministerial papers and the records left by commissions of inquiry in an effort to capture something of the reasoning or attitudes underlying particular economic policies. Some limited use was also made of newspapers and other ephemeral sources to identify popular perceptions of economic problems and issues. But the purpose has been to discover these ideas and to relate them to the events of the time. In the present state of knowledge little confidence can be placed in judgments of their intrinsic merit.

1 War, Recovery, and Management of the Provincial Economy

Ontario in 1940 was Canada's wealthiest and most economically developed province. Approximately one out of every three Canadians lived there. More than 40 per cent of the country's Gross National Product and over 50 per cent of its total manufacturing production originated in the province. Many of Canada's most important industrial activities were concentrated in Ontario, notably the iron and steel and automobile industries. Although the province lacked fuel resources, it had cheap access to high-grade coal deposits in the United States and its own highly-developed hydroelectric power system. The province's other natural resource assets were extensive and varied. Much of the country's most productive and versatile farmland was found in Ontario and what it lacked in fertility and suitability for certain large-scale farming methods, it made up for in being located close to the principal markets. Dairying was a long-established industry well integrated into the processing and manufacturing systems. Belief in the possibility of further extensions of agricultural settlement into new regions of the province remained alive, despite the unhappy experiences of the interwar years on the northern agricultural frontier. The province's forest industries were extensively developed, although much attention was being given to the problems they too had faced in the recent past. The mining industry was in a similar situation, long established, badly disrupted by the Depression, but still important. In 1940 Ontario's mineral production accounted for just under half the value of Canadian mineral output as a whole.

The province also occupied a dominant position in many of the service industries – in retail and wholesale trade, banking, insurance, and publishing. Toronto shared with Montreal dominion over much of the financial and commercial life of the nation and like its rival occupied a strategic position in the transportation and communications networks of the country. It was indisputably the business capital of English Canada and, for all its drabness in the early 1940s, its cultural capital as well.

Yet for all the commercial and cultural importance of Toronto and some of the province's smaller urban centres, Ontario in the 1940s retained much of the region's traditional rural character. The natural-resource-based industries still yielded more than a quarter of the net value of commodity production in the province, and within this natural resource sector farming was far more important than mining, forestry, or even hydroelectric power generation as a source of value. Over 38 per cent of the population lived in the countryside, and there was some substance to the cliché about farming's being the province's 'basic' industry. Economically, socially, and politically, farmers were important.

This overall economic structure supported a society that was entrenched by Canadian standards, and stable. More than 80 per cent of the province's population claimed English as the mother tongue. More than 94 per cent had been born in either Canada, the British Isles, Newfoundland, or the United States. Over 80 per cent had been born in Canada and more than 75 per cent within the province itself. Some 70 per cent claimed adherence to protestant churches.[1]

The stability of the society was particularly evident in rural areas.There, life had changed little, except for having become poorer and harder for most people during the decade just past. The number of farms had decreased somewhat since the early 1920s (declining from 198,000 to 178,000), but the amount of improved acreage was approximately the same in 1941 as in 1921. The value of farm production was recovering from the low levels of the late 1930s and in 1940 was almost back to what it had been at the beginning of the Depression.[2]

The process of agricultural mechanization had slowed during the Depression, but by 1941 25 per cent of Ontario farms had a tractor, 5 per cent a threshing machine, and 9.5 per cent a motor truck.[3] Nor had farm life yet been much altered by the introduction of modern household conveniences. Although 37 per cent of Ontario farmhouses had electric lighting (well above the national average of 20 per cent), almost 90 per cent still relied on outdoor toilets.[4]

Life in the towns and cities had also changed little since the 1920s. Because of the low levels of investment in residential and business structures and the financial plight of most municipal governments, the material fabric of urban Ontario had changed only for the worse. In many communities, especially in the resource towns of the north, social capital had actually been consumed. Most municipalities were still dumping their sewage untreated into lakes and rivers, although a few of the larger ones had succeeded in making improvements in their sewer and water-supply systems. The only other tangible evidence of material progress was in the highways and roads which the provincial government had continued to build, with the magnificent Queen Elizabeth Way between Toronto and Niagara serving as the showpiece. Airports and air passenger services were also showing some improvement. The railways were still important, but passenger services were beginning to decline, and trucking was taking over much of the short-haul freight traffic as well.

Politics and public administration were important elements in the life of the province, but quantitatively, government was not a major force in the economy.

Provincial government spending in Ontario was actually declining at the beginning of the period. The total outlays of the province and its municipalities (including school boards) fell by about 30 per cent between 1939 and 1945.[5]

In the mind of the premier, Mitchell Hepburn, the province's economic growth had reached a kind of plateau, and there appeared to be little that government could do to alter this state of affairs. The great issues of the day were of a more immediate kind: the war effort, federal-provincial relations, and the arrival of industrial unionism in the province. The government's role in the economy was essentially that of regulator, although some efforts were made to promote resource development and other industrial ventures when the opportunity arose to do so. The civil service was an insignificant source of employment (but useful, nevertheless, as part of the patronage system). The government's total spending amounted to less than 7 per cent of the estimated value of provincial production.

Under Hepburn the budgetary policies of the government were by preference conservative. Although the disasters of the 1930s had made deficits unavoidable, it was the government's intention to balance the budget and when possible to generate surpluses to be used for debt reduction. If Keynesian ideas about government financing were beginning to infiltrate the bureaucracy in Ottawa, there were no signs of a similar movement in Ontario. And with respect to the more mundane matters of day-to-day public administration in the province, there is no reason to disagree with the assessment made by Hepburn's biographer when he writes that 'on the whole, the Hepburn years at Queen's Park ... were years of efficient government.'[6]

After 1940 the economy of Ontario was almost completely transformed. Neither the nature nor the magnitude of the changes about to take place appears to have been foreseen. The expert consensus was that the end of the war would bring a return to the conditions that prevailed before it began. In Ottawa planning for the post-war period was oriented to such expectations. At the provincial level there appears to have been greater uncertainty about the likely course of events, but there is nothing in the pronouncements of the political leaders or public-affairs commentators to suggest that they anticipated the powerful changes in thought and action that were soon to alter the character of the province more profoundly than at any time since the turn of the century.

These changes are described in the following chapters. Many of the established patterns of resource development and industrial expansion that characterized earlier periods continued into the war and post-war decades. What stands out in this period, however, is the way the citizens and their elected representatives perceived the functioning of the economic system and their relationship to it.

As elsewhere, in Ontario there was a marked decline in confidence in the market system. There was a corresponding burgeoning of interest in the possibilities for deliberate management of the economy so as to achieve certain widely accepted social goals. While there remained some enthusiasm for the co-operative and other forms of voluntary collective activity, most of the responsibility for such efforts came to be lodged with the government. At the federal level interest focused on the possibility of stabilizing the economy at high levels of income and employment by utilizing the instruments of fiscal and monetary policy. The appropriate role of the provincial governments was not so clear, partly because of the constitutional uncertainties inherent in the country's federal system, but also because the theory of economic management was not articulated for subnational units in the way that the Keynesian doctrine was for a nation as a whole. Nevertheless, the provincial government, as the following account will demonstrate, did come to be held responsible for and did come to accept responsibility for intervening in the economic life of the province in a deliberate and at times aggressive manner.

While an active economic role for government at any level was far from being a new concept in Canada, the scale and openness of the intervention demanded in the 1939–75 period was unprecedented. While many of those who implemented this intervention appear to have been bound by a tacit understanding that what was being done to erode even further the system of market economy should never be recognized as such, it is difficult to find any area of economic activity in the province that was not subjected to some form of deliberate intervention during this thirty-five-year period.

The results of all this effort are difficult to identify. It is not even clear that the net effect of the provincial government's interventions was even consequential. It is interesting and instructive, however, to examine in some detail this distinctive feature of the period. What the following account will suggest is that despite the advances in economic knowledge over the period, policy-makers and their advisers lacked a sufficient understanding of the forces bringing about economic change to affect it in predictable ways. But even if they had possessed better information and all the technical ability needed to act upon it, the record set out in the following chapters will show that the root of the problem lay not in implementing policy but in determining the goals to which it should be directed.

Shortly after the war began, the Conservative party in Ontario formulated a remarkably broad and aggressive economic plan for the province, a plan that formed most of its platform for the 1943 provincial election. Thirty years later, the Conservative government, after an uninterrupted succession of election victories, renounced such interventions in the economy and dedicated itself to bringing under control not the economy but its own involvement in it.

When in 1943 the Toronto *Globe and Mail* hailed the '22 Points' declaration of the Conservatives as a 'great social document' the paper was undoubtedly playing its partisan role, but its editorial writer was right in noting that the declaration was more than just another collection of campaign promises. It could properly be regarded, he asserted, as a 'whole plan' for the future of the province, a plan through which the people of Ontario could begin 'intensively to plan the use and development' of the province's resources. There was also a broad suggestion that such an initiative would serve to return to the province the initiative in economic policy preempted by the federal government during the war.[7]

Certainly the 22 Points declaration was an eloquent invocation of the attitudes and expectations that underlay much of the economic and social policy activity of the next quarter of a century. Ideologically, it carried forward something of the tradition of the old Canadian conservatism of Sir John A. Macdonald, a tradition that incorporated the view that active government participation in the economic development of the country was appropriate, so long as it was consistent with the fostering of business enterprise and general expansion. It also owed something to the ideology, or at least to the rhetoric, of the Canadian left. While George Drew, the Conservative leader with whose name the new program was linked, greatly feared the socialists and communists of his day, he was not above appropriating the concept of comprehensive economic planning they advocated. Despite his diatribes against the intellectual leaders of the left, notably Professor Frank Underhill of the University of Toronto, a man he characterized as one of the 'evil geniuses' behind the provincial CCF party, Drew himself recognized the value of a systematic and coherent view of the government's role in the economy. By 1943 this appreciation was no longer difficult even for non-socialists. The idea of 'planning' for a better world without necessarily accepting complete collectivization was prevalent at the time. While the 22 Points program was being drafted, one of the architects of the British welfare state, Sir William Beveridge, was in Canada explaining how Keynesian principles and comprehensive social welfare programs would be combined to eliminate poverty in post-war Britain.[8] Various groups in Canada were exploring similar possibilities. The Canadian Association for Adult Education, for example, meeting in London, Ontario, concluded its deliberations on the subject of post-war Canada by accepting the 'principle of planning,' while noting that 'planning need not necessarily involve active Government ownership of, control over, or interference with industrial or agricultural enterprise.'[9]

The Conservatives' 22 Points declaration began with statements intended to define the external relationships of the province in the post-war period. First, Ontario would maintain British institutions, and the government would attempt to strengthen the British connection 'by every means within the constitutional power of the government of Ontario.' Second, Ontario would co-operate with the federal government in its war effort and in establishing a basis for comprehensive social security, health insurance, and protection in old age. However, the province would at the same time insist that the 'constitutional rights of the people of Ontario be preserved and that the Government of Ontario exercise full control of its own Provincial affairs.'[10] The declaration then went on to deal with the great worry of the time, post-war unemployment. Appropriate legislation would be enacted to provide support for all branches of the provincial economy – farms, factories, mines, forests, and personal services – so as to increase employment at good wages. Taxes would be reduced and 'bureaucratic restriction' removed so as to encourage individual initiative and hard work.

The particular problems of agriculture were addressed by the promise to create a new form of collective organization. In every county, committees of 'outstanding farmers' would be established and given authority to plan production and regulate the processing and distribution of farm output. Marketing boards, milk distributors, central produce markets, and creameries would also be put under the supervision of committees, again made up of 'outstanding farmers in each line of production.' This implied excursion into a kind of guild socialism or syndicalism was accompanied by a more conventional measure – stockyards would be taken over by the government and operated as a public utility to eliminate speculation and price manipulation and to ensure the maintenance of 'fair prices.'

Industrial relations were to be investigated by a new committee which would provide equal representation for labour, employers, and the general public. Its recommendations would be embodied in a new act which would provide the basis for 'justice, co-operation and responsibility' in the labour relations field.

The mining industry was to be aided in 'every practical way' so that it could provide as much employment as possible. Specific measures included tax reduction, appropriation by the province and municipalities of a greater share of total mining taxes, and removal of all 'restrictive measures which deny prospectors and others the inducement to find and develop new mining properties.'

The employment potential of the forest industries was also recognized, and it was proposed that they be placed under the control of an 'Ontario Forest Resources Commission.' This would be a powerful body capable of implementing policies of reforestation, long-term conservation, and soil management. Its first task would be to review all existing forest contracts and to 'cancel those which have disposed of great areas of forest resources without proper consideration.'

The housing situation in the province would be dealt with by yet another commission, which would plan 'a great housing program throughout the province' so as to create employment and bring an end to unsatisfactory housing conditions.

Property taxation would be reformed so that the 'owning and improving of homes and farms, which are the very foundation of our society will not be discouraged by excessive taxation.' The first step would be taken by the province's assuming 'at least 50 per cent of the school taxes now charged against real estate.'

The educational system would be completely reorganized so that 'every child in this province will have an opportunity to be educated to the full extent of their mental capacity, no matter where they live or what the financial circumstances of their parents may be.' Vocational training would be expanded and the 'important place of our teachers in each community' would be fully recognized. Similarly, health programs would be developed to enable every child to have 'the greatest possible opportunity to face life with a healthy body and mind.' Measures would be introduced to ensure that 'medical, dental and other health protection' would be 'available to all.'

Unemployment after the war would be reduced by a number of 'great public undertakings.' The hydroelectric system would be greatly expanded, rates reviewed and the Hydro-Electric Power Commission would be freed of 'political control.' Immediate plans were to be laid for land development and reclamation projects, so that returning servicemen could be settled 'in organized groups in areas where their economic security can be assured.' The program was also to deal with government inefficiency. Provincial departments and services that duplicated those of the federal government would be eliminated if they were not necessary 'for the purpose of preserving fundamental constitutional rights.' The civil service system would be reformed to increase administrative efficiency.

In the area of welfare, mothers' allowances and old age pensions would be increased, and the existing provisions that required the elderly to dispose of real property before becoming eligible for assistance would be repealed. Possible shortages of basic necessities were to be dealt with by 'effective organization and administrative control,' with representatives of labour, veterans' organizations, and consumers appointed to boards that would oversee such matters.

Several remaining points dealt with specific problems of the reconversion to peace-time conditions. There were to be guarantees of veterans' rights and programs to rehabilitate and retrain veterans and munitions workers.

Drew concluded the radio broadcast in which the program was made public by stating 'I pledge myself, as Leader of the Progressive Conservative Party of Ontario, to carry out each of the proposals contained in this program when you entrust me with the power to do so.'[11] The electorate gave him the opportunity and the 22 Points declaration subsequently became the basis for many important policy positions taken not only by the Drew government but by its successors. Many of the specific measures were adopted in some form or other. But while some attempt was made to establish an apparatus capable of carrying out the kind of general planning approach implied in the 1943 declaration, this aspect of the program was soon quietly abandoned.

In 1944 the Drew government created a Department of Planning and Development. This organization brought together several earlier administrative bodies which had been set up to perform certain specific types of planning such as community planning and industrial promotion. But it also had a more general planning function, at least in its conception. The new department was initially intended to serve as a co-ordinating agency which would bring together various government programs and ensure that they were working in concert to promote the government's broader economic and social objectives. As the premier explained, 'It will be the first function of this new department to co-ordinate the many planning agencies now looking to the future, and also to stimulate new planning in directions which have not yet been explored by any organized effort.'[12]

This statement suggests what the term 'planning' implies in the broad sense, the making of some 'organized effort' not only to co-ordinate certain kinds of activity but to formulate specific goals that such organized effort is then directed to attain. The socialists and communists in the provincial legislature understood 'planning' in this sense. Their expectations concerning the new Department of Planning and Development were implicit in their complaints about its performance. The department was not a year old before the CCF leader, Edward Jolliffe, was denouncing the government on the grounds that its new department had not yet indicated how it was going to deal with the expected post-war unemployment problem.[13]

In fact the new department acquired no such responsibilities. There was no support for program co-ordination in the government establishment of the time. Indeed, it was soon apparent that the new department could not co-ordinate even its own varied functions. Although vestiges of the notion that a body could be established to assist in the formulation of policies and to monitor their effectiveness remained lodged within the administrative apparatus at Queen's Park for many years, economic planning in this broad sense did not survive the immediate post-war years in the province of Ontario.

Part of the explanation for this failure must be found in the continuing uncertainty about the constitutional basis for the making of economic and social policy in Canada. The federal government retained the initiative in this field long after the war and reconstruction years were past. Despite Drew's indication in 1943 that he would willingly collaborate with the federal authorities in devising and implementing such policy, Ontario took a strongly independent stance at the 1945 dominion-provincial conference and stubbornly persisted in opposing the federal government's attempts to develop a national plan for economic and social development. Even now it remains difficult to determine what the most important points of disagreement were. Of course there was the question of 'provincial rights' and the Ontario government was obviously unwilling to sacrifice its decision-making powers to a central authority that was seen to be responsive to the particular interests of Quebec and other regions of the country. There was also a difference in the perception of what the real economic problems of the times were. Ottawa remained preoccupied with the prospect of a major post-war recession, and its policy proposals reflected a vaguely Keynesian belief that government would have to keep the economy pumped up by bolstering aggregate demand. In Ontario, the concern over unemployment, so conspicuous in Drew's 22 Points program, was rapidly dissipated by the buoyant conditions in the Ontario economy as the war came to an end. The concern in Ontario soon shifted from unemployment to the ability of the government to provide the infrastructure investment in highways, electric power generating capacity, and municipal services needed to meet the demands of a rapidly expanding and industrializing society. Concerns in Ontario, in other words, tended to be more on the supply side than on the demand side of the economic system.

The federal government's specific proposals in 1945 would have made it responsible for dealing with unemployment, old age pensions and much of the burden arising from health insurance. The provinces were asked to abandon the personal income tax, the corporation tax, and succession duties in favour of the federal government. They would in turn receive annual unconditional grants based on a fixed sum per capita, with the amount set at such a level as to make it possible for the poorest provinces to achieve balanced budgets. Owing in large part to Ontario's intransigence, these proposals failed, despite the repeated attempts of the federal government to find some basis for agreement.

When the temporary wartime tax arrangements were about to expire, the federal government sought to negotiate tax rental agreements with individual provinces. Ontario, along with Quebec, continued to resist.

While the Drew administration remained strongly opposed to the federal government's specific proposals and to the centralizing philosophy that lay behind them, the province was willing to participate in the planning of certain kinds of post-war economic activities. The premier proposed in 1945 that some kind of joint economic planning body should be established for the purpose of regulating the Canadian economy as a whole. This body, he suggested, might be called the 'Dominion-Provincial Economic Board,' and it would be supplemented by a 'Co-ordinating Committee' made up of the first ministers of the provinces and the federal government. Nothing came of this proposal at the time, but much later (in 1956), a consultative committee which resembled the body Drew had proposed was established.[14]

The departure of George Drew from provincial politics in 1948 brought no immediate change in the Ontario government's position on federal-provincial relations. The province continued to insist on financial independence and its right to formulate its own economic priorities and programs. Leslie Frost, who succeeded Drew as leader and premier (after a brief period in which Thomas Kennedy served as leader), himself had often articulated this position while serving as provincial treasurer in the Drew government, and in 1947 he reiterated it in terms that proved to be prophetic: 'Provinces cannot retain their fiscal autonomy and function with maximum efficiency if they have to depend upon the federal government for contributions and subsidies. The tendency would be for the provinces to become extravagant and subservient to the central authority.'[15] He went on to state that the Ontario government did not intend to 'undermine the strength of our province or of Confederation by consenting to the centralization of powers which will leave the development of our great heritage in other hands.'[16]

Nevertheless, circumstances were changing. By the beginning of the 1950s, the federal initiatives in economic policy were shifting from their mistaken focus on maintaining high levels of demand in the economy to supporting the rapid industrialization and expansion in productive capacity that was by then obviously underway, an approach already adopted in Ontario. At the same time, the bitter personal animosities that had aggravated the relationship between the two governments also disappeared. Frost and the new federal leader, Louis St Laurent, enjoyed a friendly relationship which contrasted sharply with the acrimony that had persisted between Drew and King.

The Frost administrations in the 1950s were preoccupied with expanding the traditional economic role of the government in Ontario, that is, creating a 'favourable investment climate' for private business in the province. This goal was to be achieved in part by running budget surpluses and reducing the provincial debt but also by undertaking major public works, especially highway construction, an activity that reached notable heights just prior to the provincial elections of 1951, 1955, and 1959. There was also a good deal of support provided to municipalities in building water and sewage systems and some increase in funding for social services, although the latter were not given a high priority.

The federal government's new policy initiatives fitted very well into the plans of the province during this period. The promotion of major social-overhead-capital undertakings such as the St Lawrence Seaway, the Trans-Canada Highway, and the gas pipeline from Alberta to central Canada were projects in which the Ontario government was happy to participate.

The new spirit of co-operation was reflected in the tax-rental agreement the province entered into with the federal government in 1952, although Ontario insisted that this was 'at best a stopgap arrangement, pending the working out of a more satisfactory distribution of tax and revenue sources.'[17]

While there are frequent references in the premier's speeches during the 1950s to the province's use of its budget to help stabilize the economy, the spending strategy appears to have been based on the perceived need for new and better public works. It was what Frost called the 'great problem' of capital spending and the planning and timing of public works which lay at the heart of his government's economic activity and motivated the province in seeking improved federal-provincial co-ordination of economic policy.[18]

Relations between the federal and provincial governments began to deteriorate, however, as the 1952 Tax Sharing Agreement neared its end in 1956. Ontario wanted a new agreement based on a sharing of the federal personal income tax, corporate income tax, and federal succession duty revenues from the province in a 15:15:50 per cent ratio. Ottawa fixed the levels at 10:9:50. When the federal Liberal government was defeated in 1957 by the Conservatives led by John

Diefenbaker, the Ontario government hoped for, and eventually obtained, more favourable treatment. The tax-sharing arrangements worked out in 1958 gave the province 13 per cent of the personal income tax instead of 10 per cent. Most of the additional revenues were allotted to municipal and other local authorities. In addition, new arrangements were made for the sharing of unemployment relief costs and for hospitalization insurance, and federal support for hospital construction was increased.

These developments foreshadowed a major change in Ontario's financial situation. The province's need for additional revenues had become sufficiently urgent, largely because of its growing involvement in the social services field, that it yielded to the temptation offered by the federal government to enter into cost-sharing arrangements. Frost's own warnings of ten years earlier appear to have been forgotten.

Although undertaking programs on a cost-sharing basis was not a new concept (federal funds had already been made available to support certain housing, welfare, and even highway programs), after 1957 the number of such programs was greatly expanded, particularly in the areas of health, education, housing, and welfare. Although Frost had complained about Ottawa's conditional grants as recently as 1955, on the grounds that they committed the province to spending its revenues on 'federally conceived projects,' by the time he was about to leave office the province had become heavily involved in just such arrangements. During the 1960s there could be little doubt that the availability of federal funding had become an important influence on the level and pattern of provincial spending.

The province's transition from spending on 'things' such as highways to spending on services is evident as early as 1958, when welfare, health, and education were emerging as major areas of provincial government activity. The following year, the focus was on the new hospital insurance scheme, by which the province, after much delay, became committed to a program requiring massive amounts of federal financial support. At the same time it introduced a 'winter works' program, in which the federal government paid 50 per cent of the labour costs involved; a housing program in which the federal government would share the costs of slum clearance and public housing construction; and a 'roads to resources' program in which the costs of building resource development roads would be shared by the two levels of government. But the most powerful demonstration of the effect of federal funding was offered by the Federal-Provincial Technical and Vocational Training Agreement of 1961 which, as will be shown in chapter 6, led the province to reorganize its entire educational system in order to maximize the potential yield.

Ontario's willingness to accept such an invasion of its traditional areas of responsibility – health, education, and resource development – was undoubtedly motivated by its need for revenues and by the relative ease with which the federal government's policy directions could be reconciled with its own. But by the end of the 1960s, the happy coincidence of interests was breaking down. The province's continuing dissatisfaction with the tax-sharing arrangements, combined with a growing uneasiness about the direction being taken by the federal government's new initiatives, particularly with respect to regional economic development, began to lead the province back towards the position it had taken on federal-provincial relations in the 1940s. These developments will be discussed further in chapter 10.

2 *Population and Labour Force*

Between 1939 and 1975 the productive capacity of the Ontario economy increased greatly. Not since the early years of the century had the province enjoyed so high a rate of economic growth, and never before had the expansion been so prolonged. Despite recessions which slowed the rate of growth at times, especially towards the end of the period, the economy of Ontario underwent almost uninterrupted growth in output for at least a quarter of a century.

The productive capacity of any economy must be limited in the short run by the available supplies of factor inputs, that is, by the quantities of raw materials, labour, and real capital (machinery, business structures, and the like) that can be drawn upon and by the effectiveness with which these resources can be used to produce the goods and services the community requires. The effectiveness of resource utilization will be influenced by factors such as the skills of the labour force, the efficiency of management, the state of technology, and the scale of production. Given sufficient time, it may be possible to increase the available supplies of productive factors. Natural increase and net immigration may cause the labour force to grow; the capital stock may be expanded through net investment (the creation of new capital goods at a greater rate than old ones are wearing out); and even the stock of raw materials available may be increased as a consequence of new discoveries, imports, shifts in tastes, or technical changes that render previously useless parts of the natural environment valuable.

Identifying and measuring increases in factor supplies are relatively simple. It is more difficult to quantify the effects of technical change, organization, and scale on productive capacity. But we know that the overall increase in total output in the economy between 1939 and 1975 was far greater than can be accounted for by the measured increases in inputs. The difference can safely be attributed to increased productivity.[1]

Quantitatively, even in industrially developed economies, labour has been the major factor input. Large increases in the size of the labour force imply corresponding large increases in the population, although over long periods of time changes in participation rates and in the age and sex composition of the population

TABLE 2
Population of Ontario and Canada, Census Years 1941–71

Year	Ontario (000s)	Canada (000s)	Ontario as a percentage of Canada
1941	3,788	11,507	32.9
1951	4,598	14,009	32.8
1961	6,236	18,238	34.2
1971	7,703	21,568	35.7

SOURCE: Statistics Canada, *Census of Canada*, relevant years.

TABLE 3
Percentage Growth of the Population of Ontario by Five-Year Periods, 1941–75

Period	Per Cent
1941–5	8.1
1946–50	11.8
1951–5	17.8
1956–60	16.0
1961–5	11.1
1966–70	9.6
1971–5	8.9

SOURCE: Calculated from *Census of Canada* data

may mean that changes can occur in the labour force independently of changes in total population.

Population Growth and Change

The 1941 census population of Ontario was 3.7 million. By 1971 it had more than doubled to reach 7.7 million. Because a similarly high rate of population growth was experienced in the rest of Canada, the province's share of the country's total population was little changed over this thirty-year period. As shown in Table 2, the rate of population growth in Ontario accelerated during the 1940s, reaching a peak in the early 1950s and remaining at historically high levels during the rest of that decade before beginning to decline in the 1960s. About 60 per cent of the growth of population over the period as a whole was caused by net migration into the province and the remaining 40 per cent by a positive rate of natural increase.

The birth rate in Ontario increased slowly during the early 1940s, rising from the historically low level of 16.9 (per thousand of population) in 1937 to 20.7 in 1943. It declined slightly during the last two years of the war but then rose abruptly in the immediate post-war years and remained at very high levels, at about 25 to 26 through the 1950s. The record high of 26.8 was reached in 1957.

Fertility began to decline in 1960 and then fell steadily to around 15 in the mid-1970s.[2]

The causes of these changes in fertility are not understood, but the Ontario experience was similar to that of Canada as a whole, the Province's rates tending to be somewhat lower than the national average. The Canadian experience was in turn similar to that of several other countries with which it could reasonably be compared, which suggests that the influences affecting fertility during the period were general.

Changes in mortality had less of an effect on the rate of natural increase than did the changes in fertility. There was a steady decline in the death rate from about 10 per thousand of population in the early 1940s to 7.5 in 1974. Again, little is known of the specific causes of the decline in the death rate, although it is assumed that more effective control of infectious diseases and other improvements in living conditions played an important part. The infant mortality rate, which is often used as a rough indicator of a society's material standard of life, fell by 50 per cent over the period.[3]

The rate of natural increase that resulted from these fertility and mortality conditions rose to a peak of 18.1 per thousand of population in 1957, remained high until 1961 and then declined steadily thereafter to less than 8 by the mid-1970s.

International immigration was the main source of population growth resulting from migration. The influx was highly variable from year to year, responding to changing economic and other conditions in Canada and abroad and also to changes in Canadian immigration policy. Except for a time immediately following the war when the Ontario government sought to promote the immigration of skilled workers from Britain, the province had little direct influence on the movement of migrants during the period.[4]

About 50 per cent of all the immigrants arriving in Canada during the period from the end of the war to the mid-1970s gave Ontario as their intended destination, and it appears that most of them did in fact find their way to the province.[5] After allowing for emigration, most of it to the United States, the net gain of population in Ontario from international migration was 154,000 between 1941 and 1951; 562,000 between 1951 and 1961; and 473,000 between 1961 and 1971.[6]

As in earlier periods, most of the immigrant arrivals in the post-war years were from Europe. In the late 1960s, new government regulations were introduced to make immigration policy less discriminatory and some increase in the numbers of non-European immigrants is observed towards the end of the period.[7] During the 1960s the proportion of total immigrants who came from Asia and the West Indies rose from less than 5 per cent annually to more than 25 per cent, but much of this percentage change is attributable more to the decrease in the flow of migrants from Europe than to increasing absolute numbers of Asians and West Indians.

TABLE 4
Components of Population Growth, Ontario, 1941-71

Components of Population Growth	1941-51	1951-61	1961-71
Natural increase	520,500	951,900	859,900
Total net migration	289,400	686,600	607,100
Net international	154,200	562,200*	473,800
Net interprovincial	135,200	124,400*	133,300
Total population increase	809,900	1,638,500	1,467,000
Natural increase/ total increase, %	64.3	58.1	58.6
International migration/ total increase, %	19.0	34.3	32.3
Interprovincial migration/ total increase, %	16.7	7.6	9.1

SOURCE: Ontario, TEIGA, *Ontario's Changing Population*, vol. 1 (Toronto, 1976), table 9, 39

Although the federal government sought to direct a large number of immigrants into rural areas during the post-war period, these efforts were not very successful, and most of the immigrants eventually found their way into the cities. In Ontario some 80 per cent of post-war immigrants settled in the larger urban centres. Toronto alone consistently attracted over 50 per cent of international immigrants giving Ontario as the province of destination during the 1960s.[8] Immigration to Ontario from other parts of Canada contributed about 13 per cent of the province's total population increase between 1939 and 1975, compared with some 30 per cent from international immigration. Most of the Canadians who moved to Ontario during this period came from areas of labour surplus, notably the Prairies and Maritimes, where the primary industries that provided most of the employment opportunities were simply unable to absorb all the labour being generated by natural increase in those regions of the country. On average, Ontario gained 12,000 to 13,000 people annually as a result of such movements. During the 1940s Saskatchewan was the principal source. In the 1950s it was Nova Scotia.

There were also important movements of population within the province during the period. About half the fifty-three counties in Ontario lost population during the thirty years between 1941 and 1971, some of it to other parts of the province, some to other provinces and some to other countries. It might be expected that much of the intraprovincial movement was away from the more rural to the urban regions, but in fact the major cities drew only a small part of their total growth from this source. One study shows that even if all the internal migration in Ontario during the period had been directed into the Toronto-Hamilton region, it could have accounted for no more than 7 per cent of the total growth of population.[9]

While intraprovincial movements of population may have been a minor factor in the growth of the main urban areas during the post-war years, they had great significance for the areas losing population, many of which had been sparsely populated to begin with. Some of the largest losses were sustained by counties in the north of the province, particularly towards the end of the period. A number of northern communities found it difficult to maintain existing public services and facilities as their population base not only stopped growing but actually began to diminish.[10]

The combined effects of migration of all types were most evident in the Toronto area, which in the course of the provincial government's regional planning exercises in the 1960s became known as the Central Ontario Lakeshore Urban Complex (COLUC). The six counties comprising COLUC (Hamilton-Wentworth, Halton, Peel, York, Durham, Metro Toronto) contained approximately half the total population of the province in the 1940s and more than two-thirds of it in the 1960s. Most of the growth was centred in Peel and Halton counties.[11] The high rate of growth in the COLUC counties was largely responsible for making the Central Ontario Region the only one of the province's designated economic planning areas to increase its share of total provincial population during the period. All the others showed a steady decline in their relative shares of total population between 1939 and 1975. This suggests that to the extent population change may be assumed to mirror economic growth and development patterns, the great post-war expansion of the Ontario economy was concentrated in a relatively small and easily identified portion of the province.

The experience of industrialization in the world at large would suggest that the growth of the metropolitan region in Ontario would have been associated in this period with a general 'rural-urban' shift of population as labour moved out of agriculture into industry. But while there is ample evidence of a large decline in agricultural employment in Ontario after 1939, the decline in the rural population is not as marked as might have been expected. The reason is that the 'rural non-farm' population increased substantially. Thus, while the farm population of Ontario fell from 694,700 to 363,600 between 1941 and 1971, the rural non-farm population, which had declined during the 1940s, grew steadily in the next two decades to stand at 995,800 by 1971.[12] By the end of the period, the rural non-farm population was almost three times as large as the rural farm population.[13]

Like these changes in geographical location, shifts in the age composition of the provincial population are significant for understanding the economic development of the province during this period. Fluctuations in fertility rates and changes in immigration levels have greatly altered the numbers of individuals in various age groups. As these effects work their way through successive generations, they may have important influences on patterns of demand as well as on factors such as the size of the labour force, the need for education, and the burden of old age dependency. As shown in table 5, the low birth rates and low levels of immigration in the 1930s meant that there were relatively few new

TABLE 5
Distribution of Population by Major Age Groups, Ontario, 1941–71

Major Age Groups	Per Cent Distribution			
	1941	1951	1961	1971
0–4	7.9	11.2	11.9	8.3
5–20	25.4	22.7	27.3	29.6
20–24	8.6	7.7	6.2	8.8
25–44	29.6	30.0	28.1	25.9
45–64	20.5	19.8	18.4	19.1
65 and over	8.0	8.6	8.1	8.3
Total	100.0	100.0	100.0	100.0

SOURCE: *Ontario's Changing Population*, vol. II, table 14, 49

entrants to the labour force in the immediate post-war period, but this dearth was soon offset by the heavy immigration of the 1950s, which brought in large numbers of working-age persons.

The increased birth rates of the 1940s and 1950s, are reflected in the sharp increases in the numbers of the young relative to the old – youngsters for whom educational and employment opportunities had to be found in the later part of the period. The percentage of the population four years of age and younger peaked in 1961. The number of five to twenty-four-year-olds as a percentage of the population was at a maximum for the period in 1971. Between 1939 and 1975 over one-third of the total growth in the population of Ontario was accounted for by the percentage increase in the five to nineteen-year-old age group.[14] But by the early 1970s this trend was ended and the average age of the population was rising.

The Labour Force

The changes in the age structure of the population greatly affected the size and nature of the post-war labour force in Ontario, but there were other important influences bearing upon it during the period as well. After 1940 participation rates were strongly affected by changes in the demand for labour, by new attitudes towards the economic role of women, by new educational needs and opportunities, and by a number of general changes in the society and culture of the province.

Between 1939 and 1975 the labour force in Ontario grew more rapidly than the population of working age. Strictly comparable data are not available until after 1954, but the most rapid growth during the post-war period occurred during the 1960s, when the labour force increased by about 35 per cent.

Female participation in the labour force greatly expanded during the Second World War because of labour shortages and new opportunities for making substantial contributions to family incomes. When the unusual circumstances of the war years no longer applied, changes in social attitudes appear to have been responsible for the persistence of higher female participation in the labour force. While the rate in Canada fell in the early post-war years from the high of over 33 per cent recorded in 1945, by the early 1950s the rate was again rising. In Ontario, the female participation rate in the early 1950s was approximatey 26 per cent. By the early 1970s it was over 40 per cent.[15]

In 1971 a total of 1,202,585 women were employed in Ontario. Although a small number were engaged in managerial and other high-ranking positions, more than one-third were still working at the clerical and relatively unskilled jobs that had been available to women in earlier times.[16]

Male participation rates declined somewhat during the period, apparently because young males began to spend more time in educational institutions before joining the work force and, at the other end of the age scale, because older males began to retire at an earlier age. The rate for the fourteen to twenty-four-year-old male age group fell from 70.3 in 1956 to 60 in 1971. The overall male rate fell from 85.4 to 78.7 over the same period of time.[17]

The total amount of labour available in the economy depends not only on the number of workers but also on the amount of labour each worker supplies. This amount may vary with changes in the conventional arrangements made with respect to the numbers of hours per day workers are expected to be on the job, the length of the working week, the number of holidays and vacations, and the amount of effort workers actually put into their jobs. Some of these factors are very difficult to quantify. We do know that there was a decrease in the number of hours worked by the average worker during the 1939–75 period. In the manufacturing industries, for example, workers put in on average 44.1 hours per week in 1945 but this figure declined gradually to just over 40 by the early 1960s and slightly under that by the early 1970s.[18] Yet it does not necessarily follow that this reduction in hours of work served to offset to any degree the effect of labour force growth on the supply of labour, because it is possible that worker productivity per hour increased, owing to the fewer number of hours worked per day.

A similarly indeterminate influence on the supply of labour during the period was the effect of improved education and training. When the Economic Council of Canada addressed itself to this question in the mid-1960s, it reported that 'A careful historical appraisal of the development of education in Canada suggests that spectacular advances were made in education from the latter part of the nineteenth century to the early 1920s' and that 'particularly noteworthy was the record of educational achievement in Ontario in the latter decades of the last century.' The council went on to note, however, that subsequently little progress was made in this direction until after the Second World War. The council's research suggested that while there had been substantial increases in the levels of formal schooling attained by members of the Canadian labour force, these changes had occurred very gradually. Between 1911 and 1961 the average number of years of schooling among Canadian male workers increased at a rate of only 0.5 per cent per year, rising from seven years of schooling in 1911 to a little over nine years in 1961.[19]

The government of Ontario joined enthusiastically in the nation-wide efforts to improve education in the 1960s, an effort justified in large part by the growing conviction that the level of education attained by the labour force was a major determinant of labour productivity.[20] At about the same time, there was a noticeable increase in the educational requirements for many occupations. Whether this was a cause or an effect of the rising levels of education that began in the 1960s was a matter of debate.[21] But even before the new educational opportunities of the 1960s could have been expected to bear fruit, the educational requirements for many jobs were already being raised. Between 1960 and 1965 the percentage of workers in the twenty to twenty-four-year-old age group with only elementary schooling or less fell from over 23 per cent to just over 15 per cent.[22]

There were substantial shifts in the occupational distribution of the labour force during the period. Because of very high gains in productivity per worker in the primary industries, notably agriculture, employment opportunities did not increase as rapidly in that sector as in other sectors and in some cases actually declined. The main source of new jobs was in the industries producing services rather than goods. The structural shifts in employment patterns during the period were not accomplished without a good deal of friction. Labour markets did not function smoothly to allocate workers where they were most needed. During the war years there were severe labour shortages, and after the war, despite the rapid growth of the labour force, certain kinds of workers were often in seriously short supply. This was particularly true of highly trained professionals. While the problem was alleviated in the short run by the immigration of such workers during the 1950s and 1960s, doubts remained about the capability of the existing system to co-ordinate education and training activities with the demand side of the labour market. 'Manpower planning' became a major interest of government at both the provincial and the federal level.

Overall levels of unemployment in Ontario were low throughout most of the period. Although the very low levels reached in the war and immediate postwar years of less than 2 per cent were not sustained, the unemployment rate never exceeded four per cent until the late 1950s, a level that most economists thought to be about the best normally attainable. The rate was again below 4 per cent during much of the 1960s. As the following table indicates, however, there appeared to be a tendency for the unemployment rate to drift upward during the later years, and in 1975 it exceeded 6 per cent. While the general unemployment rate in Ontario was consistently below the national average, the upward trend in the rate was a matter of concern, as was the fact that very much higher

TABLE 6
Average Annual Unemployment Rate, Ontario, 1946–75

Year	Per Cent	Year	Per Cent
1946	2.8	1961	5.5
1947	1.8	1962	4.3
1948	1.7	1963	3.8
1949	2.3	1964	3.2
1950	2.4	1965	2.5
1951	1.7	1966	2.5
1952	2.2	1967	3.1
1953	2.1	1968	3.5
1954	3.8	1969	3.1
1955	3.2	1970	4.3
1956	2.4	1971	5.2
1957	3.4	1972	4.8
1958	5.4	1973	4.0
1959	4.5	1974	4.1
1960	5.4	1975	6.0

SOURCE: Leacy, ed., *Historical Statistics of Canada*, 2nd ed., D494

rates prevailed for certain groups, particularly the young who were just entering the labour force.

Most of the responsibility for dealing with unemployment throughout this period was assumed by the federal government, which in 1945 explicitly accepted responsibility for maintaining high and stable levels of employment as a necessary objective for national economic policy.[23] In so far as the unemployment of the late 1950s and early 1960 could be attributed to cyclical causes, the Ontario government did not appear to be directly responsible for doing much more than co-operating with whatever federal efforts were being implemented. It was possible, however, that some of the unemployment was associated with structural changes taking place in the provincial economy, and there was accordingly some effort on the part of provincial policy-makers to devise various kinds of 'manpower policies,' particularly as they related to education and training activities over which the province exercised jurisdiction.[24] When unemployment again became a matter of particular concern to the provincial government in the late 1960s, it was prepared to supplement such activities with demand-raising countercyclical fiscal measures of its own.

Industrial Relations

The utilization of the labour force in Ontario during the 1939–75 period was at times strongly affected by the relations between workers and employers and by the efforts of the provincial government to regulate those relations. In the early 1940s industrial relations were dominated by the organizing efforts of the Congress of Industrial Organizations (CIO) and the spread of industrial unionism generally. Although the period was not subsequently marked by intensive unionization, the expansion of organized labour into new occupational areas, notably the 'essential services' gave rise to a number of difficulties.

The level of labour unrest was high in Ontario during the 1940s. The conflicts generated by strong employer opposition to unionizing activities appeared to require a more effective legal framework to contain such struggles, and the Hepburn government found itself enmeshed in a politically damaging dispute between the unions and a number of particularly obstinate employers. The premier's own unconcealed hostility to the CIO and his highly publicized interventions in several key strikes – the Campbell Soup Company strike, in which farmers and their families were brought into the factory to can the tomato crop, and the northern miners' strike in which the provincial police played an active role – all helped create a strong impression of anti-labour sentiment on the part of the provincial authorities.[25]

The labour struggles of the early 1940s were complicated by the wartime context. The Ontario government's position, and certainly the position of the premier, was strongly influenced by a conviction that much of the trouble was being fomented by 'subversive elements.' In 1942 Hepburn expressed the view that the CIO had been more responsible than any other factor for retarding the war effort in the United States, and he remained unreservedly critical of the Canadian federal government's apparent lack of will in helping him control the situation in the mining camps and factories of Ontario.[26]

Even so, in 1942 the Hepburn government undertook to develop a labour policy based on the rights of workers to organize and to engage in collective bargaining with employers.[27] But by then the real initiative in the field of labour legislation had been seized by the federal government, which was rapidly assuming the powers it needed to control the national economy in the interests of the war effort. Under the authority of the War Measures Act of 1914, the federal government had extended the provisions of its labour relations legislation, as embodied in the Industrial Disputes Investigation Act, to cover all disputes between workers and employers in industries engaged in war work. In effect, compulsory investigation and conciliation were imposed in all such circumstances. The federal government also indicated that it intended to encourage at least voluntary compliance by workers and employers of certain principles governing union recognition and bargaining practices as set out in existing American legislation.[28]

These arrangements were not entirely satisfactory to organized labour in Canada, and strong appeals were made to the provincial governments to intervene and to supplement the federal measures. In Ontario the new Conservative government responded by establishing a 'Labour Court' with responsibility for certifying unions as bargaining agents, for ensuring that workers were free to organize and that employers would bargain in good faith. While it stopped short of declaring that public policy in Ontario would actually promote unionization and collective bargaining, the Ontario government went some distance towards providing organized labour with the type of framework already developed in the United States. The labour legislation enacted in 1943 was of little immediate consequence, however, for its application was almost immediately suspended in deference to new federal regulations. Its main importance lay in establishing the foundation for Ontario's industrial relations policies through the critical postwar years.[29] These policies followed the general principles established in the federal government's 1944 Order-in-Council PC 1003, which had remained in force during the remaining war years. In 1945 the Ontario government had enthusiastically endorsed the need for a uniform national labour code during the difficult Ford strike at Windsor, and in 1948 the Ontario Labour Relations Act carried the federal government's approach (now embodied in the Industrial Relations and Disputes Investigation Act) into the provincial domain with only minor changes.[30]

Although the minister of labour in Ontario indicated that the province was not 'completely satisfied with all the provisions of the federal code,' he was willing to adopt it, he said 'to avoid confusion, uncertainty, and unprofitable litigation in industry.'[31] Administration of the provincial regulations was entrusted to an Ontario Labour Relations Board, the powers of which were expanded in 1950 with certain powers formerly vested in the Minister being transferred to the Board. The following year Ontario added a fair employment practices law and anti-discrimination regulations to ensure equal pay for men and women doing the same work.

Despite the evident trend towards more favourable treatment of labour in industrial disputes, the industrial relations situation in Ontario was far from peaceful in the immediate post-war period. The number of strikes and lock-outs shows, if anything, a trend towards more contentious and more protracted work stoppages. Part of this may have been the result of increasing jurisdictional conflict within organized labour, particularly between the CIO-affiliated unions organized in the Canadian Congress of Labour (CLC) and the more traditional American Federation of Labour (AFL)-affiliated craft unions of the Trades and Labour Congress (TLC). The merger of the CLC and TLC in 1956, however, brought no immediate relief from such conflicts.

The internal struggles within the labour movement did nothing to improve the public image of organized labour in Ontario in this period. While there was no strong anti-labour backlash in Ontario comparable, for example, to that which developed in British Columbia, there were indications that measures to strengthen further the power of the unions would be more vigorously opposed than had been the case in the 1940s. This feeling was apparent in the proceedings of the Select Committee on Labour Relations set up by the Ontario legislature in 1957.

The committee's task was 'to examine and report regarding the operation and administration of the Labour Relations Act in all its aspects.' Prompted by severe criticism in the press of the way Ontario's labour relations system was performing, the committee held extensive public hearings and collected briefs for more than a year; it reported in 1959. Although it took the position that what was needed to improve the Ontario system was more self-reliance on the part of those directly involved in labour disputes and less reliance on government intervention, the committee's recommendations were largely designed to strengthen the regulatory apparatus and to make it more difficult for employees to impose costs on the public, particularly if doing so involved the withholding of certain undefined 'essential services.' Some of the committee's ideas were embodied in a new Labour Relations Act in 1960, which set out procedures for dealing with jurisdictional disputes, for enforcing arbitration awards, and for imposing certain limitations on union security agreements. A number of measures relating to the internal conduct of union affairs were also incorporated.

The difficult issue of strikes affecting the provision of 'essential services' reached critical proportions in Ontario in 1961, when a strike by the Ontario Hydro workers appeared imminent. The government dealt with the situation by passing emergency legislation (the Ontario Hydro Employees' Union Disputes Act of 1961–2) which imposed compulsory arbitration and prohibited a strike or lock-out.

Another 'essential services' area dealt with in the mid-1960s was the hospitals. A royal commission (the Bennett Commission) was established in 1963 to study the feasibility of applying compulsory arbitration to the settlement of disputes between hospital workers and their employers. It subsequently proposed that compulsory arbitration be imposed in situations where patient care would be adversely affected or 'severely threatened' or where one of the parties had been convicted by the Ontario Labour Relations Board of bargaining in bad faith. The commission expressed confidence, nevertheless, in the principle of voluntary collective bargaining.[32] When the government came to legislate in this area, however, it explicitly prohibited strikes and lock-outs in hospitals and provided for binding arbitration of contract negotiation disputes involving hospital workers.[33]

The general issue of the effects of strike action on the public and on the economy as a whole was the subject of a careful study by yet another provincial royal commission of the 1960s. The controversial report published in 1968 by a leading authority in the field, Mr Justice Ivan C. Rand, proposed that an industrial tribunal be created and made responsible for the regulation of labour-management disputes in Ontario. Such a body would be empowered to investigate at the request of the government any aspects of labour-management relations having to do with wages, hours, fringe benefits, and picketing. It would aso have the authority to impose arbitration in strikes lasting more than ninety days when requested to do so by either party if there had been evidence of bargaining in bad faith. Above the tribunal would be an even more powerful agent, a director of enforcement, responsible only to the provincial legislature, who would make final legal decisions in all such matters.

The Rand approach to the matter of strikes in the public sector was unambiguous. Such strikes were unacceptable, and past experience had demonstrated, Rand asserted, that mandatory arbitration was a satisfactory means of settling disputes in such areas without unreasonably infringing upon the rights of workers. Strikes by public employees, Rand contended, were directed against the public and such 'irresponsible behaviour' would have to be penalized. 'Our society,' he wrote, 'is built within a structure of interwoven trust, credit and obligation. Good faith and reliability are essential to its mode of living, and when these obligations are repudiated, confusion may be the harbinger of social disintegration.'[34] Rand recommended that the government be given authority to declare any business, industry or service to be 'essential' and to ban a strike or order a return to work. Resolution of such disputes would be effected by the industrial tribunal if negotiations failed to reach a settlement.

He also made several suggestions respecting the rights of employers to hire replacements and of workers to find alternative employment during a strike. So long as the latter found only casual employment, their jobs would be protected. Employers would be free to recruit temporary replacement workers from among the unemployed. Other proposals included protection for workers against dismissal after seven years of service unless just cause could be shown; virtual elimination of the ex parte injunction; procedures for handling misconduct on picket lines; eliminating interference by international unions in Canadian settlements; and more extensive labour-management consultation.

The report was widely criticized upon its release as being impractical and authoritarian.[35] Nevertheless, some of Rand's specifics were incorporated in new Ontario legislation in 1971, particularly as it related to the situation in the troubled construction industry. When the principles of collective bargaining were extended to contract negotiations within the provincial civil service in 1972, the Rand influence was also evident in the provisions that banned strikes and lock-outs and created an Ontario Public Service Labour Relations Tribunal to handle applications for representation rights, appointment of mediators, and complaints about unfair practices. The underlying issues inherent in public sector industrial relations were far from resolved, however, as was demonstrated later in the 1970s by the disputes involving the province's school teachers.

3 Land and Capital Resources

Ontario's stocks of natural resources and man-made productive assets (real capital goods) were enlarged in the period to 1975 as a result of technical change, investments in exploration and development, and the construction of commercial and industrial facilities. The war and post-war decades were characterized by unusually high levels of real capital formation. Much of this investment activity was carried on by private business organizations motivated by buoyant expectations of profit to build new factories, to acquire new machinery and equipment and to improve facilities that in many cases had been allowed to run down in the preceding decade. Government also undertook extensive real investment by building roads, electric power facilities, schools, and hospitals and providing other kinds of social capital needed to support a growing population and an expanding economy.

Land Resources

The natural-resource base of the province was considerably altered during this period by the continuing processes of exploration, discovery, and technical change. To the extent that land resources could be imported from other regions to supply Ontario producers, there were also important developments: notably the availability of iron ore from Labrador once the St Lawrence Seaway was opened in 1959; access to western Canadian oil and gas made possible by the pipeline projects of the 1950s; and the continued availability of coal from the United States to support the iron and steel industry of the province.

Within the province the most important resource developments were the mineral discoveries of the 1940s and 1950s which added large commercial reserves of uranium and iron ore to the province's natural-resource inventory. Also important was the large base-metal discovery of Texas Gulf Sulphur near Timmins in 1964. But there were also some important depletions. Many of the established mining operations in the province were showing signs of maturity and in some cases senescence. The gold mines of the north-east were at times thought to be nearing the end of their commercial usefulness, and by the 1970s the future of even the enormous Sudbury ore bodies was becoming uncertain. The vagaries of world metal markets were such, however, that none of the worst expectations of this kind had become a reality by the end of the period.

In the case of the renewable resources the long-term trends were, if anything, more negative. While precise measurement was difficult, depletions appeared to outstrip gains during the period. Despite continued efforts to develop agriculture in the northern parts of Ontario, the overall trend was to a reduction in the quantity of land available for agricultural purposes. It proved profitable to transfer some of the province's best agricultural land to other purposes – mainly to provide building sites in the expanding urban-industrial areas – while at the same time the decreasing viability of marginal farming operations in the fringe areas of the province resulted in widespread abandonment of the poorer land. These changes stimulated much public discussion, and trying to determine appropriate uses for land became one of the provincial government's most difficult policy tasks in the later part of the period.[1] The use and abuse of the province's forest resources were also troublesome issues. While some progress was made in checking the waste and disorder that continued to characterize the industry, the forests were in no better condition by the mid-1970s than they were when the provincial Royal Commission on Forestry catalogued their sorry state in the 1940s. As the better and more accessible timber was cut and not replaced, many of the province's wood-using businesses were forced to turn to suppliers outside the province for their raw materials. By the end of the period, some pulp and paper mills in the south were importing wood from the United States.

The province's water resources remained little changed in quantity over the period, but their quality was seriously reduced. Pollution of lakes and rivers eliminated much of the inland fishery, devastated some native communities, and damaged the tourist industry in parts of the province. The problem was recognized and received considerable attention from the provincial government, but satisfactory solutions to the complex issue of managing water pollution proved hard to find. Utilization of water resources for hydroelectric power generation continued, and the system was greatly expanded in the years following the Second World War, but by the 1960s alternative forms of electric power generation were becoming more economical.

Provincial government policies with respect to the management of the province's natural resources changed substantially over the course of the period. In general, during the 1940s and 1950s policy emphasized economic growth more than what was then usually called 'conservation.' Whenever the provincial government could promote the utilization of a resource or expand the resource base by encouraging exploration and development, it continued to do so as it had in the past.[2] Although it was also the government's declared intention to 'preserve and protect' renewable resources and the natural environment in general, it is difficult to find instances of conservation's being placed ahead of tangible and immediate economic benefits.[3] There was, nevertheless, a sometimes strong opposition to this approach, which the government had to contend with.

The conservation movement had resurfaced in Ontario during the late 1930s when some of Roosevelt's New Deal measures in the United States attracted interest in Canada. This interest was sustained during the years of the Second World War by organizations involved in planning for post-war reconstruction. In 1941 a number of organizations met in Guelph to design a program that would help increase employment, control river flooding in southern Ontario, and encourage reforestation in the region. The scheme attracted federal government support, and a pilot project was undertaken to demonstrate how the Ganaraska River watershed could be managed through a co-ordinated conservation program. In 1944 the Ontario government created a Conservation Branch within its new Department of Planning and Development and two years later enacted legislation to assist municipalities to conserve renewable resources within watersheds by establishing 'conservation authorities.' The province also stepped up its efforts to enforce existing regulations concerning pollution of water supplies. Convictions under the existing legislation were so difficult to obtain, however, that little was actually accomplished.[4]

More positive action was forthcoming in the 1950s when the government offered financial assistance to municipalities building sewage treatment plants. Growing concern over pollution of the Great Lakes led to the creation in 1955 of an Ontario Water Resources and Supply Committee, which the following year was transformed into the Ontario Water Resources Commission. This body was authorized to build and operate water and sewage facilities on behalf of municipalities, which would then be responsible for repaying the costs involved over long terms and at very low interest rates. The commission even became a supplier of water when the provincial government in 1964 resolved a prolonged conflict over responsibility for the city of London's water supply by building a water pipeline from Lake Huron to London, which serviced other communities along the way. By the early 1970s the policy of requiring municipal governments to bear the full costs of such facilities was abandoned, and provincial subsidies of up to 75 per cent of the cost were provided.

Dealing with the problem of water pollution caused by industrial plants proved to be a more intractable problem. The underlying policy conflicts involved were well illustrated in the late 1940s when the Kalamazoo Vegetable Parchment Company reopened a paper mill at Espanola on a site that had been abandoned in the 1930s. The company was successfully sued for damages by fishing and tourist camp operators downstream, who obtained a court injunction ordering that the mill be closed. The provincial government sought to have the court's ruling overturned, and when this move failed, it resorted to legislation to dissolve the injunction.[5] The government's approach to the problem of reconciling industrial expansion with environmental protection was subsequently more positive, and an elaborate administrative structure was established to control industrial water pollution. Most of the responsibility for developing and applying standards in this area was assigned to an Industrial Waste Division within a new Department of Energy and Resources. By the 1970s some progress had been made in devising and enforcing waste disposal standards for industry in the province, but the underlying conflict between development and protection remained unresolved.

The same may be said with respect to other forms of pollution. Although provincial legislation made it possible to prosecute businesses creating smoke, dust, or odours that were deemed hazardous to health, these powers were infrequently exercised. During the 1950s the widely publicized concern over air pollution in Britain and in California aroused interest in the problem in Ontario, and in 1958 a new Air Pollution Control Act enlarged the scope of the existing legislation. It had little immediate effect, however, because the act made municipalities responsible for initiating action, and few had either the means or the will to attack such problems. Not until the late 1960s, when growing public concern over hidden health hazards arising from the use of insecticides such as DDT and industrial emissions once again gave such problems a political significance, did the Ontario government take further action.[6]

There was soon some perceptible improvement in the air quality in the major cities of Ontario, but again there were particular problems in cases where the economic implications of pollution abatement were particularly acute. The situation at Sudbury, where the International Nickel Company's emissions were the principal source of a major problem, provided a classic demonstration of the difficulties involved in providing a better environment and at the same time preserving employment in a community desperately in need of both.

Capital Resources

It is difficult to measure the stock of capital available in an economy and the data available for a subnational region like a province are particularly scarce and difficult to interpret.[7] The most reliable data for the modern period derive from the national income accounts and they provide us with a good indication of how rapidly or otherwise additions to the capital stock were being made. Data are also available that permit us to gain some sense of the composition of additions to the capital stock.[8] What is missing is direct evidence relating to possible changes in the quality of the capital in existence at any given time.

During the Depression of the 1930s most businesses that invested in new capital were doing so to replace machinery that had worn out. There was probably little spending on capital to modernize or upgrade machinery and equipment until the war years, when a number of industries, such as iron and steel, shipbuilding, and aircraft, were rather suddenly faced with the need and opportunity to improve as well as to expand their physical plant. Also during the war years

TABLE 7
Private and Public Capital Expenditures on Construction and New Equipment, Ontario, Selected Years 1948–75 ($millions)

Industry	1948	1950	1955	1960	1965	1970	1975
Primary and construction	153	197	259	233	360	570	1,075
Manufacturing	289	218	412	555	1,182	1,625	2,851
Utilities	230	315	347	556	690	1,334	2,635
Trade, finance, and commercial services	129	167	261	319	460	811	1,762
Housing	236	318	606	551	803	1,287	2,577
Institutions and government departments	146	205	387	640	884	1,300	2,132
Total*	1,183	1,419	2,271	2,856	4,378	6,928	13,032

* Totals do not add owing to rounding.

SOURCE: Adapted from Ontario Economic Council, *Issues and Alternatives 1978: Business Investment* (Toronto: OEC, 1979), table A27, 92–3

a number of entirely new industries, such as the synthetic rubber and electronic equipment industries, had to be completely equipped with what were necessarily the most modern types of machinery and buildings. Following the war much of the incentive for private firms to invest in new capital derived from the rapid expansion of the demand for all kinds of industrial output.[9] Government investment spending also increased to meet the new demand for roads, public buildings, and other forms of social capital. The decade following the war was consequently marked by a major boom in investment spending. Between 1948 and 1956 the rate of new capital formation in Ontario in constant dollar terms increased by 67 per cent.[10]

The sharp recession of the late 1950s checked this prolonged expansion, and the rate of investment in the Ontario economy fell in 1959 and continued to decline until 1962. Total investment spending in real terms then rose annually through the remainder of the period to 1975, except for another interruption in 1966–7.

Real capital formation may take the form of either construction, which can be classified as either 'building' or 'engineering' construction, or the manufacturing of new machinery. In Ontario during the post-war period investment in new machinery typically accounted for about one-third of total investment, although in the mid-1970s this portion increased to more than 40 per cent.

Construction and the Housing Industry

The two main branches of the construction industry are building construction, which produces residential, industrial, commercial and institutional structures,

TABLE 8
Value of Construction, Ontario, 1939–75

Year	Total Construction $ Current Value ('000)	$1971 = 100 * ('000)
1939	144,830	526,655
1941	261,239	842,707
1945	216,545	598,191
1950	1,105,503	2,074,115
1955	1,869,335	2,907,208
1960	2,332,900	3,420,675
1965	3,171,774	4,135,299
1970	4,984,865	5,301,788
1975	8,989,399	5,667,969

* Constant dollar values estimated using unweighted average of new residential and new non-residential implicit price components of GNE implicit price deflator, 1971 = 100.

SOURCES: Current dollar values from *Economic Survey of Ontario 1957*, P-4, and Ontario, TEIGA, *Ontario Statistics 1981*, table 21.10, 553; price deflator calculated from Leacy, ed., *Historical Statistics of Canada*, 2nd ed., K179 and K180.

and engineering construction, which is concerned with roads, dams, pipelines, water and sewage systems, and hydroelectric power facilities. In Ontario during the 1939–75 period the building branch in most years contributed about twice as much to the total value of construction work in the province as the engineering branch. Within the building branch, residential construction was typically the dominant element, often equalling in value the amount spent on all other types of building combined.

It would be difficult to exaggerate the contribution made by the construction industry to the changes that took place in the physical characteristics of Ontario during the post-war period. The physical fabric of the society was greatly altered by the activities of the firms and workers involved in this industry and the private and public investors who initiated and financed their efforts. While there had been a number of major public construction projects in the 1930s, notably highways, they were eclipsed in the postwar years by massive undertakings such as the St Lawrence Seaway, completion of Highway 401, the pipelines, and the vast number of new private and public structures that contributed to the extraordinary expansion, both vertically and horizontally, of the towns and cities of the province.

The construction industry was also important in the post-war period as one of the frontiers of union activity, and it was the focal point of some of the most difficult industrial relations problems of the period. It was important, too, as a source of employment for a rapidly expanding labour force, including many immigrant workers, both skilled and unskilled.

The overall structure and organization of the construction industry in Ontario changed little during the post-war period. The general level of concentration in the industry remained low. Like agriculture, it remained one of the more competitive sectors of the economy, with large numbers of producers holding relatively small shares of the total market. Some large firms existed, particularly in the area of 'general contracting.' But typically, the actual work of building was done by a shifting complex of subcontractors and individual tradesmen, many of the latter resembling small businessmen more than ordinary workers. Entry to the industry was comparatively open, particularly in the residential building sector. During the building boom of the 1950s and 1960s, it was easy to set up business as a contractor in Ontario: few assets were required, because nearly all the work could be subcontracted; licensing and other legal requirements were minimal. It was sometimes said at the time that 'any worker with initiative and a shovel' could become a contractor.[11] Yet this situation required a great deal of co-ordinating activity, and an informal but complex system for awarding contracts and obtaining the services of unionized workers grew up in the province. During the boom years the traditional constraints that operated to limit competition and maintain some kind of order in the industry often broke down, and the resulting disorder, sometimes associated with intimidation and violence, provoked demands for reform.

Another cause of public concern was the apparent inefficiency that seemed to characterize parts of the industry. The Canadian economist O.J. Firestone, who had practical as well as scholarly experience in the business, noted in 1943 that 'The construction industry ... offers a sad picture of disorganization and backwardness.'[12] Later studies of the industry found little evidence of change for the better.[13]

During the war years the federal government entertained some thoughts about possible restructuring of the building construction industry. Lorimer has suggested that the measures adopted by the Canadian government to foster large-scale housing development after the war were part of a plan to promote the creation of a small number of large companies which would develop land and build houses and related facilities on a large and presumably more efficient scale. While a number of 'development' corporations did subsequently come into being, they did not become involved in the construction end of the business.[14] Only one of the major development companies, the British-based George Wimpey firm, operated its own construction branch to perform the engineering work required in creating new residential subdivisions.[15] It appears that several factors – the absence of any great economies of scale in many types of construction work, ease of entry, and the business strategy of the development corporations – combined to permit competition and at times a good deal of disorder to persist.

Some efforts at reorganization were made from within the industry. In the building sector, which had remained almost completely non-unionized until the 1960s, there was a concerted effort to organize workers engaged in residential construction, and in the larger centres many contractors formed associations through which they could bargain with such unions.[16] These associations proliferated during the 1960s and early 1970s. Operating in collaboration with the construction union locals, they sought to control the complicated procedures for tendering, awarding contracts, and allocating workers to particular jobs. The practices involved were not always ethical and they were sometimes illegal. Particular problems were investigated by two provincial royal commissions, the Goldenberg Commission in 1962 and the Weisburg Commission a decade later; but by the mid-1970s it was still not clear whether the level of competition in the industry had been reduced or intensified by the new arrangements.

It is likely that some of the effects of organizing activity in the building trades during the period were offset by changes in building methods brought about by the introduction of new materials and techniques. Despite the traditional resistance of the building trades to new methods, during the post-war period several new materials were developed which made some of the old skills obsolete. 'Drywall' was introduced as a substitute for lath and plaster walls in the 1950s and by the early 1970s the skills of lathers and plasterers had become virtually useless. Most interior walls and ceilings in both residential and commercial buildings could be installed by unskilled workers (board men), who fastened sheets of gypsum board to the supporting studs, followed by 'tapers' who filled in the joints. The stark architectural styles of the period promoted the acceptance of this new time and work-saving material and contributed to the rejection of the ornate embellishments and detail work which were once the glory of the plasterer's craft. Similarly, the development of new types of paint, floor-covering, plumbing, and framing materials made it possible for unskilled workers to do work previously reserved for skilled craftsmen. While the craft unions resisted these developments as best they could, their ability to control work content, jurisdiction, and job qualification was seriously eroded.

The Housing 'Problem'

After the very low levels of residential construction in the 1930s, activity picked up quickly during the early years of the war. In 1941 spending on house-building in Ontario was twice that of 1939. Even so, there was a perceived housing 'shortage' in all the larger urban centres of the province.[17] The federal government took the initiative in responding to this perception by establishing a crown corporation, Wartime Housing Limited, to build houses for workers and their families near industrial plants engaged in war production. Later, rental housing was built for veterans. After the war, however, the federal government terminated its direct participation in the residential building industry and reverted to measures aimed at making it easier for prospective owners to finance the acquisition of dwellings supplied by private contractors and developers.

The principle of supporting home-ownership by providing mortgage guarantees or insurance, which had been introduced in 1935, was elaborated in the 1944 National Housing Act and continued throughout the post-war period under the direction of the Central Mortgage and Housing Corporation established in 1946. While it is difficult to determine with any certainty how much of the increase in the stock of housing in Ontario was attributable to these measures, a very large proportion of the total residential building activity carried on under CMHC arrangements was concentrated there, particularly in the southern parts of the province.[18]

Even while the federal activity in the housing field was at its peak during the early post-war years, the Ontario government was under strong political pressure to become involved as well. The opposition parties in the provincial legislature relentlessly criticized the government for its apparent unwillingness to ensure that there was 'sufficient' housing available in the province. The CCF members suggested that the government would simply have to get into the construction business itself in order to supply enough housing, because 'private industry would not.'[19] The provincial Liberals had less specific suggestions, but they too missed few opportunities to urge the government to deal with what was sometimes referred to as a 'great crisis.' While the government readily conceded that the rate of housing construction was too slow, it refused to become more directly involved in the industry except by collaborating in certain joint ventures with the federal government. The province did show some willingness to increase the supply of serviced land available for new residential building purposes.

In 1952 the Ontario legislature passed five bills to enable the province and municipalities to assemble land and to assist in arranging financing for various kinds of housing developments.[20] These arrangements were intended to increase the supply of serviced land available to private builders who would undertake to make certain kinds of housing available at 'reasonable cost' and to help the larger municipalities build rental housing for families with children. In the latter case the rental rates were to be determined by the municipalities concerned, although the province remained committed to the belief that such rates should be 'economic' and insisted that it was not becoming involved in the provision of 'subsidized housing.'[21]

During the 1960s, however, the provincial government was drawn into just such activity on a rather broad scale. In 1964 it established the Ontario Housing Corporation (OHC), which was assigned the task of ensuring that citizens of Ontario would have 'adequate accommodation.' The OHC was also obviously intended to utilize as fully as possible the funds being made available by the federal government to support low-cost housing programs. The OHC undertook surveys of housing needs throughout the province and began acquiring existing apartment buildings and constructing new ones to be operated as low-cost rental facilities by local housing councils in the case of larger communities or directly by OHC itself in the smaller centres. The 'Rent Geared to Income' program was steadily expanded during the late 1960s, with much of the activity centred in metropolitan Toronto. In 1966 OHC also became engaged in constructing university residence facilities.

Single-family housing construction was also sponsored by OHC. Several programs aimed at facilitating home building and purchasing were combined in 1967 under the 'Home Ownership Made Easy Plan' (HOME). By the end of the decade OHC was involved in more than 12 per cent of all housing starts in the province and was managing more than 22,000 rental properties located in seventy-seven different municipalities. By the early 1970s it claimed to be the second largest social housing agency in North America, exceeded only by the New York City housing authority, which dated from the 1920s.[22] In 1971 a subsidiary, the Ontario Housing Corporation Limited, was established to provide second mortgage financing to homeowners under the 'Ontario Guaranteed Mortgage Loan' program.

By the mid-1970s OHC had captured some $150 million of federal funds for use in Ontario residential construction and had made progress on several large developments, the most important of which was the long-planned Malvern subdivision in the eastern metropolitan Toronto area. In the larger centres, however, such expansion was becoming increasingly difficult owing to restrictions on the supply of building land and growing opposition in some established communities to the further development of 'subsidized housing.' The OHC nevertheless remained an aggressive participant in the provincial housing market and by the mid-1970s was making special efforts to promote housing development in the smaller centres of northern Ontario where a new program, 'Northern Ontario Assistance in Housing' was implemented to promote residential construction and lower-cost rental accommodation as part of community development efforts in frontier resource towns.

In the main population centres of southern Ontario the provincial government's role in supporting residential construction by providing more and more serviced building land was complicated by conflicting policy considerations. As the expanding suburbs, shopping centres, and industrial parks engulfed the countryside surrounding the urban areas of southern Ontario, finding ways to control and limit 'urban sprawl' began to rival supplying serviced building land as a policy object, and it became increasingly difficult to reconcile the two. The situation was complicated by the emergence of a major new private-sector industry devoted to the development of large new residential and commercial projects. This industry involved companies created for the purpose of acquiring properties, devising plans for developing them, seeking approval of public authorities for these plans, investing in the necessary utilities, such as roads and streets, water supplies, and other services, and selling or leasing the building sites so created to builders who then erected the houses or other structures on them for sale to the

Land and Capital Resources 49

final users. As this industry grew, it became increasingly concentrated, and a few large land development or combined development and building companies acquired dominant positions. During the 1950s many individual builders and developers formed syndicates, some of which in the 1960s evolved into large development companies. One of the first of these was the Consolidated Building Corporation formed in 1966.[23]

The freedom of even such large private organizations to increase the supply of building land was limited, however, by the planning system established by the provincial government to control the physical expansion of the urban areas and to limit the strains imposed on local governments by this expansion during the post-war boom. Containing urban sprawl was achieved largely by using the powers of the provincial and municipal authorities to grant subdivision approval only after it had been established that adequate provision could be made to supply major services such as water and sewage. Public authorities were often unable or unwilling to finance the provision of such services, and even very large private development corporations could not do so on their own in cases where extensive construction through areas adjacent to particular developments was required. Not until the early 1970s did the province begin to provide assistance on a large scale for major new trunk water and sewer systems. Some local authorities got around this constraint by allowing developers to build on unserviced land, for example, by permitting the use of septic tank sewage systems. But in most major jurisdictions this option was denied by local regulations enacted in response to pressure from the provincial planning authorities. Septic tank subdivisions were not permitted in Metro Toronto, for example, after 1955. Although lower servicing standards were applied in smaller centres and in rural areas, regulations concerning water and sewage systems became increasingly strict and served to limit the approval of subdivisions and the creation of individual building lots by severance. In recreational areas, too, the raising of waste disposal standards served to control growth and, as elsewhere, contributed to rising land prices.

Despite the problems of serviced land supplies and other constraints operating on the industry, the output of housing reached very high levels during the post-war period. Activity accelerated during the late 1950s, and a record level of 63,753 housing starts was reported in 1958. During the decade between 1951 and 1961 almost 460,000 housing units were added to the stock of housing in Ontario, an increase of almost 40 per cent.[24] By 1962 the provincial government could claim that 'In general, the shortage of housing accommodation has been overcome,' although it acknowledged that there remained some pockets of 'real need' among families requiring rental housing and particularly among those who cannot pay an economic rent.[25]

As shown in table 9, the housing branch of the construction industry remained active through the remainder of the 1960s and into the following decade. By the early 1970s the total housing stock in the province was 2.25 million units and

TABLE 9
Dwelling Starts, Ontario, 1945–75

Year	Number	Year	Number
1945	15,100*	1961	48,144
1946	21,300*	1962	44,306
1947	24,700*	1963	55,957
1948	29,976	1964	65,617
1949	34,023	1965	66,767
1950	33,430	1966	52,355
1951	27,349	1967	68,121
1952	30,016	1968	80,375
1953	38,873	1969	81,446
1954	46,382	1970	76,675
1955	53,456	1971	89,980
1956	48,712	1972	102,933
1957	47,739	1973	110,536
1958	63,753	1974	85,503
1959	54,158	1975	79,968
1960	42,282		

* Completions 1945–7 inclusive

SOURCE: 1950–75: *Ontario Statistics, 1977*, vol. 2, table 21.13, 628

the annual additions were still increasing, reaching a new peak of 110,536 starts in 1973. Even so, the need for housing was also growing, and the new construction did little more than maintain the housing standards existing in the early 1950s. For example, the incidence of 'crowding' (households with one person per room) was not noticeably lower than it had been twenty years earlier, although there was great improvement over the levels of the early 1940s.[26]

There was a major change in the type of housing constructed during the period. While the earlier post-war years were marked by the building of small, detached houses in new suburban areas, the 1960s brought a pronounced trend towards multi-family buildings. In the late 1950s, nearly 65 per cent of all housing starts were single-family detached dwellings; by the mid-1970s this percentage had fallen to less than 40, as rising land and labour costs encouraged the construction of larger buildings, especially the high-rise apartment structures, which by then were becoming common not only in congested downtown areas but in the suburbs as well. Legislation introduced in the late 1960s to facilitate the condominium form of ownership contributed to this trend. The Ontario Housing Corporation as well as private developers began building increasing numbers of condominium apartments in the early 1970s.

Engineering Construction

During the 1930s there was considerable investment in engineering construction, particularly of highways, despite the difficult economic conditions of the time.

TABLE 10
Engineering Construction by Type, Ontario 1939–75 ($thousands)

Type of Structure	1939	1945	1952	1955	1960	1965	1970	1975
Roads, highways, and airports	30,767	9,761	192,519	168,584	251,930	296,360	389,944	634,445
Water and sewers	3,695	2,648	47,716	57,723	99,521	122,137	207,915	518,741
Dams and irrigation	655	304	4,460	5,656	4,989	11,885	16,298	39,690
Electric power	13,207	1,534	140,368	104,730	118,422	145,270	353,096	737,175
Rail and telephone	–	–	84,849	114,077	143,053	130,008	199,388	339,648
Gas and oil	–	–	51,435	25,469	69,104	73,573	105,046	348,318
Marine	1,760	2,179	14,103	17,839	25,426	33,939	25,328	33,153
Other engineering*	8,429	3,429	12,105	48,837	103,739	140,465	263,477	580,982
Total	58,513	19,855	547,555	542,915	816,184	953,637	1,560,492	3,232,152

* Rail and telephone and gas and oil are included in 1939 and 1945.

SOURCES: 1939 and 1945: Ontario, Bureau of Statistics and Research *A Conspectus of Ontario* (Toronto, 1946), table 84, 272; 1952–72: *Ontario Statistics 1975*, vol. 2, table 20.9, 702; 1975: *Ontario Statistics 1981*, table 21.8, 551

But many projects were also deferred, particularly those for which local governments were normally responsible. During the war years the federal government's system of priorities in allocating economic resources discouraged much of this activity, except when it was deemed essential for the war effort. What could be done seldom went beyond the making of necessary repairs and provision of military and other facilities. In Ontario highway and electric power construction claimed about $10 million annually. The rate of growth in the stock of these and other basic facilities fell far behind the growth of demand. At the end of the war the government of Ontario consequently found itself with a backlog of urgently needed construction work. Yet shortages of labour and materials, combined with the rather conservative budgetary practices of the government in office made progress slow until the 1950s, when large roadbuilding, electric power, oil and gas pipeline, and waterworks and sewage system projects got under way.

Road, highway, and airport construction accounted for more than 50 per cent of total engineering construction in 1939 and for about 30 per cent through most of the post-war period to the mid-1960s, falling sharply in relative importance in the early 1970s to reach just under 20 per cent of the total in 1975. Spending on roads and highways also accounted for a substantial proportion of total provincial government spending during the period. Such investment claimed about

TABLE 11
Highway and Road Mileage, Ontario, 1939–75

Year	Total Mileage
1939	72,538
1945	72,959
1950	73,779
1955	82,271
1970	94,499
1975	97,780

SOURCES: *Ontario Statistics 1975*, table 21.4, 729; *Ontario Statistics 1977*, table 22.3, 642–3; *Conspectus of Ontario*, table 129, 313

15 per cent of the provincial budget in 1945 and approximately double that amount in the late 1940s. Thereafter the road and highways item took between one-quarter and one-third of total provincial net expenditure, with the highest level of 33.4 per cent recorded in 1957.[27]

Such spending had strong appeal for politicians and constituents alike. The outlays could be treated as a potentially self-liquidating form of investment and one that yielded tangible evidence of the efforts being made by elected officials to improve the well-being of their supporters. It could also be justified in times of prosperity on the grounds that it was needed to keep up to increased requirements for transportation, while in times of recession it could be justified as a way of creating jobs. Highways could also be seen as instruments by which other virtuous goals of government were being realized: notably the decentralization of industry and the promotion of regional economic growth objectives, although the net effect of improved transport in the latter case was not always clear. At least until the late 1960s neither the government nor the opposition parties had any doubts about the need for an ever-expanding road network in the province, although there was ample disagreement about the type of roads, their location, and the best ways to finance their construction. Thus, when the government claimed in 1949 that its five-year program of highway construction would 'facilitate the development of manufacturing, logging, mining, farming and tourism' and that it was budgeting $69 million for it that year, the opposition could only complain that such efforts were not great enough.[28] During the early 1950s the CCF repeatedly condemned the government for taking in more revenue from gasoline taxes than it was spending on highways, while the Liberals were complaining that only 200 miles of new highways had been built since 1943. The government seemed willing to agree that greater efforts were required and a spokesman proclaimed that 'No small nibbling at the highway problem will suffice.' The 1953 road budget was claimed to be without parallel in the history of the province; more than $150 million was devoted to highway construction and maintenance, so as to 'overtake the twenty-year lag' in such work.[29] By the late 1950s the outlay on highways was more than $230 million annually.

Ontario's total road and highway mileage was only slightly greater in 1949 than it had been a decade earlier: 72,847 miles compared with 72,538. Over the next twenty years the total increased by nearly 30 per cent, reaching almost 95,000 miles by the mid-1970s. By then, however, the once-universal enthusiasm for road-building was past, and there were growing doubts in the province about the desirability of building roads whenever and wherever there appeared to be a demand for them. The end of the boom in expressway construction, which had brought the province the Queen Elizabeth Way from Niagara to Toronto in the 1930s and Highway 401 from Windsor to the Quebec boundary in the early 1960s, was marked by the provincial government's decision to terminate the Spadina Expressway project in Toronto in 1972. Interest in new transportation systems was beginning to shift in the direction of improved mass transit facilities.

Electric Power Construction

Second to roads and highways, construction of electric power facilities was the largest component in engineering construction in the province over the 1939–75 period. Like highway-building it was almost entirely a publicly financed activity. Some expansion of the system had taken place even during the depression years of the 1930s and at the outbreak of war in 1939 Ontario Hydro was in the midst of a further modest expansion program, which had been undertaken in the expectation of an eventual increase in demand. New agreements had been reached with adjacent jurisdictions in the United States concerning water rights, and in 1940 a major diversion plan at the Lakehead was approved. By 1941 these expansion plans had been caught up in the wartime mobilization campaign, and the diversion schemes designed to feed water from James Bay into the Great Lakes system were expanded. In 1942 Ontario Hydro added almost 67,000 horsepower to its generating capacity, and new plants were begun at Barrett Chute and Bark Lake, both on the Madawaska River, and at De Cew Falls.

At the time, much of this work was seen as a substitute for the long-hoped-for St Lawrence River project, which would have permitted much larger developments than those possible on the Ottawa River tributaries or by diverting James Bay water to the south. A large part of the rising demand during the war years was met by increased purchases of power from other producers.

At the end of the war power requirements in Ontario increased very rapidly and the existing facilities proved hopelessly inadequate. Black-outs became common and power rationing schemes were implemented, causing much public discontent. With the St Lawrence project still bogged down as a result of political problems in the United States, Ontario Hydro had no alternative but to undertake the development of more northerly sites in the province and to improve interconnections with American systems so that in emergencies larger quantities of power could be imported when needed. Construction was also undertaken to improve existing facilities, particularly at Niagara Falls.

During the 1950s hydroelectric sites were developed in the north-western part of the province. The Nipigon, Winnipeg, and English rivers were developed, and interconnecting facilities with Manitoba Hydro were installed similar to those already built to connect the southern Ontario system to the Detroit Edison and Niagara Mohawk systems.[30]

In 1954 the long-awaited go-ahead for the St Lawrence project was received and after forty years of discussions, work officially began on the International Rapids section in August. The massive engineering program involved construction of two main dams and two power houses. At the foot of the Long Sault Rapids a dam was built to create a head pond some 125 miles downstream from the eastern end of Lake Ontario. The structure containing the power houses spanned the channel between the Canadian shore and the eastern end of Barnhart Island, about three miles west of Cornwall. The Long Sault dam was built from the end of Barnhart Island to the U.S. shore to control the water level in the head pond, while further upriver another dam, the Iroquois, spanned the river from Iroquois Point on the Canadian side to Point Rockway on the American side to provide control over the outflow from Lake Ontario. River channel realignment, dyking, and clearing some 20,000 acres to be flooded on the Canadian side added to the size of the undertaking. The town of Iroquois, six hamlets, and part of the town of Morrisburg were obliterated.

The huge construction project on the St Lawrence River combined with the other power projects underway in the province in the mid-1950s raised the level of activity in this branch of the industry to unprecedented levels. In 1957 the value of such investment amounted to almost $200 million.

By 1956 Ontario Hydro believed that it had reached the end of foreseeable hydro developments in southern Ontario. Noting that the remaining sites in the north were not large, the commission indicated that its future expansion would entail building mainly thermal plants some of which might be nuclear fuelled. Two large conventional thermal plants were constructed during the 1950s, the Richard L. Hearn plant in Toronto and the J. Clark Keith plant at Windsor.

While the commitment to thermal power and the associated development of nuclear technology subsequently were to dominate Ontario Hydro's activity, advances in high voltage transmission technology opened up new opportunities for developing several remote sites remaining in the far north. In the early 1960s the commission built four new hydro stations on the Moose River in the James Bay watershed and later added three others on the Mattagami River to the west. Late in the decade several smaller projects were undertaken near Elliot Lake and on the Madawaska River in eastern Ontario. Several of the new facilities were designed to be completely operated by remote control.

Spending on electric power construction was maintained at high levels into the 1970s because of the nuclear power station program. The first demonstration nuclear plant in Canada was built at Rolphton, Ontario and began feeding power into the grid in 1962. The first full-scale plant was subsequently constructed at Douglas Point on Lake Huron and was brought into operation in 1967. This was followed by the even larger 2,160,000 kWh station at Pickering, near Toronto, which began producing power in 1971. In the same year the first unit of the large Bruce Nuclear Station was begun at the Douglas Point location on Lake Huron.

The Size and Timing of Public Works

Much of the post-war expansion of the electric power, highway, and other social overhead capital facilities in Ontario can be explained simply by the requirements placed on the provincial and municipal governments to meet the demands created by a rapidly growing population and an expanding industrial system. Given the increase in the relative size of the public works budget and the growing acceptance of the principle that government spending could be used to help stabilize the economy, it might be expected that the scheduling of such projects would have been related to fluctuations in the overall level of activity in the economy. Such does not appear to have been the case.

By the end of the 1940s the idea of using the government's control over the level of public works activity to influence the level of employment and income was well established. Even in the 1930s the government of Ontario had found itself, however inadvertently, creating employment by such means. Through the post-war period it was common for the throne and budget speeches to refer to the employment-stimulating effects of the government's proposed spending programs, or to justify reductions in such spending on the grounds that restraint was needed to alleviate inflationary pressures. Yet studies of the construction industry in Ontario and in Canada as a whole show that outlays, even in the case of engineering construction, tended to be pro-cyclical rather than counter-cyclical in their timing and impact. No evidence has been found that any sustained effort was made to use investment spending under direct government control as a stabilizing force in the economy.[31]

4 Transportation and Communications

The national transportation and communications systems developed in Canada after Confederation endowed Ontario with a strong central position in the economic geography of the nation. The physical location of these facilities, the organization of the firms and agencies operating them, and the policies of the governments that regulated them reinforced the dominance of central Canada in the economic and cultural life of the country. In the period after 1939 Ontario's position was maintained, but important changes were taking place. The decline of the railroads, improvements in air transport, the development of the St Lawrence Seaway, the coming of interprovincial oil and gas pipelines, and the great expansion of communications facilities during the 1939–75 period had mixed effects on the economy of the province, many of them beneficial. But some of these new developments were disappointing in their immediate results, and a few raised concerns about the future.

The Railways

The transportation and communications facilities established in Ontario during the railway-building era earlier in the century provided the province not only with links to the rest of Canada and, indeed, the entire continent, but with an extensive internal network of rails and copper-wired telegraph and telephone services as well. Nearly every community of any consequence, except in the far north of the province, had its railway station and regular freight and passenger services. Communications were provided by the mails carried on the trains and by telegraph and telephone wires strung along the railway right of way. Most of these services were provided by national organizations, the Canadian Pacific Railway and Canadian National Railway companies, but Ontario also had its own provincially owned and operated railway system, the Timiskaming and Northern Ontario Railway, which linked Toronto and the mining and forest-resource towns of north-eastern Ontario.

By 1939 the dominance of the railways over other forms of transportation was breaking down. The expanding network of roads and highways and increasing fleets of private automobiles and trucks were making it possible for people and freight to travel with greater freedom and economy. Air transport was also beginning to provide an alternative to railways in the southern parts of the province, athough it was already well established as the preferred, and often only, means of modern transport in the north. Water transportation was confined to moving grain, coal, and a few other bulk cargoes on the Great Lakes–St Lawrence system and to providing some small-scale freight and passenger services on a few lakes and rivers in northern Ontario and a few recreational services elsewhere in the province. The possibility that a deep-water seaway along the St Lawrence would permit Ontario to develop direct ocean shipping facilities was a lively topic of discussion. Interest also remained alive in the possibility of developing a port at Moosonee on James Bay and utilizing the Timiskaming and Northern Ontario Railway to link such a port with the continental rail system.

In the special case of urban passenger services the continuing shift of population from the countryside to the cities and towns was creating a growing demand for improved roads to alleviate traffic congestion and to reduce travel time between downtown and the spreading suburban areas. The alternative, further development of the tramways and other established street railway systems, was not favoured. In Ontario, as elsewhere in North America, the preference of governments and their advisers was for measures that would accommodate the needs of private automobiles and the motor buses that were about to replace the streetcars and other fixed-line vehicles. The streetcars did not entirely disappear, however, and in Toronto they were eventually supplemented with an expensive underground railway system which came into operation in 1954.

The vigorous measures taken to facilitate the use of motor vehicles in Ontario during the period are reflected in the account of highway investments in the preceding chapter. What the data fail to convey is the extent to which the roads, highways, and urban expressways shaped the life-style of the post-war period, how they contributed to the decline of established commercial areas in downtown parts of the cities, disrupted residential neighbourhoods, and determined the strip developments of shopping plazas, malls, drive-in theatres, and fast food establishments of the suburbs. The immediate environment in which the post-war generations grew up in Ontario was shaped in large part by the expenditures made on road and highway construction. At the time, such developments were generally regarded as benign. When the province's first urban expressway, Mount Pleasant Road, was bulldozed through Rosedale, one of Toronto's most prestigious residential neighbourhoods, little protest was recorded.

Other forms of transportation were also becoming important in the early part of the period. As large, efficient new types of aircraft were developed, the prospect that Toronto and possibly other major centres in southern Ontario could become centres for international as well as domestic aviation was a subject of increasingly optimistic conjecture on the part of Ontario politicians and businessmen.

Despite all the interest in planning during the war years, the implications of the technical and other changes affecting transportation and communications then and in the immediate post-war period appear to have attracted no serious attention. Certainly there was no deliberate effort on the part of governments at any level to devise a new kind of transport system for the country. If there was any view as to what the future would hold, it appeared to be strongly rooted in the past. The nineteenth-century assumption that the railways would provide the core of the system persisted well into the post-Second World War period, a conceptual lag that was thoroughly documented by the several inquiries subsequently conducted into the state of the transportation industry.

Early in the 1930s the Duff Royal Commission had studied the situation of the railway companies and made recommendations intended to improve their financial position. Some of them had been incorporated in the federal transportation legislation of 1937 which gave a newly created Board of Transport Commissioners (formerly the Board of Railway Commissioners) power to regulate rates charged by air (and some water) carriers. The new regulations permitted the railways to negotiate 'agreed charges' with customers in the hope that this facility would enable them to meet more effectively the growing competition from the trucking industry.[1]

After the war the perennial discontent of Canadians, particularly western Canadians, with the structure and level of railway freight rates led to the appointment of another royal commission (the Turgeon Commission) in 1951. It devised an elaborate procedure for determining appropriate railway freight rates, but its proposals were overtaken by the course of events. The loss of freight traffic by the railways to the trucking industry was no longer so much a threat as a fact. Not just local, short-haul traffic was being taken, but longer-haul freight as well. Even as the Turgeon Commission was deliberating, the Trans-Canada Highway system was being completed, considerably facilitating such long-distance trucking. Railway freight rates no longer constituted the important political issue they had.[2] By the end of the decade, construction of other new transportation facilities, the major oil and gas pipelines, and the St Lawrence Seaway, and continued advances in air transportation carried the process further.

The railway companies were not entirely defenceless in the face of this increasingly competitive situation. They lobbied strongly for public financial support. In the later 1950s they obtained such help from a new federal government, which found it politically expedient, however, to subsidize the railways rather than grant them the rate increases they claimed they needed to offset rapidly rising labour costs.[3] In the hope of finding a more acceptable long-term solution to the problem, the government appointed another royal commission (the Macpherson Commission).

The analysis and recommendations contained in the Macpherson Commission report in 1961 were a departure from the established approach to Canadian transport policy. Accepting the fact that the railway monopoly had been broken by new forms of transport, the commission recommended that the railway companies be given free rein over their rate setting, that a single regulatory board be created with jurisdiction over all forms of transportation in Canada, and that the railways be compensated for costs that were imposed upon them as a result of broad public interest considerations. These recommendations reflected the Macpherson Commission's understanding that the nature of transportation in Canada was being fundamentally changed by 'a massive and largely undirected expenditure on roads,' an expenditure, it noted, which was taking place without reference to 'rational transport planning.'[4]

With the notable exceptions of the Trans-Canada Highway project and the resource development roads of the late 1950s and early 1960s, both of which entailed extensive federal participation, most of the road-building effort was supported by the provinces. The railways, air transport, waterways, and pipelines were mainly matters of federal responsibility. This jurisdictional difference, the markedly different technical characteristics of the various forms of transportation, and the mix of private and public firms involved – some very large, others small – made the development of a coherent and 'rational' transportation system in Canada particularly difficult, if not impossible. The implications of this lack of an overall transportation plan for the country were better understood in the years following the Macpherson Commission's report, as the issues of conflicting regional interests were more clearly articulated.

While the National Transportation Act of 1967 implemented many of the Macpherson Commission's recommendations, it did not resolve the problem of reconciling a national transportation policy with the economic aspirations of the country's various regions. The conviction persisted in the Maritimes and western Canada that the national interest in transport policy continued to be suspiciously congruent with the interests of central Canada, just as it had in the days when transportation was a virtual monopoly of the railways. To the extent that Ontario had an official position on such matters, it was one of defending the status quo. But even within Ontario it was difficult to find a consensus on transport policy. People outside the southern metropolitan area, particularly those living in northwestern Ontario, felt that they too were the victims of discriminatory rate-setting and poor service.[5]

The Ontario government made its first formal submission on the subject of transport policy in 1960, when the Macpherson Commission held hearings in the province. In his opening remarks to the commission, the premier, Mr Frost, expressed interest in the commission's task and emphasized his understanding of how fundamental were the changes taking place in the transportation industry. 'The railways which, at one time, could bend the economy to meet their operating convenience,' he noted, 'could no longer do so.' While they could still in some areas 'exercise the power of life or death over resource or business development and expansion, their near monopolistic domination of the economy at large no longer exists.'[6] Recognizing that there were a number of reasons for this change, Mr Frost expressed many of the same concerns the commissioners were to hear elsewhere in Canada. He observed that in much of the province railways had 'ceased to be of economic consequence,' and that he had himself 'seen and watched the almost total dissolution of any practical railway service to the people of vast areas of Ontario.'[7]

The theme of Ontario's submission to the Macpherson Commission was that Ontario contributed more than any other part of Canada to the revenues of the railways by virtue of the high density and relative profitability of the freight traffic carried by the railways in the province. Concern was expressed that if the commission failed to find ways to resolve the railways's financial problems without imposing higher rates on their Ontario customers, the province's trade would be restricted, which would adversely affect not only Ontario but the whole of Canada. Such fears proved groundless, it seemed; for in Ontario, as elsewhere in the country, the issue of railway freight rates appeared to die a natural death in the late 1960s. The feeling in Ontario following enactment of the National Transportation Act in 1967 was that some of the problems of the national transportation policy had been alleviated and no vital interests harmed.

Many of the problems of the national railway systems were shared during the period by the Ontario government's own line, the Timiskaming and Northern Ontario Railway (T & NO). Increasing competition from the trucking industry, rising labour costs, and sharply increased fuel prices were problems which persisted from the 1930s into the 1970s.

In 1940 the Timiskaming and Northern Ontario was in reasonably good financial condition. It was acquiring new equipment, and the organization was expanding its activities into trucking and bus transport. The railway's administrative operations were closely controlled from Queen's Park. As in earlier periods, it was not uncommon for the premier to take a personal hand in directing its affairs, and it was understood that jobs in the organization were within the government's giving. In 1944 the new Conservative leader, George Drew, appointed a three-man commission, all staunch party supporters, to run the operation.

The Drew administration actively supported the T & NO system as part of the post-war reconstruction effort. Northern development was once again seen as a convenient way to relieve the economic and social problems that were expected to afflict southern Ontario after the war ended. Mr Drew held a strong personal conviction that agricultural settlement in the north and further exploitation of northern timber and forest resources would create useful employment for returning veterans and others who might find it difficult to locate jobs in the industrial areas of the south. Despite pessimistic advice from those who knew something of the region (and also from his own minister of mines, Leslie Frost), Drew exhorted his new T & NO commissioners to explore 'every possible opportunity' to make the railway the 'backbone of a greatly expanded system of communication supporting a greatly increased population' in northern Ontario.[8] The new chairman of the commission accepted the challenge, declaring upon assuming office in 1944 that, 'We are not concerned so much with the operation of the railway, as with the opportunities it can offer in the development of the North.'[9]

During the next several years the possibilities for promoting northern development in Ontario were actively explored but to little effect. From the standpoint of the railway's own operations, one of the most promising developments would have been to utilize the lignite coal deposits known to exist in the region it served. This would provide the railway with an alternative to the imported U.S. coal supplies it had always depended upon. During the early 1940s much had been made of such a possibility.[10] But nothing came of the scheme then or on subsequent occasions when it was resurrected, often in conjunction with the much-discussed plan to construct an ocean port at Moosonee. The T & NO's fuel supply problem was eventually solved not by developing local fuel sources but like the national railways by converting from steam to diesel-electric locomotion.

The railway's name was changed after the war to the Ontario Northland Railway (ONR), apparently in recognition of the fact that the system by then extended well beyond the Timiskaming region and also to eliminate the considerable inconvenience that arose with respect to billing and boxcar retrieval when the T & NO was mistaken for the Texas and New Orleans Railway.

The conversion to diesel began shortly after the end of the war and was completed by 1957. Along with new engines, the system acquired modern service and repair facilities at North Bay and Cochrane. Extensive improvements were undertaken in the roadbed and signalling apparatus. The costs of this capital spending were met by the provincial government, which guaranteed or purchased over $17 million worth of the railway's debentures in the ten years between 1947 and 1957.[11]

The organization's financial situation in the post-war years was similar to that of the other Canadian railways. Despite rising rail freight rates and vigorous promotional efforts aimed at increasing railway traffic, revenues rose less than operating costs. Even major new mining developments in the 1960s, some of which greatly reduced the railway's former dependence on 'less than carload' freight shipments, helped less than might have been expected. Heavy capital outlays had to be made to provide the new equipment, and better operating standards were required to serve the new bulk shippers becoming established in the area.[12]

Once these improvements were made, however, the Ontario Northland system developed a hybrid operation in which the railway itself concentrated on handling heavy bulk cargoes while general freight and passenger traffic was turned over to trucking and bus lines operated by the commission as subsidiaries. A private trucking firm, Star Transfer Limited, was acquired in 1960 and with an expanded fleet enabled the Ontario Northland Transportation Commission (ONTC) to provide highway freight service from Toronto-Hamilton directly to many centres in northern Ontario once served exclusively by rail.[13] Similarly, an expanding network of bus routes operated by the commission in the north served to tie passenger service in the region into the passenger transport systems of southern Ontario. The volume of rail passenger service provided by the Ontario Northland fluctuated erratically but trended steadily downward. In the 1940s over 500,000 passengers annually were carried on the railway. By the early 1970s this figure had fallen to fewer than 200,000.

In contrast to passenger traffic, the physical volume of freight carried on the railway remained generally stable over much of the period, fluctuating between 2 and 3 million tons annually between the end of the war and the mid-1960s. The new bulk shipments of ore and concentrates thereafter generated a great increase in the volume of freight carried. By the early 1970s freight tonnage was double what it had been five years before. The first of the mining developments responsible for this expansion was the iron pellet operation at the Adam mine south of Kirkland Lake. When this site was connected to the railway by a five-mile spur line in 1965, it became possible to ship the pellets produced there directly by rail to the Jones and Laughlin Steel Company mills in Cleveland and Pittsburgh. Three years later the Sherman mine, located north of Tamagami, was brought into production by Dominion Foundries and Steel Ltd. (Dofasco) and tied into the rail system. The Kidd Creek base metal mine of Texas Gulf Sulphur was also linked to the ONR in the late 1960s.

Bulk freight traffic generated by a new poplar plywood plant established in Cochrane in the mid-1960s was added to that of the established pulp and paper mills, principally the Spruce Falls plant at Kapuskasing and the Abitibi mills at Iroquois Falls and Smooth Rock Falls, all of which continued to depend on the railway to ship out their finished products.

With this increase in bulk freight traffic and the successful adaptation of its other services to the new conditions created by the expansion of highways in the region, the Ontario Northland system was in reasonably good financial condition by the late 1960s. While it maintained relatively low rates on some of its services, such as local express, it was compensated for any losses thereby incurred through a system of government subsidies. These were in turn treated by the government as appropriate outlays to be made in the interests of encouraging northern development in the province.[14]

In the later 1960s and early 1970s the use of the ONTC as an instrument for northern development was greatly expanded when the government began to add

TABLE 12
Motor Vehicle Registrations, Ontario, Selected Years 1939–75

Year	Total	Passenger	Commercial	Motorcyles
1939	682,891	595,586	82,206	5,099
1945	662,719	556,740	100,234	5,745
1950	1,104,080	887,571	202,800	13,709
1955	1,617,853	1,317,590	287,942	12,321
1960	2,062,484	1,732,933	320,190	9,361
1965	2,516,680	2,139,696	352,914	24,070
1970	3,047,599	2,576,041	426,307	45,251
1975	3,913,452	3,255,243	615,659	72,550

SOURCE: Leacy, ed., *Historical Statistics of Canada*, 2nd ed., 171–4

new functions to the organization's agenda. Many of these, unlike the truck and bus lines which were at least marginally profitable in terms of commercial accounting concepts, clearly had little prospect for operating at anything but substantial losses. Small-scale water transport, air services, tourist facilities, electric power, and communications systems were established in small northern communities and turned over to the ONTC to operate. The government itself, by then caught up in a new mood of austerity, proved reluctant to offset fully with subsidies the losses generated by these new functions. By the end of the period the commission was faced with a financial crisis which even a record $6 million government grant in 1975 could not fully resolve. Reductions in maintenance and restrictions on service appeared to be unavoidable. And once again, plans for a massive redevelopment of the railway itself, to be carried out as part of a new plan which would finally result in the establishment of a seaport on James Bay, were quietly put aside.[15]

Road Transport

The growing popularity of motor transport as a mode of passenger travel during the period is suggested by the fact that by the end of the 1930s there was one automobile for every 6.4 persons in Ontario. By 1975 the ratio was one for every 2.6. The numbers of commercial vehicles operating in the province also increased over the period, but because of the increasing size and efficiency with which commercial vehicles were used, particularly in the decades of the 1950s and 1960s, the amount of service provided was much greater than was suggested by the increased number of commercial vehicle registrations.

The technological and economic characteristics of the commercial trucking and passenger bus industries as they developed in the post-Second World War period were markedly different from those that affected the other principal modes of transportation in Canada. Because of the relatively small capital outlays required, entry to the industry was potentially easy, and the opportunities for highly competitive market structures to develop were correspondingly great. The flexibility of truck and bus operations was such that they could be organized to provide service on a scale appropriate to the needs of a great variety of possible users. This was one of the reasons commercial road transport posed such a strong challenge to the railways. Yet this competitive advantage of the private truck and bus carriers was not allowed to develop unrestrained.

The basis for regulating the trucking industry in Ontario had been established as early as the 1920s, when, apparently in response to pressure from the railways and a few already-organized trucking companies, the provincial government enacted legislation requiring operators to obtain permits from the Department of Highways before offering 'for hire' trucking services.[16] During the 1930s the Ontario Municipal Board was made responsible for screening applications for licences to determine whether there was a need for additional services. Exemptions from this requirement were granted to private owners of commercial vehicles using them in their own businesses. Carriers of farm or forest products and 'for hire' truckers operating in urban areas were also exempted.[17] These arrangements were reviewed in 1938 by a provincial royal commission on transportation. The findings as set out in the 'Chevrier Report' of December 1938 not only confirmed the need for such regulation but sought to extend its application to 'all commercial vehicles whether they be publicly or privately operated.' The guiding principles of the report were stated as follows: 'The duty of the controlling authority should be confined to insurance of the dependability of service, protection of the public against extortionate charges, discrimination and unfair and ruinous competition, the exploitation of labour, dangerous equipment and hazardous operating practices. It should afford protection of the licensed operators in their legitimate interests.'[18]

Chevrier recommended that a separate highway transport board should be created (a recommendation not adopted for another sixteen years) and that regulation of the trucking industry be continued and expanded. It had become a 'duty' of the public authority, he concluded, to supervise the standards of equipment, service, hours, conditions of labour, and operating methods of those who would use the public highways for commercial purposes. The outbreak of the Second World War rendered many of the commission's specific recommendations at least temporarily irrelevant, but the general principles of regulation it endorsed were embodied in subsequent law and practice in Ontario. In particular, the basic method of regulating entry to the trucking industry remained in effect through the post-Second World War period with only minor changes.

During the early 1940s organized truckers in Ontario expressed great concern over 'abuses' of existing regulations. The Ontario Trucking Association was strongly in favour of stricter controls to prevent unlicensed carriers from operating and to guard against 'overloading' of trucks. At the same time, they were worried about the possibility of 'excessive' regulation of their industry. They especially feared the entry of the federal authorities into the field. Apparently, the truckers suspected that the federal government was biased in favour of the railroads, not just because of historical involvement with their early development, but because it was itself a railway owner.

Another major concern of the trucking companies in the early 1940s was the prospect of unionization. By 1944 their worst fears appeared to have been justified. American organizers appeared in the province, some of whom none too tactfully suggested to operators what they were in for if they did not co-operate.[19] But large-scale unionization of truckers did not take place until after the war, by which time there were enough operators with substantial numbers of employees to make union organization feasible. There was considerable labour unrest in the industry during the 1950s.

The authority of the provinces to regulate trucking was challenged during the 1950s, and when the Privy Council ruled against them, it appeared that the federal government might intervene. It chose not to do so, however, and instead enacted legislation delegating to the provinces responsibility for regulating extra-provincial and international freight and passenger operations. In Ontario these functions were assumed in 1955 by a newly created body, the Ontario Highway Transport Board, which was also made responsible for regulating the bus and school bus industry under the provisions of the Public Vehicles Act.[20]

These arrangements were extensively reviewed during the 1960s and 1970s, but few changes were made. Most of the pressure for change seems to have come from groups interested in having more rather than less regulation of the industry. Organized truckers were particularly interested in finding ways to prevent operators from getting around restrictions by 'leasing' their vehicles to shippers.[21] But there were also critics of the regulatory system. One study, commissioned by the Ontario Economic Council, sought to demonstrate that the regulation of commercial trucking in the province had promoted the inefficient use of resources, caused rates to be higher than necessary, reduced levels of output, and, in general, concluded that the system of regulation had exercised 'a deleterious effect on the ability of Ontario shippers to produce goods.'[22]

Urban Transit

Most of the increased urban passenger service required by the rapid growth of Ontario cities in the 1939–75 period was met by the capital expenditures on roads and expressways and the accompanying increase in private automobile ownership referred to earlier in this chapter. Public transit facilities were relatively neglected. Most of the electric tramways and street railway systems were allowed to wear out, to be replaced with gasoline and diesel buses, which permitted greater flexibility in the design and scheduling of services, especially in the new suburban areas. Toronto retained its streetcars, and trolley buses were adopted there and in some smaller cities. Toronto also began building a subway system in the 1950s. But with such exceptions, reliance on public transit diminished in Ontario during the post-war period. By the late 1960s private automobiles were being used for an estimated 90 per cent of all urban passenger miles travelled.[23]

Problems of traffic congestion and air pollution in the cities became matters of concern during the 1960s but generally it appeared to be accepted that these difficulties could be overcome by building more expressways and through technical changes in automobiles that would lessen their noxious emissions. The problems of long-distance commuters also claimed attention, and in the 1960s the Ontario government began to experiment with commuter rail services which might serve to limit the need for further expansion of what were becoming increasingly expensive highway facilities in the more heavily populated, Toronto-centred region. The lakeshore 'GO' (Government of Ontario) trains operated between Pickering and Oakville by the CNR under contract to the provincial government demonstrated that a system of subsidized rail services could divert some commuter traffic from the highways.

At the same time, an effective grass-roots campaign to limit the further accommodation of the private automobile as a means of urban transport was gaining strength in the province as it was in other parts of North America. In Ontario it was led by those who opposed construction of the Spadina Expressway in Toronto.[24] The provincial government's apparent acceptance of the position taken by these groups was marked by its intervention in terminating the Spadina project and its announcement, in November 1972, that it had developed a new urban transportation policy which would redirect activity from expressway construction to other possibilities. Subsidies amounting to 75 per cent of new equipment costs and 50 per cent of operating losses were made available to municipalities investing in public transit facilities. Grants were also offered to assist local governments in improving traffic control systems. There were also inducements for employers to implement more flexible working hours as a means of reducing the rush-hour problem. Further efficiencies were to be sought by encouraging municipal governments to collaborate in developing regional transit authorities, the first of which was the Toronto Area Transit Operating Authority established in 1974.

Some aspects of the government's new enthusiasm for public transport were more visionary. Not only would it promote the use of existing forms of public transit, but it would undertake to lead the rest of the world in the development of new mass transit technologies. To implement its plans, the government created the Urban Transportation Development Corporation (UTDC), which was to 'develop innovative transit equipment of greatly improved technical capacity; and stimulate a major transit-manufacturing industry in Canada through financing and encouraging a continuous advanced transit research and development program.'[25]

The initial efforts of UTDC to create a new system were disappointing and politically embarrassing for the government. The idea was to develop, in collaboration with the Krauss-Maffei organization of West Germany, an intermediate capacity system using aluminum-bodied vehicles, magnetically levitated over steel rails built on an elevated concrete viaduct and propelled by linear-induction motors. Early tests were discouraging and UTDC subsequently appeared to be redirecting its efforts along more conventional lines.

By the mid-1970s it was apparent that the new urban transportation policy would yield results only slowly. Despite rising gasoline prices, increased subsidies to hold down mass transit fares, and much public relations effort aimed at speeding up the public's acceptance of mass transit, the automobile remained the preferred means of urban transport. Its manufacture also remained one of Ontario's most important industries.

Air Transport

Commercial aviation in Canada was still in its infancy at the beginning of the period. Trans-Canada Airlines, which began its operations on the west coast in 1937, had only begun to develop its routes in central and eastern Canada. In July 1939 air mail, passenger, and express services were inaugurated between Montreal, Ottawa, and Toronto, via Muskoka. The following year scheduled services were established between Toronto, London and Windsor, and a transcontinental flight was routed through Toronto to Ottawa and Montreal. By the end of the war, services through Toronto had been greatly expanded both in number and in frequency. Flights were available to New York, Chicago, and Cleveland as well as to most major cities in eastern and western Canada. In the years after the war, commercial aviation in Canada expanded enormously. In the country as a whole the number of passengers carried by Canadian airlines in domestic and international service and by scheduled foreign carriers within Canada increased from aproximately 837,000 in 1946 to more than 25 million in 1975.[26] In Ontario the commercial airlines in 1939 boarded 75,463 passengers; in 1975 more than 6 million passengers boarded commercial flights at the major airports in the province (Toronto, Ottawa, Windsor, London, and Thunder Bay).[27]

Much of this expansion of commercial aviation in the province was facilitated by public investments in airports. Late in the 1930s the federal government had built a number of large fields across Canada to promote the development of the national airline system and also as an employment-creating program. In Ontario fields were constructed at Ottawa, Malton (near Toronto), Crumlin (at London), and Windsor. The Commonwealth Air Training Program during the war necessitated additional construction and some twenty-five training fields were built in southern Ontario, mainly in the south-western part of the province. Consequently, at the end of the war there were air fields available in most of the major cities and towns of southern Ontario. There were problems, however, in adapting many of these to commercial use in the post-war years. Some were turned over to local governments to operate under a leasing arrangement with the federal authorities. The fields at Brantford, St Thomas, Kingston, Gananoque, St Catharines, Welland, Goderich, Tillsonburg, and Oshawa were subject to such agreements, but there appears to have been little incentive for the municipalities concerned to initiate improvements or even to maintain the facilities. Twenty years after the war a study found that 'The potential of these fields is still awaiting development, but the assets are steadily declining.'[28] Several new municipal airfields were constructed in southern Ontario after the war, but none of these was suitable for regular scheduled commercial use. At least until the early 1970s the provincial government showed little interest in supporting the development of airports in the smaller centres.

Because of such difficulties and the technical developments that led the major commercial airlines to adopt larger jet aircraft in the 1960s, the great expansion of civil aviation after the war affected mainly the larger centres that had adequate facilities and sufficient traffic volumes to support the new generation of aircraft then coming into use. While small firms did enter the business to supply local services to many of the medium-sized communities, they typically experienced chronic financial difficulties, even in the relatively well-populated southern areas of the province. In the north the problem was particularly acute; for there, alternative forms of transportation were often scarce or non-existent.

The provincial government was under continuous pressure to involve itself in the problems of the small regional air carriers operating in the northern part of the province. A number of studies were carried out by the Department of Economics and Development in the 1960s, but the conclusions did little to establish grounds for any very substantial intervention in the business by the government. One report completed in 1963, for example, suggested that the basic problem in northern Ontario was not the lack of facilities such as landing fields, but the absence of sufficient traffic to support profitable commercial services. It recommended that instead of attempting to develop feeder air services, which would probably require continuous and heavy subsidization, the government should seek to improve existing surface transportation in the north to link the region with the air services already established in the larger centres to the south.[29] A similar conclusion was reached when the department reviewed the matter several years later. It sternly warned against a policy of using public investment to lead the growth of demand for air services in remote areas, cautioning that 'The development potential of any area has to be ascertained before access is provided.'[30]

Despite such advice, the provincial government in the early 1970s did adopt a more positive policy to promote the development of short-haul air transport in certain parts of the province. In 1971 it initiated what was to be a three-year demonstration program to show how a high standard of local air services could be provided on apparently marginal routes. The experimental service, linking Sudbury, Sault Ste Marie, Timmins, and Earlton was initially flown by an existing small carrier (White River Air Services) under contract to the government and subsequently by a subsidiary of ONTC, 'norOntair.'[31]

Even with such encouragement, the local air services in Ontario remained weak at the end of the period. Although the province was well served by the trunk carriers, Air Canada and CP Air, and by a few large regional carriers such as Transair and Nordair, the various 'third-level' carriers which tried to provide service to smaller centres were generally marginal enterprises at best. In 1974 yet another provincial government study of the problem concluded that 'Whether considered individually or collectively, this group of carriers constitutes a weak industry, with serious problems of capital, inadequate equipment, limited service networks, poor airport and navigational facilities, low service reliability and low penetration of potential markets.'[32]

Water Transport

Much of the economic history of Canada has been written around the contribution of the St Lawrence River-Great Lakes waterway to the development of the country, while the efforts of successive governments to improve the system by means of canals and other expensive public works have been part of Canada's political history as well. Such efforts continued into the post-Second World War period, culminating in the opening of the St Lawrence Seaway in June 1959.

Throughout the 1940s the Ontario government devoted considerable effort to promoting the seaway project, partly because of the increased trade a seaport was expected to bring to the province, but also because of the need to develop additional hydroelectric power. When the project eventually did go ahead in the 1950s, construction progress was rapid. By the end of the decade it was possible for ocean-going vessels with a draft of twenty-seven feet to ascend to the head of the Great Lakes. The six St Lawrence canals and twenty-two locks previously in operation were replaced by three large new canals and seven locks.

Direct overseas shipping to and from Great Lakes ports in Canada and the United States was already growing in volume before the Seaway opened. In 1955 seventeen shipping companies were operating regular ocean services on the route, carrying mainly manufactured goods such as iron and steel products, automobiles, electrical apparatus, chemicals and clay.[33] There were also a few direct shipments of grain from the Lakehead to overseas destinations. Of much greater importance to the Ontario economy, however, was the intralake traffic in iron ore, coal, and limestone from the United States to supply the steel plants at Hamilton, Welland, and Sault Ste Marie. While these large bulk shipments were not severely restricted by the existing canal system, the prospect of supplementing the declining ore reserves of the American mid-west with imports

TABLE 13
Tonnage and Transits, St Lawrence Seaway, 1959-75

	Montreal – Lake Ontario Section		Welland Canal	
Year	Number of Transits	Short Tons	Number of Transits	Short Tons
1959	7,590	20,351,711	8,252	27,156,291
1960	7,387	20,310,346	8,007	29,249,689
1961	6,639	23,417,720	7,778	31,454,803
1962	5,963	25,593,600	7,248	35,406,305
1963	5,872	30,942,890	7,182	41,303,479
1964	6,440	39,309,029	8,051	51,388,512
1965	6,751	43,382,864	8,046	53,420,179
1966	7,031	49,249,358	8,428	59,271,666
1967	6,569	44,028,638	7,192	52,809,414
1968	6,296	47,953,850	6,998	58,074,714
1969	5,970	41,014,040	6,653	53,532,336
1970	5,973	51,143,168	7,001	62,868,908
1971	5,851	52,948,322	6,761	62,909,293
1972	5,884	53,579,940	6,621	64,095,379
1973	6,013	57,634,137	6,706	67,194,684
1974	4,113	44,146,444	5,090	52,359,962
1975	4,704	48,010,403	6,041	59,849,026

SOURCE: *Ontario Statistics, 1976*, vol. II, table 22.6, 647

from Labrador via a seaway to the east coast was of great interest to the steel industry in the Great Lakes region.

The total capital cost of the Seaway was about $1 billion. Of this, the Canadian St Lawrence Seaway Authority put up $322 million, the Ontario Hydro-Electric Power Commission $300 million, the Power Authority of the State of New York $300 million, and the St Lawrence Seaway Development Corporation of the United States $132 million. The project was expected to be self-liquidating, with construction and operating costs to be met by tolls charged on shipping.

Those who expected the Seaway to turn Toronto and other major centres on the Lakes into bustling ocean ports were soon disappointed. By the end of the first shipping season it was apparent that the system would not greatly increase the amount of direct ocean shipping to and from the Great Lakes region. Ocean-going vessels were difficult to handle in the confined canals of the inland waterway, and restrictions on their draft made it impossible to load many vessels to their high-seas capacities. As early as 1960 it was recognized that the Seaway would continue to be used mainly by specialized vessels carrying grain and iron ore between lake ports and St Lawrence River ports and the large, ocean-going vessels would take on and discharge their cargoes at or below Montreal.[34]

Some local optimism survived, however, and there were still hopes in the 1960s that the Seaway would stimulate the development of several harbours in Ontario, not only in major centres like Toronto and Hamilton, but at Sarnia, Windsor, Cornwall, and Thunder Bay. Both private and public agencies undertook a number of substantial capital works to improve handling and storage facilities at these places. But a combination of circumstances and policies seemed to doom such efforts to failure.

Marine transport was undergoing rapid technological change even while the Seaway was being planned. There was a strong trend towards the use of larger and more highly specialized ocean vessels, many of which could not be handled by even the largest conceivable inland waterway and certainly could not be economically employed in such service. Even general cargo vessels were being greatly altered in size and structure. The adoption of container systems, in particular, was affecting both the kinds of ships and the harbour facilities needed to work them. By the late 1960s it was apparent that even the largest ports in Ontario would be hard pressed to justify investment in such facilities. But the problem was not simply one of finding the necessary funds – there were also problems of administration and public policy.

While all public ports in Canada during the period were under federal jurisdiction, the major harbours, such as those at Montreal, Vancouver, and Halifax were administered by the Canadian Harbours Board, enjoying an established status as national utilities. The harbours on the Great Lakes, such as those at Toronto, Hamilton, and Thunder Bay, which were operated by independent commissions, appeared to be at a disadvantage in that their operations were judged to be more of local than national significance. This led some observers to believe that part of the reason for the lack of development along the Seaway was that the federal government was discriminating against the inland ports and providing significantly more aid to the others. The effect, it was alleged in Ontario, was for the federal government's harbours policy to 'choke off the Seaway at Montreal and Halifax.'[35] A study of Toronto harbour in 1968 suggested that a combination of preferential railway freight rates and lower terminal charges at coastal ports operated by the National Harbours Board made it impossible for Toronto to capture any appreciable amount of outbound freight traffic.[36]

Another source of disappointment in Ontario with the outcome of the Seaway development was the matter of toll charges. The Ontario government had initially hoped that the Seaway would be treated as a national utility, with the capital costs borne by the federal government. The Frost administration had lobbied vigorously to have the tolls either eliminated or set at a level sufficient to cover only operating and maintenance costs. Instead, the tolls were set to cover all the costs of the project. Successive Ontario governments, supported by Great Lakes shipping and other local interests, pressed for a reversal of this policy. As one Ontario businessman pointed out early in the debate, if the toll charges were to cover the capital costs of the Seaway, it not only would harm a number of industries in the province, but would mean that the province of Ontario would bear the major burden for paying for a 'national' system.[37] And, as the premier pointed out to the federal minister of transport, industrial development in central Canada historically had been fostered by toll-free navigation through the St Lawrence–Great Lakes system, a desirable precedent which he believed should be followed in determining the rates to be charged for the use of the Seaway.[38]

As the Ontario government developed its facilities for performing more sophisticated economic analysis, studies were produced supporting its position with respect to seaway tolls.[39] Such efforts proved somewhat difficult to sustain, however; for modern economic analysis is ill adapted to providing justifications for such regional subsidization. When the provincial government got around to developing a comprehensive transportation policy of its own in the early 1970s, it specified that the province 'desires to create an atmosphere where each mode of transportation offers its services under tolls and conditions that are as close as possible to the actual costs of providing these services, including a reasonable rate of return on invested capital.'[40] The government found it possible, nevertheless, to remain firm on the matter of Seaway tolls. The premier told the Great Lakes Commission's semi-annual meeting in 1975 that the province continued to oppose tolls on the Seaway and could not accept the inequalities created by the federal government's practice of applying a different cost recovery policy to the Seaway than to other modes of transportation. Noting that efficient and competitive ports were essential to the continued growth and stability of the province, he stated that they must not be allowed to be 'strangled by artificial constraints.'[41]

Such problems of reconciling political and economic issues in national transportation policies also arose in connection with a new form of transportation which became important to Ontario in the post-war period: the transcontinental pipelines.

Pipelines

The fuel shortages experienced in Ontario during the Second World War and the immediate post-war years demonstrated the province's vulnerability to interruptions in supplies of imported coal and oil. Although a small amount of oil was still being produced in Ontario in the early 1940s and some natural gas was used for residential cooking and heating in the south-western part of the province, the prospects for developing significant domestic reserves of these fuels were known to be poor.[42] A municipal committee examining the natural gas situation in 1947 saw only three possible ways of supplementing the declining Ontario reserves: manufacturing gas, importing natural gas from Texas, or importing natural gas from western Canada. Of these, only the first appeared to be feasible at the time. Because of natural gas shortages in the United States it seemed unlikely that exports to Canada would be allowed. The possibility of obtaining gas from Alberta appeared to be only a remote future possibility.[43]

Two developments, however, which were to alter Ontario's situation with respect to fuel supplies, were already under way. One was the successful advancement in the United States of long-distance pipeline technology which was being utilized to bring oil and gas from Texas to markets in the eastern United States. The other was the realization of unexpectedly large oil and gas reserves in Alberta in the late 1940s.

Development of the Alberta oil fields depended upon the establishment of markets outside the immediate production region, and in the late 1940s Imperial Oil began planning a pipeline from Edmonton to Regina. As reserves continued to grow much faster than expected, the scheme was expanded and the company proposed to extend the line to Superior, Wisconsin, at the head of the Great Lakes. From there tankers could be used to carry the Alberta crude to the company's large eastern Canadian refinery at Sarnia. The cost of transporting the oil in this way was estimated to be less than one-quarter the cost of rail shipment.[44]

The line was built by Interprovincial Pipeline Company and brought into operation in 1950. It was subsequently extended through the United States to Sarnia and eventually to Port Credit, near Toronto, by which point it had become the longest pipeline in the world, 1930 miles in total.

With the oil pipeline from Alberta in operation, Ontario had a major new source of crude oil available to supply its refineries and petrochemical plants. But especially after the opening of the St Lawrence Seaway, the alternative of importing oil from overseas was also attractive. The choice between western Canadian and overseas oil supplies was to be dictated by forces over which the province had little control: the policies of the large multinational oil companies involved and of the Canadian government. As a consequence of the National Energy Policy adopted by the Conservative government of John Diefenbaker, Ontario soon found itself committed, for better or worse – and in terms of immediate price differentials probably for worse – to western Canadian crude.[45]

The issues involved were subsequently even more clearly displayed in the bringing of Alberta natural gas to Ontario. The large reserves of natural gas being developed in Alberta, largely as a by-product of petroleum exploration and development, obviously greatly exceeded the conceivable local uses for it. One obvious market was the western United States. At about the same time that gas producers in Alberta were investigating the possibility of building pipelines to tap western American markets, the gas distribution companies in southern Ontario, such as Consumers' Gas of Toronto, were contemplating the possibility of obtaining natural gas from the large U.S gas distributors, who were by then developing markets in the north-eastern parts of the United States. Had the companies involved been allowed to work out arrangements among themselves, it appears likely that Alberta gas would have flowed into the north-western United States, and Texas gas would have found its way into the St Lawrence region of

Canada. But on both sides of the border powerful public policy considerations stood against such a development. A more complicated and, for Ontario consumers, more expensive arrangement evolved.[46]

The political and economic considerations involved in the decision to build a gas pipeline from Alberta to eastern Canada following a route north of the Great Lakes have been described in detail in other publications.[47] The roles played by the Ontario government and by business interests based in Ontario are not easily disentangled from the complex national and international elements that contributed to this controversial undertaking. The Ontario government's position with respect to the basic issues involved was initially conditioned by the simple fact that the province needed additional fuel supplies in the 1950s. There was reason to fear that opposition in the United States to exports of U.S gas to Canada would lead to protracted negotiatons with little certainty as to the outcome. There was also the experience of the Second World War years to consider. It was possible that in another emergency the Americans would simply shut off exports to Ontario. The Frost government was consequently disposed to support any scheme that would bring Alberta gas directly to Ontario by the most secure if not the most economical route. Its preferred instrument for achieving this goal would have been a crown corporation set up to build and operate a pipeline directly connecting Ontario and Alberta. With C.D. Howe handling the project for the federal government, it might have been expected that this approach, which had been so popular during the Second World War might have appealed to the federal authorities as well. But such was not to be. The federal cabinet apparently feared that the political risks involved in having a crown corporation involved in potentially contentious intraprovincial trade would be too great. It therefore chose to devise a scheme by which a private company would be assigned the task. Ontario went along with this arrangement, but it was quick to co-operate when the federal government found it necessary to create a crown corporation to build the troublesome 'northern Ontario bridge' portion of the pipeline.

There remained the question of how the western Canadian gas should be distributed once it reached its destination in Ontario. As the NDP pointed out in the legislature, it would be reasonable for a province that had pioneered in the public ownership of electric power generating facilities to entrust gas distribution to a public agency. C.D. Howe had also proposed such a course to the premier, Mr Frost. But the Ontario government took a different view. There were already private gas-distributing companies established in the province. Two of them, Union Gas and Consumers' Gas, were large and influential. Consumers' Gas had waged a vigorous campaign against the whole Trans-Canada pipeline scheme and had lobbied strongly to promote its own plans for importing U.S gas in collaboration with the large American utility, Tennessee Gas. The provincial government's professed reason for rejecting public in favour of private ownership of the distribution facilities in the province was, however, fiscal prudence. Relentlessly goaded by the NDP, the premier took refuge in his familiar recital of the province's financial woes. Given all the other demands being made on the public credit, he told the legislature in 1957, 'the more the province can do to encourage private agencies and others to operate these vast projects the better.' The credit of the province, he pointed out, 'is so important that the minute one waters it down with more projects than it can undertake, one is inviting disaster. There is the situation.'[48]

The choice of private instead of public agencies to handle the gas supply project solved some problems but created others for both the federal and the provincial governments. At the federal level the choice led to the politically disastrous 'great pipeline debate' of 1956. For the province it led to long-lasting recriminations concerning the fairness with which gas retailing franchises were awarded and an embarrassing scandal in which government officials were suspected of profiteering in the financing of a new gas distributing company, Northern Ontario Natural Gas, which was established to supply users in the northern part of the province.

But despite the difficulties, the gas pipeline was built. Completed by the end of 1958, the line ran from the Manitoba border to Thunder Bay and from there followed a broad arc through the clay belt region of northern Ontario and south through North Bay to Toronto. There the line branched, running west along the lakeshore to Hamilton and the Niagara peninsula and east to Montreal, with branches connecting Lindsay, Peterborough, and Ottawa to the main line of the system.

Consumers in Ontario were supplied by three major distributing companies. The Union Gas Company supplied the south-west, Consumers' Gas serviced Toronto and most of the rest of southern Ontario, while the Northern Ontario Natural Gas Company brought the new fuel to most major centres in northern Ontario. The main trunk line across the north, which had been built by the Northern Ontario Pipeline Crown Corporation, was purchased in 1963 by Trans-Canada Pipe Lines Ltd.

Even with the all-Canadian line in operation, the possibility of building a shorter, more economical line south of the Great Lakes remained alive. As eastern demand expanded beyond all expected levels, the capacity of the original line proved inadequate. The question was, should it be expanded by laying additional pipe in northern Ontario to 'loop' the line or by building a new line through the United States? In northern Ontario there was strong opposition to the U.S. alternative because of fears that it might result in higher prices in the north. In southern Ontario the old concerns about security of supply were again raised. Trans-Canada and its U.S. partner in the project gave assurances, however, that the main supply of gas to eastern Canadian would continue to move via the northern route and, on the basis of this and other assurances, received permission to go ahead with the line south of the Lakes. The new line was completed in 1968.

Even with the costs imposed by considerations of national policy, the new fuel supplies were utilized on a large scale. Within a few years a large part of the industrial and residential demand for heating in Ontario was being satisfied from these sources. This reduced the importance of some existing transportation facilities that had been developed to supply coal and crude oil to Ontario users. But the coming of the pipelines did not force abandonment of these facilities, most of which remained in use. Nor did the new fuel supplies cause any marked shifts in the location of major industries in the province. The large industrial users of oil and gas expanded their operations at or near existing installations. In Sarnia, for example, the petrochemical industry easily adapted to the opportunities presented by a reliable, steady supply of feed-stocks made possible by the pipeline system. The availability of unrestricted supplies of natural gas in northern Ontario removed one of the most frequently cited reasons for the sparseness of industrial development and population growth there, but the immediate effects on economic development were not great.

Communications

The period 1939–75 was marked by a number of major changes in the communications industries, many of them dictated by the advent of new technologies. There was also an enormous expansion in the sheer volume of information handling in business and the entertainment media. This 'information revolution' was common to much of the world, and Ontario's experience was similar to that of other economically advanced regions. The most obvious changes involved the substitution of higher capacity and more efficient ways of transmitting data, such as microwave and coaxial cable systems, for the old copper-wired networks upon which the telegraph and telephone companies had formerly relied. In broadcasting the great change, of course, came with the introduction of television. There were also the improvements in radio broadcasting arising from the development of frequency modulation and stereophonic broadcasting technologies. These developments were accompanied by a general trend towards concentration of ownership and control in several parts of the communications industry and by increasing centralization of certain related activities. The central position of Ontario in the national communications systems, established in the earlier periods of railway and the associated telephone and telegraph networks was continued and in the case of broadcasting strengthened. Toronto became the main production centre for English-language television in Canada.

The only part of the communications industry to show an absolute decline during the period was the telegraph. The number of telegrams transmitted in Ontario fell from just under 4 million in 1939 to less than 1.5 million by 1975.[49] Much of this business was lost to the telephone network, which became increasingly interconnected and inexpensive for long-distance communications.

The telephone system in Ontario was greatly affected by the Depression. While

TABLE 14
Telephones in Ontario

Year	Systems	Telephones
1954	465	176,593
1960	306	179,918
1970	66	183,858
1972	42	194,942

SOURCE: Ontario Telephone Commission, *Annual Reports*

the Bell Telephone Company system, which dominated the large urban markets of southern Ontario, easily survived the difficult years of the 1930s, many of the smaller independent telephone companies did not. During the war years the problems of the smaller companies were compounded when shortages of labour and equipment made it impossible to maintain their facilities, even when the financial means to do so were available. Many gave up and sold out. By the end of the war more than 80 per cent of the telephones in Ontario were connected to the Bell network. Although there were still some 550 independent systems in the province, they were very small. The largest, operated by the Northern Telephone Company had fewer than 16,000 customers, compared with Bell's 687,000.[50]

The Ontario government intervened in the affairs of the telephone industry in the late 1940s, enacting legislation (the Rural Telephone Act) in 1948 for the purpose of allowing Ontario Hydro to seek ways of improving and extending the rural telephone system. It went further in 1954, when the new Telephone Act made it possible for the government to provide independent telephone companies with technical help through a new body, the Ontario Telephone Authority. The latter was also assigned the regulatory and other functions formerly exercised by the Ontario Municipal Board.[51]

When the new authority began its work, there were 465 independent telephone companies in the province operating approximately 176,000 telephones. Few of these companies had dial exchanges and most had fewer than 300 subscribers. By amalgamating neighbouring systems it was possible for some to make the conversion to dial exchange operation economically. But many found it more convenient to sell out to Bell than to undertake such modernization on their own.

During the 1950s and 1960s the number of independent telephone systems in Ontario declined steadily, and by the mid-1970s there were only forty left, twenty-four of which were privately owned and the remaining sixteen municipally owned.[52] The largest independent company, Northern Telephone, which served a large part of northern Ontario, was the object of vigorous competition between Bell and Ontario Northland Communications, (ONC) a subsidiary established by the provincially owned Ontario Northland Railway in 1946. The latter made several attempts to gain control of Northern Telephone in the post-war years as part of its own efforts to create an integrated communications network in north-eastern Ontario. Northern Telephone was acquired by Bell, however, and it was not until a number of agreements had been worked out between Bell and ONC that the telephone, teletype, and microwave radio services in northern Ontario were successfully interconnected.[53]

Broadcasting

Much of the national English-language radio and television broadcasting activity that developed during the war and post-war years in Canada was centred in Toronto. The prospect existed for some time, particularly after television broadcasting began, that the production and distribution of Canadian-made entertainment as well as news and public affairs broadcast material would become a major new industry for the province. The growth of this industry was severely restricted, however, by the failure of the federal government to implement a national broadcasting policy and by its eventual acceptance of a system that largely mirrored and drew most of its material from the U.S. commercial system.

Radio broadcasting in Canada was an important element in the federal government's war effort. The demand for war news was a further stimulus to expand the system, and during the early 1940s Toronto became the centre of a growing broadcast news network. The Canadian Broadcasting Corporation, (CBC) which had from its inception depended for its news on bulletins supplied free of charge by the Canadian Press, established its own news service in 1941, with the Toronto bureau operating as the central newsroom for the national system. Such centralizing trends were offset by the growing influence of private radio broadcasting interests and the subsequent retreat of the federal government from its commitment to support a single national radio broadcasting system dominated by the CBC.[54] In the early post-war years the private broadcasters strengthened their position, claiming an important victory in 1948, when station CFRB in Toronto was granted permission to increase its power to 50,000 W in compensation for moving to a less desirable frequency.[55]

The development of commercial television in the United States after the war introduced a new element into the Canadian broadcasting situation, one that greatly affected southern Ontario and other areas in Canada with heavy population concentrations adjacent to the international border. For a brief period the possibility existed of developing a purely Canadian television industry, or at least one that did not simply conform to the pattern emerging in the United States. The federal government's interim television policy announced in 1949 and the recommendations of the Massey Royal Commission which followed in 1951 apparently envisioned a Canadian broadcasting system that would be led by the CBC, would avoid domination by the needs of commercial advertisers, and would support Canadian producers, artists, and even possibly manufacturers of receiving sets and other equipment.[56] Much of the activity generated by such a system would undoubtedly have been concentrated in southern Ontario. But such was not to be. As early as 1948 avid pioneer viewers in southern Canada were tuning into U.S. television broadcasts. The funds allotted to the CBC to develop its first stations were totally inadequate, and when they eventually began operation, in Toronto and Montreal in 1952, they were poorly equipped to offer an attractive alternative to U.S. television.

In the early 1950s the federal government further weakened the possibilities for developing a strong national TV system by retreating from its proclaimed policy of refusing to license private stations in communities that did not yet have a CBC station. A private TV station was licensed to operate in Sudbury in 1953, and by the end of the decade the growth of private TV broadcasting had far outstripped that of the public system. Despite the 'Canadian content' requirements set out in the new federal (Conservative) government's legislation in 1958 as part of the new regulatory system (to be run by the Board of Broadcast Governors (BBG)), the private broadcasters, many of whom were affiliated with existing newspaper or private radio broadcasting companies, were prone from the outset to buy inexpensive U.S. programs rather than produce their own. The CBC itself became increasingly dependent on such material.[57]

By 1960 the television broadcasting system had expanded to the point where private business interests were pressing for licences to establish stations in centres that already had one station. The prize commercial opportunity was in the large Toronto market, and the licence there was eagerly sought by a number of applicants, including a group headed by John Bassett, owner of the Toronto newspaper, the *Telegram*. The Bassett group, several members of which were well connected to the federal Conservative party, then in office, were successful in obtaining the licence and, despite subsequent financial difficulties and conflicts with the BBG, were instrumental in building a private television broadcasting network, CTV, which began operating in 1961.[58] While the new network was Toronto based, it appeared to be devoted more to overcoming restrictions on its use of US programming than to producing its own. The CBC, weakened by continued underfunding and internal administrative difficulties, became increasingly dependent upon commercial sponsorship. Its lamentable condition was reflected in its comically inadequate facilities in downtown Toronto, which despite many plans for improvement remained in use through the 1970s.[59]

Educational Television Broadcasting

Several provinces, including Ontario, became interested in the possibilities of developing their own provincial educational television systems in the 1960s. Educational programming was undertaken early in the decade by the Ontario Department of Education, which used CBC and private television stations to transmit their material during early morning hours. By 1965 the department was anxious to secure its own broadcasting facilities. Despite some uncertainty about the feasibility of the undertaking, the provincial government eventually agreed to provide the necessary support. The main obstacle, however, was the federal government's established policy of refusing to grant broadcasting licences to provincial governments or to agencies under their control. In the course of the review of national broadcasting policy undertaken in the mid-1960s, the federal government proposed to assume control over educational television by establishing a federal agency for the purpose. As a result of strong opposition from the provinces and from the CBC, this plan was eventually abandoned, and the legislation introduced to implement it was withdrawn in 1969.[60]

Faced with an apparent impasse with respect to the jurisdictional issue and with pressure from the opposition parties in the provincial legislature to get on with the creation of educational television in the province, the government simply went ahead and established the Ontario Educational Communications Authority (OECA), a crown corporation with a mandate to 'initiate, acquire, produce, distribute, exhibit or otherwise deal in programmes and materials in the educational broadcasting and communications field.' In 1970 OECA began broadcasting on channel 19 in Toronto, the country's first VHF station. Additional transmitters were subsequently constructed to rebroadcast programs at other points in the province.

The reasons for the Ontario government's aggressive initiatives in developing the provincial educational television system were complex. Simple enthusiasm for the new technology was undoubtedly a factor. William Davis, then minister of education, had been much impressed during a visit to Europe in 1965 by the progress being made there in developing educational broadcasting. The professional educators in the provincial bureaucracy were also at the time highly receptive to any innovation that promised to challenge the existing educational establishment in the schools. Interestingly, no one appears to have given any thought to the possibility that broadcast television would serve to lower the costs of education in the province. The minister explicitly ruled out such a possibility, stressing that educational television would be a supplement to existing education at all levels and not a substitute for it. Public response was favourable. One journalist praised the government for keeping Ontario abreast of the times, citing Marshall McLuhan's observations about the inadequacy of the conventional educational system for meeting the needs of a new generation of students.[61]

There may also have been a longer-term consideration behind the province's move to occupy the educational television broadcasting field. By the late 1960s the Ontario government was increasingly interested in obtaining more influence over the development of the cable and other data communications systems which were by then becoming one of the great new growth areas in the communications industry. If necessary, the province was prepared to seek constitutional revisions that would enable it to grant franchises to private operators providing such services, to establish technical standards, and to regulate rates. By the early 1970s the provincial government was actively considering the development of its own telecommunications policy.[62]

5 The Services Sector, Trade, and Finance

The rapid growth of the service-producing industries was one of the most important features of the years from 1939 to 1975. While less advanced than in the United States, the process was well under way in Ontario in the early 1940s. As will be seen in table 15, the primary industries thereafter shrank significantly as a source of jobs in the province; the secondary sector, comprising manufacturing and construction, showed a smaller relative decline; while the service (tertiary) sector grew rapidly in importance, accounting for almost two-thirds of total employment by 1975. There was also a shift in the composition of total output, with the primary sector accounting for almost 27 per cent of the total value of production in 1940 and approximately 6 per cent by the end of the period. The secondary sector also declined in relative importance by this measure, but more moderately. The tertiary sector more than doubled its share, rising from approximately 25 per cent in 1940 to more than 56 per cent by 1975.[1]

Some of the growth in services during the period was accompanied by a transfer of certain types of services production, such as health care, from private to public hands. Many established public-sector service functions, such as education and public administration, grew rapidly. Indeed, much of the 'growth of government' that was so much remarked upon during this period was a consequence of the expansion of such public service undertakings. But the remaining private services sector also grew vigorously as the economy became more complex and more highly specialized. For example, many functions that had once been performed internally by business firms could now be handled more efficiently by specialized firms supplying specific kinds of business services such as accounting and recruiting.

The causes of the relatively more rapid growth of the services sector during this period are not easily identified. One possible explanation lies in the well-known tendency for people enjoying rising incomes to spend proportionately less of additions to income on such necessities as food and more on non-essentials and luxury items. While it has not been established that there are sufficiently strong differences in the income elasticities of demand for goods and services

TABLE 15
Sectoral Composition of Output and Employment, Ontario, Selected Years 1940–75

	1940	1955	1961	1971	1975
Percentage of Total Output					
Primary	26.8	14.0	9.2	5.8	6.1
Secondary	48.3	40.3	43.4	37.2	37.5
Tertiary	24.9	45.7	47.4	57.0	56.4
Percentage of Total Employment					
Primary		13.7	9.6	6.1	4.7
Secondary		38.3	33.3	33.5	30.8
Tertiary		48.0	57.1	60.4	64.5

in general to account for any large part of the growth in the service industries, there is circumstantial evidence of at least an association between the growth of real incomes in the post-war period and the changing patterns of domestic and external trade, the quantities and types of goods and services exchanged, and the organization of the economy over the period.[2]

The demand for goods and services produced in Ontario grew rapidly after 1940. The disruption of the existing patterns of international trade during the war and other unusual wartime circumstances provided a number of opportunities for some Ontario producers to claim a larger share of the Canadian market and to enter some new foreign markets as well, but such effects were soon submerged by the new patterns of trade established in the 1950s. These patterns were largely determined by economic and policy influences beyond the control of Ontario producers or the Ontario government: the formation of the European Common Market in 1959, Britain's drift into closer European ties (culminating in entry to the EEC in 1973), American military requirements during the course of the Korean and Viet Nam wars, changes in commercial policy under the General Agreement on Tariffs and Trade negotiations, and the growing competitiveness of Japanese and other Asian countries in manufacturing, all of which were important influences upon the volume and type of production carried on in Ontario.

The domestic market for Ontario production grew strongly during the period. Population growth in the province averaged 2.5 per cent annually until the early 1970s, and the high rate of family formation during the period sustained rapid growth in the demand for housing, consumer durables, education, and health services. Real income increased even faster than the population. The average real growth rate of Gross Provincial Product between the end of the war and the early 1970s was nearly 4.8 per cent annually. After making allowance for price changes, per capita real personal income rose from $1,600 in 1945 to $3,059 in 1971.

The rate of increase in per capita income was not uniform over the period,

TABLE 16
Personal Income and Personal Income Per Capita, Ontario,
Selected Years 1941–75 (constant $1971)

Year	Real Personal Income (000)	Real Personal Income Per Capita
1941	6,214	1,641
1950	9,212	2,003
1955	12,266	2,329
1960	15,626	2,557
1965	20,266	2,986
1970	28,633	3,792
1975	39,316	4,780

SOURCE: Calculated from Leacy, ed., *Historical Statistics of Canada*, 2nd ed., F96 and K174

since there were years of low or even negative growth, but such periods of recession were more than offset by years of remarkably high growth. By 1975 personal income in Ontario had reached almost $53 billion, and consumer spending on goods and services had grown to just under $38 billion. During the entire period, however, consumer outlays declined as a percentage of total spending in Ontario, falling from just under 70 per cent in the years just after the war to approximately 58 per cent in 1975. Much of the difference was made up by increased government spending, which rose from less than 2 per cent in 1947 to over 17 per cent by 1975.

These data underestimate the real gains of individuals over the period, because the large increases in real per capita income were accompanied by an increase in leisure time as well.

Rising levels of real income per capita created the possibility of higher levels of personal consumption and increased personal savings. They also created the possibility of increased taxation and government spending. Provincial government net expenditure in real terms rose steadily from 4.6 per cent of the per capita real income in Ontario in 1945 to almost 11 per cent in 1970. While personal income in the province grew at an annual average rate of about 9.4 per cent over the period from 1947 to 1975, personal disposable income (income after taxes) grew at only 9 per cent per annum. The difference was not, of course, a loss to taxpayers; for the government's expenditures program returned benefits of various kinds which must be counted as part of the real income of individuals.

The rising level of material well-being in the province is also suggested by data on household equipment. In 1941 less than a third of Ontario households had mechanical regfrigeration; by 1971 this figure had increased to more than 99 per cent. In 1941 just under 70 per cent of Ontario dwellings had water piped inside; by 1971 almost 99 per cent had inside water supplied.[3] The growth of consumer spending and the increases in real per capita incomes that supported

TABLE 17
Real Per Capita Personal Expenditure on Goods and
Services, Ontario, Selected Years 1947-75

Year	Constant $1971
1947	1,764
1951	1,803
1955	1,951
1961	2,066
1965	2,357
1971	2,901
1975	3,364

SOURCES: Current dollar expenditure data from *Ontario Economic Accounts*, annual; deflator from Leacy, ed., *Historical Statistics of Canada*, 2nd ed., K174

it were not evenly distributed in terms of either individuals or regions. Much of the increased income and spending was concentrated in the south-central part of the province. The lowest average incomes were found in the north, the highest in the major urban areas of the south. Strong growth forces were at work throughout the entire period to strengthen this regional concentration. By the mid-1960s the Toronto metropolitan region contributed more than 40 per cent of all the consumption spending done in the province.[4] Despite federal and provincial government programs aimed at diverting growth to other regions, by the mid-1970s there was little evidence that such efforts were having measurable effects.

While changes in the level and composition of income in Ontario were generally similar to those in the rest of Canada, so that Ontario production destined for markets in the other provinces was affected in much the same way as it was by the patterns of demand originating within the province itself, such was not necessarily true of the province's exports abroad. These exports consisted almost entirely of goods as distinguished from services, however, and except for the period during and immediately after the war when Ontario producers of certain manufactured goods, such as textiles, found themselves faced with unusually favourable conditions in both domestic and some foreign markets, the province's export trade continued to depend heavily on foodstuffs and raw materials in various stages of processing. The demand for such goods fluctuated with economic conditions in other countries, notably the United States, which by the end of the period was buying more than three-quarters of all the goods exported from Ontario. In the case of certain minerals that had a military application, additional instability was introduced to Ontario export markets by the vagaries of American foreign policy and military activities. Overall, however, the value of Ontario exports fluctuated within a range of 22-30 per cent of the estimated value of total provincial output during the period.[5]

Ontario imports from abroad were more stable, running consistently at just

TABLE 18
Imports and Exports, Ontario, Selected Years 1947–75
(percentage of GPE in parentheses)

Year	Exports	Imports	GPE
1947	1,526 (28)	1,270 (23)	5,444
1950	1,995 (27)	1,786 (24)	7,410
1955	2,742 (25)	2,717 (25)	10,803
1960	3,412 (23)	3,625 (25)	14,638
1965	5,633 (26)	5,165 (24)	21,661
1970	10,354 (29)	8,311 (24)	35,314
1975	19,319 (30)	15,326 (24)	65,309

SOURCE: Ontario, TEIGA, *Ontario Economic Accounts 1947–1975*

under 25 per cent of the value of all spending in the province. Although the underlying forces influencing the levels of Ontario foreign trade were largely beyond the control of the province, the Ontario government did make some attempts during the period to intervene in this as in most other aspects of the province's economic life. Indirectly it could seek to influence the commercial policies of the federal government through the usual channels of federal-provincial communications. On occasion it also tried more direct action.

During the immediate post-war years, as noted in chapter 1, the Ontario government was committed to promoting trade between Ontario and Britain. Efforts were made to interest British exporters in developing markets in Ontario and to attract British manufacturing firms that might be willing to establish plants in the province.[6] Through the 1950s this general position remained an article of faith in the province, with politicians and other opinion leaders expressing enthusiasm for maintaining and strengthening the British connection. But by the 1960s the fact of the province's increasing dependence on American markets and American capital and growing doubts about the British commitment to Empire trade (doubts that were reinforced by Britain's efforts to gain admission to the European Common Market) induced the provincial government to develop a more general policy with respect to trade and foreign investment. The 'Great Trade Crusade' introduced with a vigorous publicity campaign in 1962 was aimed at cultivating foreign markets wherever they might be found and, at the same time, attracting new industry to the province, especially from the United States, which seemed to be the most promising source then at hand.[7]

Among the various trade promotion programs and policies developed by the provincial government during the period were the purchasing programs in which government departments and agencies were encouraged to discriminate in favour of Ontario suppliers when calling for tenders and granting contracts, although by the 1970s some of these more blatant efforts were being transformed into 'Buy Canadian' instead of 'Buy Ontario' policies – a distinction of little importance in the case of most manufactured commodities. The more overt forms of provincial protectionism survived, however, in the cases of agricultural products, particularly where the interests of provincial marketing agencies were involved.[8]

Wholesale and Retail Trade

Some of the many changes in the organization of wholesale and retail trade in Ontario during the years from 1939 to 1975 may be attributed simply to the growth of markets arising from population increase and rising incomes; others appear to be related to broad social and cultural trends of the post-war period. The adoption of mass retailing methods, exemplified by the self-service meat and grocery supermarket, and the development of suburban shopping centres are perhaps the most conspicuous examples.

Wholesaling activities during the period continued to be performed by a variety of enterprises, only some of which engaged in the usual wholesaling function of obtaining goods in bulk from producers and supplying them in smaller quantities to retailers. Many were involved in assembling goods for sale to other processors or to large commercial and institutional users. Others were not so much 'wholesalers' as manufacturers' sales agents or brokers dealing with other wholesalers. While changes in census definitions of these activities make it difficult to identify even gross trends in the internal organization of the industry, the evidence suggests that the role of the 'wholesaler proper' was eroded during the period by changes taking place both at the retailing and manufacturing ends of the production cycle. As retail organizations grew in size, many began to deal directly with manufacturers, establishing their own warehousing and other handling facilities. Some manufacturers began to set up distributing systems of their own, reducing their need for middlemen. Such developments were particularly important in the food, home furnishings and home hardware lines. In dealings with commodities such as automobiles, automotive equipment and supplies, and petroleum products, where there had always been strong direct links between producers and retailers, there was no weakening of such ties. While public policy does not appear to have had an important influence on these developments generally, it is possible that the prohibition of resale price maintenance in 1952 may have been significant in certain product lines.[9]

In the area of retail trade, the 1941 census of retail stores in Canada showed few changes in the structure or character of retailing since the first survey was made a decade earlier. In Ontario, as elsewhere in the country, the Depression had taken its toll of weaker establishments and there was a perceptible trend under way towards the amalgamation of certain kinds of businesses into larger units of ownership. Smaller specialty stores, particularly the meat markets, were being absorbed into larger enterprises (then called 'combination stores') which handled both groceries and meats. These larger shops were often part of a chain, even in the early 1940s, but the growth of the chains was a very gradual process

TABLE 19
Retail Sales, Ontario, 1939-75

Year	Current Dollar Values ('000)	$1971 = 100 ('000)
1939	1,039	2,854
1941	1,407	3,457
1945	1,774	3,969
1951	4,116	6,107
1955	5,296	7,620
1961	6,207	8,082
1965	8,043	9,857
1971	11,877	11,877
1975	19,156	13,972

NOTE: Constant dollar values calculated using personal expenditure on consumer goods and services implicit price index
SOURCE: Leacy, ed., *Historical Statistics of Canada*, 2nd ed., v95 and K174

in Ontario. Between 1930 and 1941 the number of chain stores in Ontario grew from 3,269 to 3,385, and their share of total retail sales grew by less than 1 per cent.[10] The department stores and mail-order stores survived the Depression, although they lost some of their share of the market to the 'variety stores' which specialized in low unit value sales. None of these changes had much impact on the way business was conducted or on the physical nature of retail outlets themselves. Even the early chain grocery stores were indistinguishable from the independent groceries, except for the nature of their management.

Perhaps the most significant changes in the early years of the period were in the automotive field. Automobile sales were recovering with the growth of employment and incomes. In the closely related retail gasoline and 'filling station' fields the 1940s began with intense rivalry among the large gasoline and motor oil distributing companies, which were striving to establish as many outlets for their brands as possible. In the course of that struggle filling stations proliferated in Ontario, many of them operated by lessees, and their total sales in 1941 were more than double what they had been a decade before.[11] These developments were short-lived, however; for in 1942 civilian automobile production was terminated, and gasoline sales became subject to strict government control.

The face of retail trade in Ontario during the early part of the period was consequently little changed from what it had been in the inter-war period. While there was some growth of larger-scale merchandising, most of the province's retail trade remained in the hands of relatively small, usually independent merchants, who were responsible for more than 68 per cent of the total volume of retail trade in the province. Much of this traditional pattern of organization was to change in the course of the next decade.

By the early 1950s both the absolute volume of retail sales in Ontario and the organization of the trade were much altered. The 'baby boom,' rising family incomes, rapid urbanization of the population, the proliferation of private automobiles, and the growth of large suburban residential areas created conditions in Ontario suitable for the kinds of changes in retailing already well under way in the United States. Within a few years new forms of retailing were introduced to exploit the opportunities created by a rapidly expanding mass market for consumer goods. A high rate of family formation, rising real incomes, and a reduction in the hours of work, all contributed to changes not only in the volume of goods but the kinds of goods consumers were willing and able to buy. Entirely new markets developed for goods associated with 'leisure living' and the informal recreational activities of newly affluent suburbanites. The list of items was long, ranging from the backyard barbecue and its accessories to specialized clothing. The 'sport' shirt became an indispensable part of male attire. Other new goods were the products of technological change; synthetic fabrics and television receivers were perhaps the most important, although the initial assessment of the sales potential of the latter was surprisingly restrained.[12]

The retail outlets that developed to serve these new markets were exemplified by the large food stores, especially the self-service supermarkets, and the small department stores located in the suburbs, both of which were soon incorporated into one of the most distinctive institutions of the period: the suburban shopping centre. Among the first major shopping centres in Ontario were Lawrence Plaza in North York, which opened for business in 1953, and a large regional centre built in the Hamilton area by the E.P. Taylor interests the following year. In 1955 the press carried reports of a major new supermarket opening, the precursor to a large shopping centre planned as part of a new community, Don Mills, to be located 'seven miles north-east of Toronto.'[13] By then shopping centres were beginning to appear in smaller cities and towns. One of the first to be built outside the densely populated southern area of the province was located in Sudbury, where the benefits of a closed, centrally heated mall proved particularly attractive in winter. By the mid-1970s over 20 per cent of retail sales in Ontario were in shopping centres.

The negative impact of suburban shopping centre development on established downtown businesses in the cities of Ontario was less severe than it was in the United States. In most Ontario cities, the major department stores and other downtown businesses survived the competition from the suburban establishments. The reasons are complex, rooted in different patterns of residential choices, property taxation, law enforcement, and municipal government. In the case of the largest city, Toronto, the downtown retailers met the new competition with aggressive modernization and redevelopment of the main department stores, aided greatly by substantial public investment in the mass transit system which provided easy access to the downtown from at least some of the new outlying areas. Such cities also retained their downtown residential neighbourhoods. As early as 1961 there were press reports of a renewed interest in downtown housing in Toronto. Real estate values were rising, and builders of new houses in the suburbs were being forced to offer buyers amenities such as 'free' air conditioning to enhance the saleability of their product.[14]

Although they survived the growth of the suburbs and the shopping centres, the large traditional department stores faced another serious challenge in the 1960s, this time from the so-called 'discount stores,' which offered a wide range of consumer products at prices kept low by the elimination of many of the services offered by the traditional stores. Just as the grocery supermarket was seen as the main retailing innovation of the 1940s and the shopping centre of the 1950s, the discount department store was hailed as the answer to the changing consumer buying preferences of the 1960s. Aimed as they were at the 'down-market' trade, promoting what often proved to be the least durable consumer items of the day, the discount stores appear in retrospect to represent the rather dismal culmination of the mass-consumption economy so optimistically greeted in the early 1950s. Typically located in the unsightly strip developments lining the highways and major roads slicing through suburbia, they contributed a different impression of what mass retailing meant than had been foreseen when the post-war boom began. The earlier euphoria had been conveyed by a journalist writing in *Maclean's Magazine* in 1956: extolling the trends then taking place in retailing – self-service, pre-packaging and other improvements – he predicted that within the next few decades his readers would do most of their shopping at night, 'carried along on moving store aisles,' with television transforming parking lots into tomorrow's stores and robots serving as grocery clerks. 'This new revolution,' he predicted, 'will be part of the second industrial revolution, which is bringing automation to the factory,' and the result, he expected, would be that 'the shopper will get more value per dollar.'[15] By the mid-1960s such enthusiasm seemed dated, especially in the perception of a new generation of young shoppers bent on pursuing dreams of a different kind of revolution.

The changes in retailing that did take place during the remainder of the period were rather less revolutionary than foreseen and probably less appreciated. Night shopping was gradually introduced, but not without opposition from organized labour and municipal governments, who were not easily convinced that it represented an improvement in the quality of life for all those affected by it. There was also an extension of mass retailing to new lines. The principle of the grocery supermarket was applied to drug stores, to lumber and hardware outlets (many of which became 'home improvement centres'), and other commodity-line supermarkets selling specialized items such as paints, wall coverings, carpets, and draperies. The culmination of this trend, represented by the huge general merchandise warehouse (the Hyper-Marché) which emerged in Europe in the late 1960s was slower to catch on in Canada. A version of this kind of operation was opened in Oshawa in the mid-1970s.[16]

The new self-service retail outlets gained wide acceptance, and most of their customers no doubt believed that the lower operating costs implied in such operations were being passed on to them in lower prices, but it did not escape notice that the consumer was in fact being asked to do much of the work formerly done by employees. Whether or not this change resulted in a net social gain remains difficult to assess.

Implementation of the new mass-merchandising techniques was usually undertaken by large organizations which had the resources available to exploit the opportunities presented for standardization and volume operations. Both conceptual and reporting difficulties make it difficult to determine the extent to which the ownership of retail enterprises in the province became more concentrated. What is known is that the percentage of independent stores declined from more than 70 per cent of all retail stores in the early 1950s to less than 60 per cent by the mid-1970s.[17] While the large chain stores came to dominate the food retailing industry, private retailers continued to survive in other retail fields that lent themselves less easily to standardization and in which the benefits of large-scale purchasing were apparently less important. The average size of retail locations remained small, with the number of paid employees per location rising from 3.5 in 1941 to 4.6 in 1971.[18]

One factor that may have helped sustain the smaller retailers in the later part of the period was the introduction of general-purpose credit cards, which made it possible for them to offer the same convenient credit facilities as the large department stores and oil companies, which had pioneered the use of what was soon to be known as 'plastic money.' This benefit was not available to small food retailers in Ontario, however, because of a rather peculiar law prohibiting the use of credit cards for grocery purchases.

The persistence of traditional forms of enterprise in the retail trade despite the proclaimed revolution in retailing saw the revival of the department stores in the early 1970s. While discount stores such as K-Mart and Woolco had by the end of the 1960s built up a volume of sales about equal to that of the traditional department stores, the next several years saw the department stores pull ahead again. This they accomplished by adopting new merchandising strategies in their existing downtown stores and by developing new stores in the larger regional shopping centres.[19] By 1973 more than 50 per cent of the total sales of department stores were made in their shopping centre branches.[20]

The impact of these changes in retailing on the provincial economy as a whole was probably not great. The building of the plazas and shopping malls obviously contributed to the high levels of capital formation that characterized the decades of the 1950s and 1960s, but otherwise developments in the trade sector appear to have been more the consequence than the cause of underlying economic change. The pattern of employment in wholesale and retail trade changed little, with the emphasis continuing to be on the use of relatively unskilled workers.

Turnover rates remained characteristically high. The absolute growth in the volume of retail trade created new jobs, but the trend towards self-service and some early (often not very successful) attempts to mechanize certain retailing activities offset some of the employment-creating effects of this growth. There was a substantial increase in labour-productivity in retailing over the period as a whole. While the sales volume increased by some 3.5 times between 1941 and 1971 (after allowing for price changes), the number of paid employees in Ontario retailing increased by only 1.5 times.[21]

Closely resembling the retailing establishments supplying food and other tangible goods to consumers were a large number of enterprises that provided services either to other businesses or directly to consumers. Eating places, hotels, laundries, dry-cleaning plants; businesses providing entertainment; undertakers, advertising agencies, photographers, and equipment-rental establishments were all engaged in supplying retail services. As a group such businesses had changed little in their relative importance during the past forty years; although some, such as domestic service, declined, while others, particularly those providing technical services to other businesses, grew. With some important exceptions these kinds of activities were carried on by independent owners and operators. (The exceptions would include the theatres, hotels, and, towards the end of the period, the fast-food outlets and other franchised operations in which only a limited form of independent ownership and direction was practised.) Throughout the period the total number of working proprietors in the service trades was very little less than the total number of service trades establishments.[22]

As with the retailing of goods, many of the changes that occurred in the service trades during the post-war period were closely related to the development of new patterns of living. Changes in family structure, growing female participation in the labour force, increased leisure time, and changing tastes were all involved. Such changes were clearly important in the case of domestic service. Despite the increase in family real incomes, the employment of domestic servants decreased greatly. The growing affluence of the middle class was accompanied by a trend towards self-sufficiency in certain aspects of family living. Although real incomes rose, more people assumed the burdens of house-cleaning, personal grooming (the home permanent became popular), yard maintenance, and repair work around the home. Such labours were eased, however, by the availability of mechanical aids such as the dishwasher, power lawn mowers, home hair dryers, and inexpensive power tools.

Family entertainment also greatly changed during the period. The downtown movie theatres flourished during the 1940s, and their number increased from just over 400 in 1941 to more than 600 by the end of the decade. In the late 1940s, however, the drive-in movie theatre came to Ontario, doing for the movie business what the suburban shopping centres did for the general retail trade: both were outgrowths of the automobile-dependent suburban life-style of the post-war years. First developed in the United States in the 1930s, the drive-ins appeared in Canada shortly after the gasoline rationing and building restrictions were lifted after the war. The first drive-in theatres in Ontario were built at Stoney Creek, Windsor, and London in the late 1940s. By 1953 there were fifty-five in the province, half the Canadian total.[23]

The drive-ins took business away from the downtown movie palaces, which saw their paid admissions fall steadily from over 100,000 annually in the late 1940s to less than a third of that number by 1975. The business done by the drive-in theatres grew in terms of paid admissions until 1970, when a peak attendance of 5,376,708 was recorded. Thereafter they too went into decline as television began to take over as the dominant form of popular entertainment.[24]

Finance

The Canadian financial system continued to be heavily concentrated in central Canada through the period to 1975, with the head offices of most of the banks, trust companies, and insurance firms located in either Montreal or Toronto. Although at the end of the period a number of new financial institutions were becoming established in western Canada, they were still of little consequence, while the political uncertainties in Quebec were serving to strengthen Toronto's position as the centre of financial power in the east. Along with its share of the banks and insurance companies, Toronto remained the site of the country's major stock exchange. Financial business consequently remained an important and growing part of the Ontario provincial economy, the tangible evidence of which was the vertical expansion of Toronto's financial district.

During the early war years the banking system continued the contraction which had begun in the Depression. The number of chartered bank branches in Ontario declined from over 1,200 in 1940 to a low of 1,092 in 1943. Thereafter the banks began establishing new branches again, but it was 1950 before the system was as large as it had been a decade earlier. Despite a move to eliminate smaller branches and to concentrate business in the larger ones, the total number of bank branches in the province continued to grow during the 1950s and 1960s, and by the end of the period was more than double what it had been in 1940. The number of cheques cashed increased sevenfold during the 1950s and 1960s.[25] There were also some important changes in the type of business done by the banks, especially after the 1954 Bank Act allowed them to enter the residential mortgage business and to make loans for home improvements. New regulations that permitted banks to accept chattel mortgage securities for personal loans also encouraged them to establish substantial consumer credit divisions.

The expansion of banking activities after the war created new employment opportunities, especially for women, who continued to perform most of the routine front-office work of the banks. There were also the beginnings, however, of a trend towards automation of many clerical activities. By the mid-1960s the availability of more sophisticated data-processing and communications equipment was making it possible for banks to offer new types of services, to speed up cheque clearing and other routine functions, and to substitute capital for labour in some of their operations. The efficiency of banking operations was also increased by changes in the scale and organization of the business. The most conspicuous changes took the form of mergers. The Bank of Toronto and the Dominion Bank united in 1955 to form the Toronto Dominion Bank; the Imperial joined with Barclay's in 1956, and in 1961 the Imperial and the Canadian Bank of Commerce formed the Canadian Imperial Bank of Commerce. Although several new banks appeared in the later years of the period, only the Unity Bank, with seventeen branches in Ontario, was significant.

Another major development after the war was the expansion of the trust companies into the banking business. Prior to 1940 a number of trust and loan companies were the most important non-bank financial institutions in Ontario. The loan companies, however, had been declining in relative importance since the turn of the century. During the depression of the 1930s they began to disappear, many being converted to trust companies, others simply going out of business. By the mid-1950s there were only seven loan companies operating in Ontario. The trust companies, on the other hand, had grown and in the postwar years greatly expanded both their fiduciary functions and their business of receiving deposits and making loans. Many businesses and individuals, faced with the problems presented by an increasingly complicated tax system and by more elaborate regulations concerning the ownership and management of real property, found it expedient to entrust the handling of some of their affairs to such firms. Many trust companies also became aggressive in establishing new branches in the growing suburban areas, where they competed strongly with the chartered banks for deposit and loan business by offering longer and more convenient hours of service.

The chartered banks also encountered growing competition for consumer deposit and loan business from the credit unions. These organizations were just beginning to appear in Ontario during the late 1930s. The first were modelled directly on the type of credit unions already operating in the United States, most of which were to be found in large cities serving a membership based on particular occupations.[26] In 1941 a central body, the Ontario Credit Union League, was formed to link the ninety-three credit unions, whose total membership was 18,670, then operating in the province.[27] The movement grew rapidly thereafter, with membership reaching 1,422,000 in 1975.[28]

The insurance companies remained important channels for transferring personal and other savings into real estate developments and other investments. Although the high tax rates of the war years and the heavy public purchases of government bonds slowed the life insurance business during the early part of the period, the industry expanded rapidly after the war. By the mid-1950s total assets were double what they had been at the beginning of the war, and employment had risen by some 50 per cent.[29]

Regulation of most of the financial system in Canada has been a responsibility of the federal government, which, under the provisions of the British North America Act, was given jurisdiction over banking and finance. Because of a requirement that insurance and trust companies be licensed by the government of any province in which they wished to do business, however, there has been some provincial involvement in the affairs of this part of the financial system. Much of this activity during the 1939–75 period was of a routine nature. The principal exception was in connection with the failure in 1965 of the Atlantic Acceptance Corporation. One of its principal creditors was an important trust company, British Mortgage and Trust, based in Stratford, Ontario. When it appeared that this well-established 'near-bank' was likely to fail, both the Ontario and the federal governments became active in ensuring that public confidence in such financial institutions was preserved. Financial support was provided, and the province encouraged another trust company to absorb British Mortgage and Trust. The federal government subsequently introduced legislation that established the Canada Deposit Insurance Corporation. Membership in the corporation was made mandatory for chartered banks and federally incorporated trust and loan companies accepting deposits from the public. Ontario and all the other provinces except Quebec (which established its own scheme) authorized provincially incorporated trust and loan companies which accepted deposits from the public to apply for membership as well. Individual depositors were insured to a maximum of $20,000.

Provincial intervention in the securities business during the period was a more contentious matter. Although there was legislation respecting the selling of securities in Ontario as early as the 1890s, the need for a formal regulatory system was not recognized until the stock market crash of 1929. In 1930 the provincial government passed the Stock Frauds Prevention Act and a year later legislation that would permit the establishment from time to time of an organization to oversee the conduct of security trading in the province. It was not until 1938, however, that such a body, the Ontario Securities Commission, was appointed to administer the provisions of the Ontario Securities Act. This legislation was concerned with all kinds of securities trading, but appeared to be aimed mainly at the issuing and trading of mining stocks. It was vigorously opposed by mining companies and some others on the grounds that it would inhibit mineral exploration and development in the province. There were also critics who claimed that the legislation was inadequate, likely to be badly administered, and unlikely to prevent investors from being victimized by unscrupulous mining promoters as they had been in the past. The debate continued into the 1940s and the government eventually referred the matter to the Royal Commission on Mining (the Urquhart Commission), which reported in 1944.

The Urquhart Commission's findings appeared to support those who feared that regulations concerning securities trading would be detrimental to mineral resource development. Yet the commission also confirmed that the existing regulations had failed to curb fraudulent promotion of mining stocks.[30] Such fraud had reached serious proportions, the commission concluded, and it recommended that new legislation be enacted to tighten public control over brokers and dealers and to require fuller disclosure in securities offerings. Urquhart also suggested that a new securities commission should be appointed.

These proposals became the subject of a protracted and confused public debate.[31] How confused was suggested by the positions taken by one of the groups most directly concerned, the Ontario Prospectors' and Developers' Association. It had long urged that the existing securities commission be abolished, and its complaints about the ill effects of what it called 'rigid' securities regulations were widely believed to have been instrumental in causing the government to have a royal commission inquiry into the matter.[32] Yet the association, which made no submission to the Urquhart Commission while it was sitting, objected to its recommendations and appealed directly to the government *not* to abolish the Securities Commission.[33]

After some hesitation and consultation with other provinces, the Ontario government did enact new securities legislation in 1945. Because of delays in application, the new act had little immediate effect on the ways mining stocks were being promoted and traded. In fact, the Interprovincial Mining Committee noted that 'matters had gone from bad to worse.'[34] In 1947 the legislation was revised to require that company prospectuses provide purchasers with 'full, true and plain disclosure' of all material facts relating to the security at the time of its primary distribution. Until then, the main provisions of the legislation had to do with the prevention of fraud and with establishing a system for licensing those engaged in the industry.[35]

Another wave of fraudulent stock issues in the late 1940s (which victimized many American investors) motivated the government to proceed with fuller implementation of its securities laws and within a few years the system in place in the province was being hailed as a model for other provincial governments in Canada to copy.[36] While never far below the surface, the issues surrounding securities regulation were submerged during the prosperous periods of the 1950s and early 1960s.

During this period the Toronto stock market flourished and underwent some important changes in its organization. Following the war there was a trend towards increasing interdependence among various kinds of securities dealers. Many investors, institutional, corporate, and individual alike, began to acquire both debt and equity items. At the same time, improved communications made it feasible for dealers to handle a greater variety of assets, including those being traded at places remote from their own bases of operation. As a result, many dealers, including those with seats on the Toronto Stock Exchange (TSE) became more diversified in their operations. Some became associated with other markets both in Canada and further afield. There were also changes in the TSE itself. For example, until the 1950s, all firms belonging to stock exchanges in North America were organized either as single proprietorships or partnerships. In 1953 the New York Stock Exchange changed its rules to permit corporations to hold memberships and the TSE almost immediately adopted the same practice. One effect of this was to allow members to increase the scale of their operations and to expand their long-term financing capabilities.[37] By the early 1960s, almost half the TSE members were incorporated.

The volume of business transacted on the TSE increased greatly during the boom of the early 1950s. Twice as many transactions were recorded in 1955 as in 1950. Activity then fell off again until the mid-1960s when another boom began. Certain events associated with this second post-war trading boom once again called into question the adequacy of the provincial government's regulatory procedures in the securities business.

A number of take-over bids in 1963 raised concerns about how they had been arranged, and allegations of unethical practices were made. The matter received extensive press coverage, and in October the government appointed a committee, led by the newly-appointed head of the Ontario Securities Commission (OSC), J.R. Kimber, QC, to examine the province's securities laws, particularly as they related to take-over bids and insider trading. While the Kimber Committee was working, the Ontario securities market was severely shaken by events surrounding the huge Texas Gulf Sulphur discovery near Timmins. When news of this strike became public in April 1964, there was excited trading on the TSE of stocks of nearly every mining company with interests in the Timmins region. The activity became so disorderly that the attorney-general ordered the OSC to investigate. While it was doing so, public attention was drawn to an obscure mining company, Windfall Oils and Mines Limited, which had acquired some land inadvertently left unstaked by the Texas Gulf staking teams. During the summer of 1964 rumours abounded that Windfall had found a large ore deposit on these lands. Intervention by the OSC only raised the level of speculation and the price of Windfall shares rose from approximately 60 cents to more than $5. When the company finally revealed its situation, which was that it had not found any ore, its shares fell overnight from $4.15 to 80 cents. The government appointed another royal commission, the Kelly Commission, to investigate the Windfall affair and, while it was at it, to look into 'the function, role and activities of the Toronto Stock Exchange and the Ontario Securities Commission.' By the end of 1964 no fewer than five inquiries were under way into Ontario's securities laws, especially as they related to mining stocks.[38]

Both the Kelly Commission and the Kimber Commission found much to criticize in the way the Ontario securities industry was conducting its affairs. The Kimber Commission's report provided a succinct, but thorough, review of the industry's operations. The report is notable for its clear statement of the economic as well as the administrative issues involved in trying to reconcile the protection of investors with the resource-allocating functions of financial markets. Noting that secondary industry was becoming more important than the natural resource industries in Canada, the commission emphasized that capital markets must be not only efficient, but 'respectable,' if they were to serve as channels through which savers would place their money in equity investments. There could be little doubt that the public's confidence in the financial system had already been badly shaken by the events of the early 1960s. While recognizing that investors could never be fully protected against the risks inherent in equity investments, the committee suggested that the public might at least expect to have access to enough information to be confident that when it experienced losses, these would be 'genuine economic losses.'[39] Such had not been the case in Ontario during the recent past, the committee found. The ideal of a free securities market was simply not relevant to the existing real-world situation. Imperfect knowledge, impediments to free entry into the market, and restrictions on the mobility of financial resources made the existing market far from 'free and open.' Consequently, in the view of the commission, the task was to design securities legislation that would reduce the imperfections in the capital market and ensure that it would function in a way consistent with attainment of 'long run economic objectives.'[40] What these objectives might be and how they would be determined was not specified. Most of the commission's recommendations had to do with increasing the amount of information disclosed to investors. With respect to the much-publicized matter of insider trading, the commission proposed that the securities laws should make it clear that the use of information not available to the public for gain by insiders was wrong and that appropriate remedies should be made available for those harmed by such misuse.

The Kimber Commission was also critical of the way Ontario's securities laws were being administered. The Ontario Securities Commission was found to be incapable of performing the tasks assigned to it. Not only was it inadequately staffed and financed, its members, oddly enough, had hitherto not been expected to have any special knowledge of the securities industry. The commission proposed that the OSC be made more independent of the attorney-general's department and that it be provided with an adequate staff and more knowledgeable members.

A few months after the Kimber Commission reported, the Kelly Commission released its findings on the Windfall affair. Kelly was, if anything, more damning in his criticism of the existing system than the Kimber Commission had been. The OSC, Kelly found, not only lacked the capability to carry out its work, it did not even know what it was supposed to do.[41] This lack of any clearly specified function, he suggested, helped explain how the OSC had become entangled in the Windfall affair (its director apparently had personally traded in Windfall shares). He also criticized the role played by the Toronto Stock Exchange. Members of the TSE had traded so large a percentage of the Windfall shares on their own accounts that Kelly was moved to wonder whether members of the brokerage community regarded the exchange as a public securities market 'or as a private gaming club maintained for their own benefit.'[42] He was sceptical about the TSE's ability to govern its own affairs in a responsible manner. He suggested that if the governors of the exchange could not enforce their own rules to make the market function as a truly public institution, then some outside authority would have to take charge of its affairs. He recognized, however, that in the absence of a nation-wide set of rules governing securities exchanges, it would be difficult to implement stricter rules in Ontario than those applied to exchanges in other provinces.

The TSE anticipated this criticism and was already implementing new rules governing the conduct of members and their employees. The government responded to the suggestions of the Kimber and Kelly reports by creating a new ministry, the Department of Financial and Commercial Affairs, one stated purpose of which was to promote 'a high degree of public confidence in Canadian investment.'[43]

Few of the changes made either in legislation or in organization of the industry, however, altered its general character. Nor did they lay to rest the doubts that had accumulated about its capacity for reform. Indeed, the introduction of new legislation in this and related fields appeared to be a permanent feature of the provincial government's legislative agenda in the 1970s. Protection of the investor remained a matter of controversy and complaint. Concerns were raised again about business combinations. Within eighteen months of the new Securities Act, which came into force in 1966, a large number of corporate take-overs, mergers, and private acquisitions occurred. The adequacy of investor disclosure, particularly financial reporting, in several of these transactions was questioned by the Ontario Securities Commission, prompting the government to introduce yet more legislation covering various aspects of business organization, financing, and management.[44] Reaction to this proposed legislation was so unfavourable, however, that it was withdrawn and reintroduced in 1969 and withdrawn and reintroduced again in 1970. But by then a new issue had arisen. The sale of a controlling interest in Royal Securities to a 'non-resident' purchaser in 1969 brought to a head concern that had been growing about foreign ownership of Canadian business, especially Canadian financial business. The general issue of foreign ownership in Ontario was studied by an interdepartmental task force in 1971, while the more particular question of foreign involvement in the financial system was referred to a committee of the Ontario Securities Commission.[45] Even before the latter reported, however, the government set out a basic policy position on the matter. Speaking in the legislature in July 1971, the premier stated that the government considered the investment industry to be an area in which the ownership of firms should remain 'substantially Canadian.' Guidelines were to be applied to investment companies similar to those already established for trust and loan companies (and paperback book publishing firms): the capital owned or controlled by non-Canadians in such firms was not to exceed 25 per cent, and no more than 10 per cent of the capital would be owned or controlled by a single person or group of persons who were not Canadian citizens. Such measures as they applied to the investment industry, the osc committee noted in its report on the situation, could be expected to provide only an interim solution to the problem. In the long run, action would be needed at the national level to ensure that domestic sources of capital would be adequate to finance the development of natural resources and the growth of secondary industry.[46] The committee also expressed concern, however, that other provinces seemed to be showing little interest in adopting such measures. Indeed, British Columbia, Alberta, and New Brunswick, it noted, each had recently registered at least one non-resident investment company, thereby raising the possibility that Ontario might find itself with an investment industry free of non-resident control but isolated. The problems involved in developing a national policy were at the time being investigated by a commission sponsored by the Canadian Stock Exchanges and the Investment Dealers' Association of Canada.[47]

The outlook by the end of the period for an early resolution of these problems was not good. Despite widespread recognition that uniformity of securities laws was essential, Ontario itself proved most unwilling to sacrifice any of its responsibilities in this area to the federal government. When the latter moved to enact legislation to regulate mutual funds in 1974, for example, the Ontario government hastened to introduce legislation of its own which the responsible minister pointedly observed would render the proposed federal legislation unnecessary.[48] The legislation proposed in Ontario, however, proved to be totally unacceptable to the investment community in the province, and it was withdrawn.

6 *Education, Health, and Welfare*

Nothing better illustrates the growth of the services sector of the provincial economy, the expansion of government activity in the economy, or the inability of the province to develop a set of coherent economic objectives than the postwar development of the education, health, and welfare 'industries.'

Total government outlays in Ontario (federal, provincial and municipal) on education, health, and welfare services tripled between the end of the Second World War and the early 1970s, increasing from less than 4 per cent of the Gross Provincial Product to more than 13 per cent.[1] Total spending on such services was, of course, greater than this, for although the period saw more and more of the responsibility for such matters shifted from private to public hands, individuals remained responsible for financing some of their education and health requirements – for example, there were some private schools, and the costs of dental care and some other health services were still handled privately, even at the end of the period – while some welfare activities were still privately funded through charitable organizations such as the Community Chest, churches, and service clubs.

What effect did this have on the development of the provincial economy over the period? There can be no simple answer. The outputs of teachers, physicians, and welfare workers cannot be measured directly. They are typically inferred from the cost of the inputs. While it is known how many students were enrolled in formal studies, how many appendectomies were performed, and how many destitute mothers received aid, there are no direct measures of the real values of such services to the recipients or to the society at large. The fact that it was politically acceptable to shift much of the responsibility for paying for such services from individuals to the community at large suggests that the electorate expected such benefits to be positive or else was imbued with a strong sense of altruism. Of course part of the explanation must lie in the experience of the Depression, but considerations beyond a heightened concern with equity were also involved. After the war there was a revival of interest in the phenomenon of economic growth. Why were some populations rich and others poor? What forces governed the material progress of people?

Many economists who turned their attention to such questions in the early post-war period were inclined to attribute differences in the growth experience of particular economies to their rate of real capital accumulation. The fact that rich countries had more capital than poor countries[2] made the available labour supplies more productive, and consequently real per capita incomes were higher in one than in the other. The problem of poor economies consequently was seen as being largely a matter of increasing their stocks of capital – a difficult task, of course, since capital goods can be produced only if resources are shifted to such purposes from the creation of consumer goods. In situations where incomes were very low, such a shift could be close to impossible. Hence the vicious circle of poverty in what were then called the 'underdeveloped' countries of the world. In the developed 'industrial' countries the problem was not so much that denying consumption was too painful, but that profitable opportunities for investment might be wanting or that private capital markets might undervalue certain kinds of capital and cause too little to be produced.

Empirical studies undertaken in the late 1950s and early 1960s raised doubts about the validity of this heavy emphasis on investment in capital goods as the principal determinant of economic progress. Studies of economic growth in the United States, subsequently replicated in Canada, suggested that the growth of real per capita output was considerably greater than could be accounted for by increased investment in real capital.[3] Something else appeared to be contributing to productivity growth. Even after making allowance for greater efficiency arising from scale economies and the organization of production, a substantial 'residual' of productivity increase remained to be accounted for. The best guess as to what lay behind this residual seemed to be that workers and managers had become more productive because of better health, improved training, and attainment of higher levels of education. Thus arose the notion that investments in 'human capital' were possibly important sources of economic growth: that outlays made on education, and possibly on other services such as health care, could be expected to yield a stream of future benefits, just as investments in physical capital could.

The concept of human capital was quickly picked up by the media, politicians, and other opinion-makers in the 1960s. As used by economists, it was usually defined as the knowledge, skills, energy, and motivation acquired by individuals that contributed to their ability to produce goods and services. While the view survived that educational standards and health levels were high in Canada, particularly in Ontario, where there had long been a certain smugness about the quality of the province's educational system in comparison with the American, it was soon noted that one reason that productivity and incomes were lower in Canada than in the United States might be that the Canadian labour force was demonstrably less well educated.[4]

It was typically acknowledged, of course, that education, health care, and social security were necessary and desirable in themselves. They had a 'consumption' as well as 'investment' value, but this aspect of such services was typically paid only lip-service, perhaps because the economic analysis applied in studying them was better suited to handling returns in the form of income on investment than it was to evaluating the much more subjective 'greater enjoyment of life' associated with them. The efforts of economists to measure the returns to education in the early 1960s were somewhat crude, but they were important because they appeared to support the traditional assumption about the 'value' of a good education. Early studies suggested that the private returns to higher education (that is, the additional income individuals could expect to receive over their lifetime after deducting the direct expenses such as tuition fees and the indirect cost of forgone income during the years spent obtaining additional schooling) were well worth the costs. Some indicated that these returns were substantially above the returns that could be expected from investments in physical capital.[5] Canadian studies found that the returns to investments in higher education in this country were probably even greater than in the United States. Thus, the Economic Council of Canada suggested in its annual report of 1965 that the overall rate of return to investment in education, taking into account not only the private but the public costs involved, would range from 10 to 15 per cent, levels which compared favourably with even the pre-tax returns available from investments in physical and financial assets. The policy implication was clear: greater emphasis should be placed on expanding investment in education relative to investment in other assets.[6]

Much of the expansion of the educational, health, and welfare systems was dictated, of course, by the high rate of population growth and rising real incomes of the period. The importance of the new 'scientific' knowledge, especially the concept of human capital, lay in the effect it had in transforming governments, certainly in the case of Ontario, from agencies forced to accommodate such an expansion into agencies enthusiastically promoting it. Unfortunately, this enthusiasm proved to be ill founded. By the 1970s the work being done on the economics of education was showing that the earlier estimates undoubtedly exaggerated the returns to investment in further schooling, partly because they failed to take into account factors such as differences in individual ability, family background, the 'screening function' performed by the educational system, postgraduation experience and other considerations that might have been responsible for the higher incomes earned by the more highly educated.[7] Combined with generally lower estimates of lifetime earnings of university graduates, the re-estimation of the rate of return to investments in higher education, by the mid-1970s was yielding figures more in the range of 4–5 per cent rather than 10–15 per cent. At the same time, however, newer approaches to the question of identifying returns, both private and public, were being developed, which raised

TABLE 20
Total Enrolment and Teaching Staff, Elementary and
Secondary Schools, Ontario, Selected Years 1940-75

Year	Enrolment	Teachers
1940	661,563	21,829
1945	687,213	22,353
1950	749,079	26,353
1955	1,065,123	35,560
1960	1,422,821	49,292
1965	1,790,907	68,602
1970	2,073,188	93,000
1975	2,056,627	94,600

SOURCE: Leacy, ed., *Historical Statistics of Canada*, 2nd ed., w121 and w170

the possibility that the earlier estimates, while based on biased data and inadequate techniques, may have been close to the 'true' rates of return after all.[8]

Education in Ontario

By the 1940s the principle of mass, publicly supported, compulsory education was well established in the province. With only a few exceptions, all children were required to attend school until at least age fifteen. Although there were a few private schools, they served less than 3 per cent of the total number of students in the province, a figure that varied little over the entire period. There were also a number of federally operated schools for native children, but they had less than 1 per cent of total enrolment in the early 1940s and less than half that figure by the mid-1970s. Total enrolment in the elementary and secondary schools of Ontario increased from 661,563 in 1940 to 2,056,627 in 1975. The total number of teachers grew from 21,829 to 94,600 over the same period.[9] The quality of their effort defies measurement, but if the student-teacher ratio is relevant, teacher productivity clearly increased. So did their formal qualifications: in the early 1950s only a quarter of the elementary and secondary school teachers in Ontario had a university degree, but by the 1970s more than half did. While school-teaching remained a largely female occupation, after the Second World War the number of men in the elementary and secondary schools increased, their number rising from just over 30 per cent in the 1950s to nearly 45 per cent by the end of the period.

The growth of the educational system was even more notable at the post-secondary level. At the beginning of the period Ontario had three publicly supported universities; at the end it had fifteen. The number of non-university post-secondary institutions increased from a few trade and vocational schools to a system of some twenty colleges located across the entire province. Full-time university enrolment increased from 12,410 in 1940 to 159,701 in 1975; full-

TABLE 21
Full-Time Non-University Post-Secondary Enrolment,
Ontario, Selected Years 1955–75

Year	Enrolment
1955	10,861
1960	16,596
1965	21,215
1966	24,957
1967	33,670
1968	45,028
1969	48,962
1970	54,399
1971	50,345
1972	52,521
1973	55,399
1974	56,642
1975	59,640

SOURCE: Leacy, ed., *Historical Statistics of Canada*, 2nd ed., w327

time, post-secondary, non-university enrolment increased from less than 11,000 in 1955 to almost 60,000 in 1975. There were 1,179 university teachers in Ontario in 1940; by 1975 there were 12,290.[10] Total expenditures on education in the province exceeded $10 billion annually by the end of the period, about 60 per cent of which was disbursed by the provincial government, 20 per cent by the municipalities, and 10 per cent by the federal government. Fees and other sources covered the remaining 10 per cent.[11]

The role of the provincial government in the administration and financial support of the educational system changed considerably over the period, reflecting a tendency towards centralization and an increasing reliance on expert knowledge and opinion. Yet there is little evidence that the provincial government was able to formulate any set of very clear objectives with respect to the province's educational system. Neither the quantity nor the quality of educational services supplied appears to have been related to any specific objectives, either to perceptions of consumer 'demand' for education as a consumption good or to the requirements of job markets for particular types of training. While there were frequent studies of the system, including several that were supposed to answer the question of what its goals should be, and despite the aggressive action taken on occasion to meet perceived 'shortages' of particular kinds of labour, no general pattern of purpose emerges with respect to what was becoming one of the province's most important industries.

At the beginning of the period management of education in the province was relatively decentralized. Local boards of education made up of either elected or appointed trustees were generally responsible for hiring teachers, building and maintaining the schools, and raising money for educational purposes from local property owners. The provincial government provided financial support in the form of grants, prescribed certain courses of study and textbooks, and exercised control over the training and certification of teachers. It was not directly involved in the day-to-day provision of educational services, except in the case of certain special activities such as correspondence courses, travelling railway car schools serving remote communities, educating the deaf and blind, and broadcasting educational material over the radio.[12]

Post-secondary education was in the hands of the universities, whose autonomy was seldom challenged. Many were substantially self-supporting, although the University of Toronto and the other non-sectarian institutions did receive substantial grants from the province to aid them in their work.[13] Vocational education was provided by the provincial Department of Labour, which operated an apprenticeship training program and by a number of private secretarial and trade schools. Most nurses were trained by hospital schools of nursing. Elementary school teachers received their special training in provincial-government-operated 'normal' schools and high school teachers at the Ontario College of Education. Adult education, which had become popular during the Depression years, was offered by the universities through 'extension' programs and by voluntary organizations such as the YMCA and the Workmen's Educational League. Specialized organizations, such as Frontier College, also provided education to particular groups of workers.

The inability of many local school boards to meet expenses during the Depression remained a central concern of provincial government education policy well into the 1940s. One of the boldest of Drew's '22 Points' in 1943 was his promise to have the province assume 50 per cent of the school tax then being charged against local real estate. Although there were some doubts as to how this was meant to be interpreted, by 1945 the provincial government had in fact increased its grants to school boards until they were covering just over 42 per cent of their total expenses (compared with 14 per cent in 1940).[14] The financial health of the boards was also improved by the government's efforts to induce the weaker boards to amalgamate and form larger units. By the end of the war nearly half the small elementary school sections had been brought together within township areas, and some progress was being made in enlarging secondary school districts in the province as well.

The most acute problem in the immediate post-war period, especially at the elementary level, was the shortage of qualified teachers. Despite efforts to increase the numbers of graduates from the normal schools, the first entrants from the baby boom increased the need for teachers faster than they could be trained. For more than a decade the Department of Education was forced to authorize boards to hire hundreds of untrained people to teach school in the province. A large percentage of these teachers had not completed secondary school.

The need for vocational training was also recognized in other areas. The province opened a number of special schools after the war to teach particular skills. The Institute for Mining at Haileybury in northern Ontario was opened in 1945 to 'provide special technical courses in subjects relating to mining for capable boys who wish to enter the mining industry without investing the time and money which is required for technical university courses.'[15] The Provincial Institute of Textiles at Hamilton and the Lakehead Technical Institute were institutions with similar purposes and, like the Haileybury school, were closely associated with local industries. A school for retraining returning veterans in Toronto became in 1948 the Ryerson Institute of Technology, a polytechnical school offering courses at the junior college level and some of the Department of Labour's apprenticeship programs.

The returning veterans after the war flooded the province's degree-granting institutions. University undergraduate enrolment in 1945 was about the same as it had been in 1940. By 1947 it had doubled.

In the field of adult education, a 'Community Programmes Branch' was established within the Department of Education to provide services to communities that would take the initiative in organizing recreational and adult education activities.

This policy of providing support while leaving responsibility for initiating and operating programs to local bodies was in keeping with the provincial government's apparent objective of centralizing financial and administrative functions in education while decentralizing curriculum development. In 1949 the high school entrance examination was abolished, and local authorities were made responsible for moving students from one division of the school system to another. Local boards were also made responsible for choosing textbooks, and 'teachers and supervising officers familiar with the local situation' were to be given greater responsibility for curriculum development.[16]

These practices were supported by the findings of the first major inquiry in the post-war period into the workings of the educational system in the province. The Hope Commission, appointed in 1945 and reporting five years later, broke little new ground and failed to find an acceptable solution to the main problem confronting the government – the highly sensitive issue of public financial support for Roman Catholic schools in the province. The general policy position of the provincial government remained conservative in the 1950s, with much attention still being given to problems of financing education. The minister of education noted in 1950 that before any drastic changes were made in the organization of the system or in the curriculum, it would be necessary to 'scrutinize expenditures carefully to see that they are necessary and that full value will be obtained in return.'[17] As to what the purposes of the system were, the government's view appeared to be that the main task of the elementary and secondary schools was to socialize students, turning them into good citizens. The economic returns to education received little attention. Thus, the minister of education in 1952:

The objective of our work in this Department is to produce loyal, intelligent, right-thinking, religious, and freedom-loving citizens to take their places in developing, by all

TABLE 22
Total Spending on Elementary and Secondary Education in Ontario by Level of Government, Selected Years 1946–71 (per capita $1971)

Year	Municipal	Provincial	Federal	Total
1946	36	31	n.a.	67
1950	58	30	1	89
1955	81	33	1	115
1960	101	53	1	155
1962	87	74	33	194
1965	111	83	12	206
1969	156	126	6	288
1970	142	116	4	262

SOURCE: V. Lang, *The Service State Emerges in Ontario* (Toronto: OEC, 1974), table 5(a), 80

legitimate means at their disposal, this rapidly-expanding Province and Dominion. In the schools of Ontario the young people and the boys and girls are being trained to realize what true democracy really means and it is hoped that their loyalty to Queen and country will be such that they will be ready when their turn comes, to render their share of public service in the communities in which they make their homes.[18]

By the end of the decade such a position would have defied belief. Both thought and practice changed radically within only a few years. Enrolment increases in the elementary schools as the baby boom children flooded in, combined with a sharp rise in the secondary schools' retention level, severely shocked the system. Total spending on current account by elementary and secondary school boards increased from over $54 million in 1945 to more than $99 million in 1950. By 1955 the annual current outlay had more than doubled again.[19] Capital spending increased even more rapidly, rising from $7.7 million in 1945 to $35.5 million a decade later.

While demographic forces, rising per capita incomes, and a growing belief in the economic benefits of education were major factors promoting the expansion of the educational system in the province during the 1950s, another important influence was federal government policy, especially as it related to vocational and technical education. A series of federal programs, beginning with the Vocational Training Co-ordination Act of 1945, made federal funding available to provinces interested in expanding vocational and technical training facilities. To maximize Ontario's benefits under the terms of these programs, the provincial government undertook a major restructuring of the educational system in the province. In the 1960s this activity became particularly intense. Under the terms of the 1960–1 Technical and Vocational Training Agreement, the federal government's contributions were specified as a proportion of provincial government outlays for such purposes. The Ontario government promptly assumed direct responsibility for a large part of secondary school spending, thereby increasing the base on which federal grants would be calculated. Because of time limits imposed on the capital grants part of the agreement, Ontario initiated a crash program of school construction. It also launched a program of curriculum 'reform' which implemented a streaming system in which there would be three 'distinct but equal' branches: arts and science; business and commerce; and technology and trade. While sound pedagogic reasons were cited for this change, it could not escape notice that it also greatly increased the number of high-school courses eligible for federal financial support. By 1965 approximately half the secondary schools in Ontario were offering technical and vocational programs.[20]

The physical expansion of the primary and secondary school system proceeded at a remarkable pace in the 1960s. Addressing the legislature in 1963, the premier, John Robarts, claimed that 'we here in Ontario have opened a new school or a substantial new addition every day of every week of every year, Sundays and holidays included, for the past fifteen years.' The record shows that the statement was accompanied by applause.[21] Between 1945 and 1969 the province had spent more than $2.3 billion on more than 9,700 building projects to provide spaces for 1,820,000 elementary and secondary school students.[22]

The cost of operating this expanding system remained a concern, as did uncertainty about what the system was supposed to be producing. Both matters were aggressively addressed during the decade: the first through an elaborate financing arrangement known as the 'foundation tax scheme' and the second by a highly controversial inquiry carried out by the 'Provincial Committee on Aims and Objectives of Education in the Schools of Ontario,' better known as the Hall-Dennis Committee.

Real per pupil costs of education had levelled off for a time after the 1958 changes in the school grants system, but by the early 1960s they were again showing signs of increasing, and many of the smaller school boards appeared to be headed for serious financial trouble. Various measures for relieving the problem were debated in the legislature, but attention centred on a plan that had the support of the increasingly expert staff being assembled in the Department of Education. Modelled on a scheme developed in the United States, the proposal was for a 'foundation level of expenditure' of so many dollars per pupil to be determined for the province as a whole. A local tax rate of so many mills per unit of equalized assessment would then be determined, and provincial grants to boards would be scaled accordingly. In principle a simple means of making provincial grants equitable, the plan as actually implemented in 1964 was complicated by a complex system of floors, ceilings, and special grants incorporated to ensure that it would be politically acceptable to local school boards across the province.[23] It appears that there was also hope on the part of the government that the new plan would provide an acceptable way to increase public support for Roman Catholic schools.[24]

The provincial government also moved to accelerate the process of school board amalgamation. Legislation in 1964 made the township the general unit for elementary school administration, a bold stroke that reduced the number of rural school boards in the province from 1,850 to 423. Subsequent legislation forced the pace by promoting the consolidation of many separate-school boards and the formation of county-wide systems combining elementary and secondary school administration. By the end of the decade consolidation had reached the point where the government could implement yet another system for allocating provincial grants. The foundation tax plan was abandoned in favour of a more flexible system which would enable all boards to spend at a given level with the same rates of local taxation while at the same time ensuring that boards with higher levels of spending would have to levy higher local taxes. The making and implementing of this new policy reveals an interesting feature of the decision-making process in place at the time. The new plan was carefully formulated by a group of expert consultants working for the Grants Committee in the Department of Education. One of these consultants later noted that the plan they devised 'largely represented their own policy preferences or their own interpretations of what general provincial policy implied in the domain of grants to school boards.'[25] It was greatly modified, however, in the course of implementation.

By 1970 the provincial government's main concern was no longer with assisting local boards to meet their obligations, but with controlling the rate at which educational spending was increasing. Boards were put on notice that if they did not restrain their spending voluntarily, the province would subject them to direct controls. An amendment to the Department of Education Act in 1969 empowered the minister to specify which expenditures a board could or could not make, a measure that the minister indicated was to be a 'reserve power' to be used only in the event that boards proved unwilling or unable to keep their spending within some acceptable – but unspecified – limit. The 'unable' apparently referred to the matter of teacher salary negotiations. With such salaries accounting for the bulk of operating expenses and the teachers becoming organized and militant, the government was anxious to put pressure on the boards to take a hard line in negotiations with their employees. If school board financing continued to grow at the rates of the late 1960s, it seemed likely that this single item of provincial expenditure would constrain all future budget planning. According to one senior adviser to the government, continued growth in spending on education would completely abort the government's efforts to reform the provincial-municipal tax system and starve other provincial programs that might be expected to yield a higher long-term pay-off. There was also the possibility that teacher salaries would rise 'disproportionately' to those of other workers if these trends continued.[26]

Such concerns about the relative 'pay-offs' to different kinds of provincial government spending raises the question of what the pay-offs to education were expected to be. Discovering the answer was the task assigned to the Hall-Dennis Committee, which was asked to 'identify the needs of the child as a person and as a member of society, to set forth the aims of education for the educational system of the province, and to propose means by which these aims and objectives may be achieved.'

Although the Hall-Dennis Committee's report, *Living and Learning*, released in 1968, fell short of specifying what the aims and objectives of education in Ontario should be, it amply catalogued the prevailing professional ideas on the subject. The committee sidestepped the problem of defining the purposes of education by declaring that 'The aims and objectives of education are an intrinsic part of the proposed educational process, and are inherent in the very spirit of the report.'[27] Instead, it provided the government with a vividly illustrated guide to progressive thought in curriculum design and teaching methods. 'The conditions of dynamic economic and cultural growth in which we now find ourselves,' the report declared, 'demands that educational policy and practice be the result of expert long-term and short-term forecasts.' Ignoring the past failures of attempts at forecasting, the committee went on to urge that 'the lockstep structure of past times' be abandoned so that the child would 'progress from year to year without the hazards and frustrations of failure.' The fixed positions of pupil and teacher, the insistence on silence, and the punitive approach would all have to give way to a more relaxed teacher-pupil relationship. The 'new world' in which the child found himself (as the committee put it) demanded new approaches to learning. The committee made much of technical change, noting that the new child found himself in a 'technatomic' period, which 'began to show its impact upon our society after 1945' and which led to wonders such as the Ontario child's finding 'that his breakfast orange juice comes fast frozen in a throw-away can.'[28] Yet the report had nothing substantial to say about the connection between education and the fostering of technical change.

The committee accepted the prevailing view that 'money spent on education is a sound investment,' citing the Economic Council of Canada to support this view. It declared that it was neither dismayed nor surprised by the fact that in the last decade the costs of education had risen, and it suggested, not very helpfully, that new ways of financing education should be sought. Two of the seven research studies it sponsored had to do with the economic aspects of education. One involved the development of cost estimates for 'optimum educational models.' The other, by O.J. Firestone, found by means of a questionnaire survey that increased years of formal schooling and increased mobility contributed to economic opportunities in almost all categories of employment.

The report had little to say, however, about education as a preparation for work. It seemed to be preoccupied with education as a consumer commodity that would create a setting of 'unity, harmony, and peace' in which 'educational endeavour' would flourish and 'truth will make all men free.' Its great emphasis on less structured forms of education ('more child-centred') supported trends already underway in the provincial schools and was at least not inconsistent with the dismantling of the Robarts streaming system and the reorganization being undertaken by the province in the technical and vocational curriculum in the late 1960s.

One of the great practical problems of this period was the inability of labour markets to absorb the large numbers of young adults now seeking employment with specialized but low-level training in various skills and trades. One plausible remedy was to provide such new labour force entrants with further training. But while some of them could be accommodated by the existing technical institutes and a few by the universities, it seemed that additional facilities were required. As early as 1963 the Committee of Presidents of Universities in Ontario had drawn attention to the emerging problem and proposed that a major expansion of technical education facilities should be studied. Other bodies, such as the Grade Thirteen Study Committee, also saw such a need and proposed that the province establish 'a new kind of institution which will provide, in the interests of students for whom a university course is unsuitable, a type of training which universities are not designed to offer.'[29]

The government responded to these suggestions in 1965, creating the Colleges of Applied Arts and Technology (CAAT). Several of the existing technical institutes were converted to the new type of institution, and new colleges were built throughout the province. By the end of the decade twenty CAATs were in operation. The capital outlay was substantial, rising from annual expenditures of about $2.5 million in 1966 to more than $63 million in 1971. The annual operating costs rose from about $5 million in 1966 to over $100 million in the early 1970s. A substantial part of these costs was met by federal government grants to the province in support of post-secondary education and research. Even so, the burden on the province was considerable, particularly at a time when the costs of other forms of education were becoming a matter of increasing concern. The government's reasons for developing a new tier of educational facilities under these circumstances have been a matter of considerable speculation. The availability of federal funds was undoubtedly a consideration. It has also been suggested that the legacy of the Robarts 'streaming' plan had been a flood of unemployable young people who had to be either absorbed by some new kind of institution for 'upgrading' or allowed to drift into chronic unemployment.[30] There was also the model afforded by developments in other jurisdictions. In 1965 the minister of education, Mr Davis, returned from a visit to California having found that employers there 'weren't really willing to accept high school graduation as a minimum qualification for new employees, but were demanding graduation from junior colleges as the irreducible minimum.' This, he suggested, might be a 'preview of things to come in Ontario.'[31]

The creation of the CAAT system was both a relief and a threat from the standpoint of the province's universities. It removed much of the pressure they had been under to expand their own diploma and other programs of low academic content. But there was also the risk that the new institutions would siphon off much of the public funding upon which the universities were becoming increasingly dependent to expand their own operations.

The financial problems of the universities had been a matter of concern as early as 1951 when the Royal Commission on National Development in the Arts, Letters and Sciences addressed the matter and recommended that the federal government provide universities in Canada with per capita grants in recognition of their 'national importance.'[32] Universities in Ontario, like those in other provinces, subsequently obtained financial support from the federal government to help cover both operating and capital costs. After 1967 the federal government provided 50 per cent of the operating costs of post-secondary institutions under the terms of the Federal-Provincial Fiscal Arrangements Act. Federal funds to support research in the universities was also provided through the Canada Council and the National Research Council.

The provincial government's funding of university education in the early part of the period was carried out on an ad hoc basis, with the government responding to requests for money from individual universities as was seen fit. As these requests grew after the war, the government instituted a system for making grants to universities based rather loosely on the available 'surplus' in the provincial budget.[33] Church-affiliated colleges were not eligible for such public support, and as they, like the other post-secondary institutions, attempted to meet increasing enrolment pressure, many of them found it expedient to sever their religious affiliations in order to obtain provincial financial aid.

As the number of universities eligible for support increased, the government found it necessary to develop more formal mechanisms for allotting funds among them. In 1951 it hired a part-time consultant to function as a go-between in its relations with the universities.[34] Four years later the task was assigned to a committee of senior civil servants. In 1961 a larger body was formed, which included several businessmen as well as the chief justice of Ontario, the deputy minister of education, and other senior officials of the government. Representatives of the universities were eventually added, the committee was renamed the 'Committee on University Affairs' and in 1967 was given a full-time chairman, Dr D.T. Wright, a former dean of engineering at the University of Waterloo.

Many of the functions of the Committee on University Affairs were paralleled by those of the Department of University Affairs which had been created in 1964. Both were involved in the task of allocating government funds to the universities. By the mid-1960s the latter had become almost entirely dependent upon government grants both for operating and for capital needs, a situation viewed with some alarm by many academics. As one of them, J.A. Corry, observed, 'The university has become a public service institution and has fallen into basic dependence on governments for the resources it needs ... The community and university are now fated to much closer relationships than ever before. What will happen to the ivory towers and dreaming spires?'[35] What happened was that the government made clear its intention to require the universities to meet the demands placed upon them with respect to turning out trained manpower in an efficient manner. If they would not do so voluntarily, the government would be forced to 'move in and take over.'[36]

Fortunately a system was developed for allocating funds among the universities in a manner that enabled them to maintain a semblance of autonomy that was viewed as tolerably fair, and that satisfied the government's need to maintain the necessary degree of financial accountability. This was the 'formula financing' approach implemented in 1967. It involved a rather complicated system of program categories and weighting numbers for the various divisions of a university to which a basic grant for a student of 'unit weight' was applied to arrive at a total grant for each institution. Special 'extra formula' support was made available for the new universities being established. The universities were then free to apportion their income among their various divisions and faculties as they saw fit.[37] It was also possible for universities to seek funding from private sources, and this was important for the new institutions in particular, all of which owed their existence to considerable community and especially business-sector support. Even in these cases, however, the percentage of total operating expenses provided privately was small.[38]

The main problem to emerge in the later years of the period was the government's reluctance to continue increasing the total amount of money committed to these purposes. The system was by then so large, owing to the government's commitment to provide higher education opportunities for all those qualified that, as with the primary and secondary system, it seemed obvious that the rate of growth in spending had to be curtailed. By the 1970s it appeared that there was no easy way to do this – despite continued growth in enrolments, the amount of money supplied by the government to the universities would have to be cut.[39] The government did, however, make an effort to explore the possibilities. In 1969 it appointed a large committee of inquiry to investigate the whole matter of post-secondary education in the province.

The Commission on Post-Secondary Education in Ontario (COPSEO) was a microcosm of the problems and conflicts it was investigating. It comprised an odd collection of academics, 'educators,' youthful activists, businessmen, and representatives of various cultural constituencies in the province and was presided over (with much difficulty) by Dr D.T. Wright for most of its existence. When Dr Wright left to become deputy provincial secretary for social development, the work of the commission was completed under the chairmanship of one of its members, D.O. Davis, who submitted its final report in December 1972.

Full of dissension within, the commission also faced bitter external opposition, much of it from the university community, which viewed the whole undertaking with much suspicion. The fears of those who suspected that the commission had been intended to undermine the traditional values of higher education were seemingly confirmed when its first publication, a newsprint flyer, appeared. Its tone suggested that the commission intended to launch an all-out attack on the existing system. An interim report published in 1971 did nothing to quiet these fears, suggesting as it did that the government should support 'socially useful alternatives to post-secondary education,' should channel all funding for post-secondary education through a single department, and should broaden the definition of post-secondary education to include museums, theatres, schools of nursing, and 'similar institutions.'[40]

The commission's final report in 1972 was an anticlimax. The 126 recommendations included the earlier proposals to broaden the system, to increase accessibility, to promote lifelong learning, to expand French-language facilities. It also proposed that a number of advisory bodies be established and that formula financing be retained but improved by basing grants on projected enrolment data to facilitate planning. Increased student aid was also called for.[41] Most of these proposals were promptly lost, however, in the context of the provincial government's new commitment to restraining the growth of educational spending in the province.

Total spending on education in Ontario had risen from less than 2 per cent of the Gross Provincial Product at the end of the war to more than 6 per cent. By the early 1970s education had become the largest single expenditure item in the provincial budget, accounting for almost 40 per cent of total estimated general expenditure. Declining enrolment at the elementary and secondary levels, growing doubts about the economic returns to education, and the fear that the education budget would eventually consume the province's revenues if allowed to grow unchecked made the issues of educational policy suddenly rather simple. By 1975 it appeared that the educational industry of the province had been over-expanded. The practical question was how to cut it back with a minimum of political cost. What the economic costs might be seemed relatively less important in the circumstances and, given the state of the economic theory of education and its contribution to economic growth, highly speculative.

Health Care

Expenditures on health care have an investment aspect like expenditures on education; for there is a plausible expectation of future returns from enhanced productivity in a healthy labour force. In a relatively advanced industrial economy, however, where most of the epidemic and debilitating contagious diseases have been brought under control, this aspect of health care appears to attract less attention than its immediate direct benefits to the recipient do. The great

TABLE 23
Hospital Bed Capacity, Ontario, Selected Years 1947–75

Year	Public General and Allied Special		Mental		Tuberculosis	
	Beds	Per '000 Population	Beds	Per '000 Population	Beds	Per '000 Population
1947	17,077	4.1	15,864	3.8	4,023	1.0
1955	27,150	5.2	18,391	3.5	4,482	0.9
1965	40,506	6.0	23,968	3.6	1,641	0.2
1975	49,321	6.0	16,513	2.0	–	–

SOURCES: 1947, 1955, 1965: Ontario, *Report of the Committee on the Healing Arts*, Vol. 1 (Toronto: Queen's Printer, 1970), table 6.49, 192; 1975: *Ontario Statistics, 1977*, table 5.12, 138

expansion in the volume of health care services provided in Ontario during the 1940–75 period was consequently attributable to the increasing demand for such services, a demand fostered by public policies that made it easier for increasing numbers of individuals to obtain health care. These policies appear to have been based on a widely shared belief that access to health care should not be restricted by the ability of individuals to pay for it directly and that there should be carefully regulated and uniform standards applied in the supplying of such services, not only within the province, but nationally.

The growth of the health care industry in Ontario rivalled and at times exceeded that of the educational system over the course of the 1940–75 period. By the end of the period, spending on health care amounted to over 5 per cent of the GPP. The employment created greatly exceeded the ability of the province to supply the necessary trained workers, with the result that large numbers of doctors, nurses and other skilled health care personnel had to be recruited outside the province. Providing the necessary physical facilities added substantially to the construction boom of the 1950s and 1960s. As it did with post-secondary education, the federal government played an important role in the financing of this expansion, and it also participated in the reorganization of the system through its insistence on certain standards with respect to accessibility and methods of financing.

The growth of the physical facilities required in the production of health care in the province over the period is suggested by the rapid increase in the number of hospital beds available. The program of hospital construction carried out added bed capacity at a higher rate than population was increasing, at least until the early 1970s. General public hospital beds per thousand of population grew from four at the end of the Second World War to six by 1975.[42] Employment in hospitals more than doubled. No measures of the quality of hospital care are available, nor is it possible to estimate the efficiency with which hospital workers performed their tasks, but there do not appear to have been any obvious increases

TABLE 24
Patient Days, Public General and Allied Special Hospitals, Ontario, Selected Years 1953–75

Year	Patient Days ('000)	Patient Days (per '000 population)
1953	7,008	1,418.3
1955	8,013	1,521.6
1960	10,224	1,673.0
1965	12,449	1,834.0
1970	14,651	1,940.3
1971	14,768	1,917.2
1972	14,703	1,882.6
1973	14,370	1,816.9
1974	14,643	1,818.1
1975	14,696	1,798.3

SOURCES: 1953–65: Ontario, Committee on the Healing Arts, *Report*, vol. 3, 117; 1970–5: *Ontario Statistics 1981*, table 5.12, 136

in productivity over the period. Between 1953 and the mid-1970s the number of full-time hospital personnel increased from 165 to more than 186 per hundred beds. The total volume of hospital care, measured in terms of patient days, grew steadily over most of the period, reaching a maximum of 14,768,000 in 1971 after which the annual number of patient days fell. The number of patient days per thousand of population also grew steadily, increasing from 1,418.3 in 1953 to 1,940.3 in 1970, and then falling sharply to 1,798.3 in 1975.[43] The number of physicians registered in Ontario increased from 4,195 in 1941 to 14,523 in 1975, a rate of growth also in excess of the increase in population. The number of persons per physician fell steadily over the period from 903 in 1941 to 566 in 1975.[44]

The growth in the supply of nursing services in the province is difficult to quantify, because many nurses registered in Ontario did not work there. Total registration increased from 10,162 in 1950 to 77,270 in 1975, again outpacing the growth of population, so that the number of persons per registered nurse fell from 225 to 106.[45] As in the case of physicians, a large part of the additional nursing force employed in Ontario, especially in the earlier part of the period, was recruited from outside the province.[46] In addition to the registered nurses, relatively larger numbers of registered nursing assistants, student nurses, orderlies, and other attendants were also employed. Changes in definitions make an accurate estimate impossible, but in general there were probably twice as many of these other workers employed as there were registered nurses.

Not all parts of the health care systems showed such growth patterns over the period. The numbers of dentists, pharmacists, optometrists, chiropractors, osteopaths, and podiatrists increased, but typically not as rapidly as the population. The number of fully qualified dentists in Ontario increased from 1,891 in 1941 to 3,902 in 1975, but the population per dentist actually increased over much

TABLE 25
Number of Physicians, Ontario, Selected Years 1941–75

Year	Fully Licensed Physicians	Population per Physician
1941	4,195	903
1951	5,642*	835
1961	8,136	774
1971	12,445	625
1975	14,523	566

SOURCES: 1941, 1951, 1961: Ontario, *Report of the Committee on the Healing Arts* except *, which is a revised total; 1971, 1975: from *Ontario Statistics 1977*, vol. 1, table 5.4, 130

of the period, reaching 2,599 in 1966, but declining thereafter to 2,108 in 1975. It is likely, however, that technological change, notably introduction of the high-speed drill and the practice of using dental assistants, may have increased the volume of service supplied per dentist by more than these data would suggest. Some other health care specialty services, such as those provided by laboratory technicians, physiotherapists, and radiology technicians, grew rapidly, but accounted for a small percentage of the total health care labour force.

Only fragmentary data relating to the total volume of spending on health care exist for the period before 1956. The first attempt to develop such data for Canada was made in the 1950–1 'Canadian Sickness Survey,' which attempted to measure the amount of sickness, the volume of medical care received, and family expenditures on it. As health insurance programs became more common later in the 1950s, the quantification of health care spending became simpler. Two facts stand out from such data: the total amount of spending on health care was increasing and an increasing proportion of this spending was being channelled through either privately or publicly operated intermediaries. Between 1956 and 1971 total spending on medical services in Ontario increased steadily from $42 million per capita (1971 constant dollars) to $92 million. Until 1959 these figures represent entirely personal spending. By 1971 only 24 per cent of the total was paid by individuals, 48 per cent by the province, and 28 per cent by the federal government.[47]

This increase in health care spending was part of a long-term trend. Even before the Depression, spending on health in Canada was increasing, but the rate of increase accelerated dramatically in the years after the war, particularly during the 1960s. In Ontario, spending on personal health care increased from 3.76 per cent of GPP in 1960 to just under 7 per cent in 1975. The percentage of personal income spent for such purposes increased from 4.62 to 8.57.[48]

The shift in spending to health care from other possible uses of income may be explained by a number of possible forces, such as changes in consumer preferences arising from better education, relative income elasticities of demand

TABLE 26
Expenditures on Personal Health Care as a Percentage of GPP and Personal Income, Ontario, 1960-75

Year	GPP	Personal Income
1960	3.76	4.62
1961	3.95	4.98
1962	4.04	5.04
1963	4.14	5.27
1964	4.15	5.40
1965	4.18	5.47
1966	4.08	5.35
1967	4.43	5.67
1968	4.69	5.99
1969	4.76	6.04
1970	5.06	6.32
1971	5.32	6.57
1972	5.17	6.18
1973	6.56	6.05
1974	6.38	8.23
1975	6.94	8.57

SOURCES: 1960-73: OEC, Ontario Economic Council, *Issues and Alternative 1976: Health* (Toronto: 1978), table 3, 42; 1974-75: *Ontario Statistics 1981*, table 5.9, 132

TABLE 27
Per Capita Health Care Expenditures, Ontario, 1960-75

Year	Total	Hospital Care	Physician Services	Dentist Services	Drugs	Other
1960	135.84	50.72	23.18	8.09	7.77	46.08
1965	189.06	76.84	33.17	10.97	11.03	57.04
1970	316.99	130.97	59.29	16.28	18.16	92.30
1975	554.23	249.22	91.93	31.02	29.40	152.65

NOTE: Current dollar values are shown. The increase in spending on health care in real terms was much more modest. Deflating the values shown in the 'Total' column using the Current Expenditure component of the Government Expenditure on Goods and Services implicit price index gives constant (1971) dollar values of $237.07, $277.21, $336.50, and $356.42 for 1960, 1965, 1970, and 1975, respectively.

SOURCE: *Ontario Statistics 1981*, table 5.10, 133

for various kinds of goods and services, or changes in the relative prices of such goods and services. Much public and some expert opinion during the period, however, attributed the shift to the changes made in the way health care services were produced and distributed.

The provision of health care services at the beginning of the period was still largely in the hands of private practitioners working on a fee-for-service basis out of their own offices and making use of hospitals maintained by a variety of municipal, religious or other private agencies. Standards of service were set and administered largely by the physicians themselves and by hospital boards, although the general licensing and regulatory framework was established by the provincial government. The main function of the public authorities was to provide certain kinds of public health services that could not be provided effectively by the private sector. By 1940 the province had developed a system of local public health offices designed to control infectious diseases by enforcing sanitation standards, and through a number of specific programs, including milk pasteurization and chest X-ray screening for tuberculosis. The province also maintained a system of public mental hospitals and provided financial support to other specialized institutions, such as tuberculosis sanatoria and facilities serving the indigent and aged. The province paid a portion of the fees earned by physicians treating indigent patients.

During the war years the province's main concern was with expanding public health services in the more remote areas of the province and with increasing the efficiency of public health units by incorporating them into larger units. This work was hindered, however, by serious shortages of physicians, nurses, and other types of health care personnel. The government sought to increase the numbers of doctors available by providing fellowships to physicians working towards the Diploma in Health and to dentists, sanitary engineers, and veterinarians taking courses leading to various diplomas in public health offered by the School of Hygiene at the University of Toronto.[49]

In the early post-war years the province was spending about 11 per cent of its total budget on health services of various kinds.[50] During the 1940s strong pressures were building for a greater portion of total health care spending to be shifted from individuals to the public at large. The belief that maintaining full employment and providing a minimum level of basic services to individuals regardless of their incomes became widespread. There was also sentiment in favour of making such functions a responsibility of the federal government, despite the constitutional assignment of these powers to the provinces. By the end of the war there appeared to be no insurmountable obstacles to establishing some kind of national health insurance plan in Canada. Public opinion was generally favourable, a number of strong interest groups, including labour, farm, and church organizations were actively promoting such a plan, and, perhaps more important, the Canadian Medical Association had indicated its willingness to support the scheme.[51]

When the federal government presented its proposals for post-war reconstruction to the provinces in 1945, it included in the package a plan by which it would pay 60 per cent of the cost of operating health insurance plans established by the provinces. Ontario was strongly opposed to the federal government's general program, however, and the health-care proposal was rejected along with the rest of the package. The matter lay dormant for a decade.

During this time the Ontario government neither opposed nor actively promoted the development of health insurance plans in the province. Its stock reply to those who urged that it take an initiative in this matter was that the health care facilities available in the province were not yet adequate to support a broadening of the availability of services. As the minister of health explained on one such occasion, it would amount to 'taking money by false pretenses to bring in a scheme before a reasonable number of hospital beds and required health personnel were available.' At the same time, he was careful to say that as soon as the province had enough beds and staff and could give service at reasonable cost, the government would be willing to go ahead with some kind of hospital care scheme.[52]

Although the province was not yet very actively involved in expanding hospital facilities in the province, some important changes were taking place in the system during the 1950s. The dramatic effect of new drug treatments for tuberculosis on the need for sanatoria in the mid-1950s relieved the pressure on the province to expand or even maintain existing tuberculosis hospitals, many of which were soon to be converted to other uses.[53] In the case of mental health care facilities, there was a major shift in professional and public attitudes towards the type of care that should be provided. Although the government built several new 'Ontario Hospitals' in the 1950s, the idea of incarcerating mental patients in large specialized institutions was passing out of favour. The Ontario government was sensitive to such changing ideas, and in 1951 it announced that it would thereafter concentrate on promoting the development of smaller, community-based facilities, including psychiatric units to be established in public general hospitals.[54]

Such changes held out the prospect of economies in the government's support of hospitals in the province, but these were soon more than submerged by the increasing costs of care in the public general hospitals. These costs began to rise sharply in the mid-1950s, and the government found itself forced to increase its operating grants to such institutions. It consequently became increasingly interested in finding ways to control hospital spending and if possible to shift some of the burden of supporting such spending to the federal government. The most likely course seemed to be to promote a hospital care insurance plan.

There were good reasons for adopting this approach. The success of the pioneering hospital insurance plan introduced in Saskatchewan in 1947 and the adoption of similar plans in Alberta and British Columbia made it seem odd that so economically advanced a province as Ontario should lack such a progressive amenity. The opposition in the provincial legislature missed few opportunities to chide the government for its backwardness in this respect. At the same time, the popularity of hospital insurance with the public was being demonstrated by the proliferation of group medical and hospital insurance plans developed by the medical profession and the private insurance companies. Some of these, such as Associated Medical Services of Ontario, had been developed as early as the 1930s and, although they covered only a minority of the population, the size of that minority was growing rapidly.[55] With a provincial election imminent and a new round of negotiations with the federal government under way in 1955, the Ontario government rather abruptly announced that it was anxious to implement a hospital insurance scheme and that it wanted the federal government to provide financial support. Ontario insisted the matter be discussed at the 1956 federal-provincial conference, and it presented a well-prepared set of proposals whereby Ottawa would pay 60 per cent of the cost of a provincial hospital insurance scheme. The provincial share would be financed by premiums.

Despite divisions within the federal cabinet and the prime minister's personal dislike for the whole idea of government intervention in the provision of health services, the federal government responded to Ontario's initiative with a proposal to implement a somewhat less comprehensive scheme.[56] After two years of sometimes difficult negotiations a scheme acceptable to both levels of government was worked out. On 1 January, 1959 the Ontario Hospital Services Plan went into effect. For monthly premiums of $2.10 for a single person and $4.20 for a family, the 91 per cent of the province's population initially enrolled became eligible to receive standard ward accommodation in community general hospitals. The plan was administered by a public agency, the Ontario Hospital Services Commission. The private insurance companies were left with only supplementary coverage to offer. This meant that the provincial government in effect gained control over the entire hospital care system in the province; for virtually all the funds involved in paying for hospital services as well as in financing the maintenance of existing facilities and constructing new ones passed through its offices, whether they originated as insurance premiums, tax revenues, or federal government grants.[57]

With public hospital insurance in place, pressure on the government increased to extend the principle to other forms of health care. Both the CCF and Liberal parties in Ontario supported such a move.[58] When Saskatchewan went ahead with its plans to introduce general medical care insurance in 1962, national interest in this long-debated matter was revived, leading the federal government to establish another major commission, the Royal Commission on Health Services. To the surprise of those who had expected the commission to oppose 'medicare,' its 1964 report strongly supported the idea. It recommended that a joint federal-provincial plan be developed to add medical care (and eventually dental care and the cost of prescription drugs) to the hospital insurance plan in order to create a comprehensive health care insurance system for all of Canada.[59]

While apparently resigned to the inevitability of some such scheme being implemented, the Ontario government was anxious to avoid a repetition in Ontario of the ugly experience in Saskatchewan, when the physicians went on strike to resist implementation of the government medical insurance plan there.[60] The key to maintaining peace with the physicians appeared to be to devise a plan that would meet the requirements set out by the Canadian Medical Association. The latter placed much emphasis on the desirability of expanding the existing private insurance schemes and having the government pay the premiums for people who were unable to obtain even minimum coverage from the private insurers. This, the CMA argued, would preserve freedom of consumer choice and the rationing power of market forces without imposing undue hardship on the poor and indigent. This approach was attractive to the Ontario government, especially so, it appears, after John Robarts became party leader and premier in 1961.[61] Indeed, Ontario had already taken the position that the existing private health care insurance plans operating in the province were functioning effectively and, unlike the situation in other provinces, covered a large enough part of the population to meet the universality requirements proposed by the federal government.[62]

In 1963 just before the end of the legislative session, the provincial government introduced a bill to set up a medical care scheme similar to the kind endorsed by the CMA. The object would be to establish a basic health service contract which private insurance companies would provide for a prescribed maximum premium. The government would guarantee that this basic coverage would be available to all citizens, and public funds would be used to provide coverage for those unable to pay the premiums. The plan, the minister of health noted, had been worked out in co-operation with a committee made up of twenty-four physicians, eleven insurance industry representatives, and staff from the government's own departments of health and economics.[63] While the opposition parties castigated the government for its caution, there were others who found in the plan a reasonable compromise which, in the words of one newspaper editorial, would enable Ontario to avoid 'the excesses of Saskatchewan.'[64]

In fact, however, the government soon found itself embroiled in a conflict with the private insurance carriers it had been at such pains to satisfy in the early stages of developing its plan. They turned out to be opposed to the obligation placed on them to provide a 'standard contract' to all who wished to purchase such coverage. In 1966 the government agreed to remove this requirement, amending the legislation to allow the insurers to offer whatever type of coverage they wished. It was not long, however, before the implications of this concession were realized. Under the amended proposal the private companies would be in a position to single out high-risk cases and charge them very high rates, a possibility that led the *Globe and Mail* to observe that 'It is cynical to suggest that this plan will make medical care available to all in Ontario who choose to take it.'[65]

While the Ontario government was struggling with this problem, the federal government regained the initiative by introducing a new medical care proposal of its own. In 1965 it offered to pay 50 per cent of the cost of provincial plans that met certain specific requirements. They would have to provide universal coverage, comprehensive benefits, be portable from province to province, and administered by an agency of the provincial government on a non-profit basis.

There ensued a difficult struggle between Ontario and the federal government to bring the Ontario scheme into conformity with these requirements. The principal issue was, of course, Ontario's determination to preserve the role of the private carriers. Eventually Ottawa relented on this point and also agreed to allow Ontario to achieve universal coverage in stages. In October 1969 the two governments signed an agreement to bring Ontario into the federal shared-cost health insurance program, and the private insurance carriers in Ontario were enfranchised to sell basic government coverage. Although he had earlier called the federal plan 'the greatest Machiavellian fraud ever perpetrated on the people of Canada,' the premier Mr Robarts, at this point proclaimed a victory for the province, declaring that the period of hard bargaining 'had produced a scheme that takes into account special conditions within the province, where previous proposals had not.'[66] Ironically, the elaborate arrangements by which Ontario had secured the position of the private carriers proved to be administratively unworkable.[67] In 1972 a new Ontario Health Insurance Act merged the hospitalization and medical care insurance plans into a single government-operated health insurance plan for the province. Under the new arrangements, the Ontario Hospital Services Commission was disbanded and its duties transferred to the Ministry of Health. The ministry took over the provision of standard coverage from the private carriers, although the latter continued to offer extended coverage.

With most of the health care system in the province now under direct public management, it was apparent that the administration and planning of the system would have potentially large effects not only on health care, but on other parts of the provincial economy. There were obvious strong linkages between the provision of health care services and the educational system and many indirect interconnections among the system of labour relations, regulation of the professions, and intergovernmental relations. The government soon began to establish planning facilities within the Department of Health. It also created a senior advisory body on health matters, the 'Ontario Council of Health,' which was to undertake a broad range of research and planning activities relating to health care in the province. At the same time it established a special commission of inquiry, the Committee on the Healing Arts, to look into 'all matters pertaining to the preparation, education, training, control, and disciplining of all those involved in the practice of the healing arts.'[68] The chairman was Ian R. Dowie, a retired businessman. The other two members were Horace Krever, a law professor, and M.C. Urquhart, a professor of economics.

The committee's interpretation of its very broad terms of reference was conditioned by the fact that the massive report of the federal Royal Commission on Health Services had been published only two years earlier, and its far-reaching recommendations were still being analysed and debated. The Ontario committee chose to concentrate on matters of education, regulation, and the organization of health-care services.[69] Its research program reflected this emphasis. The committee's principal contribution was made in the several studies carried out on various professional groups in the province, especially a perceptive examination of the medical profession itself.[70] Oddly, while recognizing the primary importance of hospitals in contemporary medical practice, it did not undertake any systematic study of these institutions.

The report of the Committee on the Healing Arts dealt largely with matters relating to the education of health care personnel, the regulatory system for ensuring quality of practice, and the administrative structure needed to coordinate the health care system in the province. However, it also documented many of the general characteristics of the provincial health care system as it had developed to the late 1960s. Particularly valuable was its review of the economic structure of the health care sector of the provincial economy, although in this as in other aspects of its work the committee was severely handicapped by the lack of useful statistical data relevant to its subject.[71] It found, for example, that those parts of the health care system in Ontario that had remained most subject to direct market forces were declining in relative importance, while those in which government, professional, and other non-market influences were dominant had become more important. The role of the price system had declined substantially in relation to the provision of health care, the committee noted. While prices continued to influence the choices of people with respect to occupations in the field of health care, the 'introduction of public comprehensive hospital and medical insurance has virtually completed the process of removing price as a constituent in the choice of hospital and medical care by the individual member of the public.' This was not, however, simply a consequence of the growing participation of government in this part of the economy; for the committee also noted that 'the role played by professional bodies, formally and informally, places them in league with government as major constituents of the economic structure of the health care sector.'[72]

The implications of these changes for provincial public finance have been carefully studied by Professor D.K. Foot, who has shown that over the period from 1950 to 1972 the average annual real rate of growth in Ontario government health expenditures averaged 11.1 per cent for administration, 7.2 per cent for mental health and 11.6 per cent for public health.[73] Hospital spending under the Ontario Hospital Services Commission increased at an average annual real rate of 9.1 per cent between 1956 and 1972.

With the integration of hospital and medical care insurance in 1972, the Ministry of Health became the largest spending department in the provincial government, although by only a small margin exceeding the spending of the Department of Education. In the 1972–3 fiscal year the Department of Health's estimates amounted to 28.7 per cent of the government's total spending plans.[74] Concern over the rate of growth in such spending had been chronic since the early 1960s, but it was not until the end of the period that it became politically feasible for the government to undertake to check the apparently limitless growth of its outlays on health services. Much of the problem was attributed to rising costs associated with the general inflationary trends of the time. But it was also pointed out by some economists that in the absence of any overall mechanism for determining the amount of health care that was socially justifiable, and given the motivation of suppliers of health care to maximize their incomes in a situation where they also had the power to prescribe the amount of service required, outlays on such services could continue to expand indefinitely.[75] By the mid-1970s the Ontario government was redirecting its efforts with respect to the provision of health care services much as it was in the case of education – seeking to cut back the system, beginning with a determined effort to close hospitals and to restrict wage and salary increases for health care personnel.[76]

Welfare

The social welfare programs and policies in place in Ontario at the end of the 1930s still reflected many of the attitudes and objectives of earlier periods. There was still something of the Victorian concern that public welfare should be provided in such a way as to reinforce the individual's sense of responsibility for making a living and, in cases where this approach was inapplicable, to provide the necessary 'protection, custody and control,' often in an institutional setting.[77]

During the inter-war period the nineteenth-century arrangements that had gone some distance to meet the needs of the aged, the physically handicapped, the mentally ill, and dependent children were supplemented by measures intended to deal with the new problems created by a rapidly industrializing economy. Ontario led the way with its workmen's compensation legislation of 1914 under which the costs of compensation to injured workmen were met out of a fund built up by levies on employers. Means-tested mothers' allowances and support for other easily defined groups, including the blind, followed, and the provincial government gradually assumed more direct responsibility for matters that until then had been handled mainly by local governments and private charitable organizations. The two largest groups whose needs were recognized in this period were the old and the unemployed. In both cases there was an early interest in the possibility of federal government involvement. The first major shared-cost federal-provincial program was established by the Old Age Pensions Act of 1927 under the terms of which the province was reimbursed by the federal government for 50 per cent of the amounts expended on pensions to the aged.

During the Depression years, the problem of unemployment relief became the most conspicuous social issue in Ontario, as it did elsewhere in the country. At the beginning of the 1930s it was still accepted that unemployment relief was a provincial and municipal responsibility, and the Ontario government found itself forced to accept the burden of sharply increasing outlays on direct relief to the unemployed. A number of ad hoc shared-cost unemployment relief programs were introduced by the federal government, but attempts to establish a comprehensive program were frustrated by the constitution. It was not until 1940, when a constitutional amendment cleared the way, that the federal Unemployment Insurance Act could be brought into effect, providing for a system of nationwide compulsory insurance financed by contributions from employees, employers, and the federal government. In Ontario there were mixed reactions to this development. While it relieved the government of a potentially serious financial burden in the event that the expected post-war depression materialized, there was still concern over the erosion of provincial authority in the field of economic and social policy. Business response was also generally favourable, but not universally so. Although most manufacturing and other firms selling primarily in the domestic market could expect to pass along much of the cost of contributory insurance schemes to the buyers of their products, mining and other raw material exporting firms saw such additions to their costs as a threat to their competitiveness in world markets.[78] The general climate of opinion at the time, however, was favourable to such innovations, conditioned as it was by the experiences of the Depression, the wartime promises embodied in the Atlantic Charter (which established freedom from want as an objective of the governments that were party to it), the welfare state initiatives in Britain, and, not least, the gradual spread of Keynesian economic theory which implied a need for such means of bolstering aggregate demand in economies that might otherwise face chronic unemployment.

This environment was hospitable to an elaboration of a comprehensive national welfare scheme, and the case for such an undertaking was extensively studied and discussed in the course of federal and provincial planning for the post-war period.[79] Although the federal government never did fully accept the idea of a comprehensive social security system, it appeared to be moving in such a direction in 1944 when it introduced the country's first universal welfare payment program, a non-means-tested program of family allowances. Under the Family Allowances Act parents of all children up to the age of sixteen who were attending school (or were unable to attend school for medical reasons) would be eligible for monthly allowances graduated according to the ages and numbers of children they had. The purposes of the legislation were said to be to ensure that the basic needs of all children would be met and to help maintain purchasing power after the war ended.[80]

This principle of universality was extended to old age pensions in the federal government's proposals to the provinces at the 1945 Conference on Reconstruction. The suggestion was that all Canadians who had lived in the country for at least twenty years would be paid $30 a month without a means test – this pension to be financed and administered by the federal government. The federal government would also pay 50 per cent of the costs of provincially administered means-tested pensions for persons aged sixty to sixty-five. Ontario rejected this proposal along with the rest of the fiscal program offered, not because it was considered too radical, but because the province wanted a larger social security program and more money from the federal government to finance it.

After the failure of the 1945 conference, the federal government proceeded in a piecemeal fashion to work out fiscal arrangements, including the handling of the existing and several new welfare programs, with the individual provinces. In 1952, following a study of the old age pension plan by a joint committee of the Senate and Commons, and a necessary constitutional amendment, the federal government introduced the Old Age Security program, which provided $40 a month to all Canadians who had lived in the country for twenty years or more. This was to be financed from a fund to be built up from an old age security tax levied by the federal government. This non-means-tested pension was supplemented by a means-tested pension, which would be financed on a cost-sharing basis by the federal and provincial governments. This 'Old Age Assistance' pension would be available to persons sixty-five to seventy years of age whose incomes were below a specified level. A blind person's allowance scheme similar to the old age assistance program was also established on a cost-sharing basis. In 1954 the Disabled Persons Act provided shared-cost coverage on a means-tested basis for persons who had become permanently disabled and who were not covered by workmen's compensation.

Although the federal government expanded the coverage and benefits provided by the unemployment insurance system in the 1950s, Ontario also became more involved in providing support for unemployed persons. In 1956 the federal government passed the Unemployment Assistance Act, which provided for cost-sharing of financial aid to the needy unemployed by municipal or provincial governments. Subsequently there were increases in provincial support for indirect welfare measures, such as grants to local children's aid societies in the late 1950s and early 1960s, but there were no major changes in direct income support programs until the new federal Canada Pension Plan and Canada Assistance Plan legislation was introduced in the mid-1960s.

Concern over the inadequacy of existing pension programs in the late 1950s and early 1960s led to a number of proposals for reform of the old age security system. The issue was raised during the 1957 federal election campaign, and Ontario joined with other provinces in supporting a proposal by the Diefenbaker government that would have removed the constitutional obstacles to the development of a broad coverage contributory public pension system in Canada. The possibilities were explored further when the Liberals returned to office in 1963, although by then Ontario was having doubts about such a scheme and was proposing that it might be better to find ways of expanding the scope of private pension plans. By 1966, however, after extensive negotiations and study, a new plan had been worked out which was acceptable to all the provinces, although Quebec would administer its own version of the plan. The Canada Pension Plan of 1966 was a compulsory contributory pension plan covering all employees between the ages of eighteen and seventy earning certain minimum incomes. The benefits were intended to be sufficient to maintain the living standards of retiring workers, not simply to provide a minimum level of support. As implemented, there were doubts about the adequacy of the benefits and the equity of the contribution schedules, but despite such flaws, the plan appeared to offer a considerable improvement in the prospects of retired workers and the elderly.[81] It would take some time, however, before the plan could meet the needs of all retiring workers. The 'Guaranteed Income Supplement' plan was enacted to provide interim support for people retiring before they had built up sufficient contributions to the Canada Pension Plan.

The Canada Assistance Plan, also enacted in legislation in 1966 extended the coverage of the pension plan. It enabled the province to integrate many of the existing cost-sharing programs, such as unemployment assistance, old age assistance, blind persons allowances, and disabled persons allowances, into a general plan which could, in principle, cover all those in financial need for whatever reason. The Ontario government seized the opportunity presented by the new plan to reorganize the complicated administrative arrangements that had grown up in the province to handle the shared-cost programs. The Department of Public Welfare was reorganized and renamed the Department of Social and Family Service (eventually becoming the Department of Community and Social Services).

Total spending on family allowances, unemployment insurance, and old age security in Ontario increased in real terms from a post-war low of $54.34 per capita in 1948 to over $205 dollars per capita by 1971. The federal share of this expenditure amounted to 84 per cent in 1948 and almost 92 per cent in 1971.[82] By 1971 the federal government was making income transfers amounting to nearly $1.3 billion annually to residents of Ontario, an amount far in excess of the province's own outlays on health and education services. These transfers, however, were not necessarily net gains for the province. Because of Ontario's relative affluence compared with most of the other provinces and varying patterns of need across the country, the overall system of national taxing and spending probably worked to Ontario's disadvantage. Leaving aside the important consideration of Ontario's stake in the maintenance of national unity and stability, it has been estimated that in 1975 Ontario residents lost $51 per capita on the federal-provincial shared-cost programs then in effect (Hospital and Medical Insurance, the Canada Assistance Plan, and Post-Secondary Education); $41 per capita on the direct transfers to individuals (through the Family Allowance and Old Age Security programs); and $28 per capita on the Unemployment Insurance Program, compared with what the per capita costs would have been if these programs had been entirely financed within the province.[83]

By the 1970s, the welfare system in Ontario had evolved into a complex

TABLE 28
Expenditures on Income Maintenance, Ontario, 1946–71 (per capita $1971)

Year	Family and Youth Allowances	Unemployment Insurance	Old Age Security	Federal Portion of Shared-Cost Programs	Federal Total	Provincial Net	Municipal Net	Totals
1946	38.18	8.89	–	7.73	54.80	6.54	1.57	62.91
1947	37.79	4.28	–	9.02	51.09	5.67	1.89	58.65
1948	33.30	4.17	–	8.67	46.14	6.45	1.76	54.35
1949	33.45	6.91	–	11.28	51.61	6.85	1.70	60.19
1950	33.57	9.19	–	11.57	54.33	6.90	1.95	63.18
1951	30.94	6.18	9.29	8.16	54.57	5.81	1.32	61.70
1952	30.37	10.87	37.10	1.61	79.95	4.61	1.22	85.78
1953	31.54	11.85	37.99	1.61	82.99	4.96	1.43	89.38
1954	32.05	22.18	37.79	1.70	93.72	5.20	1.61	100.53
1955	32.80	17.63	37.88	2.03	90.34	4.86	1.31	96.51
1956	32.74	16.08	37.08	1.91	87.81	4.68	1.03	93.52
1957	34.31	23.65	43.36	2.78	104.10	5.49	1.04	110.63
1958	35.54	36.58	48.10	4.82	125.04	6.60	1.07	132.71
1959	35.76	29.03	50.20	5.57	120.56	6.67	1.16	128.39
1960	35.81	34.24	47.27	5.41	122.73	7.14	1.12	130.99
1961	36.01	33.48	48.34	6.25	124.08	7.74	.90	132.72
1962	35.83	25.46	55.13	7.92	124.34	8.20	1.23	133.77
1963	35.09	22.85	58.47	8.08	124.49	8.48	1.19	134.16
1964	36.80	19.09	61.60	8.62	126.11	9.37	1.23	136.71
1965	37.40	15.78	61.70	8.04	122.92	9.98	1.30	134.20
1966	35.75	14.16	66.65	11.96	128.52	4.91	1.69	135.12
1967	34.29	17.53	80.61	11.70	144.13	8.16	2.48	154.77
1968	32.83	20.37	84.25	14.42	151.87	8.06	3.67	163.60
1969	30.88	21.95	88.94	14.76	156.53	8.44	1.56	166.13
1970	30.72	32.14	95.32	18.14	176.32	11.85	2.24	190.41
1971	28.59	39.07	100.73	20.49	188.88	13.69	2.82	205.39

SOURCE: Lang, *The Service State Emerges in Ontario*, table 3, 74–5

collection of programs the logic and interrelations of which few people could be expected to understand. It was further complicated at the end of the period, when the province introduced a Guaranteed Annual Income System (GAINS), designed to supplement the incomes of persons sixty-five years of age and older and also the incomes of the blind and disabled. Minimum income levels were specified for individuals and families, and benefits under GAINS were scaled to make up the difference between these minima and the sum of the benefits received from Old Age Security, the Guaranteed Income Supplement, Family Benefits, other welfare income, and private income. This amounted to a much-modified version of an approach the Ontario government had once proposed for establishing a tax-based guaranteed minimum income scheme for the province.[84] By this time, however, it is significant that the province was operating independently

TABLE 29
Trends in Major Social Security Programs, Ontario, Selected Years 1959–75

	Fiscal Year				
	1959–60	1965–6	1970–1	1972–3	1974–5
1. Social Assistance (Family Benefits and General Welfare Assistance)					
Transfers ($ millions)	52.9	100.8	231.3	275.5	246
Number of recipients (average monthly caseload)	69,933	90,120	139,833	157,771	n.a.
2. Old Age Security					
Transfers ($ millions)	208.6	337.2	603.0	653.4	961.4
Number of recipients (thousands)	300	400	630	670	703
3. Guaranteed Income Supplement					
Transfers ($ millions)	–	–	78.5	228.0	250.3
Number of recipients (thousands)	–	–	270	330	341
4. Family Allowances					
Transfers ($ millions)	156.7	182.4	191.4	190.3	633.6
Number of children (thousands)	900	2,300	2,400	2,400	2,500
5. Day Nurseries					
Expenditure ($ millions)	0.2	0.4	3.3	14.5	n.a.
Number of places	9,865	14,760	27,150	35,565	n.a.
6. Unemployment Insurance					
Total benefits ($ millions)	125.4	81.9	253.7	637.4	676.1
Claimants (monthly average)	146,250	89,250	194,500	263,000	268,300
7. Gains					
Transfers ($ millions)	–	–	–	–	74.1
Number of recipients	–	–	–	–	36,500

SOURCE: Ontario Economic Council, *Issues and Alternatives 1976: Social Security* (Toronto: OEC, 1977), table 5, 12

again. The Canada Assistance Plan of 1966 was the last of the shared-cost programs to be negotiated between Ottawa and the province. The federal government after that date sought to limit its susceptibility to provincial pressures to increase funding for such programs by substituting arrangements by which income tax points and adjustment grants would replace the cost-sharing approach. Ontario spokesmen expressed outrage when the federal government outlined its new position in the course of the 1966 federal-provincial tax-sharing negotiations. The new federal strategy, the Ontario treasurer complained, would lead to the creation of a 'tax jungle' in Canada and a 'Balkanized economy.'[85]

The province had in place a number of additional programs by the mid-1970s that could be considered part of the overall welfare system in Ontario. In the field of housing the Ontario Housing Corporation operated a 'Rent-Geared-to-

Income' plan and a Rent Supplement Program under which developers and owners of housing were eligible for provincial subsidies under certain conditions. Free medical and hospital insurance and child dental care costs were made available to welfare recipients. Free prescription drugs were available to persons sixty-five years of age and over (the Drug Benefit Program). Free medical and hospital insurance coverage was provided for everyone over sixty-five and for persons with no taxable income. Partial medical and hospital care coverage was also available to low-income earners who met certain requirements. A provincial day care program provided funds that municipalities operating day care centres could draw upon to meet any deficits incurred by such operations. The province also paid for day care required by handicapped children and children of low-income families.[86] Minimum-wage legislation, introduced in the province in 1920, remained in effect.

The complexity of this system and the various anomalies encountered in its operation gave rise to many complaints, especially when the problem of poverty became an issue of national public policy in the 1960s. In 1968 a Senate Committee on Poverty was appointed under the chairmanship of Senator Croll. Its report in 1971 severely criticized the existing arrangements for social security in Canada and proposed implementation of a guaranteed annual income system. The possibilities of reform were explored in a succession of federal government discussion papers and at several high-level conferences. Out of these studies came a number of new perceptions of the issues involved. One was that simply being employed did not mean that individuals and their dependants would have adequate standards of living. Another was that the net effect of the elaborate system of income transfers still evolving had not seemed to alter appreciably the overall inequality in the distribution of income. In Ontario, where average incomes were higher than in all the other provinces except British Columbia, there was also somewhat less inequality in the distribution of income among individuals. The explanation appeared to lie in the fact that Ontario had relatively fewer of its workers employed in low-income, primary-resource production and subsistence farming. Yet, over time, the amount of inequality in Ontario did not seem to be declining, although one study did show that during the early 1960s there was a small decrease in the number of income recipients in the lowest income categories, although the supporting evidence of even this fact was not very strong.[87] Why there should have been so little change was not easily explained, although there were a number of popular hypotheses. One, supported by the Ontario Economic Council, was that the system of income redistribution directed much of the spending back into the hands of those who had provided the tax revenue. At least part of what the council referred to as 'the mystery surrounding the seeming inability of society to defeat poverty' was the fact that much spending on social security programs was not directed to the poor but, as in the case of Old Age Security payments, tended to accrue to the middle- and upper-income groups.[88]

By the mid-1970s the proposals for the reform of the social welfare system had met the same fate as the other social service activities discussed earlier in this chapter. As economic growth slowed, as confidence in economic management collapsed, and as a new mood of conservatism swept over the political scene, interest shifted to different and more immediate issues, including the possibility of reducing the public commitment to some welfare programs in keeping with the new policy of public spending restraint. These new developments at the end of the period are considered in chapter 10.

7 Agriculture, Fishing, Fur Production, and Tourism

Although the total physical volume of agricultural production almost exactly doubled between 1939 and 1975, farming declined in importance as a source of income and employment relative to the rest of the provincial economy during this period.[1] The great increase in output was achieved with decreasing inputs of both labour and land. The total number of people living on farms fell by more than half. The amount of land worked also declined greatly, with the amount of occupied farm land in the province falling at a rate of more than 17,000 acres per year between the early 1940s and the 1970s. Whereas almost 10 per cent of Ontario's total land area was classed as occupied farm land in 1941, by 1971 this figure had decreased to 7 per cent. Allowing for changes in the purchasing power of the dollar, total income from farming in the province was much the same in the early 1970s as it had been was in the early 1940s. Fortunately, the decrease in the number of persons dependent on such income for their living fell so much that those remaining actually became better off, with the realized net farm income per person rising from an estimated $557.30 to $994.54 in 1971.[2]

The reduction in farmland in Ontario during this period was the result of a number of forces that were working to reduce its value in agriculture relative to other uses. In the south-central part of the province there was a growing need for land to be used for urban residential subdivisions, for new industrial plant, for highway use, and as a source of gravel and other building materials. Such requirements were particularly intense near the major centres of population, especially in the counties adjacent to metropolitan Toronto. In Halton county, almost 42 per cent of the 1941 farm acreage had disappeared by 1971; in Peel the loss was 40 per cent, and in York, 36 per cent. Outside the heavily populated southern region, much of the decrease in acreage resulted from abandonment of marginal farm lands. This was particularly noticeable on the fringe of the Canadian Shield. In Haliburton and Muskoka the farm acreage reduction between 1941 and 1971 amounted to almost 80 per cent, with much of this land being allowed to revert to brush and unimproved pasture. In the later post-war period

TABLE 30
Index Numbers of Physical Volume of Agricultural Production,
Ontario 1941–75 (1961 = 100)

Year	Number	Year	Number
1941	65.6	1959	90.6
1942	77.1	1960	93.5
1943	58.4	1961	100
1944	71.8	1962	105.1
1945	64.4	1963	106.4
1946	70.4	1964	108.9
1947	66.6	1965	108.6
1948	70.3	1966	118.0
1949	73.5	1967	114.6
1950	73.0	1968	118.5
1951	75.8	1969	117.7
1952	77.5	1970	124.6
1953	77.5	1971	127.9
1954	77.6	1972	125.3
1955	78.9	1973	122.4
1956	80.0	1974	129.5
1957	84.7	1975	135.3
1958	93.2		

SOURCE: Ontario, Ministry of Agriculture and Food, *Agricultural Statistics for Ontario 1941–1978* (Toronto, 1979), table 1:4, 6

much agricultural land began to be taken up for non-farm residential and recreational use, a trend that was stimulated by the attractiveness of land as an inflation-resistant investment.[3]

These trends were accompanied by a decrease in the number of farms and an increase in average farm size. Although changes in definition make it difficult to document the change in the number of farms precisely, the overall decrease may have been on the order of 47 per cent over the period as a whole.[4] The size of the average farm in Ontario increased from 126 acres in 1941 to 169 acres in 1971. This trend was general throughout the province, and farms in the northern areas, which had always been larger than those in the south, became even larger.[5]

The great increase in the productivity of labour in Ontario farming during this period must be attributed to increasing inputs of capital, improved disease control in crops and livestock, and a number of less tangible influences such as better knowledge and organization. The mechanization of farming in the province was temporarily slowed during the war years by severe shortages of new machinery and fuels, but once these restrictions were removed, mechanization proceeded rapidly. Between 1941 and 1951 the number of tractors in use on Ontario farms almost tripled. The rural electrification program resumed when the war ended, and by the early 1950s the number of electric motors in use on farms in the province was double the 1941 figure.

TABLE 31
Census Farms Classified by Size of Farm, Ontario, 1951 and 1975

	1951		1971	
	Number	Per Cent	Number	Per Cent
Total farms	149,920	100	94,722	100
Under 3 acres	652	0.4	1,529	1.6
3–9 acres	6,733	4.5	3,619	3.8
10–69 acres	26,243	17.5	16,763	17.7
70–129 acres	53,459	35.7	26,287	27.8
130–179 acres	24,893	16.6	13,440	14.2
180–239 acres	18,780	12.5	13,051	13.8
140–399 acres	14,265	9.5	13,315	14.1
400–559 acres	3,385	2.3	4,233	4.5
560–759 acres	992	0.7	1,461	1.5
760–1,119 acres	368	0.2	715	0.8
1,120–1,599 acres	101	0.1	224	0.2
1,600 + acres	49	0.1	85	0.09

SOURCE: R.B. Campbell and R.G.F. Hill, *Trends in Ontario Agriculture* (Toronto: Ontario Ministry of Agriculture and Food, 1973), table 10, 20

Despite the financial difficulties it created for many farmers, further mechanization of their operations was preferable to relying on increasing labour inputs to expand production. The capital and operating costs of machinery were generally rising throughout the period, but not as fast as farm wages. By the late 1950s, although the costs of machinery, fuel, and oil had almost doubled their 1939 levels, wages for farm workers were nearly five times greater. These trends continued, with farm machinery prices rising by nearly 36 per cent in the 1960s and farm wages by 85 per cent.[6] The total amount of farm capital in relation to the farm population of Ontario quadrupled in real terms between the early 1940s and the 1970s.[7]

The development of large urban markets, improvements in transportation, changing patterns of retail and wholesale trade, and new requirements with respect to quality control and the standardization of products necessitated a number of changes in the organization of farming in Ontario during the period. Many farmers found it profitable to become more highly specialized in their operations so as to make economical use of increasingly expensive machinery and to take advantage of the opportunities presented by new plant varieties and more efficient techniques for handling livestock. The output of the more specialized farms typically moved longer distances to markets, thus reducing the importance of many local processors and intermediaries. While it was frequently claimed during the period that these trends were accompanied by the displacement of independent farmers by corporate enterprises, the traditional pattern of ownership does not appear to have changed much over the period.[8] In 1971 more than 95 per cent of the total farm acreage in Ontario was still being operated either in whole or in part by the owners of the land.⁹ It was undoubtedly true, however, that farmers were becoming more closely integrated into a system of production and distribution some parts of which were increasingly dominated by a few very large organizations. The kind of concern this gave rise to was expressed by F.R. Oliver, the leader of the provincial Liberal party in 1958, when he deplored the emergence of 'an integrated food industry' and the development of large farms controlled by 'packers and marketers.' He went on to express a view shared by many farmers, that producers in the province were becoming 'the hewers of wood and the drawers of water for corporate concerns over which they have no control and financial interest at all.'¹⁰ Such concerns were not new, of course, but they continued to fuel the efforts of farmers bent on finding ways to protect themselves against market structures that they believed were rigged against them.

The economic and political situation Ontario farmers found themselves in at the beginning of the 1940s must be viewed against the background of the Depression years. It was not until The Second World War was already under way, by which time the prospects for Canadian food producers generally were beginning to brighten, that the Canadian public became aware of how bad the economic position of farmers had been in the 1930s. The findings of the Rowell-Sirois Commission documented the depths to which farm incomes had fallen during the Depression and the size of the gap that had opened up between farm and non-farm incomes. The average farm income in Canada in 1936 had been only $400, compared with an average non-farm income of over $1,000.¹¹

When markets improved during the early years of the war, farmers could expect to make up for some of their past losses, but such opportunities were soon curtailed by the federal government's price controls and labour policies. In Ontario the provincial government became concerned that restrictions on the supply of labour, machinery, and fuel to farm users might actually lower farm output in the province, and it moved to implement a subsidy program for hog and cheese producers. While sceptics suggested that the government's actions were motivated more by politics than by economic considerations, Ontario farm output did drop and in 1943 was less than it had been in 1936.¹² Farmers in the province resented being exhorted to produce more while being denied what they considered appropriate opportunities and incentives to do so. Some also suspected that they were being discriminated against in comparison with farmers in western Canada, whose interests seemed to be closer to the hearts of the federal cabinet.¹³ Their preferred remedies were concisely set out by the Ontario Federation of Agriculture in 1943. Looking forward to the post-war reconstruction of agriculture in Ontario, the federation demanded more intervention by the government and specifically measures to ensure 'equitable farm labour and investment return, price stabilization tied to production costs, collective marketing, planned production in relation to market outlets, and co-operative purchase and sale.'¹⁴

As the war neared its end, the 'farm problem' in Canada became less a matter of promoting output to meet wartime food requirements and more one of finding ways to restrict output to maintain prices. In Ontario there was particular concern with the hog, butter, and cheese markets in which there was every reason to expect increasing competition in both domestic and foreign markets once peacetime conditions were restored. While part of the solution to the problems foreseen could be sought through measures to increase efficiency, it was recognized that this might mean many farmers would be forced out of the business. Such 'rationalization' of farming was economically attractive but politically threatening so far as the provincial government was concerned. In the speech from the throne in 1945 the government made its usual affirmations about the desirability of maintaining the province's agricultural industry, 'the most important basic industry in Ontario.' Yet it was no secret that there were some in the provincial Department of Agriculture who believed that there were too many farmers in the province. Editorializing on the subject of marginal farmers, the *Globe and Mail*, which only two years before had been frightening its readers with speculation that in the event of a farmers' strike they 'would all starve,' objected to the idea of weeding out the less able producers only because it might lead to an increase in the numbers of unskilled and unemployed labourers in the cities.[15]

A government commission investigating the state of agriculture in the province at the end of the war avoided the issue by recommending price supports and at the same time encouraging farmers to help themselves through co-operative and other organizational efforts and by changing their methods of operation.[16]

The main thrust of provincial government agricultural policy in the immediate post-war period was concerned with promoting the development of marketing schemes. While some encouragement was given to the farmers' co-operative movement, this does not appear to have been a high-priority item in the government's agenda. Nor was it an approach that any longer attracted much support from the agricultural community itself. There were, however, over 200 agricultural co-ops in Ontario at the end of the Second World War. Most were small local enterprises set up to distribute farm supplies, but there were also more than sixty 'marketing' co-ops, many of which were involved in the grading, packaging, and marketing of poultry products. A smaller number of local co-ops handled fruits, vegetables, grain, seed, and livestock, while some twenty-four others provided their members with services such as trucking, storage, and the rental of seed-cleaning equipment.[17] Such service co-ops proved popular during the late 1940s and remained important well into the 1950s. Along with some new marketing co-operatives, they helped keep the movement alive in Ontario. By 1962 there were about 280 agricultural co-ops in the province.

During the 1960s the agricultural co-operative movement in Ontario began to decline. Many of the smaller local organizations found it impossible to sustain member support in the face of increasing competition from the large commercial retail chains, and many of them were merged or otherwise reorganized, often with the help of the United Co-operatives of Ontario, successor to the old farmers' co-operative organization. The new body, which was established in 1948, was owned and controlled by local co-ops throughout the province. It provided a number of supporting functions, including a program to facilitate the mergers of small local units. Failing local co-ops were purchased, reorganized, and put under the management of the central organization until they were re-established. But such efforts only slowed the decline of the agricultural co-ops in Ontario. The interest of farmers in the co-operative approach to their problems continued to wane, and their attention shifted to the possibilities of compulsory marketing schemes.[18]

The legal framework for Ontario's agricultural marketing arrangements dates from legislation in 1937 that was intended to salvage programs already established under the federal Natural Products Marketing Act of 1934. This act had been found unconstitutional by the Supreme Court in 1935, a decision upheld by the Privy Council in London in 1937.

The Ontario Farm Products Control Act of 1937, subsequently amended and renamed the Farm Products Marketing Act in 1946, represented a major retreat from the principles of free-market economics. It provided for the creation of monopolistic marketing procedures to operate on the producers' side of the market, presumably to counteract the monopolistic practices of the large food-processing and retailing organizations on the other side. With the subsequent enactment of milk marketing legislation, it became possible for most agricultural production in the province to be regulated and controlled. Although the full scope of this possible coverage had not been implemented by the end of the period, by the early 1970s some 60 per cent of the cash income of Ontario farmers was derived from the sale of products covered by some kind of marketing scheme.[19] Most full-time farmers in the province, except those involved exclusively in beef production, were then likely to be registered members of at least one marketing board.[20]

The Farm Products Marketing Act provided that producers of some particular farm product could organize a marketing scheme and propose its establishment to the Farm Products Marketing Board, a body created for the purpose of administering the act. Provided that more than 15 per cent of the producers of the commodity supported the scheme, the board would consider it and, if so disposed, organize a vote by the producers affected. If a majority were in favour, the board would recommend the plan to the minister, and, once it was established, all producers of the commodity would be required to abide by whatever regulations were set up under the act.[21] Administration of particular plans would be entrusted to a local marketing board, a non-government body, normally made up of representatives of the producers involved.

An unusual feature of the Ontario legislation was that its provisions could apply not only to producers but also to processors, shippers, dealers, and others engaged in the industry. Indeed, during much of the period Ontario boards used their powers to control buyers and processors more than producers.[22] Yet only one agency, the Ontario Apple Marketing Commission, provided packers, processors, and retailers with representation on the board.[23]

Three different types of marketing plan were envisioned in the Ontario legislation: promotional schemes in which the board collected fees and carried on research and advertising; negotiating plans which brought together producers and buyers to set the terms and conditions for the sale of farm products; and agency-type boards which set production quotas and prices and arranged for the appointment of marketing agents. The first type was not popular in Ontario, but the other two were widely used.[24]

Establishing marketing boards was not always a smooth operation. Most of the inherent problems were demonstrated in the case of the hog marketing plan, one of several that grew directly out of the circumstances surrounding producers of several key agricultural products during the Second World War. During the war production and marketing of hogs in Canada was controlled by a Canadian Meat Board. In 1941 the Ontario producers organized the Ontario Hog Producers' Association to counteract what they claimed was the domination of the industry by the meat-packing companies. The organization initially enjoyed little support, but in the later years of the war the dissatisfaction of hog producers with their situation made them more militant, and by the end of 1945 more than 90 per cent of those eligible to vote supported the formation of a negotiating-type plan. However, as wartime controls continued into the immediate post-war years and meat packers resisted the efforts of the producers to negotiate, little was accomplished. In 1952 Ontario hog producers took advantage of provisions in the existing legislation to establish an exclusive marketing agency. This was the first venture of its type in Ontario and the board immediately became entangled in a web of legal and political complications. Over the next several years it came into conflict with the Ontario Farm Products Marketing Board, with the private packing companies, with a large, producer-operated, meat-packing co-operative, and with dissident hog producers, many of whom undertook to establish their own organization, the 'Free Enterprise Hog Producers.'

A frequently postponed plebiscite, eventually held in 1958, failed to resolve the conflicts, but it provided the government with an opportunity to intervene more directly in the situation. In 1960 the marketing board legislation was amended to give the provincial Farm Products Marketing Board more control over the operation of individual boards. This move, along with other changes, including implementation of a teletype auction system for selling hogs, reduced the dissension within the industry but did not entirely eliminate it.

Apart from hog marketing, the most difficult part of Ontario agriculture to bring under collective control was the dairy industry. Subject to some form or other of government regulation since the 1880s, the dairy industry subsequently displayed the problems of reconciling the interests of producers, processors, distributors, and consumers in classic form. The process was subjected to so much investigation and debate that it was thoroughly documented, the extensive record compiling a sorry account of the failure of incremental and ad hoc public intervention in this kind of market.

The initial problems of the Ontario dairy industry in the 1930s appeared to stem from the existence of competition in the industry. Prices of dairy products fell, and, while this drop pleased consumers, it prompted the provincial Department of Agriculture to set up an inquiry into the 'ruinous' conditions prevailing, particularly in cities such as London, where price competition was particularly vigorous. The outcome was the Milk Control Act of 1934 which established a public agency, the Milk Control Board, to regulate (subject to government approval) the production, processing, and distribution of milk products in Ontario.[25] These arrangements worked reasonably well through the next decade, but by the mid-1940s there were growing complaints about milk prices, this time not from producers claiming they were too low, but from consumers who believed they were too high. By 1946 the Housewives' Consumer Association in Toronto was organizing telephone campaigns to muster support for a boycott of milk, its members expressing outrage at milk prices of 15 cents or more a quart.[26] The provincial government appointed another commission to study the problem, a one-man inquiry conducted by a justice of the supreme court, D.C. Wells.

The Wells report on the dairy industry in Ontario was a well-reasoned and balanced analysis of the problems involved in regulating the market for a 'basic' commodity. The commissioner chastized the producers who appeared before him for being preoccupied with cost of production considerations and apparently ignoring the question of consumer demand. Yet he also recognized that seasonal forces operated to create periods of surplus production. His preferred method of dealing with such surplus problems was for the producers to organize voluntary marketing organizations which they themselves would operate. If this plan were feasible, Wells suggested, he would have been 'inclined to the opinion that the full play of competitive market forces would reasonably protect the consumer in the respect of distribution and would in the long run produce a much more economic and better organized system in the industry as a whole.'[27] But in fact the commissioner found that the producers were not strong enough to operate such a marketing plan themselves, and that it would consequently be necessary for the government to continue to intervene in the market and maintain a 'fixed price to the producer with the sanction of law behind it,' as provided for in the Milk Control Act of 1934. Otherwise, he foresaw that there would always be some among the 16,000 milk producers in the province who would be 'prepared to break away and cut prices or give secret rebates to distributors.'[28]

The basis for fixing milk prices was not very clearly specified in the Wells report, but it is pertinent to note that the commissioner was surprised to find that no one in the industry appeared to know how much it cost to produce and distribute this product. He observed that 'farmers as a group, or as individuals, do not know their costs of production.' Nor did the distributors, whose accounting practices he found were often 'obscure.' As for the Milk Control Board, which for a decade had been fixing the price of milk both for the producer and at retail, Mr. Justice Wells found it to be 'an amazing fact, but apparently true, that at no time in exercising its functions has the Milk Control Board had a really adequate knowledge of either producer or distributor costs.'[29]

For this or for other reasons the fixing of retail milk prices was terminated in 1948, and the government set up a collective bargaining procedure involving producers and distributors in its place, with the Milk Control Board serving as arbitrator. With some modifications this kind of procedure was continued through the 1950s, and separate marketing boards were established for fluid milk, cream producers, and cheese producers. The various groups comprising the dairy industry remained disunited and contentious, however, and there were continuing complaints, especially from producers, about the operation of the system.

The problems of the industry were again investigated. The Milk Industry Inquiry Committee, which reported in 1965, identified many of the trends then affecting Ontario farmers in general. In the dairy industry, productivity was rising rapidly, with specialization and mechanization dramatically increasing output per cow. Although there were still perhaps 40,000 milk and cream producers in the province with herds of twelve cows or fewer, the committee foresaw a decline in the number of producers. The introduction of bulk handling in 1953 had displaced the old 'eight gallon can' method of storing and transporting milk and had made it necessary for producers to invest in expensive new facilities. The processing of milk products was becoming more concentrated. Control and decision-making was coming to be dominated by a few large international companies, but the committee found this monopoly to be beneficial, contributing 'to the progress and development of the industry, without ... seriously undermining the competitive character of Ontario milk market.'[30] The number of distributors was also declining. Replacement of horse-drawn wagons by motor trucks was broadening the range of operation, and smaller distributors who were unable or unwilling to invest in new facilities were being forced out of business. Retail stores, including the new 'jug milk stores,' were taking over from home delivery. Again, there was a strong trend towards concentration, the large chain dairies assuming a substantial portion of the fluid milk business and the chain supermarkets becoming the major buyers of milk, butter, and cheese. The committee thought this trend was likely to prove beneficial, because, as in other food industries, it seemed likely to force prices down.[31]

The committee's general position on the economics of the milk industry was that of the standard market economists of the day. Government intervention in the industry was condemned because it tended to obstruct progressive change. The observations of an academic economist, H. Scott Gordon, were cited with approval by the committee. 'In my view,' Professor Gordon had stated, 'most of the difficult problems of the milk industry are due to efforts to resist and hamper the processes of progress and change.' Inefficient producers, such as the 'one man farm with ten or a dozen cows, ramshackle barns, and poor equipment' had to understand that they must either modernize their operations 'or else get out of the industry.' Manipulating markets and prices would not solve the problem, Professor Gordon had insisted, but merely 'perpetuate waste and inefficiency.'

The committee could not go all the way with this 'let the market rule' approach, however. While proposing that all southern Ontario be turned into a single marketing area and that flexibility in pricing be maintained to promote innovation, it also suggested that the time had come to establish a single producer-controlled marketing agency for raw milk. Such a plan had been proposed by the Ontario Federation of Agriculture, which had asserted in a brief to the committee that 'where the best efforts of producers have failed, governments at both provincial and national levels have a responsibility to prevent collapse of the dairy industry' and that the Ontario government should immediately establish a marketing plan to bring order to the industry.[32]

This the government did. Although there was some uneasiness about the aggressiveness implied in the committee's recommendations, the government proceeded, through the Milk Act of 1965, to set up the Ontario Milk Marketing Board (OMMB) which quickly established itself as a major force in the industry.[33] Under the strong leadership of its first chairman, George McLaughlin, the OMMB exercised an effective monopoly over the sale of raw milk in Ontario. Its control over supply and price was virtually complete in the case of fluid milk. Milk for further processing ('industrial milk') was by this time more affected by federal than provincial regulation, but even in that field the OMMB functioned as the federal government's agent in the province.

For milk production, as for other agricultural products controlled by provincial marketing boards, federal government price supports had become increasingly important influences. Under the 1958 federal Agricultural Prices Stabilization Act, butter and cheese had been made 'named commodities' along with cattle, hogs, sheep, certain grains, and eggs. This meant that producers would be guaranteed minimum prices for such goods based upon a percentage of a ten-year average. The Canadian Dairy Commission also operated a comprehensive marketing plan for 'industrial milk' (milk destined for processing rather than direct consumption) under which Ontario and other milk-producing provinces were assigned shares of the total Canadian domestic output. The upper limit to this production was set by a market-sharing quota system (MSQ). Producers were also eligible for federal government subsidies determined through a subsidy eligibility quota system (SEQ). Yet another quota system, the plant supply quota, was used to allocate industrial milk among producers of butter, cheese, and skim milk powder.[34]

Under the Milk Marketing Board, the attrition rate among Ontario dairy farmers remained high, but those producers who could adapt to the system profited from it. Despite complaints by producers about the high quality-control standards and associated capital costs imposed upon them by the OMMB, the privilege of producing milk was highly valued. Fluid milk quota was saleable and a strong market developed for it in the early 1970s. The price of 'quota' rose so sharply, in fact, that the OMMB intervened and attempted to control it, too.[35] While producers benefited under these arrangements, it is not clear that consumers were as well served. One analysis indicated that the OMMB had used its monopoly powers to hold milk prices above competitive levels and by so doing had transferred some $11 million a year from consumers to producers.[36] The OMMB defended itself against such charges by arguing that it was benefiting consumers by maintaining stability in the industry and ensuring an adequate supply of milk. Its spokesmen became eloquent expositors of the case for regulation and control and against competition in commodity markets.

The weakness inherent in the consumer position in such situations is suggested by the fact that the monopoly pricing issue attracted less attention than the working of the national supply management system. As in other areas of agricultural marketing board operations, there were growing tensions among the various provincial organizations and conflicts over national policies which were thought to favour producers in some provinces over others. Ontario's position in such matters was aggressively parochial throughout the period. In the case of milk, under the rules of the federal program if a province failed to meet its quota of industrial milk output, it would lose quota to provinces that could. In the early 1970s Ontario appeared likely to lose quota to Quebec because of such 'under-production.' This led to the anomaly of the provincial authorities urging Ontario milk producers to expand output under an 'Industrial Milk Production Incentive program,' while at the same time supporting an elaborate system of supply restriction under the OMMB. While it is true that two technically different kinds of product were involved, this distinction was becoming increasingly artificial, because most milk produced in Ontario met the high fluid milk standards set by the OMMB.

Another problem associated with the industrial milk part of the system was the effect of the processing allocation on Ontario's traditional cheddar cheese producers. While this part of the dairy industry had long been the object of 'rationalization' policies, by the 1970s it appeared likely that the system for allocating milk to different kinds of processors was likely to drive most of the remaining specialized cheddar plants out of business. While the media and

Agriculture, Fishing, Fur Production 145

provincial politicians blamed the situation on 'dunderheads in Ottawa,' the OMMB blamed the cheddar producers for not keeping up with changing demands. At the same time, the growing interest in preserving some of the traditional elements of rural life in the province, such as the small local cheese factories, brought demands for special measures to protect these vestiges of local industry.[37]

While some of this criticism of what was primarily federal government policy was only well-practised bad-mouthing of national agricultural marketing schemes by provincial politicians, it was also symptomatic of the real problem of co-ordinating provincial and federal policies in the absence of any overall planning framework. The failures of regulation were aggravated, as well, by persistently strong market forces, which even in the 1970s continued to break through and disrupt the system. Many of these forces seemed to be beyond the reach of provincial or federal administrators.

Unlike producers in many other provinces, Ontario farmers in the post-war years had become less dependent upon export markets. Except for those specializing in the production of tobacco, cheese, and a few other specific commodities such as white beans, producers in Ontario were almost entirely oriented towards the provincial market. Even in the case of the exceptions noted, exports tended to be a way of disposing of surpluses, useful mainly for stabilizing domestic markets. Although the provincial government was urged from time to time to take a more aggressive position in trying to develop export markets for Ontario agricultural products, it was reluctant to do so, apparently because of concerns over possible conflicts with federal trade policies and possible conflicts with other provinces engaged in similar lines of production.[38] This heavy dependence on local markets, however, made Ontario producers extremely sensitive to any 'invasion' of their territory by outside producers. During the 1950s this threat appeared to be growing. In 1958 it was brought to the government's attention that imports of fruits, vegetables, and processed foods were increasing and that American producers and distributors appeared to be taking a growing interest in the Ontario market. Even during the Ontario harvest season, it was noted, stores in the Niagara region were heavily stocked with fruits and vegetables imported from the United States.[39]

The problem was studied by the Agricultural Marketing Enquiry Committee established in 1959. In its report this committee depicted Ontario agriculture as a rather backward industry struggling to hold its own against growing competition from outside producers. This view was strongly suggested by an analysis provided by the Ontario Department of Economics. Its brief to the committee took the position that the principal markets for Ontario agricultural output would be generated by the growth of population within the province. Although beef, cheese, hogs, and tobacco were exported, high production costs, the prevailing exchange rates, import duties, and lack of purchasing power abroad all were factors likely to limit future growth of reliable export markets. 'High' freight rates similarly restricted opportunities for Ontario producers to develop markets in other parts of Canada. Consequently, the department brief argued, Ontario agriculture had to be seen as a domestic industry dependent upon markets within the province itself. Opportunities for growth there, however, were being restricted by a number of forces, such as the concentration of food retailing in the hands of a few large chains and the tendency towards mass production of major food items. Rising real income levels of consumers also implied an increasing demand for more highly processed foods, which were unlikely to be produced in Ontario at competitive prices because of the scale economies involved. Frozen foods and poultry were cited as examples.[40]

The Agricultural Marketing Enquiry Committee accepted this general line of analysis. It was not very optimistic about finding ways to avoid the implications of it. The committee noted that co-operatives, because of their voluntary basis, had in the past been unable to affect the prices of farm products, and that even the compulsory marketing boards seemed unlikely to be effective in keeping farm prices up in the long term, except in a few cases where Ontario producers were in a position to control the supply of a particular commodity. National compulsory marketing boards might be more effective, but the committee noted that they might make the matter worse for Ontario producers by facilitating 'the movement of products from outside Ontario into Ontario markets.'[41] For the most part, price control and supply restriction were not seen as promising long-term solutions to the problems of Ontario farmers. The rather bleak alternative favoured by the committee was a strategy of 'adjustment.' This meant that individual farmers would have to reorganize their operations, find supplementary off-farm employment, or quit farming. The overall strategy for Ontario agriculture should be to seek a larger share of the growing Ontario market, so that agriculture could develop in 'balance' with the other sectors of the provincial economy.[42]

This general approach also seems to have been favoured by the Ontario Department of Agriculture. Its position during the late 1950s and through the 1960s appeared to be that Ontario did have too many farmers and that those who could not adapt to the new economic realities would simply have to choose other lines of work. Most of the representations made to the provincial government for assistance, it had been noted, came from 'inefficient farmers,' including the leaders of some farm commodity groups.[43] The adjustment problem was not expected to be unduly great because of the growth taking place in other parts of the provincial economy. One of the department's tasks would be to help farmers redirect their interests most profitably. While official statements continued to emphasize the traditional support of farming as an industry and as a way of life, references to the family farm were now often often qualified with the adjective 'economical.'

The intellectual basis for farm 'rationalization' was found in the concept of economic efficiency. Given the existence of more rewarding alternative employment opportunities, it made sense to accept the shaking out of inefficient farm operators. But economic efficiency was not the sole criterion by which government economic policy had to be evaluated in the post-war period. Equity and growth considerations also had to be taken into account. The 'war on poverty' initiatives, which swept North America in the 1960s, complicated the development of programs which seemed, in some respects, to be unresponsive to the plight of low-income people in rural areas. Similarly, interest in promoting growth, especially in 'backward regions,' spawned a number of programs which seemed to be aimed at propping up low-productivity activities rather than facilitating their abandonment. The province's involvement in the federal programs mounted under the Agricultural Rehabilitation and Development Act (ARDA) in the early 1960s was a case in point. The minister of agriculture in 1960 urged the premier's office to avoid promoting measures that might have the effect of encouraging farming in marginal areas. Noting that in the previous forty years the province had wasted millions of dollars trying to encourage farming in northern Ontario, he urged that priority be given to promoting larger and more economical farming units in the south.[44]

Despite such advice, however, the government did enter into regional development schemes that appeared likely to encourage marginal agriculture in the interests of regional development. In the 1962 speech from the throne the government promised to carry out under the ARDA arrangements projects to develop community pastures, drainage and reforestation, and alternative land use schemes 'in co-operation with agricultural groups.'[45] One of the largest of these was aimed at developing a beef cattle industry in north-eastern Ontario by acquiring and making available to farmers on long-term leases some 16,000 acres of potentially high-quality hay pasture lands in the region. Beef production was seen as one of the few potentially profitable alternatives to the traditional small-scale farming operations in that part of the province.[46]

The problems of rural poverty posed an even greater threat to the 'adjustment' policy in agriculture. Not unexpectedly, the perception of rural poverty from the standpoint of general social welfare analysis raised doubts about the desirability of accelerating the movement of low-income farmers off the land and, by implication, into the cities. One of the strong links between poverty and farming was the tendency for many elderly people to remain on economically weak farms either in the hope of eventually cashing in on appreciating land values or more simply for purposes of residence. Some policy advisers to the provincial government were inclined to the view that it would be better to leave such people alone rather than deal with the problems that would arise when they were moved into town.[47]

The matter of farm incomes in general again claimed the attention of the government in the late 1960s, generating another inquiry which, like those conducted at about the same time in other fields such as education, seemed to reflect a general collapse of traditional views on the subject. The Ontario Farm Income Committee presented its findings in a 1969 report with the trendy, if not very original, title, 'The Challenge of Abundance.'[48] Like the investigation of a decade earlier, this one found that the main cause of the farm problem in Ontario was the organization of the food industry. Its recommendations were also familiar in that they called for more government involvement in the industry. They differed in matters of degree. One committee member unambiguously declared that 'the days of the free-enterprise farmer are gone.'[49] One of the committee's critics found that its report amounted to 'a program for implementing a planned economy for Ontario agriculture.'[50] While it urged farmers to stop looking for political solutions to their problems, it proposed that a central farm lobby be formed by amalgamating the Ontario Federation of Agriculture and the Ontario Farmers' Union. The lobby, for which the oddly Orwellian title the 'General Farm Organization' was proposed, would co-ordinate farmers' pressure group activities and advise government on farm policy. Yet the committee seemed to have no high hopes that even such a concerted effort would have much success, given what it referred to as 'the prevailing social philosophy or level of social consciousness within the Ontario farming community.'[51]

What the committee seemed more taken by was a scheme by which all food production in Ontario would be placed under the control of a central marketing body (the 'Food Supply Agency') which would establish production quotas, let contracts for production of particular commodities to selected producers, contract with wholesalers to supply farm products at predetermined prices, and act as the sole selling agency for Ontario farmers. The committee also proposed that entry into farming should be regulated, that selling of production quotas should be restricted, that food imports into Ontario should be controlled, that the selling of fertilizer and farm machinery should be regulated. In addition, farm income would be supported through a proposed federal negative income tax, better farm credit facilities, and special assistance to milk producers (!). The income support measures were defended on the grounds that it would be better to support low farm incomes than to force poor farmers to retreat to urban environments, where they would likely be worse off than if they had stayed on the farm.

While most of its recommendations were impractical, the Farm Income Committee's strongly interventionist approach was not inconsistent with the general drift of provincial agricultural policy in the early 1970s. The government continued to emphasize income support through compulsory marketing, and by the end of the period it was moving towards implementation of a voluntary stabilization plan by which the price supports of the Federal Agricultural Stabilization Program would be supplemented by payments from stabilization funds subscribed by participating producers in Ontario. By the mid-1970s, however, the attitude of the public to these matters was changing in response to the prolonged period of high inflation. While some of the increase in food prices could be blamed on structural changes in the economy, suspicion was growing that marketing boards and other agencies involved in supporting farm incomes were contributing to the problems of consumers. Although a public body, the Ontario Food Council, had been established to provide a forum for various groups involved in production and marketing, it had few powers, and its assigned task of 'monitoring' food price increases in the mid-1960s seemed unlikely to have any significant effect on the situation.

The complexity of the problem of reconciling consumer and producer interests under conditions of general price inflation was compounded by the controversy over interprovincial trade in regulated farm products. The most dramatic example was the 'chicken and egg war' between Ontario and Quebec. Ontario's poultry industry had undergone radical change in the 1950s and 1960s. The old practices whereby farmers had purchased chicks from hatcheries, produced their own feed, and sold eggs and poultry wherever and whenever they could was replaced by a much more specialized system in which eggs were produced on large, single-purpose poultry 'farms' using chicks and feed supplied on a contract basis by feed hatchery operators and feed manufacturers. By 1971 almost 86 per cent of the eggs produced in Ontario came from operators with an average of 15,500 laying hens.[52] Under the new system, producers still carried much of the risk arising from fluctuating market prices. Because of their large investments in plant and the absence of alternative uses for it, the egg producers found it difficult to adjust output when prices fell. The problem of surplus production was aggravated by the differentiation of the Ontario egg market into a number of sectors based on major population centres and the absence of a reliable export market.

Sharp fluctuations of egg prices plagued producers in Ontario through the 1960s. According to one estimate, the typical Ontario producer with a flock of 10,000 hens would have had a loss of $750 a year during the decade.[53] In the case of poultry, the vulnerability of Ontario producers to outside competition was pointed up late in the 1960s, when large quantities of Quebec poultry appeared in the Ontario market, apparently an after-effect of the capacity built up in Quebec to meet the demand generated there by EXPO '67. The result was a bitter conflict between producers and marketing agencies in the two provinces in which the federal government and several provincial governments became embroiled. The chaos was not brought under control until the summer of 1972, when the egg marketing boards of Ontario, Quebec, and Manitoba reached a price-fixing agreement, and the federal government established a system to regulate relations among provincial marketing boards.

What emerged from this experience was the understanding that provincial agricultural policies had to be designed as part of a much grander policy matrix, one that included both provincial and national interests and that could accommodate a number of policy aims at both levels.[54] Yet it was also becoming clear that these policy aims were becoming more diverse and sophisticated in their requirements. Simplistic analysis based on narrow definitions was being challenged by broader concerns. Considerations of economic efficiency in agriculture were being tempered by a growing interest in the meaning of 'community' and the preservation of whatever qualities of rural living could be accommodated within the context of an advanced industrial society.

The Commerical Fishing Industry

Many of the same underlying forces that changed farming in Ontario during the period operated on the fishing and fur-producing industries of the province. Although they were quantitatively unimportant in relation to the total provincial economy, both had some local importance in particular regions.

The commercial fishing industry in Ontario developed in two main branches: the Great Lakes fishery, concentrated mainly around Lake Erie, where ready access to markets permitted a relatively large-scale specialized type of fishing to be carried on; and the 'inland' fishery, operated mainly by part-time fishermen on the lakes and rivers of northern Ontario.

Throughout its history the commercial fishing industry in Ontario has undergone a series of major changes brought about by the impact of population growth and industrial development on the resource base. The ecological disasters of the nineteenth century, which destroyed the Atlantic salmon stock in Lake Ontario, for example, were followed in the twentieth century by the invasion of the upper Lakes by the sea lamprey and the subsequent destruction of major commercial species such as the sturgeon, blue pickerel, and lake trout. The industry survived, because operators were able to develop more economical harvesting methods and to find ways of utilizing species such as the smelt and alewife which formerly had little or no commercial value.

Between 1939 and the mid-1970s the total physical output of the Ontario commercial fisheries fluctuated greatly from year to year, depending on the supply of fish and the fishing effort expended. The former was surprisingly variable, with certain species, particularly in the Great Lakes, showing large variation in numbers over even short periods of time. For example, on Lake Erie the blue pickerel catch, which had dwindled to less than 2 million pounds in 1941, more than doubled in 1942 and doubled again the following year, before again falling to negligible volumes. Even more spectacular was the return of the herring to Lake Erie at the end of the war. In 1946 fishermen saw herring in quantities unknown since the boom years of the First World War. In 1946 they harvested 9.5 million pounds of this almost forgotten fish. But again the revival of a desirable species was brief. In 1947, despite expanded fishing capacity, the catch fell to one-quarter of the 1946 level and within a few years declined to almost nothing.

The invasion of the Great Lakes by the sea lamprey in the years following the war was a disaster for the commercial fishery. This predator reached even the upper Lakes by the 1950s and virtually destroyed the important lake trout fishery on Lake Superior within the decade.[55] A vigorous program of sea lamprey control was introduced, and considerable progress was made in reducing its population, but other problems subsequently arose which made it difficult to reestablish the Lake Superior fishery. In the late 1960s the population of yellow pickerel, one of the commercially attractive alternatives to the lake trout also began to decline drastically for reasons unknown, although over-fishing, pollution, and competition from other species were suggested explanations.[56]

The extent and effectiveness of the fishing effort on the Great Lakes also varied, largely in response to fluctuations in price and, over the longer term, to changes in techniques and the type of equipment available. As with other food producers, Ontario fishermen had to live with the fact that the demand for their product was relatively inelastic. In practical terms this meant that unexpected changes in output typically affected price, which in turn strongly affected their incomes. Abundant harvests typically resulted in lower prices and sharply reduced incomes. Smaller operators often adapted to these conditions simply by suspending their efforts for a year or two until markets improved. But larger operators with substantial overhead expenses could not adopt such a strategy.

The number of large operators increased after the Second World War, when rising labour costs and shortages of workers encouraged fishermen to invest in more efficient, diesel-powered boats equipped with improved gear for handling nets and cargoes. The result was a remarkable increase in labour productivity similar to that observed in farming. Between the late 1930s and the early 1970s employment in the Great Lakes fishery fell from about 4,000 to 2,000. Over the same period the volume of output increased by five times.[57]

As with other food producers, such as the poultry farm operators, the increased specialization and heavy investment in equipment reduced the fishermen's independence. More than ever, their ability to remain in business depended upon keeping production high, especially during periods of low prices. Yet high production in turn caused low prices. It is not surprising that individual fishermen felt themselves to be the victims of a marketing system that worked against their interests. Their resentment was often directed against the wholesalers through whom they had to market their output. These firms, faced with their own problems in remaining competitive, tended to become fewer and larger. More elaborate processing facilities were needed to meet the demands of the supermarkets and other large-scale retailing organizations. As railway service deteriorated, many found themselves forced to invest in fleets of large refrigerated trucks. Many of the older companies were unable or unwilling to adapt to these new requirements and sold out, leaving the primary producers faced with a diminishing number of potential buyers for their product.[58]

The commercial fishermen on the Great Lakes reacted to this perceived deterioration in their competitive position as the farmers did. They organized local associations, many of which supported a provincial body, the Ontario Council of Commercial Fisheries; they also formed co-operatives; and after prices collapsed in the early 1960s, they sought government aid. In 1966 the Lake Erie fishermen were brought under a price support program for yellow perch operated by the federal Fisheries Prices Support Board. This program provided modest support for the Lake Erie fishery in the latter 1960s, although steadily rising prices eventually rendered the program superfluous.

Although a substantial number of immigrants found their way into the commercial fishery in the post-war period, particularly the Portuguese in the case of the major fishery on Lake Erie, the industry continued to provide employment mainly for people who, like many farmers, simply were following family or local tradition. The actual income earned in fishing was well below that which would have been available in manufacturing employment. In 1972 the incomes of fishing boat captains on Lake Erie were less than hourly rated manufacturing employees in the area, and in the case of crew members the average annual income was one-third less than local manufacturing incomes. The differentials were offset, however, by the fact that because fishing was highly seasonal, opportunities existed for earning income from other employment and for obtaining unemployment assistance benefits.[59]

The total physical volume of production in the Ontario commercial fisheries reached a record level of almost 64 million pounds in 1963 and remained at historically high levels through the remainder of the decade. In the early 1970s, however, concern arose over the possible extent of chemical contamination in the Great Lakes system, and output dropped sharply. Several species were found to contain alarming quantities of mercury. Testing of samples from all the commercial fishing areas of the province during 1971 revealed that the problem was probably less widespread than had been feared. Nevertheless, some species taken from a number of different areas were found to contain more than the 'acceptable' 0.5 parts per million of the metal. As a result, all of Lake St Clair and the eastern part of Lake Ontario were closed to commercial fishing. Parts of Lake Erie were closed to pickerel and white bass fishing, and the Thunder Bay trout fishery was also shut down. The licensing arrangements for commercial fishing in the province were revised to restrict operations only to those species found to be free of excessive mercury.

By 1975 it appeared that some branches of the commercial fisheries in Ontario would survive the mercury pollution scare, but the underlying economic situation of the industry was such that there remained little prospect for future growth. Total physical output in 1975 was approximately what it had been twenty years before.

TABLE 32
Quantity of Commercial Fish Landed and Persons Employed in Commercial Fishing, Ontario, 1939–75

Year	Quantity ('000 lb)	Persons	Year	Quantity ('000 lb)	Persons
1939	24,817	4,206	1958	47,172	3,224
1940	19,690	4,020	1959	48,984	3,527
1941	22,783	3,608	1960	47,600	3,409
1942	18,718	3,336	1961	54,951	3,059
1943	23,786	3,610	1962	63,780	2,993
1944	22,545	3,809	1963	54,342	3,271
1945	24,478	n.a.	1964	43,508	2,952
1946	23,562	4,244	1965	52,486	2,544
1947	20,343	4,026	1966	56,344	2,445
1948	23,933	3,736	1967	54,656	2,197
1949	34,061	3,930	1968	55,707	2,044
1950	32,755	3,886	1969	63,205	1,959
1951	30,069	3,833	1970	46,081	1,836
1952	38,044	3,878	1971	42,795	1,999
1953	44,838	3,807	1972	43,195	2,097
1954	47,680	3,657	1973	53,052	2,215
1955	45,634	3,483	1974	53,225	2,208
1956	59,717	3,135	1975	45,363	2,220
1957	51,113	3,066			

SOURCE: Statistics Canada (DBS), *Fisheries Statistics of Canada*, 1939–50, annual (24-201); and 1951–75, annual (24-207)

The Inland Fishery

Although a small amount of commercial fishing continued to be done in the smaller lakes of southern Ontario, most of the inland fishing in the 1939–75 period was concentrated in the northern part of the province. The fishing activities carried on there involved a mix of subsistence fishing by the northern Cree and Ojibwa, sports fishing closely tied in with the tourist industry of the area, and small-scale commercial operations conducted by both native and some other operators. Despite the extent of the northern lake and river systems, conflicts arose during the period among the various groups involved in utilizing the fish resources of the area, particularly the commercial and the sports fishing interests. There were even more serious conflicts between industrial operations that polluted the waters of the region and all those interested in preserving and developing the fishing opportunities there.

The extent of the subsistence fishing carried on by the native population of northern Ontario became a matter of contention during the period. The facts were difficult to ascertain, but some evidence suggested that many, if not all, Indian bands in the area were reducing their consumption of local fish as improvements in transportation made alternative kinds of 'store bought' food more readily available. It was also noted that the introduction of snowmobiles reduced the dog population and the need for fish to feed the animals previously relied upon for winter transportation, and that in areas where trapping was declining in importance, the quantity of fish needed for trap bait was also reduced. Thus, one study carried out in the early 1970s very tentatively concluded that while subsistence fishing remained a part of the economic system of northern Ontario, it was of decreasing importance and in the case of the Ojibwa communities was no longer a significant feature of the local economy except in the most remote areas.[60]

Through much of the period, however, the native population of northern Ontario became increasingly involved in commercial fishing and for some communities, by the 1960s, fishing had become the chief source of earned income. Indeed, with the decline of trapping, it was often the only source of such income; for the alternatives, working as guides in the tourist industry or harvesting wild rice, were available to Indians living only in certain of the more southerly areas. This growing dependence on commercial fishing created a serious policy issue for the provincial government. Coincident with a heightened appreciation of the moral and political claims of the native population for greater self-determination and better economic opportunities, the government found itself faced with strong pressures to support certain kinds of development in the north that were obviously incompatible with the interests of the native people of the area and specifically harmful to the recently developed commercial fisheries there. The most conspicuous problem was that created by mercury contamination of several lakes and river systems by pulp and paper mills. This pollution led the government to forbid fishing altogether in many areas. There was also concern about the effects of commercial fishing on the tourist industry that was developing in north-western Ontario in the 1960s. Stricter regulations concerning the legal size of fish that could be taken commercially and the size of mesh in nets used for commercial fishing were also introduced at this time. In addition, priority was being given to hydroelectric developments, as Ontario Hydro moved into the north to utilize the remaining hydro potential of the province. In the face of such developments, the commercial fisheries of north-western Ontario appeared to face a bleak future, and both the native and non-native commercial fishing operators in the area became convinced that the provincial government was actually bent on destroying their industry. The situation was not helped by the controversy over the marketing of fish produced in the area. In 1969 the federal government enacted legislation to bring the marketing of inland fish under the control of a central agency, the Freshwater Fish Marketing Corporation, the object of which was to market fish in an orderly manner, increase returns to fishermen, promote markets, and increase interprovincial and export trade. Producers in north-western Ontario along with those in the Northwest Territories, Saskatchewan, and Manitoba were brought into the plan.[61] Unfortunately the

Agriculture, Fishing, Fur Production 155

early years of the plan's operation were marked by serious problems of mismanagement and disappointing returns for producers. So great was the dissatisfaction in north-western Ontario that a portion of the area was withdrawn from the plan.

Although production data are unreliable for the inland fishery, physical output probably peaked in the mid-1960s, when it may have reached some 8 million pounds annually. By the mid-1970s it was perhaps half that amount.[62] As to the future of the industry, it appeared unlikely to survive in competition with the tourist industry, non-renewable resource development, and hydroelectric power.[63]

Fur Production

The production of furs in Ontario during the period from 1939 to 1975 is of interest more for the prospects the industry held out for improving incomes in northern Ontario than for its actual contribution to economic activity in the province as a whole.

The production of wild furs during the period remained an important activity in the north, where it supported a number of full-time professional trappers and provided at least part of the income of native people in the area. Output varied greatly with fluctuations in the availability of animals and the response of trappers to prices. Some control over the industry was exercised by public authorities in the interest of regulating competition and to establish some degree of management for the resource base. During the 1940s the Ontario government moved away from its earlier policy of developing fur reserves on crown land in favour of establishing a system of registered traplines. The new program was first implemented in the vicinity of Algonquin Park and by the 1950s had spread over most of northern Ontario. Under the system trappers were licensed and assigned exclusive rights to take furs in specified regions. In the mid-1960s, some 9,000 trappers, including both whites and natives, held such licences.[64]

The physical volume of wild fur production in Ontario reached a peak in the years at the end of the Second World War. Output exceeded one million pelts in each of the three seasons following the war. After a sharp decline in 1949–50, output increased and again reached high levels during the early 1950s. Thereafter output remained fairly stable, fluctuating between 6,000 and 9,000 pelts annually.

Fur farming was a rapidly growing industry in the 1940s and it appeared to be capable of developing into an important new industry in the province. The market was strong for long-haired furs, and a number of new fox farms were established, producing silver and blue fox pelts. Even more important was the development of mutation mink in the early years of the decade. This created a wave of investor interest in the breeding and raising of new varieties of pastel-coloured mink, for which a strong market was quickly developing. The value

TABLE 33
Fur Production, Ontario, 1940–75

Year	Number of Fur Farms	Pelts Produced on Fur Farms		Wild Fur Production (number of pelts)
		Mink	Fox	
1940	1,841	60,355	39,167	n.a.
1941	1,613	62,281	34,769	954,362
1942	1,475	63,580	25,098	n.a.
1943	1,222	85,493	29,062	n.a.
1944	1,216	58,110	24,237	968,295
1945	1,304	58,539	23,473	909,280
1946	1,348	63,978	26,956	1,149,727
1947	1,425	79,372	27,929	1,035,189
1948	1,306	123,158	28,525	1,036,848
1949	1,104	139,095	15,339	
1950	1,063	134,093	14,292	781,879
1951	914	145,999	8,528	885,630
1952	769	153,256	4,365	959,431
1953	631	138,776	1,736	1,098,286
1954	549	154,126	1,349	1,016,672
1955	529	176,245	1,491	1,107,530
1956	542	242,504	795	786,608
1957	514	241,847	457	788,666
1958	507	263,644	337	791,175
1959	495	284,740	398	680,189
1960	495	348,480	838	641,093
1961	508	388,981	746	680,878
1962	500	384,473	603	627,283
1963	505	432,666	413	705,338
1964	498	407,085	435	757,803
1965	493	479,760	407	615,616
1966	491	566,262	539	733,761
1967	477	631,386	690	619,026
1968	417	568,089	674	123,698
1969	385	585,436	600	917,278
1970	352	534,867	547	764,763
1971	290	438,650	583	627,050
1972	253	414,139	642	584,882
1973	235	431,572	679	695,668
1974	212	473,321	950	816,836
1975	183	418,287	931	716,066

SOURCE: Statistics Canada, *Fur Production*, annual (23-207)

of fur farm production grew steadily through the 1950s and, after 1955, exceeded the value of wild fur production in Ontario. By 1960 fur farms were producing twice as much in value terms as the trappers. Most of the 500 fur farms then in operation were producing mink. Although fox farming continued, it became relatively unimportant. Mink production peaked in 1967, when over 631,000 pelts valued at more than $7 million were produced. Fox production in the same year was valued at less than $24,000.

The most conspicuous trend in the fur farming business after the war was the increasing scale of individual operations and their declining numbers. By 1975 the number of farms had fallen from 500 in the early 1960s to 183.[65] While there had once been speculation that fur farming might prove to be well suited to northern Ontario, where it could have served to broaden the economic base, by the mid-1970s little progress had been made in establishing industry there. Although fur farming requires considerable labour, it does not create employment on a casual or part-time basis. It also proved to be capital intensive and to require substantial management skill. While there were potential supplies of cheap feed available in the form of fish in northern lakes and rivers, it was possible to find even cheaper feed, such as food-industry by-products, in the south. By the end of the period, most of Ontario's fur farms were located near such southern feed sources, with the largest concentration in the counties of Wellington, Perth, and Niagara. The total number of fur farms in the north actually declined during the latter part of the period.

Tourism

While it is difficult to separate 'tourism' from other aspects of recreation and travel, most definitions of this activity stress the fact that tourists are travellers who are spending some time away from home for the purposes of experiencing living temporarily in some other place. The tourist industry consequently comprises those businesses and public agencies that are more or less directly involved in providing such travellers with lodging, meals, transportation, supplies, equipment, and entertainment.[66]

The development of the tourist industry in Ontario during the period from 1939 to 1975 was closely associated with the improvement of transportation facilities, especially highways and, after the war, of long-distance air services. Other influences included the increase in per capita incomes, which made it possible for more people to travel and make use of resort facilities and similar amenities and the effect of urbanization on the demand for recreational services outside the cities. Rising levels of education may also have strengthened interest in travel to historical and cultural points of interest.[67]

Structurally the tourist industry of Ontario has been characterized by a predominance of small, privately owned firms. The provincial government and to a much smaller extent the federal government sought to encourage the industry by building roads, sponsoring advertising programs, and establishing standards of service. So did local governments and voluntary agencies, many of which viewed tourism as a relatively promising way to increase employment and income and to diversify local economies. 'The tourist industry promises the community and the Province more returns faster than any other industry,' the provincial director of travel research claimed in 1963. The same official argued that while much had been made of secondary manufacturing as a source of new jobs in Ontario, it was clearly declining in importance as a primary source of employment, giving way to the service industries of which tourism comprised an important part.[68]

Like many of the service industries, tourism was a relatively heavy user of low-paid workers. It was also an export-based industry drawing upon local resources, typically land resources, to supply the experiences 'consumed' by non-residents of the area. What comprised 'the area' and who were to be considered 'tourists' were difficult to assess when attempts were made to quantify the activities involved in the industry. Most of the tourism statistics collected in Ontario for the period were based on counts made of Americans entering the province for recreational purposes. There were also various estimates of interprovincial tourist travel, for example, the numbers entering the province from Manitoba to vacation in the resort areas of north-western Ontario. International travellers arriving by air in major centres such as Toronto have also been routinely counted as part of the immigration control process. Visitors to the national capital in Ottawa and to other specific attractions could be estimated with varying degrees of reliability. While such data provide an approximate sense of how much tourist activity went on in the province, they are far from satisfactory for most purposes. Most of the difficulties arise from problems of definition. Some attempts to standardize definitions have been made, particularly at the international level. For example, the League of Nations in 1937 proposed a definition of the term 'tourist,' which would mean 'any person travelling for a period of 24 hours or more in a country other than that in which he usually resides.'[69] But such a definition has not been of much use in a country as large as Canada, where particular regions may attract more tourists from other parts of the country than from abroad. Even with the efforts made in the post-war period to measure border traffic exchanges between provinces, the often important intraprovincial flows of recreational travellers could be estimated only by less direct methods.

Because of these problems of definition and counting, estimates of the volume of tourist travel and of the amounts of tourist spending are unreliable, with wide variations in different sources. Local estimates, for example, may reflect a tendency for local groups to exaggerate the importance of tourist activity in particular areas. As one survey of the literature on tourism notes, 'Much of the existing literature comes from local booster associations and is extremely optimistic about the potential riches that tourism can bring. Some consulting firms have specialized in the production of reports and projections with local groups as their clients. Unfortunately, many of these reports appear to have been stamped from the same mold and are of relatively low quality.'[70] At the same time, there has also been a tendency to underestimate the value of domestic travellers, if for no other reason than that they are more difficult to count than foreign visitors. This tendency is reflected in the emphasis given in the official provincial government reports of the 1950s and 1960s, which were dominated by the counts of U.S. cars entering Ontario, the average length of stay of such visitors, and their average expenditures. In 1953, for example, the *Ontario Economic Review* reported that the United States was the province's most important source of tourists, with 1,534,135 American cars entering the province directly and some 56,000 entering via other provinces, an increase of 12.6 per cent over the year before. Another 717,637 American tourists came into the province by rail, boat, bus, and air in 1953.[71] Such data do suggest the growth of at least this part of the tourist business in the province over the course of the period. The number of American cars entering the province directly from the United States in 1974, for example, was 7,829,376.[72] Other parts of the industry are also well documented statistically, notably the use made of the growing system of provincial parks in the post-war period. We know from these data that from 1957 to 1972 the number of provincial parks increased from 55 to 115; that the number of developed campsites grew from 1,849 to 19,983; and that the number of vehicle entries to such parks increased from 629,666 to 3,652,935. Certain trends are also evident in such statistics: Ontario residents made by far the greatest use of the provincial parks over the period, but the out-of-province visitors increased from 18 per cent of the total in the mid-1950s to approximately 33 per cent in the early 1970s.[73]

While there are no general historical series that enable us to identify long-term trends in Ontario's tourist industry as a whole, what is beyond question is that the industry, however defined, grew rapidly during the post-second World War decades and by the mid-1970s had become an important part of the provincial economy, employing about 165,000 persons and generating revenues of some $2.6 billion.[74] It thus accounted for perhaps 10 per cent of total employment in the province and, in terms of value, could be considered one of the three or four leading industries. But even more important is the role it has played in the development of certain regions of the province, particularly the southern fringe of the Canadian Shield.

Tourism in Northern Ontario

Two main types of tourist business are often distinguished, one catering to relatively small numbers of affluent travellers seeking exotic locales and facilities and the other devoted to the mass tourism market, providing services to large numbers of people seeking out popular attractions. Northern Ontario has catered to both kinds of tourists, providing remote 'fly-in' hunting and fishing camps for (mainly American) 'sportsmen' and cheap camping and park facilities accessible by road for vacationers from other parts of the province and the rest of the continent. Ontario's natural resource endowment in the northern regions of the province is not particularly distinctive, resembling in most respects the Canadian Shield regions of the adjacent provinces of Manitoba and Quebec. Northern Ontario's main competitive advantage has been its proximity to major population centres and the relatively good transportation corridors, both rail and road, which traverse its northern 'wilderness' areas. The intensive road construction of the early post-war period considerably increased the number of northern Ontario tourist attractions accessible from other parts of the continent. The 'tourism potential' of the province was enhanced. This was particularly noticeable in north-eastern Ontario, which was largely untapped for such purposes until the 1950s, when a considerable increase in provincial road-building outlays in the area and a determined attempt on the part of the government to promote local tourist development began to stimulate commercial interest in its possibilities for mass tourism. During the 1950s the government spent some $16 million a year on highways in the north-east, and this figure rose in the early 1960s to well over $22 million.[75] The province also amended the Ontario Travel and Publicity Act to enable the government to provide grants to approved regional tourist organizations for maintenance, promotion, and development of the tourist industry in the north-east as well as in other regions of the province.[76]

Unlike the north-east, the north-western region of Ontario was by 1939 already established as a tourist area, with a number of vacation resorts and extensive cottage development in the Lake of the Woods vicinity. The area was originally opened up for such activities by the railways, with railway towns such as Kenora and Keewatin on the CPR line attracting summer vacationers from Winnipeg, the nearest centre of large population. Construction of Highway no. 17 in the early 1930s and later of Highway 71 through International Falls along with the route from Winnipeg to Kenora made the Kenora–Keewatin area an important vacation centre for residents of the United States and Winnipeg. The two major railway companies had also been active during the interwar period in developing the area's tourist potential, the CNR building a luxurious lodge at Minaki, north of Kenora on the Winnipeg River, while the CPR built a summer lodge at Devil's Gap on Lake of the Woods just south of Kenora. During the war years there was little growth because of restrictions on road construction and the scarcity of gasoline, but the level of utilization in some areas served by rail continued to be high. The beginnings of the post-war boom in the early 1950s brought a burst of activity: new cottage construction, road improvements, and a number of new fly-in sport fishing camps reached by small float-equipped aircraft operating out of bases in Kenora, Nestor Falls, and, later on, Red Lake and Sioux Lookout.[77] Completion of the TransCanada Highway through the Kenora region in the mid 1960s further stimulated the industry, making it one of the region's main sources of income. By the late 1960s it was second only to the forest industries in terms of revenues generated. While pulp and paper remained the largest source of employment and income in north-western Ontario, generating over $70 million dollars worth of value annually in the later 1960s, the estimated revenue associated with the tourist industry was about $30 million.[78] The only other industry of importance was lumbering, with the value of timber cut running at about $22 million. Commercial fishing, trapping, and farming provided insignificant amounts of income in the area by comparison.[79]

The potential of tourism as a possible alternative to the traditional resource-based activities in promoting northern development in Ontario was well recognized at both the local and provincial levels. The efforts to reduce regional inequalities in the province during the later years of the period gave considerable prominence to this potential, especially after some evidence was found suggesting that the multiplier effects of some kinds of tourist spending were less likely to 'spill-over' into the central core of the provincial economy than was true of increased spending in some other kinds of activities.[80] There were also indications from input-output analysis of the provincial economy that the income multiplier associated with tourist spending was large, exceeded only by twelve out of forty-nine sectors of the Ontario economy.[81] By the mid-1970s the provincial government was collaborating with the federal authorities to develop policies to promote tourism and on its own was utilizing tax concessions and small-business loan programs to stimulate private investment in the industry. There were, however, the usual policy conflicts. The province was inclined to favour airline fare deregulation and the development of tourist facilities in and adjacent to national parks to stimulate tourist development, matters on which the federal government appeared likely to hold different views. Within the province, tourism was not universally held to be the most desirable means of creating employment and income opportunities, especially in the north, where the aspirations of the native population to become less rather than more dependent on economic activities controlled from outside the region were unlikely to be fulfilled thereby.[82]

8 Mines and Forests

Mining

Throughout the period from 1939 to 1975 Ontario remained by far the most important mineral-producing province in Canada and the province with the most varied mining sector. Its lead in these respects declined, however. Between the end of the war and 1960 the value of mineral production in Ontario increased by 6.5 per cent compared with a national rate of increase of 5.6 per cent. But between 1960 and 1975 the corresponding growth rates were 3.9 and 5.3 per cent, respectively.[1] This was due in part to the changing composition of total mineral production over the period. The large gains in national mineral production in the 1960s and 1970s were in fuels, potash, and iron ore, all of which had higher production levels in other parts of Canada than in Ontario. Another factor that contributed to some deterioration in Ontario's pre-eminence in mining was the old age of many of its principal mining camps, such as Cobalt, Kirkland Lake, and Porcupine. Despite some remarkable new operations, the rate of mine openings in Ontario after the boom years of the 1950s fell sharply. The growth of the industry failed to keep pace with that of the economy generally, with the result that the value of mineral production fell from about 6 per cent of the Gross Provincial Product in the 1950s to just over 3 per cent by the mid-1970s.

Even so, mining remained important in Ontario, particularly for the contribution it made to the local economies of the north, and also because parts of the mining industry were well integrated with other industrial sectors of the provincial economy. Although the importance of mining to the economy was brought into question in the later years of the period, the industry still received considerable government support in the form of tax concessions, scientific and technical support, and public investments in transportation and electric power facilities. The overall level of activity in the industry, however, was determined more by external forces, such as fluctuations in foreign demand, than by domestic conditions or policies.

The main internal change in the Ontario mining industry after the Second

World War was a shift from precious to base metals. There were also important technical innovations, with new types of equipment becoming available, and new methods of finding and developing mining properties. While individual prospectors and specially formed small financial syndicates continued to play a role, the greatly increased cost and difficulty of finding new mines in Ontario led to the adoption of large-scale mine-finding operations by the mining companies themselves.

Gold-mining

The gold-mining camps of north-eastern Ontario were stagnating in the late 1930s. Despite relatively favourable gold prices, operators were complaining bitterly about 'oppressive' taxes and high labour costs, which they claimed were forcing them to limit operations to only the highest-grade ores still available to them.[2] Over 90 per cent of production was from mines that had been staked more than a decade earlier.

The mining community tended to blame the situation on the government, not only because of taxes, but because of tougher new securities legislation.[3] Blatant fraud and misrepresentation in the sale of mining stock and shares in exploration ventures had led the government to require that small mining syndicates register with the provincial Securities Commission. Shortly after the outbreak of war, the Ontario government hinted that it might relax these requirements to stimulate mineral exploration in support of the war effort. It was expected at the time that Canada would have to increase gold production to finance the purchase of war materials from the United States. In December 1940, the federal minister of finance called for such an increase in output, indicating that gold mining would be given the status of a high-priority wartime industry. This caused a flurry of activity in the Ontario gold-mining camps, as they prepared for a new era of expansion. At the same time, mining interests in the province seized the opportunity to launch a vigorous lobbying campaign against the regulation of mining securities issues. They were supported by the Toronto *Globe and Mail*, which did its part by urging the government to give up its restrictive policies and 'blaze a trail back to sanity and mining prosperity.'[4] This campaign continued into 1941, but within a few months the anticipated boom in gold-mining was over. Once it became apparent that the United States would enter the war, the immediate need for increased gold production disappeared. The Hyde Park Agreements of 1942 eliminated most of the concern over the American position, and the Canadian prime minister promptly announced that gold-mining would not be one of the wartime priority industries after all.

The false dawn in the gold-mining camps had a number of important side-effects. It coincided with the Kirkland Lake miners' strike of 1941, one of the landmark struggles in Canadian labour history. It also encouraged a premature expansion of municipal and other public service facilities in the gold mining towns of northern Ontario, aggravating their already serious financial situation. It was also significant in that it revealed several interesting aspects of the Ontario government's relations with Ottawa in connection with natural-resources administration.

The Ontario (Liberal) government of the time appears to have had no great interest in the future of the gold-mining industry in the province. Most of the tax revenues generated by the industry went to the federal government (an 18 per cent federal income tax compared with a 5 per cent Ontario corporations tax and a 1–6 per cent Ontario mining tax based on profits). Yet most of the infrastructure costs associated with the industry fell upon the province. The federal call at the beginning of the war for expanded gold production gave the provincial government an opportunity to wash its hands of the problem. As one provincial official declared publicly, the Ontario government 'could not and should not' be asked to do anything with respect to the gold mining industry, because it had been created largely for the purpose of meeting the requirements of the Dominion and he was satisfied that the federal government would accept any financial burdens of readjustment in northern Ontario that might result from its policies.[5] Nor did the Ontario government appear to have much confidence in the industry's commercial prospects. The premier, Mr Hepburn, wrote to a union official in 1942 that he expected that the gold mining industry would 'be a victim of the war.'[6] The gold-mining industry of Ontario survived the war, however, although physical output fell from the more than 3 million ounces produced in 1940 to less than 2 million in 1945. Shortages of labour were a major restraint. In addition to the loss to military service and other higher priority jobs, some operators noted that workers who had come from western Canadian farms during the Depression were returning to farming.[7] These labour shortages were aggravated by difficulties in obtaining mining equipment, much of which had to be imported from the United States, where war-production priorities discriminated against the manufacturing of such equipment.[8] Federal government policies in Canada forbade the opening of any new gold mines in Canada for the duration of the war.

When these restrictions were removed after the war, the industry expanded gradually, with several new mines opening in both north-eastern and north-western Ontario. Some federal assistance was provided through subsidies paid under the provisions of the Emergency Gold Mining Assistance Act of 1948, but production levels remained low. Physical output averaged 2 million ounces per year from the late 1940s to the mid-1960s, when it fell to approximately 1 million ounces. With the breakdown in the fixed U.S. dollar gold price regime that begain in the late 1960s, culminating in the abandonment of convertability by the U.S. government in 1971, gold prices rose sharply. But even with this stimulus, the Ontario industry seemed incapable of further expansion. By 1975 the physical output of gold in Ontario fell to a record low of 755,000 ounces.

TABLE 34
Volume and Value of Gold Production, Ontario, 1939–75

Year	Volume of Production		Value of Production (dollars)
	Troy Ounces	Grams	
1939	3,086,060	95,987,195	112,114,762
1940	3,261,688	101,449,837	125,579,597
1941	3,194,309	99,354,115	122,977,102
1942	2,763,822	85,964,473	106,413,978
1943	2,117,214	65,852,716	81,517,998
1944	1,731,838	53,866,183	66,675,000
1945	1,625,367	50,554,564	62,576,089
1946	1,801,294	56,026,506	65,998,448
1947	1,939,317	60,319,501	67,876,390
1948	2,095,424	65,174,971	73,339,904
1949	2,354,510	73,233,447	85,269,362
1950	2,481,113	77,171,240	94,216,874
1951	2,462,978	76,607,179	91,105,477
1952	2,513,701	78,184,840	87,540,620
1953	2,182,438	67,881,409	75,388,307
1954	2,361,387	73,447,345	80,460,251
1955	2,523,040	78,475,316	87,223,660
1956	2,513,912	78,191,403	86,489,962
1957	2,578,206	80,191,170	86,621,067
1958	2,716,514	84,493,030	92,192,231
1959	2,683,449	83,464,593	90,083,383
1960	2,732,673	84,995,631	92,774,248
1961	2,637,720	82,042,262	93,533,551
1962	2,421,249	75,309,262	90,578,924
1963	2,338,854	72,746,491	88,291,739
1964	2,155,370	67,039,500	81,365,217
1965	1,946,003	60,527,459	73,420,747
1966	1,660,750	51,655,099	62,626,883
1967	1,495,385	46,511,672	56,450,784
1968	1,379,779	42,915,924	52,031,466
1969	1,229,666	38,246,887	46,346,112
1970	1,162,042	36,143,546	42,484,255
1971	1,133,987	35,270,938	40,079,636
1972	1,019,303	31,703,867	58,720,007
1973	922,303	28,686,829	89,843,380
1974	801,105	24,917,150	124,427,629
1975	755,148	23,487,728	123,678,894

SOURCE: Ontario, Ministry of Natural Resources, *Ontario Mining Statistics: A Preliminary Compendium*, Mineral Policy Background Paper No. 11 (Toronto, 1979), 11.3 (MNR series data)

Iron-mining

Ontario's iron-ore-mining industry had been dormant for almost two decades following the closing of the Magpie Mine in 1921. In 1937 the provincial government sought to support the revival of the industry by offering bounties on iron production, and by the end of the decade there was extensive exploration activity in the Michipicoten Range north-west of Sault Ste Marie and one new mine, the New Helen, which began operations in 1939.[9] These developments were important to the local economy of the Algoma region in north-western Ontario, but there was some doubt about the long-term feasibility of iron-ore-mining there. The companies involved in the work appeared to expect that the Ontario government would continue to subsidize their operations, and this the government appeared reluctant to do, for at least two reasons. One was that the mining operations would likely be carried on by subsidiaries of steel-making companies which were unlikely to allow the mining operations to show a profit if this would jeopardize the subsidy program.[10] The second was that the Ontario government was inclined to view iron-mining, as it did gold-mining, as a matter primarily of federal government concern, particularly in view of the strategic importance of iron during wartime. The government consequently was not very accommodating in its dealings with the private companies involved in the Michipicoten and Algoma undertakings. It repeatedly rejected their appeals for financial aid, although it did indicate that it might be willing to reconsider its position once the war was over.[11]

A much more complex interaction of private developers and government, one that presaged the 'mega-projects' of later years, was involved in another iron-ore-mining project of the late 1930s in north-western Ontario. Steep Rock Lake, located about 140 miles by rail west of the Lakehead (Thunder Bay), was the site of known high-grade iron ore deposits, the extent and potential value of which was confirmed by a group of Canadian geologists and mining promoters who staked claims in the area in 1938. The discovery was of great potential significance; for it suggested the possibility of developing the first major domestic source of iron ore for the Canadian steel industry. There were, however, formidable obstacles in the way of developing the property. The main ore bodies lay under the floor of a deep, fifteen-mile-long lake. The lake received water from a river that had already been developed as a hydroelectric power site. Before mining could begin, it would be necessary to divert the river, pump out the lake, relocate the hydro station, and remove extensive overburden from the ore deposit. There were also organizational and political difficulties to be overcome, including the Canadian government's wartime ban on new mining undertakings.[12]

All these difficulties were swept aside, however, when the United States entered the war. The Canadians attempting to promote Steep Rock had already sought financial backing in the United States, and the Cleveland industrialist, Cyrus Eaton, had taken an interest in the project. His organization had the means available to arrange much of the necessary financing and also to guarantee markets for the ore. Eaton also proved to be an effective advocate in selling the idea of developing Steep Rock to the United States government. Given growing fears in Washington that the United States might run out of iron ore if the war lasted more than a few years, the necessary public support was forthcoming.

Much of the investment required for Steep Rock was subsequently provided by public agencies. The United States Reconstruction Finance Corporation and the Export-Import Bank provided most of the financial capital initially required. The Canadian government provided ore docks at Port Arthur and a rail connection to the mine site. Ontario Hydro built a 130-mile-long power transmission line. There were also a number of tax concessions which, in the words of a company publication, were 'intended among other purposes to recognize the value of the contribution made by Steep Rock, its officials and associates, in a situation of serious emergency.'[13] In fact, however, there was no emergency. As with similar undertakings in other parts of Canada, such as the Alaska Highway and the Alcan Oil Pipeline, by the time the project was in operation, the military concerns that had prompted it no longer existed.

With Steep Rock in production and the New Helen mine at Michipicoten continuing in operation, Ontario entered the post-war period with two established iron-ore-mining centres. The Steep Rock facilities were greatly expanded during the 1950s, partly as a result of further development on the main deposits worked by the Steep Rock Company itself and also through development of adjacent deposits leased to Caland Ores, a subsidiary of Inland Steel of Chicago, which wanted the additional production to supply its steel-making operations in the United States. There appeared to be no opposition in Ontario to such integration of iron ore mining in the province and steel-making in the United States.[14] Most of the iron ore used in the Ontario steel mills was still being imported from the established American suppliers.

During the 1950s the search for additional iron ore in Ontario was pursued actively, aided by the availability of new exploration methods. In 1949 an airborne magnetometer survey conducted by the Geological Survey of Canada at the request of the Ontario Department of Mines revealed a magnetite deposit near Marmora in central Ontario, near an area that had supported a number of small iron works in the nineteenth century. The property was subsequently developed by a subsidiary of Bethlehem Steel to supply the parent company's plant near Buffalo. Later in the decade another magnetite deposit was discovered at Bruce Lake in north-western Ontario, about thirty miles south-east of the gold-mining camp at Red Lake. This find and a low-grade deposit in Boston Township six miles south of Kirkland Lake in north-eastern Ontario were brought into production, contributing to the steady expansion of iron ore output in the province which continued through the 1950s and 1960s.

The province's iron ore production was also increased in the late 1950s by the development of plants designed to recover iron from ores mined primarily

TABLE 35
Volume and Value of Iron Ore Production, Ontario, 1939-75

Year	Volume of Production		Value of Production (dollars)
	Short Tons	Tonnes	
1939	123,598	112,126	341,594
1940	404,752	367,184	1,183,861
1941	516,037	468,140	1,426,057
1942	545,119	494,523	1,516,142
1943	498,850	452,549	1,452,250
1944	553,252	501,901	1,909,608
1945	1,135,444	1,030,057	3,635,095
1946	1,549,523	1,405,703	6,822,947
1947	1,919,366	1,741,219	9,313,201
1948	1,336,565	1,212,511	7,482,860
1949	2,011,736	1,825,016	13,192,781
1950	2,435,716	2,209,644	17,562,059
1951	2,841,984	2,578,204	21,205,152
1952	2,717,490	2,465,265	19,632,551
1953	2,832,090	2,569,228	23,137,997
1954	2,416,911	2,192,584	20,341,203
1955	4,362,191	3,957,313	34,340,897
1956	5,558,203	5,042,316	44,177,246
1957	4,867,105	4,415,363	41,317,629
1958	3,644,952	3,306,644	36,851,421
1959	6,018,089	5,459,518	50,830,404
1960	5,325,197	4,830,937	48,399,442
1961	5,772,664	5,236,872	62,350,773
1962	6,414,936	5,819,532	64,479,510
1963	6,749,617	6,123,149	70,033,690
1964	8,046,769	7,299,906	85,613,354
1965	8,475,218	7,688,588	94,209,236
1966	8,144,289	7,388,374	91,700,740
1967	8,649,763	7,846,932	99,903,925
1968	10,907,197	9,894,842	127,137,824
1969	10,516,786	9,540,667	128,166,423
1970	11,828,337	10,730,486	144,765,483
1971	11,178,670	10,141,118	136,205,400
1972	11,755,336	10,664,261	139,514,537
1973	12,424,318	11,271,151	152,468,574
1974	12,021,608	10,905,819	180,089,730
1975	10,476,161	9,503,813	219,024,019

SOURCE: MNR, *Ontario Mining Statistics: A Preliminary Compendium*, 12.2

for their other mineral content. One of the largest of these was the iron recovery plant built by International Nickel (INCO) at Sudbury.

Changes in the technology of steel-making and shifts in the pattern of demand in the 1960s led Ontario steel-makers to utilize more Canadian iron ore. Through the acquisition of existing mines and development of new properties at Bruce Lake, Ontario steel-makers became capable of obtaining most of their iron ore requirements domestically. When the large Sherman mine near Temagami was opened in 1965, the Ontario minister of mines announced with satisfaction that it was 'an all-Ontario project' since all the property owners and companies involved were incorporated in the province and because the ores mined would be pelletized and shipped on the Ontario Northland Railway for processing into steel at the Dofasco plant in Hamilton.[15]

Total iron ore production in the province increased from just over 1.1 million tons in 1945 to about 5.5 million tons annually in the mid-1950s. Expansion continued and by 1968 approached 11 million tons. Future development appeared to be promising.

Early in the 1970s, however, the growth of iron-mining in Ontario faltered. The depressed condition of the U.S. steel industry, combined with a revival of activity in the old American mining ranges reduced the export demand for Ontario ores. By the mid-1970s it was beginning to appear that iron ore capacity in the province was excessive, and there was considerable reorganization and retrenchment in the industry.[16] The newer by-product operations were sharply curtailed, with the private firms involved putting much of the blame on the provincial government's pollution-control standards. Most seriously affected were the INCO operations at Sudbury, where output was reduced and expansion plans abandoned. In 1972 Falconbridge Nickel Mines Limited gave up its attempts to bring a similar plant into operation at Sudbury.

Uranium

When the United States developed the atomic bomb during the Second World War, almost overnight a demand for uranium was created. Because of the established mine at Great Bear Lake in the Northwest Territories, from the outset Canada was involved in the supplying of this metal. The subsequent development of uranium-mining in Canada was closely linked to American military requirements.

Because of its strategic importance, the mining, processing, and marketing of uranium was strictly controlled by the federal government. Even prospecting for the metal was controlled, a restriction not lifted until 1947. Attempts to find new uranium mines in Canada were initially confined to the Great Bear Lake region, but when the search proved disappointing, attention shifted to the Lake Athabaska region in northern Saskatchewan. In the early 1950s, a group that had been successful in developing properties in the Lake Athabaska field carried the search to northern Ontario. They eventually found and staked an enormous field in the Algoma region about half-way between Sudbury and Sault Ste Marie. The Joubin-Hirshhorn holdings in what was to become known as the Elliot Lake field were subsequently acquired by the large British mining conglomerate, Rio Tinto, in 1955. Other portions of the field were taken over by Stephen Roman's newly organized Consolidated Denison Mines Limited.[17]

The uranium-mining industry in Ontario boomed in the early 1950s. Within five years eleven mines, several of which were among the largest ever developed, were brought into full production. What made this expansion possible was the determination of the American government to establish an unchallengeable lead in the production of nuclear weapons in the shortest possible time. The most immediate source of supply for uranium was Canada, and the Canadian government co-operated fully in promoting the development of production capacity. Operating through a crown corporation, Eldorado Mining and Refining, the federal government contracted with prospective uranium-mining companies to buy specified quantities of uranium concentrates at guaranteed prices in return for their commitment to supply the product within specified time periods.

By the fall of 1956 Eldorado had signed contracts or given letters of intent to companies operating in the Elliot Lake field covering the sale of more than $1 billion worth of uranium precipitates for delivery by 31 March 1963.[18]

The prices paid under these early contracts were sufficient, it appears, not only to cover the operating costs of the mines, but to enable the companies to recover their entire capital investments.[19] Just how favourable this arrangement would prove to be for the companies involved would depend on their prospects for further sales after the initial contracts ran out. Although there was reason to suspect that U.S. military demand would prove less than infinite, private investors seemed to feel that the industry's future was secure. Several mines, notably the enormous Denison complex, were built with capacities greater than existing contracts warranted. Both the provincial and the federal governments also demonstrated confidence in the future of the industry. There were heavy public as well as private investments in infrastructure, including the elaborately planned and executed model community of Elliot Lake.

While Elliot Lake was booming, a second uranium-mining area was established in east-central Ontario near the town of Bancroft. By the late 1950s four mines and three mills were in operation. Unlike the Elliot Lake project, the Bancroft development was located near well-established transportation and other facilities, and relatively modest investments in infrastructure were required.

Production of uranium precipitates in Ontario peaked in 1959. In that year the United States announced that no further contracts for Canadian uranium would be let after the existing contracts expired in 1963. With no appreciable market yet developed for uranium in civilian uses, the industry appeared to be doomed. Despite the Canadian government's efforts to soften the blow by stretching out production arrangements, the Ontario uranium-mining industry, which produced nearly 80 per cent of total Canadian output of the metal, collapsed.

The local impact was severe, especially in Elliot Lake, which the International Union of Mine, Mill and Smelter Workers referred to as 'the most modern ghost town in history,' when it submitted a brief on the situation to the Ontario government.[20] As hundreds of miners and their families left the new model community, many merchants and other local entrepreneurs were ruined. The elaborate attempt to create a permanent, middle-class community instead of the traditional rough-and-ready mining camp seemed to have backfired, and doubts were raised about the adequacy of the planning procedures by the various agencies, both public and private, which had been involved.

Termination of the U.S. uranium contracts also raised questions about the nature of Canada's economic and political relationships with that country. A new wave of nationalist sentiment in Canada, coinciding with a deterioration in U.S. prestige abroad, and renewed concerns about conservation and the environment, were already prompting a reconsideration of Canada's apparent commitment to non-renewable resource development and reliance on export markets for such commodities. In the particular case of uranium, there was some feeling that Canada had been unfairly used by the Americans. While the unwillingness of the United States to renew the uranium contracts could be explained at least in part by the improvement then taking place in U.S.-Soviet relations, it was also true that by the late 1950s the United States had managed to develop its own uranium-mining industry. By then more than twenty U.S. uranium mines were in operation with a combined daily capacity of more than 20,000 tons of ore.[21]

There were also recriminations at the federal-provincial level in Canada. The Ontario government held the federal authorities responsible for encouraging a boom and failing to ensure a reasonably secure future for the companies and individuals involved. It also suggested that the federal government had allowed its own agency, Eldorado, to continue operations in competition with private producers, whereas Eldorado should have been required to give them its remaining undelivered contracts.[22] Ontario also expressed concern that some of the firms operating in the province might be tempted to accelerate their shutdowns in Ontario and transfer their remaining production to operations they controlled elsewhere in Canada.[23]

While optimists suggested that atomic-power technology would soon create a new demand sufficient to restore the market for Ontario uranium output, it was not until the early 1970s that demand began to pick up. In 1972 shipments of uranium precipitates began to increase, prices rose, and the Elliot Lake mines began to reopen. As producers began to negotiate long-term contracts with atomic power agencies, the market situation appeared likely to reverse, as policy-makers in the province turned their attention to the possibility that provincial sources of uranium might become inadequate to meet future needs.[24]

TABLE 36
Volume and Value of Uranium Production, Ontario, 1955–75

Year	Volume of Production*		Value of Production† (dollars)
	Pounds	Kilograms	
1955			487,054
1956	906,614	411,233	9,361,867
1957	7,970,598	3,615,402	82,940,763
1958	19,970,136	9,058,301	210,149,700
1959	25,492,171	11,563,054	268,529,993
1960	19,793,727	8,978,283	211,983,533
1961	14,970,593	6,790,546	151,060,610
1962	12,805,203	5,808,342	118,283,081
1963	12,770,421	5,792,565	102,951,146
1964	11,805,143	5,354,722	63,606,944
1965	6,825,046	3,095,788	47,234,892
1966	5,875,698	2,665,171	42,758,135
1967	5,450,639	2,472,368	41,418,268
1968	5,361,460	2,431,917	39,163,777
1969			40,307,489
1970	6,676,841	3,028,564	
1971	7,009,985	3,179,675	
1972	8,428,053	3,822,900	
1973	8,114,567	3,680,705	
1974	8,442,966	3,829,664	
1975	10,569,539	4,794,262	

* Volume of production figures for 1955 and 1969 are confidential.
† Value of production is confidential for 1970–5.
SOURCE: MNR, *Ontario Mining Statistics: A Preliminary Compendium*, 1979, 24.1

Silver-Cobalt

The old Cobalt camp, the 'cradle of the Canadian mining industry,' appeared to be near its end in the 1930s. The richest silver veins had been worked out and low world demand for silver made revival seem unlikely. When the Second World War began, however, the fortunes of Cobalt improved because of a growing demand for the cobalt component of its ores. Contracts with the U.S. government permitted some mining to continue through the war years, but because of strong competition from more easily processed African ores, the volume of production remained small.[25]

The Ontario government was pessimistic about the future of Cobalt and stoutly resisted proposals to subsidize operations there. The official position was that such aid would generate unwarranted optimism about the future of the region and discourage workers from relocating to find alternative employment.[26]

After the war the demand for cobalt showed unexpected strength, as new uses

TABLE 37
Volume and Value of Cobalt Production, Ontario, 1939–75

Year	Volume of Production		Value of Production (dollars)
	Pounds	Kilograms	
1939	732,561	332,284	1,213,454
1940	794,359	360,315	1,235,220
1941	263,257	119,411	255,904
1942	83,871	38,043	88,444
1943	175,961	79,814	191,407
1944	36,283	16,457	34,106
1945	109,123	49,497	90,026
1946	75,848	34,404	64,471
1947	578,403	262,359	955,917
1948	1,545,744	701,137	2,624,410
1949	619,065	280,803	952,469
1950	583,806	264,809	964,003
1951	951,607	431,641	1,999,612
1952	1,421,923	644,973	3,226,903
1953	1,602,545	726,902	4,013,077
1954	2,252,965	1,021,927	5,912,997
1955	3,296,270	1,495,162	8,510,314
1956	3,392,543	1,538,831	8,781,626
1957	3,750,596	1,701,241	7,541,258
1958	2,436,064	1,104,980	4,866,767
1959	2,835,684	1,286,244	5,414,246
1960	3,258,401	1,477,985	6,312,921
1961	2,884,420	1,308,350	4,309,912
1962	2,649,193	1,201,653	4,765,808
1963	2,156,732	978,277	4,409,262
1964	2,212,016	1,003,353	4,259,215
1965	2,620,810	1,188,779	5,511,436
1966	2,684,235	1,217,548	5,464,495
1967	2,929,470	1,328,785	5,967,044
1968	3,221,025	1,461,032	6,957,851
1969	2,553,583	1,158,285	5,421,046
1970	3,692,529	1,674,902	8,211,391
1971	3,511,207	1,592,656	7,650,337
1972	2,593,814	1,176,534	6,387,560
1973	2,528,297	1,146,816	6,913,957
1974	2,775,392	1,258,896	8,141,841
1975	2,399,759	1,088,512	10,277,852

SOURCE: MNR, *Ontario Mining Statistics: A Preliminary Compendium*, 9.2

were found for the metal in both military and industrial applications. Silver prices also rose, and the production of silver from ores in the Cobalt field increased from less than 500,000 ounces to more than 4 million ounces between 1945 and 1951. In the early 1950s the Korean War again stimulated the demand for cobalt, which by then was being used to make jet engine alloys, armour-plating, and electronic components. The Canadian government introduced a system of price incentives to promote the production of this metal. Although some cobalt was produced as a by-product of nickel-refining, most of the additional output was supplied by a new smelter built at Cobalt in 1954.[27]

After the incentive program expired in 1954, the Canadian government undertook to purchase limited quantities of the metal on behalf of the United States. When the Korean War ended, output of both cobalt and silver from the Cobalt mines declined once again. Production of these two metals increased at Sudbury, however, and in the 1960s new silver supplies were opened up with the development of base-metal-mining at Manitouwadge and Timmins.

When the huge Kidd Mine of Texas Gulf Sulphur came into production at Timmins in 1967, total silver output in Ontario doubled and in 1969 reached a record level of more than 22 million ounces. By then, silver produced in conjunction with base-metal-mining exceeded that produced from the precious metal ores at Cobalt, and the demise of Cobalt once again appeared imminent.[28]

Nickel-Copper

The strong military demand for nickel during the war made possible a further expansion of the already large Sudbury operations of INCO and Falconbridge. By the fall of 1941 all nickel production in Canada was allocated to war uses, and copper production was sacrificed to permit maximum extraction of nickel from the Sudbury ores. Under the system of wartime controls the producers agreed to expand production at prevailing prices, except for an escalator provision intended to cover 'unavoidable' increases in operating costs. Despite labour shortages, ore lifted increased from approximately 8 million tons in 1939 to nearly 13 million in 1943. Output fell somewhat in the later years of the war, but in 1946 rising prices brought about a new period of expansion which continued through the following decade. In 1947, when nickel, copper, and gold together accounted for more than 75 per cent of the total value of mineral production in Ontario, the value of nickel production exceeded that of gold for the first time since 1920.

Both INCO and Falconbridge undertook major expansion programs at Sudbury in the 1950s. At INCO the main effort went into converting entirely to underground mining, and by 1952 more than 300 miles of underground passages had been developed. The expansion at Falconbridge was facilitated by large contracts the company entered into between 1952 and 1962 to supply nickel, copper, and cobalt to the United States Defense Materials Procurement Agency.

The base metals boom of the 1950s brought Sudbury to record levels of production, but it also stimulated developments elsewhere. One of the most important of these was INCO's own major nickel mining and processing venture

TABLE 38
Volume and Value of Silver Production, Ontario, 1939–75

Year	Volume of production		Value of Production (dollars)
	Troy Ounces	Grams	
1939	4,633,589	144,120,727	1,860,728
1940	5,083,671	158,119,843	1,852,110
1941	4,756,679	147,949,254	1,787,633
1942	4,311,631	134,106,714	1,748,491
1943	3,152,765	98,061,953	1,360,417
1944	2,947,871	91,689,037	1,239,961
1945	2,861,188	88,992,894	1,321,491
1946	2,608,365	81,129,220	2,171,545
1947	2,413,827	75,078,412	1,715,401
1948	2,776,544	86,360,171	2,155,682
1949	2,941,433	91,488,793	2,209,831
1950	4,925,337	153,195,105	4,082,207
1951	6,115,694	190,219,346	5,781,939
1952	6,017,665	187,170,303	5,021,323
1953	5,154,619	160,326,572	4,331,199
1954	5,443,721	169,318,649	4,530,484
1955	6,051,017	188,207,666	5,337,163
1956	6,626,447	206,105,540	5,940,586
1957	6,910,130	214,929,068	6,034,598
1958	9,815,257	305,288,618	8,529,142
1959	10,540,856	327,857,270	9,252,763
1960	11,220,823	349,006,607	9,976,434
1961	8,870,402	275,900,342	8,361,240
1962	9,383,445	291,857,763	10,931,713
1963	9,601,621	298,643,796	13,288,643
1964	9,929,858	308,853,107	13,901,801
1965	10,822,213	336,608,450	15,151,098
1966	10,900,204	339,034,242	15,249,385
1967	14,309,391	445,071,810	24,783,864
1968	21,844,592	679,442,760	50,526,541
1969	22,260,439	692,377,047	42,962,647
1970	19,876,430	618,226,079	36,771,396
1971	18,681,633	581,063,738	29,143,347
1972	19,587,694	609,245,385	32,711,449
1973	19,617,406	610,169,532	49,553,568
1974	17,852,419	555,272,300	82,638,847
1975	14,908,138	463,694,924	67,176,070

SOURCE: MNR, *Ontario Mining Statistics: A Preliminary Compendium*, 1979, 19.3

at Thompson in northern Manitoba. In Ontario the most important new developments were the Texasgulf Sulphur mine near Timmins and the copper-zinc mines opened at Manitouwadge in the north-western part of the province.

The nickel-mining boom slowed in 1958, and after eight years of near capacity

TABLE 39
Volume and Value of Nickel Production, Ontario, 1939–75

Year	Volume of Production		Value of Production (dollars)
	Pounds	Kilograms	
1939	226,110,293	102,561,903	50,922,521
1940	245,563,497	111,385,728	59,804,359
1941	282,280,122	128,040,109	68,644,405
1942	285,312,432	129,415,542	70,001,165
1943	288,078,241	130,670,092	71,670,432
1944	274,656,574	124,582,126	69,214,036
1945	245,146,145	111,196,420	61,982,659
1946	192,132,195	87,149,697	45,386,533
1947	237,256,892	107,617,915	70,780,556
1948	263,257,078	119,411,401	87,409,043
1949	257,379,216	116,745,248	99,351,785
1950	247,317,867	112,181,497	112,292,202
1951	275,806,272	125,103,620	151,217,865
1952	281,117,072	127,512,558	151,666,687
1953	287,385,777	130,355,995	160,491,126
1954	316,019,050	143,343,829	176,556,296
1955	322,322,355	146,202,960	198,489,258
1956	335,152,371	152,022,558	208,099,454
1957	354,792,843	160,931,326	243,518,138
1958	254,286,784	115,342,545	177,168,918
1959	347,929,183	157,818,022	240,053,265
1960	403,300,283	182,933,931	277,924,234
1961	392,435,773	178,005,872	295,423,149
1962	333,163,344	151,120,350	274,219,955
1963	298,178,570	135,251,524	246,252,488
1964	324,187,190	147,048,835	267,764,039
1965	382,566,712	173,529,341	316,332,366
1966	320,428,750	145,344,036	269,461,584
1967	380,117,521	172,418,407	352,238,885
1968	407,493,447	184,835,918	405,168,184
1969	293,561,275	133,157,154	329,076,314
1970	448,509,011	203,440,265	608,428,298
1971	431,506,689	195,728,141	583,946,348
1972	378,855,007	171,845,740	519,935,356
1973	393,293,298	178,394,839	574,786,081
1974	460,879,205	209,051,290	749,782,101
1975	394,836,613	179,094,875	811,328,713

SOURCE: MNR, *Ontario Mining Statistics: A Preliminary Compendium*, 16.3

operation INCO reduced production at Sudbury. Unstable world supply and demand conditions in the 1960s resulted in fluctuating levels of production in Ontario, but a generally upward trend in nickel output continued until the early 1970s. Partly as a result of deliberate attempts by INCO to stabilize its level of operations at Sudbury, nickel production in the province settled down to an annual average of about 400 million pounds for the remainder of the period. By the mid-1970s, however, the long-term outlook for the Ontario nickel-mining industry was bleak. Slower than expected rates of growth in world demand combined with massive investments in nickel-producing capacity abroad threatened to render much of Ontario's nickel-mining capacity obsolete.

Copper production in Ontario continued to increase during the 1960s despite the uncertainties affecting the operations at Sudbury. Until then some 90 per cent of Ontario's copper production had come from the Sudbury mines, but this situation was altered with the development of the base metal operations at Manitouwadge and Timmins. Largely because of the high volume of production at the Kidd Mine, annual copper shipments by Ontario producers in the early 1970s ran at double the annual averages of the 1950s.

One of the peculiarities of the copper-mining industry during the period was the insensitivity of output to declining prices. Part of the explanation may be found in the fact that copper is normally mined as a co-product with other metals. Another possible explanation is that the larger copper-producing firms were willing to accept short-term losses to preserve the market for copper against growing competition from plastics, which were coming into use in plumbing applications, and aluminum, which was gaining some acceptance as a substitute for copper in electrical wiring.[29] One side-effect of this strategy may have been an increase of concentration in the industry, since many small producers found it impossible to survive at the prevailing price levels.[30]

Zinc

There was no significant zinc production in Ontario until 1957, when new mines at Manitouwadge, near the old gold-mining town of Geraldton, north of Lake Superior, began making shipments. Staked by local 'weekend prospectors' in 1953, the copper-silver-lead deposits at Manitouwadge Lake were developed by two companies, Geco and Willroy. A model townsite and the necessary rail and road facilities were provided. Development was rapid and by 1965 a third mine, the Willecho, was brought into production. Until 1967 these mines produced virtually all Ontario's zinc output, which increased from almost nothing in 1953 to more than 165 million pounds in 1966. In 1967 the Kidd Mine of Texasgulf Sulphur began production, and the level of zinc output in the province more than tripled.

The Texasgulf development at Timmins was possibly the most important mining development in Ontario during the post-war period. It established the province as one of the country's principal sources of base metals; it revived the declining mining region around Timmins; and, in conjunction with the new iron-mining industry, it shifted the balance in Ontario's mineral production from precious to base metals. It also broke new ground in the area of public policy.

One of the noteworthy features of the Texasgulf development was that it had

TABLE 40
Volume and Value of Copper Production, Ontario, 1939–75

Year	Volume of Production		Value of Production (dollars)
	Pounds	Kilograms	
1939	328,429,665	148,973,190	32,637,305
1940	347,931,013	157,818,852	34,742,229
1941	333,829,767	151,422,635	33,192,644
1942	308,282,415	139,834,551	30,625,404
1943	277,840,533	126,026,345	32,194,369
1944	285,307,278	129,413,204	33,845,632
1945	239,457,242	108,615,977	29,772,270
1946	179,430,423	81,388,270	22,503,827
1947	227,873,343	103,361,609	46,019,294
1948	240,687,191	109,173,873	53,366,733
1949	226,085,423	102,550,622	44,658,786
1950	234,420,544	106,331,370	54,411,033
1951	257,616,806	116,853,017	70,861,788
1952	250,715,175	113,722,490	70,981,618
1953	261,164,653	118,462,293	77,587,440
1954	281,552,361	127,710,002	81,343,536
1955	292,813,108	132,817,791	107,251,943
1956	312,541,701	141,766,530	128,552,450
1957	343,406,269	155,766,463	98,488,877
1958	284,069,476	128,851,746	71,267,895
1959	376,544,371	170,797,653	110,547,037
1960	412,544,528	187,127,050	123,750,235
1961	423,293,547	192,002,723	122,421,860
1962	377,990,690	171,453,692	116,347,723
1963	357,919,536	162,349,570	112,048,454
1964	395,833,331	179,546,978	131,458,795
1965	432,544,119	196,198,712	161,665,138
1966	405,951,287	184,136,406	181,375,552
1967	552,291,827	250,515,358	261,814,899
1968	581,236,227	263,644,317	278,313,194
1969	477,619,761	216,644,679	244,300,501
1970	590,184,892	267,703,363	340,839,782
1971	604,739,883	274,305,396	317,527,865
1972	579,445,166	262,831,906	293,493,836
1973	574,646,559	260,655,294	365,305,858
1974	625,886,355	283,897,275	483,995,146
1975	568,303,206	257,777,998	361,431,937

SOURCE: MNR, *Ontario Mining Statistics: A Preliminary Compendium*, 10.3

been planned and executed by a single large company which bypassed the traditional involvement of intermediaries until then characteristic of frontier mining development in Canada. While it was greeted as the likely precursor of other successes using modern mine-finding techniques, the Texasgulf development also raised some concerns about the way in which a single large organization, and a foreign-owned one at that, was able to manage and control so closely a project of such magnitude. Welcome as it was, particularly in a depressed region of the province, the project challenged the provincial government's newly strengthened resolve to ensure that natural resource development would be seen materially to benefit the province and its people more than had been the case in the past. The central issue was the extent to which the ores mined would be processed in Ontario. Given the enormous growth potential foreseen for zinc, the situation could appropriately be compared with the struggle over nickel-refining earlier in the century.

The position taken by the provincial government was seemingly unambiguous. It insisted that the company build a smelter to process zinc concentrates in Ontario, and it expressed a strong interest in having such a smelter located in the Timmins area. But it also indicated a willingness to grant the company large inducements to get it to comply with these wishes. Special concessions with respect to allowances for writing off pre-production expenses, special electric power rates, and special ONR freight rates were offered.[31] Many of these provisions were subsequently embodied in legislation governing mining development generally in Ontario.[32] The Texasgulf smelter was constructed at Timmins and began producing in 1972. By the mid-1970s some 40 per cent of the zinc mined in Ontario was being refined to the metal stage in the province.

Platinum Group Metals

A large number of metals have been produced in Ontario as by-products of nickel-copper-refining. The metals of the platinum group (platinum, palladium, iridium, ruthenium, rhodium, and osmium) produced in the province made Ontario the world's third most important source of these materials (after the USSR and South Africa). The level of production through the post-Second World War period was relatively stable, averaging about 300,000 ounces annually during the early 1950s and increasing to about 400,000 ounces per year by the end of the period. Virtually all the output was exported for refining.

Non-metallic Minerals

During the period salt was the most important non-metallic mineral mined in Ontario, accounting for about half the total value of such products. Others included arsenic, asbestos, barite, calcite, gemstones, gypsum, nephaline syenite, phosphate, silica, sulphur, and talc. In total these non-metallic minerals accounted for less than 3 per cent of the total value of mineral production in the province, a figure that remained roughly constant over the entire period.

TABLE 41
Volume and Value of Zinc Production, Ontario 1939–75

Year	Volume of Production		Value of Production (dollars)
	Pounds	Kilograms	
1939	0	0	0
1940	0	0	0
1941	1,100,949	499,382	37,553
1942	4,710,394	2,136,598	160,671
1943	3,299,812	1,496,769	131,992
1944	2,429,176	1,101,855	104,455
1945	237,799	107,863	15,314
1946	42,628	19,335	3,329
1947	0	0	0
1948	0	0	0
1949	0	0	0
1950	0	0	0
1951	0	0	0
1952	744,920	337,890	130,630
1953	171,787	77,921	20,546
1954	1,420,048	644,122	170,122
1955	3,095,640	1,404,158	422,555
1956	2,454,297	1,113,250	364,218
1957	22,591,677	10,247,412	2,731,334
1958	92,478,339	41,947,468	10,061,643
1959	89,963,215	40,806,627	11,011,498
1960	90,459,368	41,031,679	12,076,326
1961	103,874,146	47,116,520	13,077,755
1962	126,264,684	57,272,697	15,278,027
1963	132,939,970	60,300,556	16,989,728
1964	144,152,666	65,386,549	20,426,433
1965	121,349,121	55,043,035	18,323,817
1966	164,789,837	74,747,412	24,883,265
1967	537,064,861	243,608,523	77,820,698
1968	693,515,176	314,573,192	97,785,640
1969	720,571,567	326,845,764	109,743,049
1970	680,484,067	308,662,380	108,401,112
1971	731,450,664	331,780,440	122,371,696
1972	807,219,666	366,148,681	153,944,862
1973	912,729,270	414,007,032	220,387,609
1974	960,117,440	435,501,945	335,080,986
1975	740,427,997	335,852,489	277,660,498

SOURCE: MNR, *Ontario Mining Statistics: A Preliminary Compendium*, 26.2

Public Policy and the Mining Industry in Ontario

The resource development policies of the provincial government in the period prior to the 1940s have been studied in detail by the historian H.V. Nelles, who sought to show that successive Ontario governments were zealous in promoting development. 'As far as help with getting on with the job was concerned,' Nelles writes, 'no developer could ask for a better, more attentive partner than the government of Ontario.'[33] He also found that when the government intervened, for example, by imposing processing requirements on mining companies, it did so in response to business pressure. When the government regulated the companies, it became complicit, and the regulated group seemed to have 'greater success in bringing the regulator under control than the other way around.'[34] While some of the subsequent experience covered in the present volume is difficult to interpret in these terms, notably the government's apparent indifference to the problems of the gold-mining companies and some of the iron ore promoters early in the period, it remains true that government policy towards mining development was more often supportive than not. It would be remarkable if it had not been, for there was a consensus that mining was good – it created jobs, earned foreign-exchange credits, and yielded at least some small amounts of public revenue. Business interests, organized labour, municipal officials, and provincial administrators behaved as if they believed they would benefit from having more rather than less mining activity in the province. To the extent that anyone was concerned about mining in the 1940s, attention focused on the matter of fraudulent securities manipulation. Taxation was also a matter of concern, not because it was too light, but because it was too heavy. The provincial government also predictably complained from time to time that too large a share of mining revenues was going to the federal government instead of to the province.[35]

In the provincial legislature at the end of the war the government was more frequently attacked for not doing enough for the industry than for doing too much. The CCF did criticize the government for allowing the gold-mining industry to develop too rapidly, but its complaint was that this was causing 'unbalanced development,' and its general position on the matter appeared to be that 'vigorous, aggressive and practical exploitation' of mineral resources in Ontario was called for.[36] The government defended itself by claiming that it was doing as much for the mining industry as it could reasonably be expected to. In the budget speech of 1946 Mr Frost was at some pains to convince the legislature that the government was indeed spending more to support mining than it was collecting in taxes from the industry.[37] Some time in the 1950s, however, the climate of opinion with respect to mining began to change.

One of the first signs of change came in connection with a familiar complaint: that there was insufficient processing of minerals in the province. What is of interest is that the complainer was not a known spokesman for private business interests in the prvince, but one of the able representatives of the Labour Progressive party. During the 1953 budget debate he urged that the mining act be amended 'so that the iron ore dug up in this province be not exported so completely as is now the case.'[38] Two years later the Labour Progressives were still pursuing the issue, deploring the government's failure to end the 'sell-out' of natural resources and the subsequent 'exporting of jobs.'[39] American interests, it was suggested, were motivated more by the desire to gain control of Canadian resources than by considerations of profit; their strategy was to construct a market for their own surplus production in Canada and to this end sought to keep the country undeveloped.

While this was very much a minority position at the time, easily dismissed as predictable Marxist rhetoric, the question of how much Ontario was actually netting from mining and other resource developments in the province began to attract attention. In the provincial legislature, the CCF led the way, attacking the government for being too generous in its treatment of the mining companies, many of which were foreign owned. The socialists also argued that depreciation allowances and other tax concessions encouraged excess investment and waste, distorted the allocation of capital and labour resources, and promoted monopolization.[40] At the national level, the Resources for Tomorrow Conference in 1961 provided a larger forum for the discussion of issues relating to natural resources policy.

During the 1960s the taxation of mining and other non-renewable natural resource extracting operations was closely examined by a number of academic economists and two major commissions of inquiry, one at the national level and the other in Ontario. The intellectual apparatus employed was not new, some of the basic concepts employed deriving from the classical economics of the early nineteenth century, but the application of these ideas was now bolstered by empirical research and quantification of the values involved. What was at issue was simply the extent of the benefits realized by society from the development of natural resources and the distribution of these benefits between the owners and the developers. Because nearly all mineral and other non-renewable resources in Ontario were owned by the province, the latter question translated into whether or not the public was receiving a fair share of the returns arising from the development of its natural resources. In more technical terms, were the royalties and taxes imposed on mining companies by the provincial government capturing an appropriate share of the economic rent generated through the use of the public's resources?[41]

The studies referred to generally answered this question in the negative. Eric Kierans, one of the major contributors to the subject argued pursuasively that the combination of federal tax concessions to mining firms and the tendency for the provinces to compete with one another to attract mining firms resulted in most of the economic rents arising from the utilization of the public's resources being left in the hands of the private operators.

Each province vies with its neighbor to attract the large corporation that will employ a few hundred more workers in the process of extracting its wealth. In this contest, the initiative and the flexibility lies with the corporation. They can pick and choose between the offers, compare the tax exemptions and the subsidies and prolong the bidding until the last concession has been gained. By then little of the surplus remains to the owners. The provinces, competing with each other, have given away their right to the super-profits, i.e., profits in excess of the returns needed to attract capital and which economists call 'economic rent.'[42]

A similar conclusion was reached by the federal Royal Commission on Taxation (the Carter Commission), appointed in 1962. Its detailed studies led to a strong recommendation that federal tax concessions to the mining industry be greatly reduced, largely on the grounds that they were in effect causing far too many labour and capital resources to be allocated to mining, when they could be yielding higher real returns in other uses. The Ontario Royal Commission on Taxation made similar recommendations and for the same kinds of reasons in its report to the Ontario government in 1967. It pointed out that because of the nature of economic rents, 'in theory, if it wished to do so, the province might tax away the full amount of ... economic rent without adverse effect upon the allocation of resources to mining.'[43] It recommended that a special mines profits tax be imposed 'as a means of securing for the province a share of the economic rent for the use of its resources.'[44]

The mining companies were outraged by such a challenge to their established position, and the larger ones hastened to enlist the aid of economists to destroy the credibility of the analysis upon which the new policy initiatives were based.[45] Such efforts were not very effective, however, and the provincial government announced in its budget speech of March 1969 that 'The government believes ... the mining industry has been taxed too lightly in relation to the taxes borne by other industries and sectors of the Ontario economy.' It proposed therefore to increase the mining tax 'to correct this defect and to secure for all the people of Ontario the revenues which should logically accrue to them from this province's natural resources.'[46] While the tax increase announced in 1969 failed to satisfy all critics, some of whom continued to claim that mining taxes were still too low, within the next few years the higher provincial taxes and the changes in federal tax policy introduced following the report of the Carter Commission threw the mining community into a state of shock, a condition aggravated by the imposition of anti-pollution regulations and renewed demands that higher levels of processing be done on mineral products before export.

It seems that the government remained unshaken by the protests of the mining companies; for in 1974 it pushed its new approach a step further. It increased the mining profits tax, removed the mine and mill allowance under the capital tax, and disallowed for purposes of calculating the corporation tax the existing mining tax and royalties exemptions.

These changes coincided with the OPEC oil shocks and the beginning of the great slow-down in economic activity generally in the world economy. Not surprisingly the level of output and expenditures on exploration work in the Ontario mining industry fell.

Early attempts to assess the extent to which the decline in activity in the industry was attributable to the policy changes were inconclusive.[47] What was becoming clear, however, was that provincial economic policy-making was a more complicated matter than had been the case in the past. The shortcomings of piecemeal policy-making were becoming increasingly evident. The old view that more growth of any kind was desirable was now being challenged. It appeared necessary to defend specific policy measures by showing how they would affect not only their specific target but the rest of the economy as well. In the face of the shrinking mining sector, the older habits of thought would have led to measures to stimulate it. Now the question was, 'How large a mining industry should the province have?' A larger mining industry was not necessarily desirable if it meant that the manufacturing sector would be smaller. Special pleading supported by partial analysis survived, of course, with private firms, individual communities, and even government departments attempting to demonstrate that they or their clients deserved favourable treatment.[48]

Yet by the end of the period the more comprehensive view was becoming better established, suggesting that the level of understanding of fundamental economic principles was indeed rising. Even the once sacrosanct belief in the virtues of further processing was held up to question. Increased processing in the province would entail a cost in the sense that the resources so employed would not be available for use in alternative kinds of production. Just because it was economical to mine certain metals in the province did not mean that it would also be economical to process them there. If the objective was to maximize the total value added from all economic activities in the province, it did not logically follow that value added should be maximized in any particular industry or group of industries. The application of such elementary economic logic was recommended by the Ontario Economic Council, which noted in the particular case of mineral resources, 'A decision to undertake further processing does not automatically guarantee a net economic benefit.'[49] What remained unresolved in this area of economic policy as in others, however, was how the desired overall mix of economic activities in the province should be determined – by the unguided operation of highly imperfect market forces, as implied in much of the economic analysis being done, or in some other way?

Forestry

Ontario's once-extensive forests have been utilized to supply raw material for two main types of primary manufacturing activity, sawmilling and pulp and

TABLE 42
Primary Forest Production, Ontario, 1939–75

Year	Cubic Feet ('000)	Year	Cubic Feet ('000)
1939	474,388		
1944	461,507	1960	541,329
1945	479,298	1961	494,048
1946	564,501	1962	519,414
1947	613,919	1963	535,077
1948	654,268	1964	569,767
1949	632,202	1965	567,131
1950	516,316	1966	600,922
1951	600,396	1967	607,085
1952	564,349	1968	590,964
1953	504,180	1969	621,645
1954	497,261	1970	593,315
1955	542,031	1971	559,340
1956	547,354	1972	613,100
1957	565,010	1973	651,400
1958	483,544	1974	666,300
1959	531,528	1975	502,000

SOURCES: Statistics Canada (DBS), *Operations in the Woods, 1950* (25-201), N11; 1939–49; *Ontario Statistics, 1977*, vol. II, table 18.1, 521

paper-making. These activities will be discussed in the following chapter along with other manufacturing industries. Here attention will be confined to the basic operations carried on in the woods, the production of 'round wood.'

More than in other parts of Canada, the forest-based industries have been strongly integrated vertically, with much of the activity in the woods directly controlled by the firms subsequently utilizing the raw material produced. While raw wood has been exported from the province, particularly pulpwood and to a lesser extent saw logs, public policy has generally sought to discourage this practice. In the post-Second World War period there was also some importing of wood as declining domestic supplies of certain species combined with lower production costs in other parts of the continent led wood-using industries in the province to turn to alternative sources of supply.

Over the period 1939 to 1975 the total volume of primary forest production in Ontario showed no discernible trend. The amount of wood cut annually in the early 1970s was the same as in the late 1940s. However, several important changes were made in the methods of producing wood during the period. Although small contractors, settlers, and others operating on private land continued to use traditional labour-intensive methods, productivity was greatly increased by the availability of lightweight but powerful chainsaws and, particularly after the Second World War, various kinds of motorized vehicles capable of operating in rough terrain. Larger operators, especially the logging divisions of the major wood-processing companies turned to new and often very expensive, mechanical tree-harvesting machinery, although these innovations came rather more slowly to Ontario than they had come to British Columbia, where the size and type of timber being harvested made the use of such equipment even more economical.

Mechanization also changed the way labour was used in the industry. There was a general trend after the war to longer work weeks and less seasonal variation in employment levels. The effects of this pattern were particularly noticeable in north-eastern Ontario, where the forest operations had traditionally employed large numbers of seasonal workers, many of them drawn from adjacent parts of Quebec. With the development of year-round logging, numbers of such workers moved with their families to live permanently in Ontario, settling in towns that began to lose their earlier frontier character and take on features similar to small towns in the south.[50] Year-round logging also created some new problems, however, particularly in areas where summer logging operations interfered with recreational uses of the forests.

Road construction was another important factor influencing primary forest operations during the period. While river-driving of logs continued in some areas because of its cheapness, an expanding road network in northern Ontario made it possible for operators to use heavy diesel trucks to get wood from the logging sites directly to the mills. In addition to the provincial government's general road-building efforts, special forest access roads were in some cases built and maintained by the Department of Lands and Forests. Annual expenditures for such purposes in the late 1960s and early 1970s averaged $1.5–2 million dollars.[51] Several hundred miles of roads were also built under the federal 'Roads to Resources' program of the late 1950s.

While the level and type of activity carried on in primary woods operations in the province were affected by such developments and to some extent by changing patterns of market demand, the critical issues relating to the industry during the period had to do with the management of the resource base itself. It was already apparent in the early 1940s that the days when timber could be considered a plentiful resource in Ontario were nearing their end. Most of the forest in southern Ontario was gone, cleared to increase the supply of agricultural land, leaving only isolated woodlots, many of which were in a sad state of neglect and deterioration. Beyond the more populated part of the province there was a wide band of commercial forest, almost entirely publicly owned, which continued to support most of the sawmilling operations. The prime species for producing lumber, the red and white pine, were becoming scarce, however, and little progress was being made in developing other species for such uses. The growing scarcity of saw wood was aggravated by the presence throughout most of this area of the pulp and paper companies, which through a complex series of agreements with the provincial government had obtained cutting rights on large tracts of forest. The vast pulpwood concessions were justified on the grounds that the companies required the assurance of adequate wood supplies to support the required scale of investment in manufacturing facilities. Despite provisions in these agreements to reserve timber suitable for use as saw logs, the pulp and paper companies preferred to cut everything for pulping, and they strongly resisted the attempts by lumbermen to enter the concession areas to cut saw logs.

Further north, the forests were still little developed in 1940. In remote regions, such as north and west of the Lakehead, there remained large stands of virgin forest, reminiscent of the conditions found in central Ontario in the nineteenth century.

The policies of the provincial government with respect to the utilization of its forest resources were the subject of much debate and controversy. The government had become heavily involved in the disastrous financial affairs of the pulp and paper companies in the 1930s and was faced with the thankless task of trying to resolve the difficulties faced by the large Abitibi organization, then in receivership. The Department of Lands and Forests itself was in disorder, and critics of the administration charged that the department was 'rotten to the core,' although a sympathetic history of the department claims that it was simply 'encumbered by a structure adequate in the 1890's, but in the 1930's overloaded with responsibilities and functions unheard of forty years before.'[52] The Conservatives, in opposition, were demanding an inquiry into the state of the forest industry and the department. There were even suggestions that the government should try to take timber administration 'out of politics' by turning it over to an independent agency modelled on the Hydro-Electric Power Commission.[53] While the Commission recommendation subsequently resurfaced from time to time, the immediate effort at reform in this area of the government's responsibility involved reorganization of the existing departmental structure. Much of the work was done by the new deputy minister, F.A. MacDougall, who sought to restore the department's credibility by establishing its operations on a 'professional' basis, thereby (according to the department's official history) removing 'the suspicion of corruption and incompetence that hung over the Department' and demonstrating that control had been brought back from the business interests involved to the government.[54]

This proved to be a formidable undertaking. In the eyes of MacDougall, the root of the problem lay in the fact that power in the industry had shifted away from the old, well-established lumbering families, such as the Gillies and the Booths, to the new pulp and paper companies. While the former had been cooperative and friendly towards the provincial government, the latter, MacDougall found, were antagonistic, bringing with them American attitudes and practices which MacDougall found inimical to the established forms of business-government relations in Ontario. For MacDougall, the struggle in resource administration was between a department dedicated to managing the forests as a trust on behalf of the people of the province against an industry now dominated by a group of hostile foreigners. American capital had built much of the pulp and paper industry of Ontario, American foresters had been brought in to run the logging operations, and the loyalty of the latter, MacDougall believed, was only to their bosses. They persistently resisted the efforts of the department to bring the forests under long-term management and, again in MacDougall's view, throughout the 1940s were largely responsible for making the government's efforts in this respect ineffective.[55]

Unhappily, not all the lumbermen in the province were co-operative either, although again most of the trouble appears to have been with another newcomer, an American lawyer, E.E. (Eddie) Johnson, who was well-connected with both the logging business and the Ontario Liberals. In the early 1940s Johnson devised a plan to develop a large sawmilling operation at the Lakehead using saw logs taken from pulp concessions in accordance with the regulations that reserved large-diameter trees on these concessions for the crown. His scheme had been accepted by the Hepburn government, which assured Johnson's financial backers that timber would be made available, other than spruce and balsam pulpwood, to support a sawmill to be built at the Lakehead by one of Johnson's firms, the Great Lakes Lumber Company. The province would benefit, Mr Hepburn claimed, because the plan would promote the development of sawmilling based on species other than the depleted white and red pine.[56] The federal government was also interested in the project, and C.D. Howe himself urged Johnson on, suggesting that he should try to establish 'permanent outlets' in the United States for Canadian lumber products and at the same time contribute to the war effort in Canada by increasing the domestic production of lumber.[57]

The pulp and paper concessionaires affected by Johnson's plan were less enthusiastic. They insisted that they could hardly be expected to manage the resources assigned to them unless they had exclusive cutting rights on their limits. It was obvious, however, that they had every incentive to waste wood by pulping large logs along with the small.

The change in government in 1943 brought little change in the forestry policies of the province. Many of the worst practices continued to be tolerated and in some cases may have been encouraged in the effort to meet short-term war requirements for wood products. Relations between the government and the pulp and paper companies continued to be strained. When the provincial and federal governments joined forces in an attempt to increase lumber production, the pulpwood companies became less co-operative than ever. Even faced with direct orders to make saw logs available to lumber-makers, they resisted, complaining that to do so would interfere with their own operations. But despite this unhappy relationship, when the war ended and producers found themselves facing unexpected strong markets for their products, the government appeared eager to promote expansion of the industry. Several large new pulp and paper operations were launched in the immediate post-war period based on timber concessions once controlled by companies that had for one reason or another abandoned them. The limits once occupied by the Pulpwood Supply Company were taken over by the Kimberley-Clark Paper Company, the General Timber Company limits by the Marathon Paper Company, the old Espanola operation of Abitibi by the Kalamazoo Vegetable Parchment Company, and the Lake Sulphite limits by the Brampton Paper Company. The latter redevelopment was hailed by the Department of Lands and Forests as a victory in its efforts to stabilize the situation at the Lakehead, where the struggle among various timber interests continued into the post-war years.[58]

The continuing uncertainty about forest policy was an embarrassment for the Drew government during the election campaign of 1945, and upon its return to office Drew appointed a Royal Commission on Forestry (the Kennedy Commission) to 'investigate, inquire into and report upon the forest resources of Ontario and their conservation, management, development and beneficial utilization for all purposes.' The professional foresters in the Department of Lands and Forests were initially dismayed when the government chose Major-General Howard Kennedy to head the new commission. Kennedy's background included involvement in the logging industry, and there was little reason to suspect that his approach would be anything other than the 'cut and get out' attitude characteristic of others in the industry. He had also been associated with what the department considered one of the least co-operative pulp and paper companies in the business, the Ontario Paper Company, which was a wholly owned subsidiary of the McCormick newspaper empire in the United States.

The Kennedy Commission, however, proved to be more impartial and sympathetic to the objectives of 'scientific' forest management than expected. The commission's inquiry and Kennedy's own notes recording his impressions of the areas he visited depict a sad record of waste and mismanagement. At Pembroke and Algonquin he found no evidence of forest management on a sustained yield basis and noted that seed trees were left only because of the inefficiency of the loggers. At Kenora he found evidence of high-grading and cutting of good jackpine and spruce for firewood. At Timmins he was dismayed by the carelessness of the operators and found barren wastes left behind wherever forest operations had been carried on. At the Lakehead, 'wastefulness was everywhere evident,' and the best resources that had existed at the turn of the century were now destroyed as a result of high-grading, fire, and disease. Many of these situations he attributed to a lack of management control. Not only was the department unable to control the companies, but the latter in turn appeared to have little control over their workers.

Kennedy proposed a revolutionary remedy. He suggested that all existing agreements and permits be terminated and that all the timber lands in the province be reallocated among twelve companies, which would be responsible for cutting and managing the timber resources on concessions laid out to correspond to the natural watersheds. These companies would then distribute the cut wood to the various wood-using industries according to their needs. A board representing these users and the provincial government would be set up to ensure that supplies were fairly allocated. In this way the tendency for the existing operators to overcut and waste wood could be eliminated. It would also be possible to rationalize the geographic distribution of logging operations to make better use of species that under the existing arrangements were often wasted because they were remote from the mills operated by the company doing the logging.

The public received these proposals favourably when the Kennedy Commission reported in 1946. There were approving comments in the press about the proposed 'new deal for forestry' and for at least a year there was extensive public discussion in the province about the need for improved management of the forest resources and the extent to which Ontario had fallen behind the countries of northern Europe in this respect. The provincial government's reception of the report was cordial, and many of Kennedy's more specific recommendations were eventually incorporated into provincial forest policy. But the general plan advanced for reorganizing logging in the province proved too radical.

The government's strongest measures following the Kennedy inquiry had to do with the old question of pulpwood exports. In 1947 it announced that it would restrict exports of spruce and balsam pulpwood cut under licence on crown land with the ultimate object of eliminating such exports within a period of ten years. This policy had only lukewarm support within the Lands and Forests bureaucracy, where the prevailing opinion was that restrictions on export of pulp logs was justifiable only if the combined cut for domestic and export purposes exceeded the productive capacity of the province's forests – a situation the Division of Timber Management in the Department of Lands and Forests did not believe was imminent.[59] The policy was endorsed, however, by the Advisory Committee to the Minister of Lands and Forests, which had been established on the recommendation of the Kennedy Commission. Opponents of the policy, including the pulp and paper companies, argued that exports of pulp provided a hedge against unemployment which might arise from recessions in the domestic economy; that restriction of such exports represented a 'loss of business' to the province; that any surplus over the allowable cut would be wasted if exports were curtailed; and that if the object of the policy was to encourage more American companies to locate mills in Ontario, it was futile, because they were now more interested in other parts of the continent.[60]

The government did not retreat from its general position with respect to the export of pulpwood, but as the end of the ten-year period approached, it decided that it would 'retain the flexibility' of determining the appropriate level of exports of raw material on a year-to-year basis.

The province's overall forest policy was outlined in some detail by the premier, Mr Frost, in 1950. It was the government's purpose, he indicated, to provide adequate protection to existing forest areas to ensure a continuing yield; to make sure that forest resources were fully and wisely used; to develop, conserve, and improve forests by the latest methods in research and management; and to regenerate areas that had been cut over or used up.[61] Progress over the next twenty-five years in achieving these goals was mixed at best. The fire control system, which had been organized on a systematic basis after the disastrous Mississagi fire of 1948, was steadily elaborated and achieved some success in controlling certain kinds of situations. Protecting the forests against insect damage was also pursued, but most of the effort appears to have come from the federal government. Ontario was one of the first provinces, however, to experiment with large-scale aerial spraying of insecticides, which for some years appeared to be a particularly promising way of controlling insects. By the 1960s, however, the ecological effects of such activity were becoming a matter of concern, and there were growing doubts about its long-term consequences and effectiveness.

The possibilities of making 'full and wise use' of the existing forests were strengthened somewhat in the 1950s through a consolidation and simplification of the Crown Timber Act and the regulations for granting timber rights. Provision was made for imposing penalties on operators found guilty of wasteful practices, and the perennial problem of making the pulp companies leave large-diameter timber for sawmill operators was again addressed. The pulp companies were now to cut such timber themselves for sale or exchange to established producers of lumber, ties, and poles. While there was at least token compliance with the department requirements in this respect, even that was achieved only with frequent exhortations and reminders.[62]

Implementing a sustained-yield forest management policy was the most difficult of the government's declared forest policy objects and the one that appears in retrospect least likely to be realized. When the government introduced a white paper on forest management in the legislature in 1954, it was acknowledged that in many parts of the province the rate of cutting was either well above or well below the level at which the rate of forest growth would be balanced with the desired level of utilization. In the more accessible regions spruce and red pine were being severely overcut. If the existing rate of utilization continued, the white paper predicted, the red and white pine supply would be exhausted by the early 1970s. Similarly, spruce pulpwood cutting appeared to be near its maximum and the white paper predicted that the spruce pulpwood industry would soon meet the same fate as the white pine saw log industry had met early in the century. The problem was that instead of being regenerated, the disappearing stands of spruce were being replaced with poplar and other inferior species. While such overcutting was prevalent in the southern regions, however, in the northern areas forests were being underutilized, particularly in the case of the balsam and jackpine species.

A number of measures were outlined in the 1954 white paper to remedy these conditions, the most significant of which was a program by which the logging companies would be held responsible for reforesting cut-over crown lands.[63] Within the next ten years it became apparent that the private operators were not doing the job and that little progress had been made towards regenerating the provincial forests. The government thereupon determined that responsibility for reforestation should be assigned to the Department of Lands and Forests. Under the new arrangements the department would plan reforestation programs and then arrange with private operators to carry out the work on a cost-sharing basis. This system did not work either. By the late 1960s the reforestation program was still clearly inadequate to bring the forests into anything approaching a sustained-yield state. The reasons were not difficult to discover. The private operators had the men and equipment necessary to do large-scale reforestation but no commercial incentive to do it. The provincial government wanted the work done but lacked the means to do it. And even the workers involved in the industry, who understood that their jobs depended upon the resource-base being maintained, preferred the work of cutting trees to planting them. Reforestation work was understandably unpopular, because it was considered to be 'back-breaking and poorly paid.'[64] By the mid-1970s the government was once again attempting to develop a reforestation program in which the work would be done by the operating companies themselves. In the budget speech of 1975 the treasurer announced that a 50 per cent rebate on taxes would be allowed to companies engaged in managing forest properties. The department was at the same time developing plans to offer automatically renewable 'evergreen licences' to companies willing to assume responsibility for regeneration and to meet regular performance audits conducted by the ministry. The policy cycle had once again come full circle.

9 Manufacturing

Manufacturing in Ontario comprises a broad spectrum of activities ranging from the production of steel and other heavy industrial goods to a great variety of finished consumer products, such as processed foods, clothing, and household equipment. These activities may be classified in different ways. The most common approach is to distinguish between 'primary' operations, which entail only rudimentary processing of raw materials, and 'secondary' manufacturing, which yields end products ready for sale to final users.[1] Primary operations usually rely upon domestic resources and sell their output in foreign markets. They are typically large-scale, capital-intensive enterprises which tend to locate near the sources of their principal raw materials. Metal-smelting, sawmilling, and the pulp and paper industry are good examples. Secondary manufacturing operations, by contrast, are often dependent upon raw materials from outside the province and their sales tend to be concentrated in domestic markets which are often protected by tariffs. The plants engaged in secondary manufacturing tend to locate near the centre of their market area rather than near sources of supply. Textiles, clothing, electrical appliances, furniture, and automobiles are examples.

While this classification system has flaws, it is well suited to the discussion of certain policy issues relating to the manufacturing sector in Canada. Just as the relative expansion of manufacturing generally has been taken as evidence of economic progress, the growth of secondary or 'higher' levels of manufacturing activity has been valued as an indication of further progress. This view was implicit in Canadian commercial policy from the mid-nineteenth century on. Whether or not much of the manufacturing activity that subsequently developed in Canada was the result of the protective tariff is a matter of continuing debate among Canadian economic historians, but what is beyond dispute is that the intention of policy was to cause Canada to have a larger manufacturing sector than it was thought likely to have otherwise. By the mid-1970s attention was being given to the possibility that yet another level of manufacturing activity was developing, the 'high technology' industries, and that policy would have to be used to ensure that Canada did not fall too far behind other countries in developing such lines of production.

TABLE 43
Value of Manufacturing Production, Ontario, 1939–75

Year	Current $ ('000)	Constant $ (1935–9 = 100) ('000)	Constant $ (1971 = 100) ('000)
1939	791,117	776,366	–
1942	1,669,191	1,349,386	–
1945	1,719,951	1,325,078	–
1950	3,068,142	1,454,096	–
1955	4,426,655	1,971,784	–
1960	5,215,229	2,153,274	6,344,561
1965	7,881,825	3,016,389	9,143,649
1970	10,524,756	3,527,063	10,728,599
1974	18,128,835	3,963,453	13,108,341
1975	18,357,809	3,643,868	11,943,923

NOTE: Data are not consistent over the period shown. The current dollar totals are for 'Census Value Added by Manufacture' in 1939–60 and for 'Census Value Added: Manufacturing Activity' thereafter, which makes the data from 1960 on slightly lower in value than they would have been if the earlier definition was applied throughout. There were also changes in concept of 'manufacturing establishments' in the period from 1957 to 1962 which affect the data to some extent. See Leacy, ed., *Historical Statistics of Canada*, 2nd ed., the introduction to section R. The constant dollar estimates are based on the Wholesale Price Index for 'Fully and Chiefly Manufactured' goods, which results in lower constant dollar values, particularly in the later period, than is appropriate. The values shown in column 4 are obtained by applying the more suitable Industry Selling Price Index for manufacturing industries, which is available only for the period since 1956.

SOURCE: Leacy, ed., *Historical Statistics of Canada*, 2nd ed., R97, K45, R91

The events of the 1939–75 period did little to alter the established pattern of manufacturing activity in Canada. Ontario retained its pre-eminence as the major manufacturing province. The province continued to benefit from its proximity to major markets, from the organization of the transportation system in the country, and from its ease of access to a variety of productive inputs. Manufacturing output in Ontario expanded in step with the growth of the national economy. There were signs that manufacturing in the province was becoming better integrated and that some of the gaps in the manufacturing sector were being filled in by, for example, the growth of the chemicals subsector and other new industries, which reduced the need for other Ontario producers to rely upon imported production inputs. But not all the changes taking place during the period were favourable. The locational advantages that had favoured Ontario in the past continued to attract new industries to the province, but there were indications that these considerations were weakening. Certain kinds of manufacturing activity developing in the post-Second World War period had different kinds of locational requirements, and this fact was reflected in a more rapid growth of some types of manufacturing in outlying regions of the country. In Ontario there was increasing concern, for example, with the extent to which petrochemical-based industry was being attracted to western Canada.

Another source of worry in the province was the change in commercial policy in Canada after the war. While federal trade policies continued to support the established industries in central Canada, the movement to freer trade, the development of the European Economic Community and other trading blocks, and the emergence of Japan and south-east Asia as major producers of clothing, footwear, and consumer electronics created increasing uncertainty about the future of many Ontario producers of secondary manufactured goods.

The established pattern of extensive foreign ownership and control of the manufacturing industries was also a source of uneasiness during the period. The issues were complex, but the debate over foreign ownership during the 1960s and 1970s raised fundamental questions about the adequacy of the manufacturing system as it had developed in Canada. A spate of studies and reports suggested that Canadian manufacturing was weakly based, excessively dependent upon primary processing for export, and ill equipped to maintain, let alone improve, its position with respect to the production of high-unit-value finished commodities for sale in even the domestic market. Many of these perceived deficiencies were attributed by some observers to the extent of foreign ownership in the manufacturing sector.

Such worries dominated the literature and policy debates of the period, undermining the surface impression of growth and vitality created by the absolute increases in output and by the relatively good performance of manufacturing in relation to the rest of the economy.

During the Depression production of manufactured goods in Ontario had fallen to a low of just over $465 million in 1933 but by 1939 had already recovered to more than $791 million. The increasing demand associated with the Second World War then stimulated a remarkable growth of output, which was briefly interrupted towards the end of the war but otherwise lasted well into the 1950s. The data on manufacturing production from the 1950s through the remainder of the period are difficult to interpret because of changes in industry classification and the high rates of inflation that occurred, especially in the 1970s.[2] But the general trend is clear. In constant dollar terms, the value of manufacturing output in Ontario dropped sharply during the recession of 1959, but thereafter increased slowly but steadily, with only a brief interruption in 1970, until 1974 when it reached a peak for the period of over $13 billion, slightly more than twice the 1956 value. In 1975 the value of manufacturing production in Ontario fell sharply to under $12 billion.[3]

The growth of employment in manufacturing was strong during the early part of the period. The number of jobs available in Ontario factories increased rapidly in the early 1940s and reached a wartime peak in 1943. Manufacturing employment sagged briefly near the end of the war but then grew steadily until the recession of the late 1950s. The recovery of the economy in the early 1960s initiated a new period of growth in manufacturing which lasted, with only brief

TABLE 44
Manufacturing Establishments and Total Employment, Ontario, 1939–75

Year	Establishments	Employees ('000)	Year	Establishments	Employees ('000)
1939	9,824	319	1958	11,858	599
1940	10,040	373	1959	11,727	609
1941	10,250	468	1960	12,090	594
1942	10,711	543	1961	12,419	639
1943	10,587	570	1962	12,585	663
1944	10,730	564	1963	12,489	691
1945	10,869	518	1964	12,781	729
1946	11,424	598	1965	12,766	774
1947	11,860	538	1966	12,986	820
1948	12,118	552	1967	13,076	818
1949	12,951	557	1968	12,932	811
1950	12,809	567	1969	12,971	826
1951	13,025	599	1970	12,736	807
1952	13,172	610	1971	12,740	800
1953	13,114	635	1972	12,589	822
1954	13,178	599	1973	12,397	862
1955	13,276	614	1974	12,662	884
1956	13,215	641	1975	12,245	850
1957	12,162	636			

NOTE: Data are not directly comparable before and after 1957 because of the adoption of the revised Standard Industrial Classification and the new 'establishment' concept. Employment data are not comparable before and after 1961 because of the distinction adopted between 'manufacturing activity' and total activity of manufacturing firms.

SOURCES: 1939–50: *Economic Survey of Ontario, 1957*, table 20.1, 0-2; 1951–75: *Ontario Statistics, 1981*, table 20.1, 510

interruptions in the late 1960s and the early 1970s, until 1974, when manufacturing employment in Ontario reached its highest level for the period with almost 884,000 workers employed, approximately double the 1940 number.

The productivity of labour in Ontario manufacturing appears to have increased steadily over most of the period, although reasonably comparable data are available only for the last part.

Total manufacturing value added per employee increased from $10,550 in 1961 to $16,394 in 1973 but fell thereafter to $16,299 in 1974 and to $15,398 in 1975.[4] Both the growth of productivity and the sudden decline at the end of the period are difficult to explain with any certainty.[5] It is apparent that short-term fluctuations in output per worker may be strongly influenced by the business cycle, with reductions in the work forcing lagging considerably behind any slump in demand for output. It is also evident that the longer-term growth in productivity over most of the period was associated with an increase in the capital stock employed in manufacturing, associated improvements in technology, and changes in the scale of many manufacturing operations. Technical change was a conspicuous feature of the period, particularly in some of the larger primary manufacturing industries such as steel-making. The use of increasingly sophisticated labour-saving devices, some of them utilizing automatic control mechanisms, attracted much attention during the period, especially from organized labour. Less attention was paid at the time to other changes taking place in the manufacturing sector, which may also have affected productivity following the war. One of these changes was the steady growth in the size of manufacturing establishments. While the number of such establishments grew from just over 10,000 in 1940 to more than 13,000 by the early 1950s, the trend thereafter was for the number to decline. By 1975 there were fewer manufacturing establishments in Ontario than there had been in 1951. While the average manufacturing establishment in 1939 had 32.5 employees, by the end of the period it had more than double that number.

Ontario's traditional domination of the national manufacturing scene continued unchanged over most of the period. During the Second World War the province's position was temporarily eroded by the federal government's wartime measures, which stimulated unusually high levels of production in some other parts of the country. But by the 1950s Ontario's pre-war share of total manufacturing value added, approximately 50 per cent, was restored. The highest level, 54.1 per cent, was recorded in 1971. These gross data underestimate the importance of Ontario as the manufacturing centre of Canada. As table 45 shows, for a typical year in the post-war period, many of the country's largest manufacturing industries were almost exclusively located in the province.

As would be expected, Ontario also accounted for a major share of total manufacturing employment in Canada. The data also suggest that manufacturing workers were more productive in Ontario than elsewhere in Canada. Productivity has varied greatly in different types of manufacturing activity; in 1960, for example, the net output per worker in Ontario was higher than the Canadian average in more than two-thirds of the 175 manufacturing industries for which such data are reported.[6] Part of the explanation appears to lie in the larger scale of manufacturing in Ontario. In most of the industries listed in table 46 in which Ontario output per employee was higher than the national average, the Ontario establishments were larger. Ontario also had more of the high-productivity industries than the rest of the country, industries such as chemicals and chemical products, primary metals, and transportation equipment in which output per worker tends to be relatively high.

Despite the important geographical and policy influences that gave Ontario such an advantage over the rest of Canada in the development of a manufacturing sector, the province remained far from self-sufficient in the production of manufactured goods. The years of the Second World War were unusual in this regard, however, for wartime circumstances cut off many imports, with the result that domestic producers of goods such as textiles, clothing, and shoes found them-

TABLE 45
Ontario's Share of Certain Large, Medium, and Small
Manufacturing Industries in Canada, 1957

Manufacturing Industries	Per Cent
Large Industries	
Motor vehicles	98.8
Motor vehicle parts	94.5
Heavy electrical goods	90.7
Primary iron and steel	77.4
Telecommunications equipment	77.0
Iron castings	69.9
Fruit and veg. preparations	67.6
Sheet metal products	59.1
Industrial machinery	58.9
Misc. chemical products	58.2
Printing and bookbinding	57.8
Brass and copper products	57.5
Acids, alkalies and salts	55.3
Aircraft and parts	54.8
Medium-sized industries	
Agricultural implements	90.0
Soaps and washing compounds	88.4
Major household appliances	80.7
Household and office machines	79.7
Hardware, tools, cutlery	74.0
Heating and cooking apparatus	68.3
Confectionary	57.7
Small Industries	
Machine tools	100
Tobacco processing	94.7
Bicycles	90.0
Prepared breakfast foods	90.6
Leather tanneries	85.0
Batteries	70.7

SOURCE: Statistics Canada (DBS), *Manufacturing Industries of Canada 1957*, section D (31-206), 5–6

selves suddenly relieved of import competition. A number of entirely new industries were developed as well, largely as a result of federal government initiatives. Items that had never before been manufactured in Canada, such as synthetic rubber, optical glass, certain electrical goods, and specialized metals, became available from new domestic producers.

Many of the new industries, as well as those that had expanded their operations during the war, survived the return to peacetime conditions. Some, however, experienced several difficult years during the period of transition. In industries such as manufacture of motor vehicles and of electrical apparatus, 1944 levels of production were not exceeded until nearly a decade later. In others, such as the textiles and clothing industries, the change-over was initially easier; for it

TABLE 46
Position of Ontario's Twenty Leading Industries in Canadian Manufacturing, 1960

Ranking*	Industry	Net Value Per Employee		Net Value Per Establishment	
		Ontario	Rest of Canada	Ontario	Rest of Canada
1	Motor vehicles	$12,366	$ 8,363	$30,001,781	$ 1,188,693
2	Iron and steel mills	11,343	7,464	16,744,772	2,463,302
3	Smelting and refining	21,836	14,134	27,603,628	18,506,955
4	Pulp and paper mills	11,446	12,774	5,814,209	6,579,301
5	Miscellaneous machinery and equipment	8,148	7,422	548,777	502,879
6	Industrial chemicals	14,660	14,540	2,459,364	1,366,793
7	Electrical industrial equipment	8,872	7,399	1,875,171	528,648
8	Printing and publishing	9,010	7,846	441,159	293,115
9	Motor vehicle parts and accessories	8,411	7,951	1,392,019	178,103
10	Metal stamping, pressing and coating	8,351	8,345	374,589	292,132
11	Printing and bookbinding	7,311	6,001	119,528	66,415
12	Fruit and vegetable canners and preservers	8,171	6,049	534,015	187,192
13	Rubber tires and tubes	10,475	20,925	10,479,886	1,443,833
14	Breweries	29,717	21,248	4,515,388	3,027,210
15	Bakeries	5,132	5,036	92,688	61,870
16	Slaughtering and meat packing	7,942	8,152	1,055,077	966,812
17	Miscellaneous metal fabricating	7,842	6,868	381,787	288,597
18	Soap and cleaning compounds	21,778	12,161	1,084,330	117,439
19	Communications equipment	6,943	7,345	746,246	2,489,100
20	Petroleum refining	13,332	30,613	9,749,837	6,851,414

* Industries are ranked by net value of production in Ontario.
SOURCE: C.R.A. Khan, 'The Structure and Concentration of Ontario Manufacturing and Its Relative Position in Canada,' *Ontario Economic Review*, 1 (May 1963–April 1964), n.p.

was not until the 1950s that they began to feel once again the full force of foreign competition. Between 1946 and 1959 the constant dollar value of manufacturing output in Ontario increased by two and a half times, considerably more than the GPP.

By the later 1950s, however, many Ontario manufacturing concerns found themselves facing shrinking shares of the domestic market and growing difficulties in maintaining the shares of export markets that some of them had built up in the early post-war years. Exports of secondary manufactures in general were on a declining trend as the decade drew to an end.[8] Imports of manufactured goods grew rapidly. By the mid-1970s the value of non-edible end-products imported to Ontario exceeded the value of the province's exports of such items by nearly $4 billion.[9]

The growth of manufacting in Ontario during the 1939–75 period was considerably greater than the growth of the primary sector of the economy, with the result that the value of manufacturing output rose from 54 per cent of the net value of goods produced in the province in 1939 to over 70 per cent in 1975. However, in relation to the output of the total provincial economy, including the services sector, manufacturing showed no relative growth during the period. Although there were years when the value of manufacturing output rose to as much as 40 per cent of the GPP during the period as a whole the average value was near one-third, with no clear trend evident in the year-to-year fluctuations.

Just as the manufacturing sector showed little overall change in relative significance in the provincial economy, it underwent few changes in its internal structure. Some industries declined or even disappeared, victims of changing tastes and technologies, while a number of new ones emerged; but the overall impression is that the structure and organization of the sector remained surprisingly stable. A small number of industries remained dominant: automobiles, pulp and paper, iron and steel, non-ferrous metals, smelting, and refining led the list of the province's principal types of manufacturing activity. Automobile parts and accessories, heavy electrical equipment, and other types of machinery occupied conspicuous places in terms of their share of total manufacturing value added. Various food product manufacturers also remained consistently important. The most notable additions to the list after the war were some of the chemical industries and petroleum refining.

The twenty most important industries, ranked in terms of value added, together accounted for more than 50 per cent of total manufacturing output. As table 47 shows, there were some substantial shifts in the relative importance of some of these leading industries during the course of the period, but there is little indication of any 'changing industrial structure,' especially when changes in definition and classification are taken into account. Automobile-making and the processing of certain staple raw materials predominate throughout. There is no obvious trend in the relative importance of 'primary' and 'secondary' manufacturing activities. Pulp and paper, primary iron and steel, and smelting and refining contributed an increasing share of total manufacturing output during the earlier part of the period, their contribution rising from about 11 per cent in the early 1940s to over 15 per cent by 1961. But their share declined thereafter, falling to approximately 9 per cent by 1975.

Established patterns of ownership in the Ontario manufacturing industry continued through these years. While individual proprietorships and partnerships remained numerous, especially in industries such as food and beverages, printing, publishing, and wood products, the corporate form of ownership became even

TABLE 47
Twenty Leading Manufacturing Industries, Ontario, 1941 and 1971

1941	1971
1. Automobiles	Motor vehicles
2. Electrical apparatus and supplies	Iron and steel mills
3. Machinery	Motor vehicle parts
4. Pulp and paper	Misc. machinery
5. Non-ferrous metal smelting, etc.	Pulp and paper
6. Primary iron and steel	Misc. food industries
7. Automobile supplies	Industrial chemicals
8. Rubber goods, incl. footwear	Rubber products
9. Aircraft	Metal stamping, pressing
10. Hardware and tools	Commercial printing
11. Iron castings	Electrical indus. equipment
12. Sheet metal products	Communications equipment
13. Brass and copper products	Publishing and printing
14. Biscuits, confectionary, etc.	Scientific equipment
15. Hosiery and knitted goods	Misc. metal fabricating
16. Bread and other bakery products	Distilleries
17. Fruit and vegetable preparations	Dairy products
18. Shipbuilding and repairs	Slaughtering and packing
19. Acids, alkalies, and salts	Breweries
20. Butter and cheese	Petroleum refining

NOTE: Ranking in 1941 by 'Net Value of Production'; in 1971 by 'Value Added by Manufacture'
SOURCE: Statistics Canada, *Manufacturing Industries of Canada*, 1941 and 1971 (31-206)

more typical of the manufacturing sector than it had been in the past. Between 1946, when comparable data first become available, and 1975 incorporated companies increased from just under 40 per cent to over 85 per cent of all the business firms in manufacturing. The number of co-operatives, which accounted for 1.6 per cent of the total in 1946 declined to less than half of 1 per cent by 1975. As would be expected, the incorporated firms were the largest in terms of both output and employment. In 1946 corporations employed about 90 per cent of the manufacturing labour force in Ontario. By 1975 the figure had increased to 99 per cent. A large proportion of these corporations were owned or controlled by non-residents. During the 1940s and 1950s many new manufacturing firms established plants in Ontario, particularly in the heavily populated Toronto-Hamilton area. The influx of foreign investment was welcomed and encouraged by the provincial government. When the extent of foreign ownership and control in the Canadian economy became a popular issue in the 1960s, the most dramatic evidence was that related to the manufacturing sector, particularly industries producing commodities characterized by significant amounts of 'product differentiation.'[10] A number of important manufacturing industries in the province were either completely or substantially foreign owned.

With the exception of several new resource towns that grew up in northern Ontario as a consequence of forestry or mining operations, most of the expansion of manufacturing in Ontario during the 1939–75 period was concentrated in the established industrial areas to the south. The scale and character of this growth was a mjaor factor in the overall economic and social transformation of this region in the post-Second World War period. The most conspicuous change was the shift of manufacturing activity from the central areas of the major cities into new suburban locations. While there had been similar shifts in earlier periods, when major industries built new plants on the outskirts of large cities, the postwar changes were unprecedented in their scale and impact on such areas. While some kinds of manufacturing enterprises, such as printing and publishing firms, continued to occupy their traditional city-centre locations, the trend was for firms to leave their multi-storeyed downtown buildings in favour of sprawling suburban facilities. New plants, including the proliferating branch plants of American firms, located almost exclusively in the suburbs, using up large quantities of land in the process.[11] In the City of Toronto proper, for example, manufacturing employment, which had grown steadily during the 1940s, reaching a peak of 160,000 in 1950, thereafter actually declined in absolute terms. By 1964 only 35 per cent of total manufacturing employment in the four counties comprising the metropolitan area was in the City of Toronto itself, compared with approximately 65 per cent in the early 1950s.[12]

The trends in Ontario manufacturing just outlined may be illustrated further by looking at developments in several specific industries which are representative of the different kinds of manufacturing activity carried on in the province during the period.

Automobiles

The automobile industry was the most important form of secondary manufacturing in the province during the years from 1939 to 1975. While it did not consistently rank first in the list of most vital industries in terms of value of production, so many other activities were directly related to it that it must be considered almost a sector of the economy in its own right. The total automotive-related activities were closely integrated with the rest of the economy, providing markets for a wide range of other manufactured commodities such as steel, glass, and textiles. Yet for all its importance to the provincial economy, the motor vehicle industry also displayed many of the shortcomings of Canadian secondary manufacturing in general, shortcomings that became increasingly apparent in the latter part of the period. The industry was entirely American owned and performed relatively few of the management, research, product development and marketing operations carried out by the sometimes smaller automotive industries of countries such as France and Sweden. It displayed most of the symptoms of 'truncated development' lamented by critics of American investment in Canadian branch-plant operations.[13]

In addition to its obviously dependent status in terms of technology, management and marketing, the auto industry in Ontario reflected the structural characteristics of the parent industry in the United States, notably a high degree of concentration, extensive product differentiation and related oligopolistic marketing policies.[14]

During the 1930s the industry was severely affected by the low levels of demand for consumer durables. Output fell sharply from the 1929 record level of 262,000 vehicles to 60,000 in 1932, about 15 per cent of capacity. Aided by tariff revisions in the 1930s, the industry began a slow recovery, but in the latter part of the decade growing import competition clouded the prospects of future expansion. Huge military orders during the early war years transformed the situation. Almost overnight the industry went from a position of surplus capacity to one in which plant could not be expanded rapidly enough to meet the demand. Output reached 271,000 vehicles in 1941, but the following year civilian production was stopped, and all available capacity was devoted to the production of military vehicles and parts. During the war years a total of 816,000 mechanized transport vehicles and more than 50,000 armoured vehicles were built.

In the immediate post-war years passenger car production in Ontario expanded rapidly in response to high levels of pent up civilian demand. In 1948 the 1929 level of output was surpassed and the domestic market remained buoyant until well into the 1950s. Output peaked in 1953 at 481,000 vehicles, declined sharply in 1954, but recovered and remained at high levels from 1955 until the recession of 1958. The sensitivity of the industry to the business cycle was aggravated in the late 1950s by a resurgence of foreign competition in both domestic and export markets. In 1949 Canada had experienced its first deficit in overall automobile trade with the rest of the world since 1914, but it was not until almost a decade later that North American auto-makers became aware of how serious the challenge of European products was likely to be. By 1957 even the United States had become a net importer of motor vehicles.[15] The causes were fundamental. European manufacturers had new and technically advanced production facilities, relatively low labour costs, and a product that appealed to a growing segment of the North American public. Producers in Britain had the added advantage of duty-free access to the Canadian market, granted as part of the 1932 trade agreements. Total imports of vehicles to Canada rose from 58,000 in 1955 to 180,000 in 1960, giving foreign producers approximately one-third of the Canadian market.

During the 1958 recession Canadian vehicle production fell to 298,000 units and remained at relatively low levels during the uncertain period of recovery which lasted until the end of the decade. These low production volumes created more than the usual difficulties for the manufacturers, since, under the tariff arrangements of 1936, they were allowed to import parts duty free if they maintained certain agreed levels of production. During the 1950s, the need to import parts increased in relation to total car production because of the growing popularity of cars equipped with automatic transmissions, all of which were produced in the United States. As total output fell in Canada, producers found themselves facing the prospect of having to buy imported parts in excess of the duty-free allowance. The situation prompted demands that the government intervene to assist domestic auto-makers.

The Ontario government was not notably responsive. As in the case of the mining industry, there was a tendency on the part of Ontario politicians to see such problems as primarily a matter of federal government concern. Furthermore, the premier, Mr Frost, was inclined to the view that the auto-makers had contributed to the predicament they found themselves in by over-expanding during the early post-war boom. He spoke out against the companies and in 1958 wrote to an official of one of them complaining about how the industry had created problems in Ontario by pushing sales too aggressively, attracting workers from smaller centres to Windsor, Oshawa, and Oakville, and then when demand slackened, laying off large numbers of workers and cutting the wage bill by tens of millions of dollars.[16]

The federal government had reason to take some action in the matter, however; for the poor performance of the domestic auto industry was contributing to concerns about the country's balance of payments on current account. The total deficit on automotive trade in 1960 was $528 million, automotive imports amounted to 10.5 per cent of all merchandise imports, and automotive exports were a negligible part of total merchandise exports.[17] In 1960 the federal government appointed Vincent Bladen of the University of Toronto as a one-man royal commission to study the problem and make recommendations. Bladen's inquiry brought out a number of different views concerning the auto industry, many of which were representative of attitudes held about the secondary manufacturing industries of Canada in general. According to some who appeared before Bladen, the solution was to be found in more protection for producers in Canada. The Automotive Parts Manufacturers' Association took the position that the industry could not survive without tariff protection and proposed that existing rates be increased, that the British preferential arrangement be eliminated, and that Canadian content provisions be increased. There were less orthodox suggestions, such as that the auto industry in Canada should be fully integrated into a rationalized North American industry. Such an approach was favoured by several of the auto companies and also by organized labour. The United Auto Workers, supported by the Canadian Labour Congress, opposed tariff protection and suggested that some type of free-trade arrangement in automobiles and parts be studied as a possible way of expanding production opportunities in Canada.

In his report Bladen concluded that the industry's basic problem was inefficiency in production arising from low production volumes and an inability to realize economies of scale. Manufacturers' prices for cars in Canada were on average 10 per cent higher and, in the case of luxury models, as much as 30 per cent higher than in the United States. Canadian auto-workers were paid 30 per cent less than their American counterparts, and their productivity, measured by value added per worker, was 40 per cent lower. There was also some evidence that the rate of return on capital invested in the Canadian operations was lower than the comparable rate on investment in US operations.

Bladen made a number of recommendations that he thought would encourage the auto-producers in Canada to increase their production and achieve greater specialization, thereby reducing their production costs and, possibly, prices. A central element in his plan was the 'extended content' concept by which auto-producers in Canada would be allowed to import cars or parts duty free to the extent that their Canadian production remained at some specified level in relation to their total sales of vehicles and parts. The government did not adopt Bladen's recommendations, but in 1962 it did bring in a measure that reflected some of his ideas.

To alleviate the problem Canadian manufacturers faced with respect to imports of automatic transmissions, the government introduced a new scheme by which they could 'earn' drawbacks on the normal 25 per cent duty on such parts by increasing their own exports of new parts. This tariff remission approach provoked controversy both in Canada and in the United States. The eventual outcome was a series of negotiations aimed at warding off a potentially damaging round of retaliatory trade measures. These negotiations in turn led to the Automotive Products Agreement, signed in 1965.

This agreement provided for duty-free movement of vehicles and original-equipment parts between manufacturers in Canada and the United States. Despite opposition by some American interests, the only condition required by the American negotiators was that all vehicles entering the United States duty free have at least 50 per cent Canadian content, thereby preventing European makers from funnelling cars into the United States via Canada duty free. The conditions required by Canada were much more elaborate. Both the formal agreement and supplementary letters of understanding submitted by Canadian auto-makers spelled out various safeguards to ensure that the Canadian industry would not become worse off under the terms of the new arrangements than it had been before.

The effects of the agreement between 1965 and the early 1970s appeared to be highly satisfactory from the Canadian standpoint. If either party had cause for dissatisfaction it was the American producers. In the course of the renegotiation of the treaty in 1968, the Americans sought the removal of the various protective conditions that had been built into the original. Although differences in the statistical concepts used in the two countries and serious reporting problems made an objective measure of the outcomes of the agreement difficult, it appeared that the Canadian industry was becoming larger and more active than it would have been without it. Between 1964 and 1971 the Canadian industry grew faster than the parent industry in the United States. The number of vehicles assembled in Canada more than doubled, and production grew at an average annual rate of nearly 11 per cent. Employment in the auto factories in Canada increased at an annual compound rate of 6.3 per cent during the same period. There were also some indications that the Canadian producers were becoming more efficient. Value added per man-hour increased by 54 per cent between 1964 and 1971 and value added per production worker by 46 per cent. Exchange rate fluctuations obscured the effects of such changes on manufacturers' price differentials on completed vehicles, but Canadian estimates put the decrease at about 6 percentage points over the 1965–71 period. Most satisfactory of all, from the federal government's point of view, was the apparent effect on the current account deficit. By 1971 the balance on automobile account had gone from a large deficit to a small surplus.[18]

Such satisfaction turned sour, however, towards the end of the period. Both the Ontario and federal governments became concerned over trends developing in the industry. There were growing suspicions that Canada was not getting a 'fair share' of the benefits being generated in the North American auto industry as a whole. In Ontario there was concern over the possibility that the industry was about to become more decentralized, with some parts of it perhaps planning to move out of the province.[19]

There was particular concern over the apparent failure of the Canadian automakers to increase investment, employment, and productivity in the Canadian industry at a rate comparable with the growth in the market. Canadian producers appeared to be concentrating on the relatively labour-intensive assembly functions and neglecting development of parts production. There was also some evidence that they were relying more than ever on the 'in-house' parts production of their American parents and that nearly all the research and development work was being concentrated in the United States. Engines and automatic transmissions continued to be made mainly in US plants, although the independent parts-producing companies in Canada, many of which were branches of large multinational corporations such as Rockwell, Eaton-Yale, and Budd, were apparently doing well under the terms of the agreement, manufacturing large volumes of the simpler types of parts and assemblies.[20] Thus, while it appeared that the auto industry in Canada was performing well by historical standards, it was possibly not yielding the province as large an amount of manufacturing activity, investment, and employment relative to total North American auto-making operations as the size of the Canadian car market warranted. By 1975 the Canadian industry was supplying 11 per cent of the North American market but was accounting for only 7.7 per cent of total value added. Adding to the disenchantment with the auto pact, Canada's automotive current-account trade balance had declined from a surplus position in 1972 to a deficit in 1973 and larger deficits in the following two years.[21]

Such concerns about 'fair shares' were soon submerged, however, in a more alarming prospect, the possible collapse of the North American automobile industry as a whole in the face of a massive onslaught from foreign, especially Japanese, producers. By the mid-1970s trends that had been developing throughout the post-war period appeared to be leading to a situation in which nothing short of a radical restructuring of the North American industry would enable it to avoid a massive curtailment in the scale of its operations. Given the importance of this single industry to the Ontario economy, no greater threat to the province's future as an industrial region could easily have been imagined.

Textiles

The textile industry has not been an important source of manufacturing value added in Ontario. It is of interest, however, because it is typical of a number of secondary manufacturing industries that have relied heavily on tariff protection in the domestic market and have had little success breaking into or maintaining export markets.

The main trend in the industry over the 1939 to 1975 period was a shift away from high labour content and low-volume production by a large number of independent producers to more capital-intensive, large-scale production. There was also a tendency for domestic producers to be forced out of the lower end of the market into more expensive products, a trend reinforced towards the end of the period by federal government policy. Technical change also played an important role in the industry, with major new products, notably the synthetics, displacing the traditional wool and cotton products. Changes in taste were also important, affecting the markets for a wide range of products from women's hosiery to types of carpeting, all of which induced changes in the pattern of demand for the basic materials used to produce them.

In the early 1940s about half the textile-producing plants in Canada were located in Ontario, with most of the rest located in Quebec. The Ontario plants were typically concerned with manufacturing woollen fabrics, while the emphasis in Quebec was more on cottons. The relatively small production of synthetics was concentrated in Quebec, where ready access to suitable sources of wood pulp and electric power facilitated the production of rayon yarns.

During the Second World War Ontario textile-producers enjoyed boom conditions as a consequence of heavy military orders and the virtual elimination of import competition from Britain in the domestic woollens market. There was also a large demand during the war for cotton fabrics of all descriptions. In 1942 the output of cotton, wool, and rayon goods for both war and civilian purposes reached a new peak. Although the synthetics then available were not suitable for military clothing, the output of rayon was supported by the increased spending power of women, who bought increased quantities of rayon dresses, lingerie, and household goods. Restrictions on imports of some types of wearing apparel may also have stimulated domestic demand for Canadian-made rayon. With such unusual market conditions, the biggest problem facing Canadian domestic producers was obtaining sufficient labour to keep their factories operating at capacity levels.[22]

These favourable conditions did not last long after the war ended. In the immediate post-war years more efficient U.S. cotton textile-producers entered the Canadian market in force. In the case of woollens, British manufacturers launched an aggressive expansion into world markets in the 1950s. The ability of textile-producers in Canada to respond to such challenges was temporarily weakened by the high value of the Canadian dollar at the time, but they faced more fundamental difficulties. Cotton mills in the United States had a particularly strong competitive advantage because of their large production runs and the relatively mild seasonal fluctuations in the demand for their output. The Ontario market for cottons was both small and, because of the climate, highly seasonal. Woollen textile producers in Ontario were faced with a number of specific problems, one of which was the difficulty of obtaining suitable raw material. Wool prices had fallen sharply in the late 1940s and the profitability of sheep-raising in the province fell to the point where local supplies were greatly reduced. Another difficulty was that despite substantial investments in new labour-saving equipment after the war, labour shortages remained a problem, although the opening of the Provincial School of Textiles in Hamilton helped by making numbers of more highly trained operators available. An even more fundamental problem for the traditional textile-producers, however, was the effect of the income elasticity of demand for their products. As the real incomes of Canadian consumers rose, they spent more, but not proportionately more, on textile-using commodities. To some extent this trend was mitigated by changing fashions, which after years of austerity were dictating that clothing would be more sumptuous and more fabric consuming – the 'new look,' with longer skirt lengths for women and broader shoulders for men. But consumers were also becoming more interested in novelty and variety, which Canadian producers, already suffering from short production runs, found it difficult to supply.

The growing affluence of Canadians also created problems with respect to traditional supplies of unskilled workers. In the smaller centres of eastern Ontario, women with few alternative employment opportunities and displaced farm workers had provided a supply of cheap labour. As better employment possibilities opened up and workers became better organized, wage rates were driven up in such places. In 1941 the average wage in primary textile mills in Ontario was approximately one-third lower than in Ontario manufacturing establishments as a whole. By 1961 the difference was more like one-fifth.

Under such difficult conditions, firms had either to increase productivity, obtain government aid, or go out of business. Some did invest heavily in new plant and equipment, installing automatic looms, modern dyeing equipment, specialized knitting machinery and the like. But many of the smaller mills could not justify such outlays and closed down or sold out to the larger concerns. Federal government assistance was forthcoming in some cases, as, for example, when a temporary quota on U.S. cotton goods imports was imposed in 1947; but the general drift of the post-war commercial policy was toward freer trade. Textile producers found this difficult to understand. Speaking in Hamilton in 1949 the director of industrial relations of the Primary Textiles Institute observed that 'These continual reductions in tariff and the enormous increase in textiles imports have resulted in primary textiles products manufactured in Canada by Canadian workmen securing less and less of Canadian domestic business. In 1938, Canadian products accounted for 71% of the home market while in 1948 the Canadian mills' share of the domestic market had been reduced to 59%.' He went on to conclude that no other major textile-producing country had granted so large a share of its domestic market (about 61.4 per cent of total apparent consumption) to foreign producers.[23]

Although changes in statistical reporting procedures during the period exaggerate the trend, the number of primary textile manufacturing establishments in Ontario decreased sharply during the 1950s, falling from ninety at the beginning of the decade to fifty-one by the beginning of the 1960s.[24]

Despite the considerable local distress caused by these plant closings, not all those concerned saw the trimming of the primary textile industry in the province as a bad thing. In 1954, for example, the Eastern Ontario Associated Boards of Trade submitted a brief to the provincial government observing that the textile industry had enlarged its facilities 'many times beyond requirements' during the immediate post-war period and proposed that the current trends in the industry be encouraged rather than resisted.[25]

During the 1960s the traditional textile industry, or what was left of it, made a strong recovery from the desperate years of the preceding decade. Part of the recovery was attributable to the increased productivity achieved in the larger mills as a result of investment in new equipment and processes. There was also extensive reorganization of production, with the output of individual plants co-ordinated to serve larger market areas. The larger units were increasingly managed by professionals, and the older type of family management disappeared.[26]

Federal government policy was also supportive. The feared reductions in the tariff were less drastic than anticipated, and anti-dumping regulations were tightened up and some temporary relief arranged in particular circumstances. The depreciation of the Canadian dollar, a temporary surcharge on certain imports in 1962, a decline in U.S. textile exports, and Japan's acceptance of voluntary export restraints helped support the domestic producers. There was also the strength shown by the synthetic producers. There were only twelve nylon, terylene, and rayon plants in the province at the beginning of the 1950s. By 1975 there were forty-five, and their total employment exceeded that of all the cotton and woollen mills in the province combined.

The Primary Iron and Steel Industry

Primary iron- and steel-producers in Ontario were already making a good recovery from the low levels of production recorded in the early years of the Depression when the burst of demand associated with Canada's entry into the Second World War provided further stimulus. The production of armoured vehicles, ships, and other military goods required large quantities of basic products such as steel plate, while tool-makers and the manufacturers of electrical apparatus and other equipment required a number of new iron and steel products capable of meeting high standards of uniformity and other technical specifications. Most of this demand was met by expanding iron and steel production in Ontario.[27]

The federal government supported this expansion through direct financial assistance to companies that were willing to increase their plant capacity. Accelerated depreciation allowances were offered to firms that were able to finance such expansion on their own. Ontario's two large integrated producers, Steel Company of Canada (Stelco) at Hamilton and Algoma Steel Corporation Limited at Sault Ste Marie used both types of aid, Algoma relying mainly on federal financial help to expand its basic steel-making facilities which had been run down during the interwar years, while Stelco made more use of the accelerated depreciation arrangements to improve its rolling, ore handling, coke, and iron-making facilities.[28]

Most of the new plant constructed by the iron- and steel-makers during the war was adaptable to peacetime uses. Domestic markets for Ontario steel grew with unexpected vigour in the late 1940s and early 1950s. High levels of demand for automobiles, household appliances, and other consumer durables combined with strong demand for structural steel and capital goods of all kinds to build markets faster than output could be expanded. Instead of having surplus capacity as had been feared, Ontario steel-producers found themselves faced with opportunities for further expansion in the post-war period. The growth of physical output is shown in table 48.

The 1950s were marked by continuing high levels of investment in new facilities as the producers not only increased capacity but added new production processes. Stelco, the largest producer, spent more than $370 million to expand its main complex at Hamilton, while its smaller neighbour, Dofasco, brought its first blast furnace into production in 1951 and spent more than $200 million to expand other parts of its plant. Algoma spent similar sums in the 1950s and early 1960s to expand its ore facilities and improve its steel-making and rolling mills.[29]

TABLE 48
Production of Steel Ingots and Castings, Ontario, 1939–75

Year	Net Tons ('000)	Year	Net Tons ('000)
1939	1,014	1958	3,504
1940	1,512	1959	4,905
1941	1,872	1960	4,609
1942	2,207	1961	5,431
1943	2,183	1962	5,965
1944	2,254	1963	6,752
1945	2,116	1964	7,618
1946	1,782	1965	8,485
1947	2,254	1966	8,580
1948	2,335	1967	8,364
1949	2,365	1968	9,401
1950	2,527	1969	7,960
1951	2,619	1970	10,129
1952	2,802	1971	10,010
1953	3,264	1972	10,768
1954	2,537	1973	12,040
1955	3,717	1974	11,926
1956	4,267	1975	11,652
1957	4,005		

SOURCES: 1939–64: *Ontario Statistical Review, 1967,* 44;
1965–75: Statistics Canada, *Iron and Steel Mills,* (41-203) annual

The most important technical advance of the post-war period was Dofasco's introduction of the 'basic oxygen furnace' process to North America in 1954. Originally developed in Europe, this process reduced the amount of scrap required in steel-making and permitted charges with greater pig iron content to be used. It was also faster than other methods. The advantages of the process were so great that Algoma abandoned the new Bessemer-type plant it was installing to convert directly to the new type of furnace. By the mid-1960s Algoma and Dofasco had five such furnaces in operation.[30] Stelco remained committed to its open-hearth furnaces but improved their efficiency.

The other notable innovation of the period was made by a small company, Atlas Steel. Established at Welland in the 1930s to make stainless steel using electric heat, Atlas introduced continuous casting in 1954, a process that was subsequently widely adopted in the industry throughout North America.

Other technical developments in basic steel-making included methods that reduced the inputs of coke and limestone required, and some of these processes were facilitated by the availability of large supplies of natural gas once the pipelines to western Canada were completed. During the 1960s and 1970s automation was widely adopted in basic steel-making processes and in many secondary processes, such as rolling, annealing, and galvanizing.

Industrial relations were a matter of particular concern in the steel industry during the period. In the immediate post-war years the industry was the focal point of labour organization, beginning with the protracted Stelco strike of 1946, the outcome of which advanced the cause of large-scale industrial unionism in the province and ultimately served to move the steel companies, which had evolved highly paternalistic programs of labour relations, towards a more interactive relationship with their employees.[31]

A similar change occurred in the style of management, especially in the case of Stelco. By the 1960s Stelco had moved, in the words of the company's official historian, from 'personal rule to elaborate administrative management.'[32]

But even with these changes, the overall organization of the Ontario iron- and steel-making industry changed little in the thirty years following the Second World War. Stelco remained the main producer, not only in the province but also in Canada, accounting for more than 40 per cent of total Canadian primary iron and steel output. Its processing operations spread beyond the province, and, despite the appearance of many small, independent firms operating electric furnaces to process scrap in locations scattered across the country, Stelco continued to rule the industry. It functioned openly as the price-setter in a mature oligopoly situation, and its role aroused little controversy. The fact that it enjoyed a good public image through most of the period may be attributed to the fact that it was an almost fully owned Canadian company; it was relatively efficient, as is suggested by the fact that Canadian steel prices compared favourably with U.S. prices over much of the period; and it had a reputation for sound management and prudent financial practices in the Canadian business community. There were, however, occasional outbreaks of rebelliousness within the industry. One small producer, Interprovincial Steel and Pipe in Saskatchewan, actually dared wage a price war with Stelco in the late 1960s, but it was quickly put in its place, its president stating in an interview for a trade publication that it would thereafter stay in line and accept that fact that 'Stelco sets the price and we follow.'[33]

The dependence of the Ontario steel industry on foreign sources of raw materials was reduced in the 1940s and 1950s by the development of domestic sources of iron ore as described in chapter 8. Nevertheless, the companies continued to rely upon large volumes of imported raw materials, mainly coal for their blast furnaces and, at times, ore as well. The integration of the industry on a continental basis may have been a major source of its strength during the post-war period. Although Canadian steel-makers developed export markets for their products during the period, they did not attempt to supply all the Canadian market, which continued to absorb substantial quantities of imported steel. This practice was partly a matter of specialization, but it is also possible that the major producers in Canada maintained their relatively high levels of productivity by relying upon imports to meet peak demands rather than risk building up capacity that might have gone unused when demand was lower. Nevertheless, by the 1970s the major producers in Ontario were faced with the need to undertake major expansions in their facilities. Because both Stelco and Dofasco were running out of space in their Hamilton locations, they began to plan in collaboration with the provincial government a vast new steel-making complex at Nanticoke, across the Niagara peninsula on the north shore of Lake Erie, which was expected to become a major new centre for heavy industry in the province later in the decade.

The Wood-Using Industries

Unlike the primary iron and steel industry, which only in the post-Second World War period began utilizing natural-resources obtained within the province, Ontario's pulp and paper, lumber, and furniture-making industries traditionally depended upon local sources for their principal raw materials. As the forest resources of the province were depleted in the post-war period, these industries were faced with the problem of adapting to new sources of supply. In the case of the pulp and paper industry this was accomplished largely by making more efficient use of available wood supplies, although by the end of the period raw pulp wood was also being imported from the United States to feed some paper mills in southern Ontario. The lumber industry was less successful in adapting to the declining availability of the preferred types of wood and had to make do with inferior quality inputs and by developing new products in which small pieces of wood were joined together or processed into sheets. The furniture industry followed a pattern more like that of the woollen textile industry – when local sources dried up, furniture manufacturers turned almost entirely to imported materials.

Lumber

During the Second World War the demand for lumber increased greatly, but labour shortages hampered the efforts of producers to expand their output. High levels of demand continued with the post-war boom in construction, but again Ontario producers of lumber found it difficult to take advantage of these opportunities because of the depletion of readily accessible good-quality timber. As noted in chapter 8, the most desirable species, red and white pine, were disappearing by the 1950s, and while some lumber mills were able to convert to other species, conversion was often hindered by the fact that large quantities of suitable wood were tied up in pulpwood concessions. Although a number of sawmills were built after the war, some by pulpwood companies expanding their operations laterally, there was little incentive for investors to support expansion or modernization of existing plant, given the timber supply situation in the province. The number of sawmills operating in Ontario increased from 741 in 1939 to 1,340 by 1951 but declined thereafter to about 700 by the mid-1970s.

Although there was an overall trend towards larger mills, most remained small, producing less than 1 million board feet of lumber annually. Most were equipped with obsolete machinery, and for accounting purposes most were fully depreciated.[34] Some of the larger, more efficient mills were able to begin using waste products such as wood chips to supply pulp mills and plants making particleboard, although many difficulties were encountered in co-ordinating such efforts.

The increasing scarcity and cost of good-quality lumber and changes in building techniques after the war promoted the development of plywood and veneer materials. Plywood, an insignificant product in 1940, became increasingly popular after the war. Initially produced only from birch, techniques were subsequently developed that permitted the use of other species as well. Even the once-useless stands of poplar proved adaptable to this technology, and by the 1970s more than half the plywood manufactured in Ontario was made from this species. These new products served to offset the virtual disappearance of markets for certain traditional wood products such as shingles and lath, made obsolete by new building methods. To the extent that they utilized wood that was previously wasted, they also served to stretch Ontario's timber supplies.

Pulp and Paper

The pulp and paper industry is the outstanding example of a primary manufacturing activity in Canada. It utilizes a plentiful natural resource, its principal product is newsprint, which is a basic input in another industry, and most of this product is exported. Foreign ownership and control is extensive in the industry, and there has been much government involvement in its affairs because government owns most of the relevant forest resources and is interested in promoting certain public goals such as job creation, regional development, and environmental protection.

During the 1930s both the provincial and federal governments became involved in the pulp and paper industry because of the disorder it fell into with the collapse of markets.[35] The continuing financial and management problems in the industry and the relatively low priority given it in the wartime allocation of labour resources made it difficult for the surviving producers to expand output until the war was over. By the late 1940s, however, several new mills had been established and the Ontario government was actively involved in promoting further expansion of the industry. Much of this was growth accomplished through the reorganization of existing pulp and paper concessions as described in chapter 8. The subsequent steady growth in physical output is shown in table 49.

Structurally the revived pulp and paper industry in Ontario was little changed from what it had been in the interwar period. What changes there were came slowly: a trend towards integration of pulp- and paper-making with other forestry operations, a gradual adoption of new technologies, and a gradual increase in the use of the sulphate pulp process.

TABLE 49
Production of Wood Pulp, Ontario, 1940–75

Year	Tons ('000)	Year	Tons ('000)
1940	1,369	1959	2,758
1941	1,507	1960	2,967
1942	1,519	1961	2,981
1943	1,491	1962	3,052
1944	1,316	1963	3,074
1945	1,469	1964	3,317
1946	1,838	1965	3,357
1947	2,100	1966	3,587
1948	2,226	1967	3,619
1949	2,138	1968	3,644
1950	2,298	1969	3,961
1951	2,485	1970	3,969
1952	2,309	1971	3,800
1953	2,324	1972	3,938
1954	2,421	1973	4,044
1955	2,602	1974	4,274
1956	2,735	1975	2,800
1957	2,746		
1958	2,736		

SOURCE: *Canada Year Book*, 1941–77

The trend towards integration of forestry operations in Ontario followed similar developments elsewhere. Despite efforts by the provincial government to encourage more rational use of the timber resources of the province, the long-lived rivalry between the lumber companies and the pulp and paper companies made innovation difficult. Not until the 1960s did the obvious commercial benefits of integration begin to overcome the legacy of mistrust among the private interests involved. Within a few years some integration of operations had been achieved, with waste wood from lumber mills being utilized for pulp-making along lines that had been long established in the more progressive British Columbia forest industries.[36]

On the output side of its operations, the most notable change in the Ontario industry after the Second World War was the rapid growth of sulphate pulp production. This process, which permitted the use of a greater variety of timber species, grew steadily in application throughout the period and by the mid-1970s was yielding almost as much pulp as the more traditional groundwood process. As shown in table 50, a third process, sulphite pulping, accounted for a relatively constant share of a total output throughout the period. It was used to produce a type of paper specially suited to high-quality magazine reproduction.

In view of the uncertainties surrounding the ability of Ontario's forest resources to sustain higher levels of cutting during the post-war period, it is noteworthy

TABLE 50
Production of Wood Pulp by Process, Ontario, 1946, 1966, 1973

Types	1946 Tons ('000)	Per Cent	1966 Tons ('000)	Per Cent	1973 Tons ('000)	Per Cent
Groundwood	1,069	58.1	1,625	45.3	1,686	41.7
Sulphite	581	31.6	707	19.7	613	15.2
Sulphate	157	8.6	1,038	28.9	1,541	38.1
Other	31	1.7	217	6.1	204	5.0
Total	1,838	100.0	3,587	100.0	4,044	100.0

SOURCE: Ontario, MNR, *The Forest Industry in the Economy of Ontario* (Toronto, 1981), 16

that the expansion of pulp and paper production during the period was achieved without any comparable increase in the total amount of wood cut. As petroleum and natural gas came into common use for heating in the province after the war, the wood once cut for fuel became available for pulping. The use of wood chips and other waste materials and the adoption of new processes, such as the high-yield digesting method, also permitted increased output in the industry without corresponding increases in the amount of wood cut. In some mills the new techniques increased fibre yields by nearly 50 per cent.[37]

Even with these changes the Ontario pulp and paper industry retained much of its earlier character. The total number of mills operating in the province was much the same in 1975 as it had been in 1940. The industry's dependence on crown-owned timber was, if anything, greater than before, since the amount of wood available from privately owned timber lands diminished greatly after the war. Its involvement in the political process of the province was undiminished. The industry continued to solicit government aid in dealing with its production problems during periods of declining demand, while individual companies sought special consideration in return for undertaking or maintaining the level of their operations. The internal organization of the industry also remained much as before. Most of the companies fell into one or the other of the two dominant organizations, the largely Canadian-owned Abitibi group and the American-owned Kalamazoo Vegetable Parchment group. In the 1970s about 50 per cent of the timber limits conceded in Ontario were in the hands of foreign-owned firms, several of which were subsidiaries of large U.S. newspaper chains.[38]

The United States remained the principal market for Ontario pulp and paper output, most of the province's output going into the nearby mid-western states where Ontario's producers retained their advantage over competitors located in British Columbia, the Maritimes, and the American south. During the latter part of the period there was growing uneasiness in Ontario over the security of this established position. There were indications that productivity in the Ontario industry was rising more slowly and production costs more rapidly than in many other pulp- and paper-producing regions of North America. By 1970 the cost of pulpwood at mill rate in Ontario averaged $43.20 per hundred cubic feet compared with $39.63 in Quebec, $29 in British Columbia, and $34.84 in the southeastern United States. Electric power costs in Ontario were also higher than in these other areas, in part because Ontario Hydro had adopted a rate structure that removed the advantage pulp and paper producers had once enjoyed through their proximity to the generating sites. In addition, Ontario's timber resources, never the richest or most productive, were declining relative to those of other regions, where climate and forestry practices permitted easier regeneration. Despite the steady expansion of output, Ontario's share of total Canadian paper production declined over the period, falling from 28 per cent in 1950 to 21 per cent in 1975.

These conditions created serious problems for the provincial government, when it found itself forced to impose stricter pollution controls on the industry to reduce the already extensive damage that had been done to the water resources of the province. Faced with the choice of levying the costs of such measures against the operators and risking considerable disinvestment in the industry, or of shifting the burden to the public by way of the tax system, the government sought a compromise that leaned somewhat more heavily towards the latter than the former.

Problems and Policies in the Manufacturing Sector

During the 1939–75 period the government of Ontario actively promoted the development of manufacturing industries in Ontario. The motives, objectives and instruments were familiar and well practised by provincial governments across Canada. The promotion of manufacturing was pursued in this period in much the same way and for the same reasons as in earlier periods. Politically, aiding manufacturers continued to make good sense – it won support from an important segment of the business community, it provided demonstrable evidence of the province's ability to contribute to local communities by helping them attract new industries, and it appeared to create employment. Economically, such aid to industry continued to be justified by the traditional association of growth in manufacturing and economic progress.

If there was anything new in the policies of the period, it was the government's effort to incorporate aid to manufacturing into a broader policy context. For much of the period, this effort could be seen in the juxtaposition of industrial promotion and references to 'planning.' By the mid-1970s, when planning had acquired less favourable connotations, industrial promotion began to find a place in something called 'industrial strategy.'

As shown in chapter 1, a good deal of thought had been given in the 1940s to the possibility of devising some kind of broad overall economic plan for the province. It was recognized that there would have to be some co-ordination of town-planning and industrial promotion efforts, which would require involving local authorities in the policy-making process. While an attempt was made to do so by bringing 'regional development councils' made up of local businessmen, municipal, and other local interests into contact with planners at the provincial level along lines practised in Britain, this approach was not very successful. The most tangible results came from the efforts of local governments, many of the larger ones setting up 'industrial development' departments which worked full time at the task of attracting new industry.[39] These departments were often particularly active in promoting the development of suburban 'industrial parks' to which they sought to attract light manufacturing firms by offering serviced land and favourable tax arrangements.

The province supported these municipal programs and also a number of specific locational policies for its own industry. These policies included special efforts to promote the establishment of new manufacturing industries in hinterland areas, where they would serve to broaden the economic base and at the same time take the pressure off the Toronto-centred region, where industrial growth threatened to become 'excessive.' While such projects were related to the government's regional planning exercises of the 1960s, specific goals were never clearly defined. In this respect they resembled the more traditional industrial development goals of the provincial government: to increase the total amount of manufacturing in the province, to reduce the province's reliance on imported manufactured goods, to encourage further processing of primary products prior to export, and to promote secondary manufacturing in general.

After the war responsibility for these policies was assigned to the Trade and Industry Branch of the Department of Planning and Development established in 1945. As outlined by the minister at the time, this organization would provide municipal and industrial statistics, advise manufacturers about establishing or expanding their industries, and assist business in finding suitable locations, in obtaining raw materials, and in developing both domestic and foreign markets. It was also to collaborate with the Ontario Research Foundation to provide scientific and technical information to industries in Ontario.[40]

During the period of rapid industrial expansion after the war the provincial government attributed some of the growth of manufacturing in the province to these programs. By the late 1950s the minister of planning and development could report that his department had played a part in attracting 1,200 new manufacturing enterprises to the province, in the expanding of 3,500 manufacturing enterprises already established, and in creating 160,000 jobs during a period of some twelve months.[41]

Efforts to attract manufacturing firms to the province during this period were not very selective, except for the special efforts made to attract British firms. This preference reflected something of the nostalgia lingering in the province for economic ties to the 'old country.' As late as 1958 the minister of planning and development was moved to declare in the legislature that while some seemed prepared to abandon such efforts, for his own part he was prepared, as he put it, to nail his political colours to the mast and declare that 'There shall always be an England and England shall be free, if England means as much to you as England means to me.'[42] But such sentiments not withstanding, by the late 1950s it was obvious that British branch-plant investment in Ontario would be trivial compared with U.S.-based activity of this kind. Ontario was, in fact, the first province in Canada to establish an industrial promotion office in the United States, when it opened a branch of its trade and industry office in Chicago in 1952.

Early in the 1960s changing patterns of world trade and increasing concern over Ontario's competitive position in domestic and export markets prompted the government to renew its efforts to improve the quality and quantity of manufacturing activity in the province. As part of a general reorganization of the economic policy-making apparatus, the principal responsibilities for industrial promotion were assigned to the new Department of Economics and Development established in 1962. At the same time another new body, the Ontario Economic Council, was created to provide independent advice and research support for the government in this area.

One immediate result of the work undertaken by the province's enhanced economic intelligence system was confirmation of the important role played by manufacturing in the provincial economy. Until 1962 there were no direct measures of the sectoral structure of the provincial economy. New estimates of Gross Provincial product in the early 1960s indicated that manufacturing activities accounted for 32 per cent of the total, prompting the minister of economics and development, Robert Macaulay, to assert that manufacturing was 'the key to the future growth and development of this country and this province.'[43] At the same time he announced that the government's policies toward manufacturing were being changed, that in the future measures would focus on the expansion of markets, rather than on directly stimulating new investment in manufacturing. 'The balance of payments problem, the economic growth problem and the unemployment problem all find a common denominator in this one simple proposition – Canadian industry does not sell enough goods and services at home or abroad ... It is my contention that this country and this province are not going to move ahead until our industries capture a larger share of the domestic market and expand into foreign markets with vigour.'[44]

Noting that Canadian imports of consumer goods in 1962 amounted to one-quarter of all retail sales, while imports of processed industrial materials, component parts, machinery, and equipment, represented a similar amount, Mr Macaulay concluded that there was a proven market for manufactured goods in Canada which domestic manufacturers were simply not taking advantage of. As for exports, the potential was unknown, but he was optimistic about this as well. While conceding that if a nation wants to sell it must also buy, the minister nevertheless concluded (he in fact claimed that 'It can be proven beyond a shadow of a doubt') that Canadians had been buying more than they had been selling. He pursued this line of reasoning to the conclusion that the province could and should work to reduce imports 'whilst on the other hand, increase our exports so as to bring both of these into a reasonable balance.'[45]

The proposed strategy was to stimulate import substitution activity and to raise the level of processing of exports: 'Let's start exporting more flour instead of wheat, more specialty steels and basic shapes instead of iron ore, petroleum products instead of crude oil, furniture instead of lumber, and manufactured goods of all kinds instead of industrial materials and raw food products.'[46] At the same time, reasoning that if Ontario producers could not compete in their own domestic markets, they could hardly hope to do so in foreign markets, he went on to propose a number of measures 'to assist our manufacturing industries to capture a larger share of the domestic market and to expand their export markets.' Thus was launched the government's great 'Trade Crusade' program, which was aimed at nothing less than re-educating Canadian consumers and manufacturing firms alike.

Denying that this was simply another crude campaign to promote local business, the government undertook to counter the effect of U.S. advertising on Canadian consumers by launching its own advertising offensive. It also held a number of special trade shows – 'manufacturing opportunity shows' as it called them to help Ontario business people overcome 'habits of purchasing that are detrimental to the economy.' Many were misguided in their decisions to import goods, the government suggested, simply because they lacked information about the availability of similar goods from Canadian sources. Others were inclined to be too timid about seeking export markets.

It is rather surprising that the Ontario government itself avoided developing the kind of formal 'purchasing policies' to favour domestic suppliers that were popular among some of the other provincial governments at the time. There had been some tentative moves in that direction in the late 1950s, when there were suggestions that government departments and agencies might try to buy Canadian or British goods, but no formal directives to this effect appear to have been issued. One reason was that the government feared that American firms might become 'annoyed or angered' by such a policy.[47]

The Trade Crusade was dismissed by some observers of government policy at the time as simply another opportunity that the government had created for itself to indulge an evident enthusiasm for large-scale public relations campaigns. Others saw in it a thinly disguised xenophobia. But the government countered such criticism by arguing that the campaign had been successful. Without addressing the basic issue of whether the outlays would have been more beneficial if directed to other purposes, the government drowned criticism in a flood of statistics purporting to demonstrate that millions of dollars' worth of new business had been developed and thousands of new jobs created in the Ontario manufacturing sector for relatively small outlays of the taxpayers' money.[48]

Promotion of manufacturing during the 1960s was not limited to the Trade Crusade. Despite the minister's derogation of the view that investment was an important problem, the government expanded its programs to assist new manufacturing firms with their financing. The Ontario Development Agency was set up with a fund of $100 million to provide loan guarantees and other assistance to new industries becoming established in the province, especially smaller ones. This was the precursor to the Ontario Development Corporation established in 1973 along with two regional bodies, the Eastern Ontario Development Corporation and the Northern Ontario Development Corporation, which provided financial assistance in a variety of forms: interest-free performance loans to firms locating in designated regions of the province; term loans with flexible repayment options for smaller firms seeking expansion; venture capital loans to help Canadian-owned firms utilize new technology; loans to assist firms installing pollution-control equipment; export loans to cover warehousing costs; and industrial mortgage and lease-back arrangements to help firms set up new manufacturing facilities.

The Ontario Development Corporation was also involved in the establishing of new industrial parks and in the development of the Sheridan Park Research Community in Mississauga. The latter project was central to the government's effort to raise the technological level of manufacturing in the province during the period. It was launched in 1963 for the purpose of providing facilities for private companies engaged in industrial research work and for the publicly funded Ontario Research Foundation. By the early 1970s ten privately owned firms were operating at the centre with over 1,500 employees.

Such attempts to encourage more 'high-technology' manufacturing in the province may be viewed as extensions of the traditional efforts to encourage higher-level manufacturing activities in general. The older policies of promoting domestic processing of raw materials continued through the period, as noted in connection with the base-metal-mining industry in the preceding chapter.

It is difficult to identify, let alone assess, the economic rationale underlying all these attempts to promote manufacturing in the province. Although they were numerous, they were probably relatively inexpensive. The direct subsidies to businesses of all kinds from the Ontario treasury were trivial through most of the period and did not become substantial until the 1970s. By the end of the period, in 1975, such subsidies amounted to about $80 million annually, although they were clearly on an upward trend. The cost of the indirect measures to support industry is elusive, in part because of the almost continual reorganization of the government departments concerned over the period.[49] What evidence there is, however, suggests that the costs were not a significant part either of the provincial product or of the provincial government's total expenditures even in the 1970s.[50]

What the province gained from such programs and policies is even more difficult to estimate. Whether or not Ontario manufacturers were more numerous, more efficient, or larger as a result of them is not clear. Nor is it known whether the people of Ontario had a higher per capita real income at the end of the period than would have been the case if such policies had been absent. If some labour resources were utilized in manufacturing rather than in lower-productivity employments, there could have been such a gain. If workers already in manufacturing retained their jobs instead of becoming permanently unemployed, there could also have been net gains. But whether or not these were indeed the alternatives that would have applied is not known.

Another fundamental difficulty is that none of these industrial development programs was developed within a comprehensive plan for the growth of the provincial economy as a whole. At no time did the government articulate what it believed would be an ideal industrial structure for the province. Policy, in fact, sought to promote everything and consequently made little sense in terms of simple resource-allocation criteria. For example, while the government sought to promote secondary manufacturing, it also sought to promote primary manufacturing. And as shown in earlier chapters, it sought to promote every other kind of economic activity carried on in the province, including agriculture. If there can be any understanding of this policy, it must be sought beyond economics in the broader areas of politics and public administration.

10 The Economic Role of the Provincial Government

Throughout the preceding chapters frequent reference has been made to specific provincial government programs and policies directed towards the promotion and regulation of particular industries. Attention has also been given to the entrepreneurial functions of the Ontario government in providing health care, education, and social services. The purpose of this chapter is to summarize the important developments in provincial government economic functions and relate them to changes in the structures, processes, and attitudes affecting public policy in the province during the years from 1939 to 1975.

Ontario government spending was actually falling at the beginning of the period, declining from $130 million in the 1939–40 fiscal year to $117 million in 1940–1. Most of the initiatives in public spending during the war years came from the federal government, which had assumed a dominant role in the economy because of the wartime emergency, but also to some extent as a consequence of the experience with the Depression which preceded it. In Ontario the government was preoccupied with its financial problems, which centred on the belief that the debt was too high and that annually balanced budgets were the norm to be aimed at after the financial legacy of the Depression was disposed of.

At the end of the war, however, spending by the Ontario government began to increase, at first only in absolute terms, but soon as a percentage of the Gross Provincial Product as well. During the 1930s Ontario's public spending amounted to about 5 per cent of the GPP. The percentage declined during the war years and in 1945–6 amounted to only 2.7 per cent. By the late 1940s the province was spending just over 4 per cent of the GPP, and this trend continued, reaching slightly more than 5 per cent by the late 1950's.[1] Using data adjusted for inflation, provincial government spending exceeded 5 per cent of the GPP for the first time in 1954–5, 6 per cent in 1957–8, and 7 per cent in 1959–60. Through the early 1960's provincial government spending kept pace with the growth of the provincial economy but in 1965 began to outstrip it. By 1972–3 government expenditures reached 16.7 per cent of the GPP, the highest percentage during the period.

Over the next several years it appeared that this trend had been broken, with annual increases in government spending falling below the rate of growth in the provincial economy.[2] Foot's study of the post-war period shows that whether expenditures are measured according to the public accounts 'estimates' or in terms of actual spending, deflating the series, or expressing it as a percentage of the GPP, there was a marked acceleration in spending between 1965 and 1971. He concluded that the data 'generally indicate that deflated expenditures of the provincial government doubled over the decade of the fifties and then doubled again in each of the subsequent five-year periods.'[3]

In absolute terms, over the years between 1945 and the early 1970s, provincial government spending in real terms increased from $73 per capita to $324.[4]

This growth of government spending in Ontario was not unusual in the context of Canadian experience as a whole during these years. The general trend in the country was for government spending to grow substantially as a percentage of total economic activity, but for most of this growth to be accounted for by increased spending channelled through governments for items such as education and health care, as well as by straight transfer payments of the kind involved in income support programs. Actual government spending to produce other kinds of goods and services customarily provided privately did not increase greatly in comparison. On a national basis the actual amount of real government spending on goods and services changed relatively little from the early 1950s to the mid-1970s, even when the large health and education items are included. The largest increases in such spending were at the provincial and municipal levels.

During the years from 1951 to 1975 Ontario government spending on goods and services, including capital formation, increased in relation to the overall level of income and expenditure in the provincial economy, rising as a ratio with Gross Provincial Expenditure from 0.074 in 1940 to 0.171 in 1975.[5] But this rise was modest in comparison with the increase in total government spending.

While it grew rapidly, total public spending in Ontario during the period was not remarkable when compared with that of other provinces. Perhaps because of efficiencies of scale in providing public services and possibly because of the province's relatively well-developed municipal system, Ontario government spending remained somewhat below the national average whether expressed on a per capita basis or in terms of a percentage of personal income.[6] It was also the case that successive Ontario governments prided themselves in keeping tax rates in the province low in comparison with other provinces.

Another indicator of the growth of government activities during the period is the size of the civil service. Following the housecleaning done by Premier Hepburn when he took office in 1934, the provincial civil service gradually expanded until the war years, when it levelled off at about 7,700 employees. After the war, provincial government employment grew gradually until the mid-

TABLE 51
Ratio of Government Spending on Goods and Services and Capital
Formation to Gross Provincial Expenditure, Ontario, 1951–75

Year	Ratio	Year	Ratio
1951	0.074	1968	0.148
1952	0.077	1969	0.149
1953	0.071	1970	0.166
1954	0.083	1971	0.169
1955	0.087	1972	0.168
1956	0.088	1973	0.159
1957	0.093	1974	0.159
1958	0.100	1975	0.171
1959	0.103		
1960	0.106		
1961	0.123		
1962	0.131		
1963	0.135		
1964	0.128		
1965	0.131		
1966	0.138		
1967	0.141		

SOURCE: Ontario Economic Council, *Issues and Alternatives 1977: The Process of Public Decision-Making* (Toronto: OEC, 1977), table 5, 68

1950s, when the rate of growth increased sharply. While growth was more gradual during most of the 1960s, it accelerated again towards the end of the decade, with total departmental employment (which excluded people employed by government enterprises such as the Liquor Control Board) reaching 88,622 in 1972. Departmental employment then actually fell in 1973 and 1974 but in 1975 increased again to a total of 93,262.[7]

The growth of the provincial civil service over the period was impressive in absolute terms, but it was not out of keeping with the growth of the provincial labour force as a whole. Even by the mid-1960s the provincial government was employing only 1.65 per cent of the total labour force in Ontario. This figure increased to 2 per cent in 1970–1 and then declined slightly to the end of the period. Given the increase in provincial government activity as reflected in its total spending, the growth of the civil service is also remarkably modest. While the popular wisdom seldom credits government employees with leading the way in productive efficiency, the fact is that while the government's total spending increased sharply in the latter part of the period especially, in relation to it, government employment decreased by approximately 50 per cent.[8]

The growth of the Ontario government's economic functions during the 1939–75 period is easier to document than to explain. There is certainly reason to believe that much of the growth that took place was dictated by forces over which the successive Ontario governments of the time had little control. Much of their activity may consequently be viewed as a relatively simple response to circumstances. Critics and some objective observers too have remarked on the 'pragmatism' displayed by these successive provincial administrations and the apparent absence of any consistent ideological commitments that might explain their overall course of action.

Of the autonomous influences bearing upon provincial government policy none could have been more important than the growth of the provincial economy itself. While the government could take some credit for not stifling this growth and possibly for stimulating it on occasion, it cannot be credited with causing it. Most of the underlying economic forces as outlined in earlier chapters were clearly beyond provincial government control. The rise in real per capita incomes in Ontario created both a demand for government services and the tax base by which the provision of such services could be financed. The importance of population growth and rising levels of per capita income as determinants of provincial government expenditure has been convincingly demonstrated by D.K. Foot for the period 1947 to 1973. Using a formal econometric model, Foot arrived at the conclusion that 'it is probably the desired demand for public expenditures, which is determined by population and income levels, that determines expenditures in the various categories.'[9] He also tested a number of other hypotheses, such as the influence of urbanization, the processes of federal-provincial financial transfers, the province's attempts at counter-cyclical budgeting, the influence of elections, and the government's observed tendency to occupy itself with particular types of activity from time to time.

Only a few of these hypotheses lent themselves to the kind of empirical testing Foot's model and data sources permitted. One that did, the influence of urbanization, was found to have a relatively small influence on overall provincial government spending during the period, although it had a recognizable effect on certain types of spending, such as hospital care and income maintenance. The other hypotheses showed only weak explanatory power, but they are of interest none the less as a means of exploring certain aspects of provincial government economic policy-making during these years.

Federal-provincial relations in the early 1960s showed signs of regressing as the congenial atmosphere created during the expansion of the 1950s began to deteriorate into something resembling more the situation of the 1940s. By the end of the 1960s Ontario was once again asserting its determination to be financially independent. This new mood followed upon a period of rapid budgetary expansion. The heavy capital outlays of the Frost era were submerged by a great increase in current-account spending under the Roberts administration, which took office in 1961.[10]

If provincial economic policy under Frost had been primarily concerned with promoting and supporting the industrial and natural resource development of the province during most of the 1950s, the following decade under John Robarts saw the effort swing to combatting recession and unemployment. The cautious budgetary policies of the early Frost years were replaced by a remarkably bold policy which entailed using the provincial budget as a major instrument by which the provincial government would seek to manipulate the short-run performance of the provincial economy. This new view of the budgetary process in Ontario was made possible by the expansion of the provincial budget noted above; since the budget assumed a proportionately greater share of the provincial total product and was growing faster than federal expenditures during the period as well, it was plausible to think that it could be used as a stabilizing force in the economic system. Accordingly, the provincial treasurer set out his 1967 budget proposals in a new form, with a separate budget statement supported by detailed 'budget papers' explaining that this was warranted by 'the substantially changed position of the provincial government in the economic and financial life of this country.' While recognizing the existence of constraints dictated by the federal-provincial framework and the need for policy co-ordination between the two levels of government, the Ontario government indicated that it was embarking upon a program of economic analysis and forecasting upon which it would base its budgetary policies, using its expenditures 'to remove economic bottlenecks and to contribute to productivity throughout the private sector of the economy' and its fiscal policy in general to 'achieve a high degree of economic development, and at the same time, the most rapid rate of economic growth.'[11]

What the provincial government and its newly expanded staff of expert advisers apparently had in mind at this time was an arrangement by which the province and its municipalities would use their budgets to effect a long-term growth policy, leaving the primary responsibility of maintaining short-run stability to the federal authorities.

With expenditures growing rapidly, the Ontario government's conviction that Ottawa was dealing unfairly with the province in tax matters continued to harden. In 1968 the provincial treasurer complained that the federal government was using the yields from the progressive taxes to 'impose' costly programs on the province which the Ontario government then had to finance with the proceeds from the regressive tax fields available to it, a condition, he warned, that would lead to a taxation 'catastrophe' unless Ottawa yielded more of the personal and corporate income tax fields to the province.[12]

The federal government, however, showed no disposition to move in such a direction. At the meeting of the finance ministers late in 1968 and again at the constitutional conference in February 1969, the federal authorities were unwilling to negotiate new tax-sharing arrangements, proposing instead that each level of government should establish its own spending priorities and revenue programs. Even worse, the federal government's own budget contained a number of new tax measures which, in the province's view, would alleviate the federal government's financial problem while making the province's situation more acute. The most galling of these proposals was the imposition of a new federal 'social development tax,' the apparent purpose of which was to finance the federal share of the medical care insurance program. There were also cut-backs and delays in federal funding for several shared-cost programs which, partly because of their direct impact on the province's finances and partly because of the way they were implemented, added further strain to the federal-provincial relationship.

The province's own efforts at the end of the 1960s were ostensibly directed to reforming the tax system in the light of recommendations made by the Ontario Committee on Taxation and to bringing total provincial spending under stricter control. To this end, the budget of 1969 was designed to restrict the growth of spending to keep it 'in line with anticipated revenue growth.'[13] The municipalities were put on notice that they too were expected to curtail spending, especially in the field of education. On the revenue side, apart from reference to the proposed broad reform of the tax system being planned, the treasurer used the 1969 budget to announce that the province would begin levying its own income tax. Three developments were cited as leading to this decision: 'the province's need for greater access to fast-growing revenue sources in order to maintain its existing programmes and undertaking essential reforms; the impasse in federal-provincial tax sharing; and the inadequacy of the present income tax abatement system to serve Ontario's long-run finance and reform objectives.'[14]

This proposal was overtaken by the debate over the federal government's tax reform proposals set out in the federal minister of finance's white paper on tax reform. The province's own initiatives in the field of tax reform appeared to be weakening. Growing opposition to some of the related changes, notably the reorganization of municipal government on a regional basis, suggested that the technically oriented restructuring of government in the province that had gained momentum during the Robarts years had outstripped the growth of political support for such change.

By the time John Robarts was about to step down from the leadership in 1970, the tone of the government's economic policy declarations was noticeably less positive. Confidence in the budget as an instrument of economic control seemed to be waning. There was actually little evidence that it had to that point been used with an effect to influence the level of activity in the provincial economy.[15] It is possible that it could have been. At least one analyst, T.A. Wilson of the University of Toronto, has argued that the Ontario budget was large enough at this time to have exerted a significant influence on economic activity in the province and, because of the strong links between Ontario and other parts of Canada, especially Quebec, on other regions as well.[16] The same authority has contended that it would have been economically justifiable for Ontario to have used its budget policies either to support federal fiscal policy or even, in the event that it was having a disproportionately large impact on employment in Ontario, to counteract it. Even so, the logic of such an approach appears to reside as much in the political need to assert such power as in its practical impact on the system. Wilson notes that it would have been difficult for any government of a large province such as Ontario to concede that it was unable to deal with the problems of unemployment and inflation and that 'Even if their own policies were in fact futile, such governments would nevertheless feel that they must be *seen* to be doing something about these problems.' At the same time he concedes that it would have been politically and economically foolish for Ontario to have tried to assume 'major responsibility' for fiscal policy during this period.[17]

There is also little evidence that the provincial budget had any unusual impact on the long-term economic development of the province after its potential for such a role was perceived in the mid-1960s. By the end of that decade, spending on capital works was constrained by the government's need for financial room in dealing with the high levels of current spending on health, education, and welfare. While increasing taxation would have been economically justifiable given the concern with inflation at the time, such a policy was no more politically attractive than it had ever been. The retail sales tax of 3 per cent that had been imposed in 1961 was raised to 5 per cent in 1966, but complaints about this regressive and unpopular tax were becoming louder. It was raised again in 1973 to 7 per cent, by which time it was the government's most important source of tax revenue, oustripping even the personal income tax. But further revenue expansion along these lines was becoming increasingly difficult to countenance. Getting spending under control was consequently becoming a more attractive alternative.

The possibility of controlling the growth of spending could not be easily envisioned given the institutional framework of government that had haphazardly evolved over the preceding several decades. Much of the problem had to do with the ways in which spending priorities were being established and appropriate levels of specific outlays determined and administered. While this was not a new problem in the province, it had been easily ignored during the period of vigorous growth after the war. As growth slowed and the economic outlook became more uncertain, the need to re-examine the budgetary and decision-making processes at Queen's Park became increasingly obvious. It also appeared necessary, given the size of the municipal component in total spending, to look again at the possibility of rationalizing local government in an attempt to raise its efficiency and, perhaps even more important, to incorporate local government decision-making into the broader structure of provincial policy determination.

The latter prospect brought the government's attention back to the whole issue of local and regional 'planning,' much of which in the past had focused on physical planning of urban areas. Under the Planning and Development Act of 1937 municipal government would develop a general plan showing existing and proposed highways, parks, and other public improvements and submit the plan to the Ontario Municipal Board for approval. One of the principal uses of this procedure was to regulate the approval of subdivisions. During the post-war period the province became more directly involved in such physical planning exercises, notably through the creation in 1953 of Metropolitan Toronto, North America's first metropolitan government system, and subsequently in the creation of new resource towns such as Elliot Lake and Manitouwadge.[18] At the local level, however, planning remained voluntary and was neither as widely practised nor as effectively implemented as the government had apparently expected it to be. In 1959 community planning was shifted out of the Department of Planning and Development and turned over to the Department of Municipal Affairs. In the years following, the province tried to induce local governments in the province to do more planning, threatening on occasion to step in if they did not.[19] But there was little active support for such planning at the grass-roots level. Planning appeared to connote provincial control of local affairs and few elected municipal officials appeared to be enthusiastic about it.

These local issues soon became entangled in the provincial government's regional planning exercises of the 1950s and with its related efforts to restructure local government units in the interests of greater fiscal, administrative, and planning efficiency. Regional planning in a formal sense was implemented in 1954, when the first of an eventual ten regional development councils was established in the province.[20] These were individual corporate entities made up of representatives of local governments and private groups, run by boards of directors, one member of which was appointed by the provincial government. Financial support was provided by the municipalities and supplemented by provincial grants.[21] The purpose of the councils was to discuss problems of regional development and advise the government accordingly. While they had some enthusiastic supporters, they seldom appear to have accomplished much in the way of developing regional priorities or practical policy recommendations. Some effort was made to involve them in specific functions, for example, by having them assist in the work of Industrial Planning Branch officers taking businessmen to prospective sites for new enterprises, but their relations with the provincial planning bureaucracy were seldom very positive.[22]

The problems of transportation in the Metropolitan Toronto area led to another involvement of the province in regional development work. What began as a study of the Metropolitan Toronto and Region Transportation System (MTARTS) situation grew into a massive, six-year inquiry, one of several demonstrations during the period that it was difficult, if not impossible, to plan a specific function without having some knowledge of the broader situation within which it was to operate.[23]

Provincial government involvement in planning for regional development was carried further in 1968, when the premier issued a statement called 'Design for

Development,' which declared that the government was accepting responsibility for 'guiding, encouraging and assisting the orderly and rational development of the province.' Until this time the federal government had the initiative in promoting regional development activity under the joint Federal-Provincial Rural Rehabilitation and Development Agreements of 1962 and 1964. The earlier agreement had emphasized ways of promoting resource development in regions with low incomes and poor employment prospects. In the course of the agreement the provincial authorities began to incline to the view that in most of the areas they were working in the problem was not so much that resource development was inadequate, but that the technical and economic changes of the post-war period had been responsible for generating rural unemployment and underemployment. Consequently, in the later joint agreement the province sought to have attention redirected to ways of creating employment and income in such regions rather than to resource development per se.[24]

In 1965 the Department of Economics and Regional Development produced a white paper on regional development in which emphasis fell on the need to approach the problems of low-income areas within the framework of a 'plan for provincial development.' The source of regional problems was believed to be 'pockets of low income,' 'strains brought about by rapid rural-urban shifts,' and 'resource-base problems.' The paper cautioned that the government's role should be to encourage, not to compel, action on the part of those involved; that it should assist the free operation of supply and demand in the labour market; and that there should be effective planning and co-ordination of programs by an interdepartmental working committee.[25]

Coincident with the premier's subsequent announcement of the Design for Development program, the Regional Development Branch of the Ministry of Treasury and Intergovernmental Affairs produced a series of planning papers establishing the broad outline of what was represented as a 'comprehensive' regional planning system for the province.[26] These planning exercises were not particularly well received by the public, and scepticism about their usefulness was particularly acute in the hinterland regions, where the objectives of the plans fell far short of local aspirations. This was clearly the case in north-western Ontario, where the plan seemed to imply continued reliance on raw material extraction, little prospect for the development of secondary manufacturing activity, and a major effort to promote tourism which local opinion saw as an industry of limited potential.[27] The problem involved was fundamental – how to incorporate appropriate political processes for determining objectives in a technically sound economic framework of policy.

But whatever its shortcomings, by the early 1970s, a regional development program had been evolved in Ontario and the final responsibility for the formulation and recommendation of development projects was entrusted to the Cabinet Committee on Policy Development. The Interdepartmental Advisory

Committee on Regional Development had also been created to bring together the deputy ministers involved in decisions affecting economic and physical planning. Regional advisory boards were constituted to facilitate discussion among civil servants in regional field offices, while the regional development councils were to provide inputs from the municipalities and other local interests. The Regional Development Branch of the Department of Treasury and Economics served as a secretariat for the system, doing research and technical work.[28]

This elaborate apparatus incorporated and continued the kind of 'industrial promotion' activity described in the preceding chapter. Despite repeated use of the word 'planning' and the elaborate studies generated as part of the process, the activity involved appears to have been little more than the co-ordination of various promotional programs. This function was not unimportant, given the increasing complexity of such undertakings caused by the proliferation of environmental protection regulations, land-use restrictions, and local 'planning' activities. There was an obvious need for such co-ordination. Yet the setting of specific development goals and the scheduling of measures to attain them seemed to get lost somewhere between the political and the merely administrative parts of the system. This was recognized, and the solution appeared to lie in reorganizing the system of local government to bring it into line with the new approach to regional economic policy. It was also apparent that the efficient delivery of health, education, and welfare services to the public required similar measures.

The government had begun to move in the direction of municipal reorganization on a regional basis when it established the Ottawa-Carleton regional government (which had jurisdiction over a 1,100 square-mile territory and a population of more than 400,000), but by the mid-1960s it had avoided making a general commitment to overhauling the whole provincial local government system on this basis. It was urged to do so, however, by a Select Committee on the Municipal Act and Related Acts in 1965 and two years later by the Ontario Committee on Taxation.[29] The latter recommended that the province establish twenty-two units of local government in southern Ontario and another seven in the north. The southern regions would vary in size, ranging from the small, densely populated metropolitan regions to large rural ones, but the object would be to have a population of at least 150,000 to 200,000 in each, a number that was thought to be optimum for the delivery of local government services. The committee proposed that the restructuring of local government in the province along these lines be completed in five years' time.

The Committee on Taxation avoided specifying in any detail the relationship between these regional governments and the matter of regional economic development. It did suggest, however, that the proposed units of regional government should be coterminous with the province's economic regions, although the economic regions (which would by then be reduced from ten to five) would contain more than one regional government. The committee suggested that the new regional governments would be effective instruments for the execution of the provincial government's economic development policies. This suggestion was quite at odds with the government's stated position in the Design for Development and later pronouncements in which the premier had insisted on treating regional development and regional government as quite separate matters.[30]

There were other suggestions that the two be linked. In a progress report on local government reorganization to the cabinet in 1970 the minister of municipal affairs urged that the existing municipal structure be replaced, because it was characterized by an implied policy of 'planning for assessment' that put immediate municipal financial gains ahead of long-run planning and environmental considerations. Local government reform would have to parallel the development of economic planning in the province, he suggested.

The reform of local government at about this time became submerged in a more general review of government organization in the province. Near the end of his period in office, Robarts had become convinced that a thorough re-examination of the whole process of governing in Ontario was needed. In 1969 he appointed the Committee on Government Productivity (COGP), instructing it 'to inquire into all matters pertaining to the management of the Government of Ontario.' The idea was not original; for there had recently been similar investigations at the federal level (the Glassco Commission of 1961) and in a number of other provinces. The Ontario committee was notable, however, for the directness with which its recommendations were dealt with, many of them being discussed and implemented as it went along.

The Committee on Government Productivity in Ontario consisted of five senior civil servants and five senior business executives. The heavy representation of the private sector was significant, for the premier was convinced that government could be made more effective by adapting the up-to-date management techniques being used in modern business enterprise.

The committee laboured for more than three years, investigating every aspect of the government's organization and activity, except those relating directly to the operations of the legislature, which was declared out-of-bounds to the committee. It produced nine published interim reports containing over 200 recommendations and a final summary report. Its own reorganization and procedures were meticulously planned (the committee referred to matters such as 'structuring our organization for project evaluation') and it was itself a model of modern managerial efficiency.

While the committee was at work, a number of fundamental changes were taking place in the political life of the province. The long rule of the Conservative party in the province appeared to be threatened by growing doubts about the state of the economy, the adequacy of the government's economic policies, and the effectiveness of the administration. Some observers also found the change of leadership to be unpromising, one chronicler of the period noting that William

Davis, the new premier, appeared to be 'uncertain and fumbling' when he took office in 1971.[31] There were many uncertainties facing the new administration: a relatively weak position in the legislature; virulent opposition to regional government; criticism of the expansion of education which the new premier had presided over as minister of education; and new insecurity in the field of economic policy. The conventional wisdom on the subject of the government's appropriate role in the economy was once again undergoing a fundamental change.

The 'new' view reflected a resurgence of conservative economic ideology already manifest in the United Kingdom and the United States. In Ontario, as elsewhere, there were expressions of disillusionment with government management of the economy, a growing sense that government spending was 'out of control' and that government intervention, instead of improving the performance of the system, was at least partly responsible for its perceived 'failures' to maintain full employment, stable price levels, a high rate of economic growth, and a 'fair' distribution of the fruits of economic effort. The Ontario government picked up on this loss of confidence in the positive economic role of government with remarkable agility. It may, in fact, have seen the opportunity it was offered to deal with what was otherwise an increasingly untenable position. The budgetary impasse that seemed to have been reached in 1969 could have been seen as an indication that the province had failed in its long struggle to wrest enough discretionary budgetary power from the federal government to permit it to continue with further expansion of major programs. The tone of the provincial government's statements concerning federal-provincial finance indicated that a new level of frustration had been reached in this respect. In 1971 the provincial treasurer, Darcy McKeough, charged that the federal government was trying to centralize power in its own hands and went on to declare that Ontario had been 'singled out for a reduced role in the building of our nation.' Ottawa was not only disregarding Ontario's needs, he claimed, it was also 'pursuing policies which are seriously reducing our economic strength.'[32]

While the government continued in the early 1970s to justify its own budget deficits on the grounds that they were needed to alleviate unemployment, which was being generated by Ottawa's spending restraints, by 1973 the provincial treasurer was taking the position that Ontario was no longer able to afford such large deficits and that it had no choice but to leave full responsibility for the poor performance of the economy to Ottawa. He could also suggest, however, that reduction in the rate of growth of provincial spending in the major social policy fields was warranted on grounds of controlling inflation.

What was particularly novel by the end of the period, however, was the frequent reference government spokesmen made to the desirability of restricting the growth of government activities and the need to promote the growth of the private sector.

In the first budget speech under the leadership of Mr Davis the government proclaimed as its first priority the restoration of 'full employment growth' in the province, but it went on to indicate that this would be achieved by measures to encourage the expansion of the private sector. The government would attempt to 'maintain firm control over public spending in order to contain tax levels and the generation of inflationary pressures.'[33] The same theme was reiterated the following year when the treasurer of the province declared that the budget would seek 'to foster maximum expansion in private sector activity and investment,' would slash the growth in provincial spending, and would reorder priorities to meet urgent social needs. There would be 'rigorous restraint on spending to make room for expansion of private sector activity and curb inflationary pressures.' But there would also be a substantial deficit to 'stimulate economic recovery.'[34]

By the mid-1970s the government was going further, asserting that it would seek not only to control the growth of the public sector, but actually to shrink it.

The logical possibility of such a program depended heavily upon a fundamental tenet of the new conservatism, that it would be possible to maintain the necessary level of social services while at the same time reducing the level of public spending. This feat was to be rendered possible by greatly increasing the efficiency of the public sector and simultaneously stimulating private sector growth (and the tax base) by 'getting government off the backs' of private enterprise. In Ontario the groundwork for such a program was established by the Committee on Government Productivity.

The committee's major recommendations bearing on economic policy functions of the government led to the grouping of ministries into 'policy fields,' each of which would be under the direction of a 'policy minister.' The latter would have no administrative responsibilities but would be free 'to concentrate on the development of policy and priority setting.' Ordinary ministers would continue to be accountable to the cabinet and to the legislature for the ministries in their charge. Ministers within a policy field would also meet with the policy minister, however, to 'deliberate on policy issues.' The policy ministers themselves would be members of a 'Policy and Priorities Board' which would make recommendations to cabinet for final approval.

The logic of the COGP approach seemed to indicate that there would be four policy fields, one each for 'resources,' 'social services,' 'justice,' and 'economics.' Only the first three such groupings were formed, however, with economics organized into a composite department called Treasury, Economics and Intergovernmental Affairs (TEIGA), and a separate Revenue Department. The new organization was accepted by the premier in December 1971.

The Committee on Government Productivity designed an elaborate mechanism for monitoring the performance of the new structure, although it conceded that 'the majority of the criteria are of necessity intangible and subjective.'[35] But it was soon evident that the logic of business organization failed to take into account the subtleties of political life. The new 'super ministers' in practice turned out to be less influential than had been intended, having little in the way of specific responsibilities and little power. It has been noted that in the first instance those appointed had been the premier's rivals in the 1971 leadership contest. Only the minister of the omnibus department, Treasury, Economics and Intergovernmental Affairs, remained politically effective, although the incumbent for whom the position appears to have been designed was inconveniently forced to resign from the government because of a conflict-of-interest situation.

To the extent that the 'new conservatism' was influential within Treasury, Economics and Intergovernmental Affairs, the pre-eminence of that department within the line ministries may have helped shape the path along which the government's restraint program was implemented. Given speculation at the time that the next major area destined for expansion was social welfare, much as highways, education, and health had been in earlier periods, it was perhaps relevant that this field of activity was particularly susceptible to restraint.

Within the realm of social policy the education and health ministries were by the 1970s well-developed administrative empires with powerful cadres of professionals, well equipped to defend their established scale of operations. The position of the health ministry was further enhanced by the ease with which community groups could be aroused to resist the loss of local health care facilities, especially hospitals. The 'Communities and Social Services' part of the social policy field had few such defences. Its professional support was relatively weak, and new trends in professional thinking were already weakening the case for strong, centralized administration of welfare programs. Fashionable views on how best to care for the indigent, disabled, abandoned, or otherwise dependent members of society were now in favour of decentralized, local, community-based support rather than the institutional forms of care that had once been relied upon.[36] It was consequently possible to argue that cut-backs at the provincial level in this area were part of a deliberate and professionally sanctioned attempt to decentralize responsibility and to strengthen the role of the community. As the Ontario Joint Committee on Economic Policy – a group of senior civil servants, business executives, and one labour leader – advised the premier in 1974, such decentralization was desirable and so was the 'deconditionalization' of provincial-municipal revenue transfers to allow local governments more flexibility in determining their own spending priorities.[37]

Another policy trend that began to receive attention in Ontario during the 1970s and was also conveniently compatible with the neo-conservative rhetoric was the prospect of 'reprivatization.' The term was used by the Committee on Government Productivity, which noted that while 'government contracts for services with the private sector' were not new, having long been used in highway construction, printing, and the procurement of office supplies, there were other areas in which the government could invite 'public and / or private agencies to bid on the delivery of services.' The committee suggested that this could result in 'significant reprivatization, that is, the delegation of responsibility for program delivery to agencies outside the government.' The main advantage seen for such a development would be more flexibility and the possibility of tapping 'community skills and resources needed to meet policy objectives.'[38]

The principle was further endorsed by the 1974 joint committee, which recommended that 'where possible, government should receive services from the private sector through competitive tendering rather than providing the services itself,' thereby enabling the government to achieve 'significant cost savings.'[39]

The potential of the new conservatism with its emphasis on decentralization and scaling-down of provincial government involvement in the economic life of the province was also evident in the particularly troublesome matter of local government reform. By the early 1970s it appeared that the resistance to the regional government approach was hardening, and provincial policy-makers were showing signs of exasperation with the slow progress being made in their efforts to negotiate changes with well-entrenched local government interests in the province. Faced with such opposition, the government seemed to vacillate between imposing regional government and easing off in its efforts. In the legislature this uncertainty gave the opposition parties frequent opportunities to criticize the government both for what it was doing and for what it was not doing. In 1971 the Liberals advised the government to develop a plan for all Ontario similar to the regional plan being proposed for the Toronto area and to allow the municipalities to do their own planning within such a framework, thereby elminating the need for regional governments. By 1975 they were proposing that the regional government program should be halted and that the right of local councils to set their own planning goals and to implement their plans without provincial supervision should be affirmed.[40] By the end of the period the government had not resolved the dilemma presented by local government reorganization, but it had at least found a justification for delay, taking the position that such reorganization must continue, but making a virtue of the fact that no overall plan was about to be forced upon the unwilling.

This eclecticism was even more evident in the government's adroit withdrawal from the process of implementing province-wide economic planning in general. While it would continue to embrace the principles of 'planning,' it could also advocate a belief in the free market system as the best means of achieving its planning objectives. The approach developed by the mid-1970s was hauntingly familiar, evoking the language used in the early years of the Frost administration. As expressed in the speech from the throne in 1976, the government held that 'We must face the fact that government spending at all levels is a major cause of inflation' and went on to assert that 'It is time for the government, for the Legislature, for agencies receiving public funds and for the people to reassess programmes and define priorities in terms of needs rather than wants.' It appeared that special interest groups, agencies, and local authorities would be given scope in which to exercise their ingenuity in reducing their claims on the province for financial support. The government for its own part undertook to cut back on its services and on construction activities, not in order to solve its taxation dilemma, but to set free capital and labour for its use in what it claimed would be an expanding private sector. The best way to preserve the social and material environment that had been built up in the province in the future would be through 'maintaining a healthy climate for free entreprise.' As for social security, the position now was that 'Employment security is the only real income security a free society can afford for the vast majority of its citizens.'[41] (And that, it went without saying, was a federal government responsibility.) As for the provincial budget, the first priority, once again, would be 'to keep the province's finances in good order,' and this would be accomplished by slashing the growth in provincial spending, reordering priorities, trimming the cost of government, and reducing the number of civil servants.

The Ontario government reiterated its conviction that there was a need for 'a national economic policy for Canada,' but this, it was now added, should be based on 'a recognition that it is the free market economy, not bureaucratic regulation, upon which our present standard of living was achieved' and on which future growth would depend. Yet the Ontario government also proceeded to table documents in the legislature supporting its budget proposals advancing plans to establish an economic and social planning framework for the province as a whole as well as for selected regions.[42] It appeared that a new synthesis of seemingly contradictory elements had been forged, the tenuous logic of which could be found only in the neo-conservative doctrines of the time.

11 Conclusion

Both the economy of Ontario and the society it supported underwent remarkable growth and change in the years between 1939 and 1975. Most obvious was the sheer growth in population and in the volume of production. As a consequence of heavy net migration into the province, most of it from abroad, and high levels of natural increase in the earlier part of the period, the population of the province grew at an average annual rate of 2.3 per cent, with the highest rates recorded in the 1950s.

As in earlier periods of rapid population growth, the age composition of the population changed markedly. Whereas in the late 1930s persons under twenty years of age accounted for less than one-third of the total, by the early 1970s they made up 38 per cent. The high level of immigration also greatly affected the ethnic character of the population. The percentage of Ontario residents claiming English or French as their mother tongue had fallen from almost 89 per cent at the beginning of the period to less than 60 per cent by 1975. Despite the efforts of immigration authorities to direct immigrants into rural areas, most of the newcomers found their way into the cities of southern Ontario. Toronto and other major cities were socially and culturally transformed in the process, their earlier atmosphere of Upper Canadian Protestantism quite altered by the influence of hundreds of thousands of migrants, some from the United Kingdom, but most from southern Europe and the Mediterranean countries.

In the countryside the social and cutural changes were associated mainly with the huge reduction in the farm population. The traditional character of small-town, rural Ontario was greatly altered. Many of the focal points of rural community life were destroyed by the technical and economic changes affecting agriculture. Abandonment of marginal farmlands, the closing of local cheese factories and creameries, the trend to larger farms, the expansion of school districts and other local government units all weakened and, in some areas eliminated, established patterns of rural community life. Yet the decrease in farm population did not lead to any corresponding depopulation of the Ontario countryside. Throughout the period the rural non-farm population increased steadily.

As many urban workers found less expensive living accommodation in rural areas and as farmers took up part-time or seasonal off-farm employment, the old distinctions between the rural and urban populations became blurred. The differences in interests and outlook did not entirely disappear, as frequent conflicts between farmers and the new non-farming neighbours showed. But by the mid-1970s the dominant social and cultural characteristics of southern Ontario were clearly those of the metropolis, its urban values and preoccupations relentlessly disseminated by the greatly expanded media networks that grew up over the course of the period.

If the character and quality of life are much affected by the nature of the work people do, life in Ontario was considerably altered between 1939 and 1975. There were large shifts in the structure of employment in the province. While not so dramatically as the decline in farming, employment in other natural-resource-based industries also fell relative to other kinds of employment. In mining and forestry machines tended to replace workers, and the industries themselves declined in relative importance. While several new centres of industrial activity were created in northern Ontario as a result of new resource developments, much of the primary sector remained based on the developments of earlier periods. The northern resource frontier of the province became more a locus of intensive than extensive investment.

The aura of economic maturity with strong intimations of incipient decline surrounding the primary resources sector through much of the period was also discernible in manufacturing. As a source of jobs, manufacturing held its own in relation to the rest of the provincial economy. While several important new types of manufacturing were developed during the war years and after, the manufacturing sector as a whole was not a leading source of growth in the provincial economy. That function was performed by the service industries, as a growing part of the labour force found employment in industries such as trade, finance, business, and personal services, and health care.

While the relatively greater employment opportunities being created in the service industries did not transform Ontario into a province of 'pen pushers and paper shufflers,' it did create a favourable environment for increased female participation in the labour force, one of the major economic and social changes of the period.

There was also an important change in job requirements, with the general level of education and skill requirements rising in most occupations. Apprenticeship and other on-the-job training tended to decline in favour of more formal instructional techniques, one important side-effect of which was to keep young people in school longer. This trend increased the pressure on an educational system already faced with the large bulge in the post-war youth population, and created severe problems of financing, curriculum design, and conflicts over issues of educational philosophy.

Once in employment, most workers in Ontario were much better off in terms of working conditions, job security, and retirement prospects in 1975 than they had been in 1939. Although by the end of the period little more than one-quarter of the provincial labour force was unionized, industrial relations legislation had advanced to the point where the bitter struggles of the 1930s and 1940s for union recognition and orderly collective bargaining had been largely forgotten. Serious problems remained, however, particularly in the construction industry and in the case of government employees and other workers in 'essential services.' Strikes and lock-outs were common throughout the period, but progress towards a reasonably effective system of industrial relations seemed to have been made. A framework existed within which the interests of workers and employers could be sufficiently reconciled to keep the system functioning. Other improvements in the labour field included better safety standards and somewhat more adequate protection against occupational health hazards (although the seriousness of such problems was becoming more widely recognized); and hospitalization and other health care insurance schemes became universally available in Ontario as they were in other provinces.

Perhaps the most remarkable aspect of the economy's performance after 1939 was its ability to create enough jobs to employ a labour force expanding at historically record levels, which was at the same time becoming more productive. No one in the late 1930s could have been optimistic enough to foresee such a performance of the system. Few expected that even the existing labour force would be fully employed after the war. Yet unemployment in Ontario did not exceed 4.5 per cent until the recession of the late 1950s and early 1960s. Even with that interruption and a number of special problem areas, the spectre of mass unemployment was absent during the entire period. Indeed, shortages of labour, particularly of skilled workers and professionals, were more of a problem, although such shortages were greatly alleviated by the immigration of highly trained workers from abroad and in some cases from other parts of Canada. Despite Ontario's large and better developed facilities for training and professional education, the province was surprisingly dependent through much of the period on other jurisdictions to supply it with such workers.

The overall increase in labour productivity was an outstanding feature of the period. Some of the reasons for this phenomenon seem obvious. Most types of work were greatly affected by mechanization and associated technical changes which made labour more effective. The productivity gains from these changes were at least as great in activities such as farming and woods operations as in secondary manufacturing, communications, and other fields, where automation commanded more popular attention. The associated growth in the stock of real capital required a high level of performance on the part of the financial system through which funds were channelled from savers to those responsible for making the actual investments. However, not all the savings tapped for this boom in private and public investment spending were found within the province. Many were accumulated outside Ontario and outside the country. Toronto's position as one of Canada's main centres of financial intermediation may have facilitated the attraction of funds to the province, as did the province's high credit rating in international capital markets. For whatever reasons, investment flowed into the province, encouraged by provincial government policies and by the competitive bidding of municipal governments and local business organizations bent on attracting new industry. Throughout most of the period investable funds were cheap, with yields on provincial government bonds running between 3 and 6 per cent and the real returns to savers often running at zero or less after inflation was taken into account.

Increased scale was another obvious source of productivity gains during the period. The expansion of domestic markets brought about by rapid population growth and rising per capita real incomes permitted many producers to grow to a more efficient size. At the same time, however, investment in transportation and improved communications helped to widen individual markets, greatly increasing competition among widely dispersed producers for shares of the market. These conditions encouraged a trend towards concentration in most of the goods-producing industries in the province. In farming, forestry, mining, and manufacturing, producing units became larger and in most cases the number of firms fewer, a process that was further encouraged by the larger capital requirements needed if firms were to be competitive in wider markets. In wholesaling and the retail trade and in some of the other service areas, including parts of the financial system, a similar trend was apparent. The construction industry was an important exception to this general pattern, and in some other areas of the economy small independent operators remained viable.

The great increases in productivity over the period resulted in increased real incomes for workers and the population as a whole. Some of the gains in output were siphoned off to non-residents, and rents, interest, profits and dividends flowed out of Ontario to lenders and owners abroad. Some of the real value produced also leaked out of the province to Canadians in other parts of the country through the system of federal-provincial financial arrangements. Both types of 'leakage,' especially the latter, held the attention of provincial officials, but throughout most of the period, while real incomes were growing strongly, these leakages were seldom seen as serious problems. They appeared to be reasonable expenses which had to be accepted to maintain the political and economic framework within which the province was growing and prospering.

The prosperity was evident. Personal real income per capita tripled between 1939 and 1975. Taxes of course also increased, yet so did the benefits of public spending which brought value back to individuals and their families in the form of protection, education, and health care at levels of service clearly far above those available in any earlier period of the province's history. All these income and other benefits were widely shared, although in the 1960s it was perceived that a surprising number of individuals and families remained 'poor' in relation to some admittedly arbitrary minimum standard of material well-being.

The large increase in per capita real income over the period was all the more remarkable in that it was earned with less time spent at work. The total number of hours worked by the average employee in manufacturing, for example, fell from nearly forty-two at the end of the Second World War to thirty-nine in 1975. Given the improvements in working conditions, the influence of unions, and the extent of mechanization, it seems unlikely that the intensity of the work effort was correspondingly increased. There was also a trend towards longer vacations, formal sick-leave arrangements, and earlier retirement, which meant that the total time spent by a worker on the job during his or her working lifetime decreased. In short, the amount of leisure time available to workers increased substantially. How workers spent this time is difficult to document, but there is evidence of increased travel and utilization of recreational and entertainment facilities.

In the home and on the farm, housewives and farm workers also gained relief from much of the drudgery and physically demanding labour of earlier times. The mechanization of farming, electrification, conversion from solid to liquid or gaseous fuels for heating, and new household appliances still coming into more general use all helped to transform the more mundane aspects of everyday life. The new life-styles were also promoted by the increased availability and acceptance of prepared foods, the convenience of pre-packaging, and other innovations in the production and marketing of goods that made it possible for consumers to shop less frequently and at more convenient times. In 1939 retail stores still handled many everyday commodities in bulk – sugar, flour, fruits and vegetables, vinegar, kerosene, all were scooped or ladled out at time of purchase. By the 1970s only a few specialty stores catering to health faddists or the very affluent affected such methods.

Other benefits of the post-war prosperity that manifested themselves in Ontario were the increased availability of education, access to cultural opportunities, and the expansion of recreational opportunities. Adult and continuing education programs were greatly expanded along with the rest of the educational system in the province, especially in the 1960s. The urbanization of the population created new opportunities for individuals to find a range of entertainments and diversions far greater than could have been imagined in the more rural atmosphere of earlier times. Restaurants proliferated as dining out became feasible for more than travellers or family groups celebrating an event at the local hotel. Liquor licensing laws were relaxed, and it became possible to obtain alcoholic beverages with meals. In most parts of the province 'cocktail lounges' and bars were gradually introduced, supplementing the 'beer parlours' which nevertheless retained considerable custom. The sale of alcohol continued to be heavily regulated and taxed by the provincial government, but consumpion rose steadily, increasing from half a gallon per capita in the early 1940s to nearly two gallons by the end of the period.

Other possibly dangerous but much desired diversions became available to the population of Ontario over the period. In 1960 it became possible to attend moving picture shows on Sundays, although the public continued to accept a clumsy censorship of films designed to guard it against excessive sexual titillation. Radio entertainment became almost universally available and, beginning in the 1950s, so did television. By 1975 fewer than 3 per cent of Ontario households lacked TV.

Travel also became a mass consumption item. Summer vacations became commonplace, and easy access was provided by the still-growing highway system to recreational areas throughout the province and, indeed, to the continent. Increasing numbers of residents in southern Ontario became cottage owners, flocking to areas once the preserve of the more affluent middle classes. Even more remarkable was the increase in foreign travel, as relatively inexpensive, long-distance air service made Europe and even more remote destinations accessible to many. The growth of such traffic was attested to by the development of Toronto's airport from a desolate collection of sheds beside a runway at Malton into the imposing, if not very functional, Terminals One and Two.

These gains in living conditions were not free of cost, and there were failures as well in the performance of the economy over the period. The improvements in productive efficiency and the increased security of individuals were made possible in part by the concentration of decision-making power and the creation of large and complex organizations which were often troublesome to deal with. There were concerns, but little hard evidence, about possible deterioration in the rights of individuals, privacy, and the impact of advertising on consumer behaviour. Some of the elements of the 'welfare state' introduced during the period alleviated many of the risks of living, but at the same time necessitated higher taxation and compliance by individuals with bureaucratic routines and procedures.

For businesses the bureaucratization of economic processes meant an increase in paperwork to comply with tax laws (especially the retail sales tax), employee benefits, and the growing list of requirements concerning land use, pollution abatement, and occupational health. In addition, the requirements imposed by unions, trade and professional associations, producers' organizations, and other private and public bodies grew in number and influence during the period.

While much of this erosion of business independence after 1939 may be traced to measures designed either by governments or by businesses themselves to restrict the free functioning of markets, the operation of 'normal' commercial forces also tended to reduce competition and in many cases to undermine the role of independent producers, including farmers. Throughout the industry-by-industry accounts of earlier chapters runs a persistent trend towards concentration of ownership and control, as small producers in many kinds of business were forced out of business, bought out, or absorbed by larger enterprises. Small, independent business did not disappear from the Ontraio scene and in some areas of the economy showed great persistence and vitality, but the overall trend appears to have been towards concentration.

One reason was the increasing capital requirements of many kinds of production. This point is clear in the cases of farming, fishing, forestry, and many kinds of manufacturing, where larger producing units not only had lower per-unit operating costs but could better finance and utilize capital in the process. Government policies recognized this trend, offering aid in various forms to smaller businesses – to what effect it is difficult to ascertain.

The economic costs of the increasing interdependence in personal and business life are elusive. Some are easily imagined, all are difficult, if not impossible, to measure. Consumers often appeared to be convinced that they were being exploited by producers, and there were attempts to organize more effective consumer groups and to enact legislation to curb such abuses. But most consumers apparently felt that the benefits of large-scale production and distribution outweighed the cost, judging from how little resistance to business concentration was forthcoming. The provincial government certainly did little in this respect. Apart from ritual affirmations of its commitment to free enterprise, the provincial government's policies do not appear to have been used to discourage bigness and the pursuit of technical efficiency. It is difficult to find a specific government policy during the period that sacrificed such considerations to promote smallness and competition.

The great increase in the production of goods in the decades following the Depression was accompanied by some increase in the production of 'bads' as well. Whether the external costs of increased per capita output were greater or only more clearly recognized in this period is debatable, but such costs are substantial and, once pointed out, conspicuous. The depletion of non-renewable resources at what may have been suboptimal rates of utilization; waste and mismangement of renewable resources such as the forests; water and air pollution; crowding; traffic congestion; noise; contamination of land with industrial wastes – all these effects must be counted among the real costs of the great expansion of the economy during the period.

In the mining industry, there was no effective system for determining the appropriate timing of development or most economical rate of depletion. Even in the important new mining projects of the period in which large elements of public control were possible, as in the case of uranium, the elements of public planning involved were probably counter-productive. The conversion of farmland to other uses was similarly governed by forces that appeared to be almost entirely haphazard. The forest industry was pushed further into the remoter regions of the province, but most of the best timber disappeared and was not regenerated.

The fish resources of the lakes and rivers were severely reduced in value by industrial pollution. Much of the land that was retained in agricultural production was subjected to practices that threatened its future fertility, as farmers sought to meet the immediate commercial pressures imposed upon them by increasing their reliance on chemical fertilizers, pesticides, herbicides, and heavier equipment to extract ever-increasing yields per acre.

In the cities, air pollution became a cause of increasing concern, but considerable progress was made in bringing the problem under control, largely through the implementation of national policies that reduced noxious automobile exhaust emissions and restrictions at the local level on certain industrial operations. In Hamilton, for example, the maximum air pollution reading recorded in 1970 was 56. In 1975 it was only 28.[1]

Housing standards were also a source of discontent. There were some students of the period who were highly critical of the suburban housing and the kind of life it supported. S.D. Clark, for example, argued in his definitive study of suburban development in the Toronto area, *The Suburban Society*, that the kind of growth that took place there after the Second World War was 'appallingly wasteful' and that 'there was something almost fraudulent about the whole vast enterprise directed to the object of persuading people to move to the suburbs,' because of the hidden or deferred costs involved – the costs of municipal services, transportation, government aid to housebuilders, and mortgage financing.[2] But with such possibilities acknowledged, the suburbs did provide housing and a life-style with which many people appeared to be contented. In 1968 the Gallup Poll found that 69 per cent of its respondents in Ontario were generally satisfied with their housing situation.[3]

Despite the facts that the physical production of housing in the province was increasing faster than the number of new families during the 1960s and early 1970s and that incomes were rising faster than housing costs in most but not all locations in the province, there was, nevertheless, a perceived 'housing shortage.' The problem appeared to be more one of expectations than physical accommodation. As one of the several studies of the situation done in the early 1970s reported, 'The physical condition of housing in Ontario is by and large satisfactory in that it meets accepted standards. Some persons are housed badly, in a physical sense, and in some cities some people are living in accommodation which is physically adequate but overcrowded. In general the housing problems of Ontario do not appear to relate to the physical condition of accommodation but mainly to its amount and its cost.'[4]

There were other areas of disappointed expectations. Despite the much-remarked-upon expansion of health, education, and welfare services, it is not obvious that the benefits were greatly in excess of the costs or that the aspirations that underlay the post-Depression reform movements were realized. It is true that most people were living longer – the average life expectancy for males at birth rose from less than sixty-seven years at the end of the 1940s to almost seventy in the early 1970s, with the female expectation of life rising from about seventy-two years to seventy-seven years over the same period. Infant mortality and maternal mortality, both indicators of health standards, declined and were lower in Ontario than in Canada as a whole. Several great scourges were virtually eliminated – tuberculosis, polio, and diptheria, for example, almost disappeared. Much pain and suffering were alleviated by improved treatment of traumas and other emergency conditions. Perhaps more significant than any of these indicators was the perception that progress in health care had been made. It is unlikely that many people at the end of the period would have been willing to accept a return to the health care financing and delivery systems of the 1930s or 1940s.

Yet worrisome problems remained. There were growing doubts about the 'cost-effectiveness' of many medical procedures and of the 'fee for service' system still in effect. There were also doubts about the ability of the authorities to control costs in a field where supply seemed able to create its own demand and where practitioners had both the opportunity and the financial incentive to oversupply their services. There was concern about the rise in morbidity associated with affluent living – obesity, alcoholism, automobile accidents – and the health effects of smoking and exposure to carcinogenic materials present in the food supply and the environment generally. An added concern was the fact that as population growth slowed in the later years of the period, the population was aging and seemed likely to require increased amounts of medical and other forms of assistance.

In the field of education the expansion of opportunity for more years of formal instruction was associated with changes in the system that not everyone believed were desirable. While falling standards of education have been bemoaned by every generation of teachers, the concerns arising in the late 1960s and early 1970s were quite specific. While the professional preparation of teachers was much improved, increased crowding of classrooms and dissatisfaction with salaries and working conditions were beginning to affect morale. But such observations remained at best anecdotal; for, as the report of the Hall-Dennis Committee had demonstrated, no one in the province was able to formulate sensible goals for the educational system or define operational performance criteria to assess its effectiveness.

The great emphasis placed on education as a source of economic growth during the early 1960s had been justified by inference rather than direct evidence. By the early 1970s the hypothesis that education was economically beneficial to the community and to individuals had not been refuted, but the subject seemed to have slipped quietly out of the public consciousness as easily as it had entered it a decade earlier. Although most educational requirements for jobs were raised, as unemployment re-emerged as a serious social problem in the later years of the period, it became apparent to many young people that such qualifications were a necessary but not a sufficient condition for getting a job.

Just as the greatest success of the economic system in the post-war period was the amount of employment it created, one of its greatest failures was the reappearance of substantial and persistent involuntary unemployment in the latter part of the period. By 1975 it was becoming clear that under conditions in which the economy was subject to strong, but not easily identified inflationary forces, governments could not utilize the tools of economic management that had seemed so promising in the earlier years. At the same time, however, the conviction that governments should be held responsible for the performance of the system, another legacy of the 1930s and 1940s, remained intact.

Yet another disappointment with the performance of the economy was the persistence of poverty. By the 1960s it was recognized that even with high levels of employment and a large, if ill-co-ordinated income support system in place, a substantial portion of the population seemed destined to remain 'poor' relative to the rest. Again, this situation seemed particularly distressing in the country's richest and most developed province. However poverty was defined, its presence was unmistakable. Large pockets of poverty appeared to be the result of special circumstances such as the situation of the native people, family disintegration, the immobility of parts of the rural population. But a surprising amount seemed to be found among the fully employed living in relatively 'normal' circumstances. While much attention was directed to this phenomenon and a variety of remedies proposed, by 1975 little of practical value had been accomplished. Attempts to reorganize the welfare system became bogged down in federal-provincial conferences and negotiations. By the end of the period it was surprising how little the actual distribution of income in the economy had changed since the 1930s.

But even when all these failures and disappointments are taken into account, the overall performance of the Ontario economy during the thirty-five years following the Depression must be judged a success, the gains by any reasonable calculus far outweighing the losses. It was a period of great prosperity for a rapidly growing population, and it is difficult to avoid saying that some kind of economic 'progress' had been made.

It is interesting that none of this progress had been anticipated. The unexpectedness of the boom that followed the Second World War was not simply a product of uninformed pessimism or the unwillingness of observers to try to see beyond the contemporary scene. For those interested in the 'conditions of economic progress' in 1939 the prospects for development in any advanced industrial economy were far from bright. It was not only the Marxists who foresaw chronic failure lying ahead. A basic tenet of Keynesianism, which was winning attention in Canada as well as in Britain and the United States, was that contemporary capitalist economies faced inevitable chronic mass unemployment because of a tendency for private investment spending to fall short of what was needed to offset saving. The Keynesian prescription, which in its broader version has sometimes been referred to as 'collective conservatism,' included proposals that would bolster demand and, if necessary, replace private investment with public spending to preserve the desirable features of capitalism and hold at bay the alternatives of fascism and communism.

In America the theoretical underpinnings of this approach had been taken up and popularized by Alvin Hansen, who supplemented the short-term Keynesian analysis with his own explanation of the longer-term course of events, which he thought had brought even American capitalism to the sorry state it seemed to be in by the late 1930s. In his 1938 presidential address to the American Economic Association Hansen sketched an account of American growth in which the vigour of the nineteenth century was sapped in the twentieth by a declining rate of population growth; the closing of the western frontier of settlement; and the exhaustion of the technical innovations that had brought about the railways, the automobile, and electrical power. Even when new inventions did come along, Hansen reasoned, they would not as easily be implemented because of the restraining influences of labour unions, monopolistic business organization, and the reduction in price competition among producers.[5]

The relevance of this analysis to the Canadian situation and the situation in Ontario was obvious, not only because of the similarity of the economic systems, but because of the direct links between them, a matter that had become all too apparent during the collapse of the 1930s. Of course the analysis failed miserably to predict what was about to happen. At least for a quarter of a century or more the causes of secular stagnation identified by Hansen were cancelled out by unforeseeable events. The rate of population growth in the industrialized countries confounded demographers by inexplicably rising instead of continuing to decline. No new land frontiers comparable to the west opened up, but natural-resource development accelerated, particularly in the region of the Canadian Shield. As for innovation, entirely new technologies and industries based on them once again emerged: petrochemicals, synthetic fabrics, electronics, data processing, jet aircraft, atomic power.

There was also a substantial change in the economic role of government, and public spending rose for a variety of reasons. There was a change in outlook and expectations too. The 'animal instincts' of at least some entrepreneurs were miraculously revived.

Yet for all the new ideas about the economic role of the government and the widespread loss of confidence in the ideal of a self-regulating market economy, there is little reason to believe that the great expansion of the 1939–75 period was deliberately engineered or even very effectively manipulated. Few people in the early part of the period could have held much hope for the reconstruction of the economy along unmanaged, free-market lines. It appeared obvious that governments would have to intervene on a broad front if the expected post-war return to depression and unemployment was to be avoided, if producers were to be ensured incomes adequate to maintain them in their chosen lines of business, if wage earners were to obtain 'fair' wages under reasonable working conditions, if smaller centres were to have a share of new industry, if natural resources were to be properly utilized, if children were to have access to adequate education, if individuals were to have the health care they needed, if the poor were to be supported at some minimum level of existence, if transportation facilities and services were to be adequate and 'fairly' priced, if electric power was to be available in sufficient quantities at an acceptable price, if water and sewage systems were to be built and maintained, and if there were to be adequate supplies of milk and other necessities of life available to consumers.

While the avowed socialists in the CCF-NDP led the way in proclaiming the need for state intervention to ensure that such objectives were met, even the Conservatives freely dedicated themselves to such a point of view. As the period progressed, successsive Conservative governments in Ontario became if anything more rather than less interventionist in relation to specific areas of economic life in the province – attempting to control the use of land, to redirect the location of private industry, to manage the supply of manpower, to influence the rate of technological change and, in the 1960s, even adopting the Keynesian policies of counter-cyclical budgeting in an attempt to control inflation and unemployment. Such active participation by a government in economic life was not particularly novel in Canadian experience; what was new was the dawning perception that if such efforts were to make any sense, they would have to be directed to the attainment of some identifiable goal. This fact was becoming apparent even in the early 1940s, as the formulation of Drew's 22 Points attests. If the market system was to be supplanted in any substantial way by conscious direction either by the government or by other bodies such as the producers' associations, rate-setting tribunals, or the like, an overall framework was needed within which decisions could be co-ordinated and, perhaps more important, conflicting values reconciled. This was what economic planning connoted. And this, as Harold Innis may have foreseen early in the 1930s, was where the whole endeavour was destined to break down. As Professor Neill has argued, Innis believed in the need for social policy and the 'inevitability of planning,' but he had little hope for any easy solution to the problems of the time. Neill notes that for Innis, 'The concept of planning meant an explicit role for social value judgements, which are arrived at through some political process,' but there seemed to be no way to prepare such judgments objectively; for in his view contemporary economics 'was little more than the intellectual dimension of the problems to be solved.'[6]

Despite the expansion of economic intelligence facilities within the government bureaucracy and its external advisory bodies and despite the growth of knowledge about how economic systems work, no overall rationale for the non-market elements in the system was developed. The failure of planning in this sense was complete. In the absence of such purpose, partial planning exercises were doomed to be nothing more than responses to particular requirements and pressures: land-use planning became mired in conflicting priorities, manpower planning foundered on the failure of forecasting; regional planning became a battleground for opposing interest groups; and industrial strategy became an empty declaration of good intentions. The inability to develop any set of coherent goals for the economy as a whole was of course partly a consequence of the federal-provincial division of powers, and the extent of this problem was well recognized. The need for a reconciliation of federal and provincial interests was frequently acknowledged by provincial spokesmen, but despite occasional progress in specific areas, by 1975 no general solution of this constitutional obstacle to serious planning was in sight.

Within the province there was also an inherent conflict between the established political institutions and processes and the idea of planning. The federal-provincial conflict was mirrored in the relations between the province and the municipalities, although the province admittedly had more influence with the latter than the federal authority had. By the end of the period, despite persistent efforts to resolve the problem by way of local government reorganization and the creation of alternative decision-making mechanisms, local and regional planning efforts still were unreconciled with provincial-municipal 'politics.'[7]

There were also problems with the reconciliation of values and interests within the provincial government apparatus itself. The legislature provided an inadequate forum for even the discussion of economic objectives. The level of debate on economic issues was generally very low, with ministers on occasion displaying remarkably little understanding of basic economic processes and a surprising willingness to perpetuate popular misconceptions and beliefs. The backbenchers, with a very few but notable exceptions, could and did do much worse.

At the cabinet level, the work done towards the end of the period by the Committee on Government Productivity showed that the inadequacy of the cabinet as a policy-making body was recognized. Many of the changes subsequently brought about promised to make the cabinet more effective in this role, particularly in establishing broad policy priorities. But the inherent conflicts between recommendations based on economic reasoning and the gut instincts of successful politicians persisted, as did conflicts between the legislature and the bureaucracy as competing channels through which policy recommendations would flow to cabinet. It is significant that the COGP was not allowed to examine even the functions of the legislature (although a separate body was established to perform this task). The COGP was almost a caricature of the 'scientific' approach to decision-making. The legislature was just the opposite. The two could not be reconciled.

Even if administrative solutions to these differences in approach could have been worked out, the implementation of planning in the full sense of the term would still have failed, if for no other reason than the fact that no one, with the possible exception of some people in the NDP, wanted it. As all observers of

Ontario governments over the period had agreed, they were without exception non-ideological and uniformly pragmatic in their approach to governing. Nor is it helpful to characterize them as lackeys of private business interests. Often they were highly responsive to the wishes of business, but they could also be aloof. Given the backgrounds of the individuals involved, the size of the political contributions made by business to the ruling party, and above all, the prevailing conventional beliefs about the benefits to be derived from promoting business activity, it is surprising that they were as independent-minded as they were on occasion. They were responsive to other interests as well.

If they were pragmatic and non-ideological, it is not true that the Ontario governments of the period were beyond the influence of ideas. On the contrary, they were remarkably quick to pick up new ideas, including fads and fancies of the time, whenever it suited their purposes. They embraced, without evident concern for consistency, 'planning,' conservation, public ownership, education, health insurance, regional government, industrial promotion, urban transport, counter-cyclical budgeting, the war on poverty, the fight against inflation, and neo-conservatism, as the occasion and practice elsewhere recommended such policies. They were often more trendy than conservative.

But this same facility, like their pragmatism, was inimical to planning. The Ontario governments of the period moved through more than three decades responding to events, to new ideas, and to the public's changing perceptions of what governments could be expected to be and do. They had some effect on the course of these events. Either deliberately or inadvertently, provincial government policies deflected growth in some sectors at the expense of others; raised land values in some areas and lowered them elsewhere; increased the supply of certain kinds of skills; expanded the education system; and had a host of different effects as a result of taxation policies, highway expenditures, zoning laws, subsidies, and grants. Yet at the end it is difficult to conclude that the net effect of all this on the growth and development of the Ontario economy of the period was positive or negative, let alone estimate its magnitude.

To the extent the expansion of the economy after the Depression was 'controlled,' it probably was so mainly by forces originating outside the province. As long as the expansion continued, this control was not as apparent as when it began to slow. When the long period of growth was checked in the early 1970s, it was propitious that the Ontario government was in a position to renounce economic management and make a virtue of its need to adapt to the new economic realities being forced upon it.

The slowing of the great post-Depression expansion in the 1970s was as unexpected as its beginnings had been in the 1940s. Stagnation again appeared to be a possibility. Population growth was even lower, with the Net Reproduction Rate approaching zero and immigration sharply curtailed. The process of urbanization appeared to be at least temporarily in check, with a surprising shift toward the countryside taking place. As the business cycle reasserted itself, private investment predictably fell, but rather than expanding public investment vigorously, the government talked as it had in the 1930s of the need to restrict public spending to preserve confidence in the economy. After decades of trade liberalization, demands for increased protection to avoid mass unemployment in the land were once again being voiced.

Prospects for continued growth in the traditional resource industries were also not immediately promising. The government was indicating to private investors that it was prepared to insist on a more direct public role in the development of new resources. The establishment of three new ministries – Natural Resources, Energy, and Northern Affairs – and, at the cabinet level, creation of a resource development policy committee seemed indicative of a more active and possibly restrictive approach to resource development in the province. Added to this impression were the issues of environmental protection and the social impacts of resource developments. Although the government proved to be pliable when faced with conflicts between enforcing environmental protection standards and maintaining jobs and investment in polluting industries, the political pressure from environmentalists could not be ignored, as was demonstrated by the enactment of legislation in 1975, the 'Environmental Assessment Act,' which was intended to provide for a comprehensive review and evaluation of all large-scale projects with significant environmental effects. Not even the province's own great agency, Ontario Hydro, was exempt from the re-examination of traditional arrangements in this type of activity. The principle of growth and expansion without concern to cost implicit in earlier practices would no longer go unchallenged.[8]

The perennial dream of expanding the northern resource frontier was also fading perceptibly by the end of the period. Despite elaborate studies of the economic base of north-eastern and north-western Ontario and the implementation of various federal and provincial programs to promote development in those regions, the census evidence of the late 1960s indicated that for some time to come they were likely to remain declining regions rather than centres of growth. By 1975 the population of northern Ontario was actually declining.

Prospects for further economic growth resulting from technological change were also becoming dim, although it must be admitted that little more was known about the causes of invention and innovation in 1975 than in the 1950s, when the beeping of the Soviet Union's Sputnik aroused interest in the matter. If it were a matter of education, as was believed in the 1960s, the trends in the early 1970s were not promising. Once again doubts were being raised about the quality of education in the province, particularly at the higher levels, where the government's efforts to control the growth of educational spending were creating serious funding problems. The impact of funding cuts on graduate education and closely related research activities was severe and in the view of many, deleterious.

In the case of industrial applications, as distinguished from the production of new basic knowledge per se, the apparent weakness in the research and development programs of branch plants operated by multinational corporations was becoming a topic of great interest.

With the slow-down in population growth, the restrictions on natural-resource development, the apparent failure of northern settlement policies, and growing evidence that the sources, domestic and foreign, of new technologies and products were drying up, many of the concerns of the late 1930s appeared to be reviving. The prospect that public spending and other government initiatives could take up the slack or that a new economic order could be designed within the traditional democratic political framework was bleaker than it had been in the preceding thirty years. Instead of new and more aggressive government measures to stimulate economic growth, the government of Ontario was preoccupied with inflation and its own financial situation, problems it proposed to attack by restraining public spending. As the government declared in the 1975 speech from the throne, 'for the first time in many years the long prevailing prosperity and buoyant growth of the Province of Ontario has been challenged.'[9] The government's approach to the problem would be to reduce its role in the economic life of the province. The liberal economic philosophy of the post-Depression years was clearly on the wane. Although as late as the mid-1960s the provincial government had been proclaiming the wisdom of Keynesian budgetary principles, by the mid-1970s the position was quite the opposite: government spending would have to be reduced, there would have to be less government 'interference' in the economy, and the budget should be balanced. Faith in the possibility of economic management was failing rapidly.

Confidence in Ontario's relative position within the Canadian economy was also showing signs of erosion. Ontario was still the dominant province, and it retained its central position with respect to markets, transportation, manufacturing, finance, and proximity to centres of North American economic power. Yet its pre-eminence was less secure than it had been. The province's share of Canada's personal income reached 42 per cent in 1970 but by 1975 had dropped to 39.6 per cent.[10] At the beginning of the decade unemployment in Ontario was lower than in any other province. By 1975 three other provinces had lower unemployment rates. Such indicators were responding, of course, to short-time trends and reflected the particular susceptibility of Ontario's manufacturing sector to cyclical fluctuations in demand, while the unusual features of the energy boom were strongly influencing the situation in western Canada. But there were other indications that longer-term trends were shifting the centre of growth from Ontario to provinces such as Alberta and British Columbia, notably changes in internal migration patterns, which substantiated fears in Ontario that more than temporary shifts in the balance of economic advantages were taking place nationally.

The economy of Ontario, while well balanced and prosperous, was beginning, like the economies of some adjacent regions in the United States, to appear distinctly middle-aged, with an industrial core showing signs of obsolescence along with its maturity. The possible sources of rejuvenation were not in sight, although comfort could be taken from the fact that in 1939 the outlook had been at least as bleak and the existing state of the economy very much worse.

Notes

INTRODUCTION

1 This period is almost totally neglected in the standard Canadian economic history texts. Two sources published after the present study was substantially completed may be recommended. A collection of original articles edited by M.S. Cross and G.S. Kealey, *Modern Canada 1930–1980's* (published as vol. 5 in the series Readings in Canadian Social History [Toronto: McClelland and Stewart, 1984]) provides an overview of the country's social and economic history since the Depression. The first section, containing articles by Paul Phillips and Stephen Watson ('From Mobilization to Continentalism: The Canadian Economy in the Post-Depression Period') and David Wolfe ('The Rise and Demise of the Keynesian Era in Canada: Economic Policy, 1930–1982'), is particularly useful. For the period after 1945 much useful information and a contrasting perspective on national economic events and issues will be found in R. Bothwell, I. Drummond, and J. English, *Canada since 1945: Power, Politics, and Provincialism* (Toronto: University of Toronto Press, 1981).
2 See F.H. Leacy, ed., *Historical Statistics of Canada*, second edition, (Ottawa: Statistics Canada, 1983), K172–3.
3 Many academic economists in Canada believed that the high unemployment and the current-account deficit in the balance of payments in the late 1950s were being aggravated by the restrictive monetary policies favoured by Mr Coyne, reasoning that easier credit would stimulate demand and reduce unemployment and that the current-account deficit would be corrected once the U.S. recession ended and demand for Canadian exports picked up. Mr Coyne argued, on the contrary, that Canadians were 'living beyond their means,' as indicated by the current-account deficit and the large capital inflows, and that restrictive monetary policy was required to prevent the problem from becoming worse. See H. Scott Gordon, *The Economists versus the Bank of Canada* (Toronto: The Ryerson Press, 1961).
4 The fixed-exchange-rate regime of the post-war years was clearly incompatible with the effective use of monetary policy to stabilize the domestic economy. In the particular circumstances cited, when the Bank of Canada had to purchase foreign currency to support the fixed value of the Canadian dollar in the exchange market, its payments for this currency found their way into the cash reserves of the commercial banks, thereby increasing the banks' capacity to expand the money supply. Thus, in order to maintain a given level of external stability as represented by the exchange rate, the ability to restrain domestic inflation had to be sacrificed.
5 See D. Walters, *Canadian Economic Growth Revisited* (Ottawa: Economic Council of Canada, 1970); also E.F. Denison, *The Sources of Economic Growth in the United States and the Alternatives before Us* (New York: Committee for Economic Development, 1962), and his later study, *Accounting for United States Economic Growth 1929–1969* (Washington DC: Brookings Institution, 1974).
6 A. Blomqvist, P. Wonnacott, and R. Wonnacott, *Economics, First Canadian Edition* (Toronto: McGraw-Hill Ryerson, 1983), 397

7 M. Denny and M. Fuss, *Productivity: A Selective Survey of Recent Developments and the Canadian Experience* (Toronto: OEC, 1982), 35
8 For a representative sample see Canada, *Foreign Ownership and the Structure of Canadian Industry* (Ottawa: Queen's Printer, 1968) (the 'Watkins Report'); K. Levitt, *Silent Surrender* (Toronto: Macmillan, 1970); A.E. Safarian, *The Performance of Foreign-Owned Firms in Canada* (Montreal: Canadian-American Committee, 1969); H.G. Johnson, *The Canadian Quandary* (Toronto: McGraw-Hill, 1963); A. Rotstein, *The Precarious Homestead* (Toronto: new press, 1973), 8–15; D. Walters, *Canadian Income Levels and Growth: An International Perspective*, Economic Council of Canada, Staff Study No. 23 (Ottawa: Queen's Printer, 1968); Science Council of Canada, *Innovation in a Cold Climate: The Dilemma of Canadian Manufacturing*, Report No. 15 (Ottawa, 1971); P.L. Bourgault, *Innovation and the Structure of Canadian Industry*, Science Council of Canada, Background Study No. 23 (Ottawa, 1972).
9 The standard reference on the subject is V.R. Fuchs, *The Service Economy* (New York: National Bureau of Economic Research, 1968). The applicability of Fuchs's analysis to Canada is examined in D.A. Worton, 'The Service Industries in Canada, 1946–1966,' in V.R. Fuchs, ed., *Production and Productivity in the Service Industries* (New York: Columbia University Press, 1969), 237–81.
10 One of the more surprising difficulties encountered in this study was the inability of the Ontario government to supply statistical support. While the province's statistical service resources were made accessible, they proved to have little to offer, and despite the co-operative attitude of those directly involved, the means were not available to construct the kind of historical series needed to provide the empirical base required for this type of work.
11 See K.A.H. Buckley, 'The Role of Staple Industries in Canada's Economic Development,' *Journal of Economic History*, 18 (1958), 439–50, and M.H. Watkins, 'A Staple Theory of Economic Growth,' *Candian Journal of Economics and Political Science*, 29 (1963), 141–58.
12 See M.H. Watkins, 'The Staple Theory Revisited,' *Journal of Canadian Studies*, 12 (1977), 83–95, and 'The Innis Tradition in Canadian Political Economy,' *Canadian Journal of Political and Social Theory*, 6 (1982), 12–33.

CHAPTER 1: *War, Recovery, and Management of the Provincial Economy*

1 All data in this paragraph are from the 1941 *Census of Canada*.
2 Ontario, Bureau of Statistics and Research, *A Conspectus of the Province of Ontario* (hereafter *Conspectus of Ontario*) (Toronto, 1946), table 26, 219
3 Ibid., table 36, 234
4 Ibid., table 34, 233
5 Ontario, Ontario Committee on Taxation Report, vol. 1, (Toronto, 1967), table 4:4, 124
6 N. McKenty, *Mitch Hepburn* (Toronto: McClelland and Stewart, 1967), 258
7 Toronto *Globe and Mail*, 10 July 1943, editorial
8 Toronto *Globe and Mail*, 26 May 1943, 1 and 5
9 Toronto *Globe and Mail*, 22 May 1943, 2
10 All references to the 22 Points program are based on the report of the original broadcast as published in the Toronto *Globe and Mail*, 9 July 1943, 1 and 2.
11 Toronto *Globe and Mail*, 9 July 1943, 1
12 Ontario Legislative Assembly, *Debates* (hereafter *Debates*) 22 Feb. 1944, n.p. Also see Ontario Economic Council, *Subject to Approval: A Review of Municipal Planning in Ontario*, (Toronto: OEC, 1973), appendix B, 155.
13 *Debates*, 28 Feb. 1945, 422–3
14 PAO, A. Careless to T.M. Russell, Taxation and Policy Branch, Treasury and Economics, 3 Jan. 1972, series VIII-1, Box 16, Joint Economic Planning
15 *Debates*, budget speech, 11 March 1947, 61–89
16 Ibid.
17 *Debates*, speech from the throne, 12 Feb. 1953, 11–12
18 See, for example, the reference to the need for an 'Economic Committee' to co-ordinate provincial and federal capital projects, thereby avoiding conflicts in economic stabilization programs; *Debates*, 11 March 1954, 501.

Notes to pages 26–35   259

CHAPTER 2: *Population and Labour Force*

1 Breaking down the productivity increases and attributing them to the various possible sources, such as technical improvements, large-scale operations, education, and the like, was a lively scholarly activity, particularly in the 1960s. For a succinct account see Economic Council of Canada, Second Annual Review, *Towards Sustained and Balanced Economic Growth* (Ottawa: Queen's Printer, 1965), 45–69.
2 Ontario, Ministry of Treasury, Economics and Intergovernmental Affairs (hereafter TEIGA), *Ontario Statistics 1975* (hereafter *Ontario Statistics (year)*, vol. 1, Social Series (Toronto, 1976), table 3.2, 98.
3 The number of infant deaths under one year of age per thousand of population, which was still as high as thirty in 1951, had decreased to approximately thirteen by the mid-1970s.
4 Ontario's recruitment campaign at the end of the war appears to have been largely a consequence of the premier's personal initiatives. 'Drew's Airlift' brought several thousand British immigrant workers and their families directly to the province.
5 This amounted to 290,000 immigrants in the 1940s, 800,000 in the 1950s, and 766,000 in the 1960s. See Ontario, TEIGA, *Ontario's Changing Population*, vol. 1 (Toronto, 1976), appendix B, 81.
6 Ontario, TEIGA, *Ontario's Changing Population*, vol. 1, table 10, 41
7 For a discussion of Canadian immigration policy in this period see F. Hawkins, *Canada and Immigration: Public Policy and Public Concern* (Montreal: McGill-Queen's University Press, 1972).
8 Ontario, TEIGA, *Ontario's Changing Population*, vol. 1, table 11, 43
9 Ibid., 49
10 Ontario, TEIGA, *Statistical Appendix, Northeastern Ontario Planning Region* (Toronto, 1976), table 1.1.1
11 A detailed analysis of these regional growth patterns in the province is provided in M. Amyot and M.V. George, *Intraprovincial Migration Streams in Quebec and Ontario* (Ottawa: Statistics Canada, 1973).
12 Ontario, TEIGA, *Ontario's Changing Population*, vol. 1, 26 and table 5, 27
13 There are some difficulties with definitions changing over the period discussed, but the general pattern is well documented. See J. Punter and G. Hodge, 'The City on the Periphery,' in L.S. Bourne, E.D. MacKinnon, and J.W. Simmons, eds, *Urban Futures for Central Canada: Perspectives on Forecasting Urban Growth and Form* (Toronto: University of Toronto Press, 1974).
14 Ontario, TEIGA, *Ontario's Changing Population*, vol. II, table 15, 50
15 See Ontario Economic Council, *Ontario: A Society in Transition* (Toronto: OEC, 1972), 38–9.
16 *Ontario Statistics 1975*, vol. II, table 10.17, 422
17 Ontario, TEIGA, *Ontario's Changing Population*, vol. II, appendix 1, 168
18 Leacy, ed., *Historical Statistics of Canada*, 2nd ed., E128–35
19 See G.W. Bertram, *The Contribution of Education to Economic Growth*, Staff Study No. 12 (Ottawa: Economic Council of Canada, 1965).
20 This belief was fostered by contemporary research into the sources of economic growth. See E.F. Denison, *The Sources of Economic Growth in the United States and the Alternatives before Us*, Supplementary Paper No. 13 (Washington, DC: Committee for Economic Development, 1962).
21 See, for example, Ontario Economic Council, *Ontario: A Society in Transition*, 36; and Statistics Canada Special Labour Force Study No. 3, *The Job-Content of the Canadian Economy 1941–61* (Ottawa, n.d.), E. and F.
22 Statistics Canada, (DBS), Special Labour Force Survey, 1965, as cited in Ontario Economic Council, *Ontario: A Society in Transition*, 37
23 As set out in the *White Paper on Employment and Income* (Ottawa: King's Printer, 1945)
24 See H.L. Madge, 'Ontario Labour Markets 1953–1963,' *Ontario Economic Review*, 2 (1964), n.p.
25 'Strikes and the CIO,' *The Canadian Statesman*, Bowmanville, 18 Sept. 1941, PAO, Hepburn Papers, Box 311, CIO

26 PAO, Hepburn Papers, M.F. Hepburn to R.H. Gale, Montreal, 14 Jan. 1942, Box 321, CIO
27 PAO, Hepburn Papers, J.P. MacKay, MPP, to M.F. Hepburn, 1 Sept. 1942, Box 327, J.P. MacKay
28 H.D. Woods and S. Ostry, *Labour Policy and Labour Economics in Canada* (Toronto: Macmillan, 1962), chap. 3
29 PAO, Frost Papers, L. Frost, Remarks on the Labour Relations Act, 1950, Box 19, Subject Files, Labour Relations 1, and F.G. Gardiner, Memorandum with Respect to Labour Relations Policy of the Conservative Party, Box 29, Subject Files – PC Labour 1942–3
30 The province's position in 1945 was clearly spelled out by the attorney-general in a radio broadcast of 23 Nov. 1945; PAO, Drew File, Box 443, Department of Labour – Ford Motor Strike.
31 PAO, C. Daley, Minister of Labour, Radio Address on Labour Relations, 24 Feb. 1948, RG7, Series II-1, Box 46, Press Releases 1948
32 *Labour Gazette*, 65 (1965), 1176
33 The Ontario Hospital Disputes Arbitration Act 1965, Statutes of Ontario, cap. 48
34 *Labour Gazette*, 68 (1968), 688
35 See, for example, the debate on the speech from the throne, *Debates*, 25 Nov. 1969, 112.

CHAPTER 3: *Land and Capital Resources*

1 The issues as they affected agriculture are discussed in Chapter 7.
2 For an account of the established policies, see H.V. Nelles, *The Politics of Development: Forests, Mines and Hydro-Electric Power in Ontario 1848–1941* (Toronto: Macmillan, 1974).
3 This appears to be confirmed even in the sympathetic treatment of the provincial government's policies set out in R.S. Lambert and P. Pross, *Renewing Nature's Wealth* (Toronto: Ontario Department of Lands and Forests, 1967).
4 W.R. Smithies, *The Protection and Use of Natural Resources in Ontario* (Toronto: OEC, 1974), 15–16
5 The KVP Co. Ltd. Act, 1950, Statutes of Ontario, cap. 33
6 The growing public concern with such issues was illustrated by the attention given to a CBC television documentary, 'Air of Death,' broadcast on Sunday evening, 22 October 1967, in the time slot normally occupied by the popular 'Ed Sullivan Show.' See Canadian Broadcasting Corporation, *Air of Death: The Audience and Its Reaction to a CBC Documentary on Air Pollution*, Research Report No. 13 (Ottawa: CBC Research Department, 1967).
7 The term 'capital' is used here in the sense of real goods that are produced for the purpose of producing other goods, not, unless indicated, in the financial sense of stocks, bonds, etc.
8 The term 'investment' will be used here to refer to the creation of new capital goods, either for the purpose of replacing worn-out capital (offsetting 'depreciation') or to add to the capital stock ('net investment').
9 W.C. Hood and A. Scott, *Output, Labour and Capital in the Canadian Economy*, a study prepared for the Royal Commission on Canada's Economic Prospects (Ottawa: the commission, 1957), chap. 6
10 Ontario, Department of Economics, *Economic Survey of Ontario, 1957* (Toronto, 1958), F-4
11 *Report of the Royal Commission on Certain Sectors of the Building Industry*, 2 vols (Toronto: Queen's Printer, 1974) (The Waiseberg Report), 4
12 O.J. Firestone, *The Organization of the Construction Industry and the Construction Labour Force* (Ottawa: King's Printer, 1943), 10
13 See B.A. Keyes and D.M. Caskie, *The Structure and Operation of the Construction Industry in Canada* (Ottawa, 1975).
14 See J. Lorimer, *The Developers* (Toronto: Lorimer, 1978), 19.
15 R.A. Muller, *The Market for New Housing in the Metropolitan Toronto Area*, Ontario Economic Council, Occasional Paper No. 5 (Toronto: OEC, 1978), 72–3
16 See H.C. Goldenberg and J.H. Crispo, eds., *Construction Labour Relations* (Toronto: Canadian Construction Association, 1968).
17 Toronto *Globe and Mail*, 22 March 1941, 16

18 For an evaluation of the effects of the federal program on the supply of housing in Canada see L.B. Smith, *The Postwar Canadian Housing and Residential Mortgage Markets and the Role of Government* (Toronto: University of Toronto Press, 1974), 9.
19 *Debates*, 14 March 1946, 288–9
20 These were The Housing Development Act, The Planning Amendment Act, The Rural Housing Assistance Act, The Junior Farmer Establishment Act, and The Elderly Persons' Housing Act.
21 PAO, Frost Files, W. Griesinger, Minister of Planning and Development, to R.H. Winters, Minister of Resources and Development, June 1951, and Memorandum on Meeting on Housing, 28 Jan. 1952, Box 72, GC Federal and Provincial and RG3, C-1-1-a, Box 12, Housing
22 Ontario Housing Corporation, *Annual Report* (Toronto: Ministry of Municipal Affairs and Housing, 1971), 4
23 Ontario Economic Council, *Subject to Approval: A Review of Municipal Planning in Ontario* (Toronto: OEC, 1979), 35
24 *Ontario Statistics 1977*, table 9.1, 281
25 *Debates*, 1 March 1962, 694
26 *Ontario Statistics 1977*, table 21.13, 628
27 D.R. Richmond, *The Economic Transformation of Ontario 1945–1973* (Toronto: OEC, 1974), table IV, 45
28 *Debates*, 4 March 1949, 556
29 *Debates*, 12 March 1953, vol. 21, A-11
30 Ontario Hydro-Electric Power Commission, *Annual Report No. 48*, 1955, x
31 See Ontario Economic Council, *A Society in Transition*, 49; and L. Auer, *Construction Instability in Canada*, (Ottawa: Information Canada, 1975), 57. Also see Ontario Economic Council, *Issues and Alternatives 1978: Business Investment* (Toronto: OEC, 1978), 9

CHAPTER 4: *Transportation and Communications*

1 In 1944 the Aeronautics Act transferred the regulation of air transport from the Board of Transport Commissioners to the new Air Transport Board.
2 H.J. Darling, 'Transport Policy in Canada: The Struggle of Ideologies versus Realities,' in K.W. Studnicki-Gizbert, ed., *Issues in Canadian Transport Policy* (Toronto: Macmillan, 1974), 22
3 Ibid., 28–9
4 F.W. Anderson, 'The Philosophy of the Macpherson Royal Commission and the National Transportation Act: A Retrospective Essay,' in K.W. Studnicki-Gizbert, ed., *Issues in Canadian Transport Policy*, 56
5 See D. Scott, 'Northern Alienation,' in D.C. Macdonald, ed., *Government and Politics of Ontario* (Toronto: Macmillan, 1975), 235–48.
6 Ontario, Department of Economics, 'Submission of the Government of Ontario to the Royal Commission on Transportation, Opening Remarks by the Hon. Leslie M. Frost, March 14, 1960,' mimeo, 2
7 Ibid., 3
8 Cited in A. Tucker, *Steam into Wilderness: Ontario Northland Railway 1902–1962* (Toronto: Fitzhenry and Whiteside, 1978), 156
9 Ibid., 157
10 PAO, Drew Files, Memorandum for Lt-Col. George A. Drew from H.M.R., 2 April 1940, Box 496, Lignite Fields
11 Tucker, *Steam into Wilderness*, 178–9
12 Ontario Northland Transportation Commission, *Annual Report*, 1966, 3
13 Ibid., 1963, 6
14 This strategy was not supported by some of the government's own economic analysis. A 1963 study opposed the policy of using the ONR's freight rate structure as a means of promoting development in the region on the grounds that such rates were only one of several factors affecting production costs in the north, and that even massive rate reductions would have little

262 Notes to pages 63–72

impact on the costs of most established producers in the area and would do even less to attract prospective firms. See Ontario, Department of Economics and Development, 'The Ontario Northland Railway in Relation to Economic Growth,' typescript, 1963.
15 This perennial plan was frequently referred to during the prosperous period in the 1960s. It had, in fact, been announced as imminent in the speech from the throne in 1960. See *Debates*, 26 Jan. 1960, 9.
16 The Public Commercial Vehicles Act, 1927, Statutes of Ontario, cap. 8 (proclaimed 1928)
17 In 1936 The Public Commercial Vehicles Act was replaced by The Commercial Vehicles Act, which classified commercial vehicles as either 'public' or 'private,' but licensing of private vehicles was not implemented.
18 Ontario, Royal Commission on Transportation, *Report*, Dec. 1938, n.p.
19 Ontario Trucking Association, *The Golden Years of Trucking*, Rexdale, Ont.: the association, 1977), 78–9
20 For a detailed account of these developments see Ontario, Select Committee on Highway Transportation of Goods, *Interim Report*, 30 Sept. 1976, 7–9.
21 Canadian Transport Commission, *The Canadian Trucking Industry: Issues Arising out of Current Information* (Ottawa, 1975). Also see Ontario, Select Committee of the Legislature on the Highway Transportation of Goods, *Final Report* (Toronto, 1977).
22 N. Bonsor, 'The Development of Regulation in the Highway Trucking Industry in Ontario,' in Ontario Economic Council, *Issues and Alternatives 1978: Government Regulation* (Toronto: OEC, 1978), 130–1
23 Ontario, 'Transportation and Economic Policy: Review of Current Issues,' Ontario Background Paper, Fifteenth Annual Premiers' Conference, 12–13 Sept. 1974, mimeo 6
24 See D. Nowlan, *The Bad Trip: The Untold Story of the Spadina Expressway* (Toronto: Anansi, 1970) and *Anatomy of an Expressway Evaluation* (Toronto: Collier-Macmillan, 1972).
25 Ontario, 'Transportation and Economic Policy,' 7
26 Leacy, ed., *Historical Statistics of Canada*, 2nd ed., T195
27 1946 data from *Conspectus of Ontario*, table 123; 1975 data from *Ontario Statistics 1977*, vol. 2, table 22.4, 645
28 N. McArthur, *Airport and Community* (Ottawa: Department of Transport, 1965), 3–7
29 Ontario, Department of Economics and Development, 'The Problems of Air Transportation in Northern Ontario,' mimeo, Toronto, October 1963, n.p.
30 Ontario, Department of Economics and Development, Applied Economics Branch, 'Commentary on Transportation in Northern Ontario,' mimeo, August 1967, 8
31 See the account of the ONTC's financial problems given earlier in this chapter.
32 Ontario, Ministry of Transportation and Communication, 'Northern Ontario Air Services System Plan,' mimeo, March 1974, 19
33 *Canada Year Book, 1949* (Ottawa: King's Printer, 1950), 824
34 S. Judek, 'The St Lawrence Seaway in Operation,' *Canada Year Book, 1960* (Ottawa: Queen's Printer, 1961), 855
35 PAO, H. Banning to W.D. McKeough, Work of the Economic Planning Branch, April-July 1971, Box 103
36 K.W. Foley, 'St Lawrence Seaway – Impact on Ontario,' *Ontario Economic Review*, 7 (1969), 8–9.
37 PAO, D.J. Forgie, Ontario Paper Company, to G. Gathercole, Department of Economics, 20 May 1959, Box 243, St Lawrence Seaway–Welland Canal
38 PAO, L. Frost to G. Hees, 7 July 1959, Box 243, St Lawrence Seaway–Welland Canal
39 PAO, 'The Effect of Seaway Tolls on the Economy of Ontario,' Box 64, Miscellaneous Memoranda and Box 243, St Lawrence Seaway–Welland Canal
40 PAO, Banning to McKeough, Work of the Economic Planning Branch, April-July 1971, Box 103
41 PAO, Premier Davis, Abstract of a Report on Great Lakes Commission Semi-Annual Meeting, Toronto, 16–18 June 1975, RG1 AA-1-3, Box 1, ADM, Lands and Water
42 PAO, L. Frost, Minister of Mines, to W.E. Maybee, Norfolk and Niagara Peninsula Natural Gas Association, 17 Dec. 1941, Box 28, Subject File, Natural Gas Situation 1

43 PAO, Frost Files, Report of a Municipal Committee Investigating Gas Situation, 23 Sept. 1947, Box 28, Subject File, Natural Gas Situation 1
44 *Canada Year Book, 1954* (Ottawa: Queen's Printer, 1955), 864
45 Until 1963 another pipeline, the Trans-Northern, brought oil products from Montreal refineries to storage depots in eastern Ontario. In that year the new national oil policy prohibited such deliveries in areas west of Brockville.
46 See L. Waverman, *Natural Gas and National Policy: A Linear Programming Model of North American Natural Gas Flows* (Toronto: University of Toronto Press, 1973).
47 See especially W. Kilbourn, *Pipeline: TransCanada and the Great Debate: A History of Business and Politics* (Toronto: Clarke Irwin, 1970).
48 *Debates*, 6 Feb. 1957, 204
49 *Conspectus of Ontario*, table 175, and *Ontario Statistics 1977*, vol. 1, table 10.4, 319
50 *Conspectus of Ontario*, tables 178 and 181
51 The Ontario Telephone Authority was subsequently renamed the Ontario Telephone Commission.
52 Ontario Telephone Commission, *Annual Reports*, for the years indicated
53 See R.D. Tennant, *Ontario's Government Railway: Genesis and Development* (Halifax: Tennant Publishing House, 1972), chap. 4.
54 See D. Ellis, *Evolution of the Canadian Broadcasting System: Objectives and Realities 1928-1968* (Ottawa: Department of Communications, 1979).
55 It had until then been understood that a basic premise of Canadian broadcasting policy was that stations had no proprietary right to the channel they were allotted, in which case such compensation was not called for, especially if it involved violating another principle, the reservation of high-power stations to the CBC national service.
56 Canadian Broadcasting Corporation, *A Brief History and Background* (Ottawa: CBC Information Services, 1972)
57 The CBC station in Toronto, CBLT, had acquired a microwave link with Buffalo in 1953 to bring in U.S. programs to support its own programming efforts; CBC *Annual Report 1952-53* (Ottawa: Queen's Printer), 26.
58 Some of the story is told in M. Siggins, *Bassett* (Toronto: James Lorimer, 1979).
59 The Fowler Committee on Broadcasting studied the problem of the CBC's physical plant in Toronto in some detail. See Canada, *Report of the Committee on Broadcasting* (Ottawa: Queen's Printer, 1965), 208-9.
60 See F.W. Peers, *The Public Eye: Television and the Politics of Canadian Broadcasting 1952-1968* (Toronto: University of Toronto Press, 1979), chap. 13.
61 Toronto *Financial Post*, 2 Oct. 1965
62 PAO, 'An Overview of Ontario Telecommunications Policy,' Dec. 1970, Box 66, Telecommunication, Sept.-Dec. 1970

CHAPTER 5: *The Services Sector, Trade, and Finance*

1 The service industries have received surprisingly little attention given their importance in the development of modern economies. With the exception of the rather general literature cited on the subject in the Introduction, the observation made by the authors of a study for the Royal Commission on Canada's Economic Prospects in 1957 remains true more than a quarter of a century later: 'Although the service industries as a whole form a large and growing section of the Canadian economy, representing more than one-third of total employment, there appear to be no definitive or satisfactory background studies of them relating either to Canada or the United States and the available statistics and source material for Canada are fragmentary and scattered.' Bank of Montreal, *The Service Industries*, A Study Prepared for the Royal Commission on Canada's Economic Prospects (Ottawa: the commission, 1957), 2-3
2 V.R. Fuchs, *The Service Economy* (New York: National Bureau of Economic Research, 1968), chap. 1
3 Ontario, Treasury Department and Department of Economics, *Economic Survey of Ontario* (Toronto, 1957), C-1 and *Ontario Statistics 1977*, tables 9.18 and 9.19
4 R.H. Frank and I.M. Rash, 'The Pattern of Consumer Expenditures at Provincial and Regional Level,' *Ontario Economic Review*, 6 (1968), 6, table 4

5 The provincial export data are estimates by the Ontario government.
6 This was an explicit element in the Progressive Conservative party's political program of the time: PAO, Drew files, Implementation of the 22 Points and General Records, Ontario Progressive Conservative Association, 8 Dec. 1944, Box 454, PC Party.
7 *Debates*, 10, Feb. 1965, 421
8 These programs and policies are considered in more detail in the chapters on agriculture and manufacturing (chaps. 7 and 9, respectively).
9 See G. Rosenbluth and H.G. Thorburn, *Canadian Anti-Combines Administration 1952–1960* (Toronto: University of Toronto Press, 1963), L.A. Skeoch, 'The Abolition of Resale Price Maintenance: Some Notes on the Canadian Experience,' *Economica* 31 (1964), 260–9.
10 Statistics Canada (DBS), *Census of Canada*, 1941, xviii
11 Ibid., table 2, 9
12 By 1952 some 80,000 television sets had been sold in the Toronto-Hamilton area to customers able to pick up signals from the United States. There was uncertainty as to whether the advent of Canadian broadcasting would stimulate much additional interest in these devices. See Toronto *Financial Post*, 19 July 1952, 2.
13 Ibid., 19 Feb. 1955, 43
14 Ibid., 3 June 1961, 1
15 P.C. Newman, 'Revolution in Retailing That's Changing Your Shopping Habits,' *Maclean's Magazine*, 1 Sept. 1956, 11–13
16 See D.J. Tigert, 'The Changing Structure of Retailing in Europe and North America,' Mimeo, Faculty of Management Studies, University of Toronto, Jan. 1974, 10.
17 Leacy, ed., *Historical Statistics of Canada*, 2nd ed., v225
18 Ibid., v326
19 Tigert, 'The Changing Structure of Retailing,' 7
20 M.S. Moyer, 'Shopping Centres in Canada: Their Impact, Anatomy and Evolution,' *The Business Quarterly* 38 (Summer 1973), 23–31, and Statistics Canada, *Shopping Centres in Canada 1951–1973*, occasional (63–527)
21 Leacy, ed., *Historical Statistics of Canada*, 2nd ed., v236, deflated by GNE implicit price deflator for consumer spending on goods and services
22 In 1971 there were 43,883 such locations and 40,625 working proprietors in the service trades; Leacy, ed., *Historical Statistics of Canada*, v443.
23 Toronto *Financial Post*, 30 May 1953, 1
24 Paid admissions data are from Statistics Canada, *Motion Picture Theatres and Film Distributors* annual, 1951–75 (63–207).
25 *Ontario Statistics 1975*, vol. 2, table 13.9, 507
26 Ontario, Select Committee on Company Law, *Credit Unions* (Toronto, 1969), 9
27 *Ontario Credit Union Yearbook 1971* (Toronto: Ontario Credit Union League, 1972), 20
28 *Ontario Statistics 1977*, vol. 2, table 14.19, 442
29 Bank of Montreal, *The Services Industries* (Ottawa: Royal Commission on Canada's Economic Prospects, Studies, 1956), 81–2
30 Ontario, Royal Commission on Mining, *Report*, vol. III, 3–6, and vol. II, 18–19 (Toronto, 1944)
31 The debate was well documented in the press. See issues of the *Financial Post*, 27 Nov. 1943, 11 Dec. 1943, 1 Jan. 1944, 26 Feb. 1944, 24 June 1944, 25 Nov. 1944, and 6 Jan. 1945. Also see the *Rouyn-Noranda Press*, 2 Dec. 1944, and the *Northern Miner*, 2 Dec. 1944.
32 *Northern Miner*, 20 April 1944
33 PAO, Prospectors' and Developers' Association, 'A Brief Concerning Prospecting and Early Stage Development in Canada,' Box 3, Prospectors' and Developers' Association
34 PAO, Department of Mines, 'Financing Mining Prospects,' 12 April 1945, Box 2, Interprovincial Mines Committee, Notes
35 J.P. Williamson, *Securities Regulation in Canada* (Toronto: University of Toronto Press, 1960)
36 E.A. Royce, Chairman, Ontario Securities Commission, 'Securities in Ontario: The OSC – Its History, Its Composition, Its Organization,' a speech delivered to the Empire Club, Toronto, 1971, 3

Notes to pages 97–106   265

37 Toronto Stock Exchange, *Brief to the Royal Commission on Banking and Finance* (Toronto, 1962), 13–14
38 In addition to the Kimber Committee, two committees of the Ontario Securities Commission, and the Kelly Commission, a select committee of the Ontario legislature was looking into the subject. The federal Royal Commission on Banking and Finance (the Porter Commission) had also undertaken to examine the operation of securities markets.
39 Ontario, Attorney General's Committee on Securities Legislation in Ontario, *Report* (Toronto, March 1965)
40 Ibid., 7
41 Ontario, *Report of the Royal Commission to Investigate Trading in the Shares of Windfall Oil and Mines Limited* (Toronto, 1965), 97
42 Ibid., 101
43 *Debates*, 25 Jan. 1967, 6
44 The view of the Ontario Securities Commission was set out in the *Report of the Committee on the Problem of Disclosure Raised for Investors by Business Combinations and Private Placements*, also known as the 'Merger Study' (Toronto: the commission, 1969).
45 See Ontario, Department of Treasury and Economics, *Report of the Interdepartmental Task Force on Foreign Investment* (the Honey Task Force) (Toronto: 1971).
46 Ontario Securities Commission, *Industry Ownership Study* (Toronto, 1971), 99
47 See Investment Dealers' Association of Canada, *Report of the Committee to Study the Requirements and Sources of Capital and the Implications of Non-Resident Capital for the Canadian Securities Industry* (Toronto, May 1970). (This publication was also known as the report of the Moore Committee and of the Joint Industry Committee.)
48 Toronto *Financial Post*, 15 June 1974, 1

CHAPTER 6: *Education, Health, and Welfare*

1 See V. Lang, *The Service State Emerges in Ontario*, The Evolution of Policy in Contemporary Ontario Series, No. 3 (Toronto: OEC, 1974), chap. 4.
2 The term 'capital' is used here in the sense of 'produced goods for use in further production,' that is, machinery and equipment, structures and inventories.
3 See the reference to studies by Walters and by Denison, Introduction, n. 5.
4 See, for example, the discussion in chapter 4, 'Education and Economic Growth,' in the Economic Council of Canada, *Towards Sustained and Balanced Economic Growth*.
5 See, for example, G.S. Becker, 'Underinvestment in College Education,' *American Economic Review*, Supplement, 50 (1960), 346–54.
6 Economic Council of Canada, *Towards Sustained and Balanced Economic Growth*, 91
7 See J. Mincer, 'The Distribution of Labour Incomes: A Survey with Special Reference to the Human Capital Approach,' *Journal of Economic Literature* 8 (1970), 1–27; Z. Griliches, 'Notes on the Role of Education in Production Functions and Growth Accounting,' in W.L. Hansen, ed., *Education, Income and Human Capital* (New York: National Bureau of Economic Research, 1970); J.E. Stiglitz, 'The Theory of "Screening," Education and the Distribution of Income,' *American Economic Review* 65 (1975), 283–300.
8 For a review of this literature see G.K. Douglas, 'Economic Returns on Investment in Higher Education,' in H.R. Bowen, ed., *Investment in Learning* (San Francisco: Jossey-Bass Publishers, 1978), 359–87.
9 Leacy, ed., *Historical Statistics of Canada*, 2nd ed., W118–21 and W170
10 Ibid., W481
11 Funds transferred from the federal government to the provincial government for the purpose of post-secondary education are classed here as provincial expenditures; *Ontario Statistics 1977*, vol. 1, table 6.33, 201.
12 For a general history of the educational system in Ontario see R.M. Stamp, *The Schools of Ontario, 1876–1976* (Toronto: University of Toronto Press, 1982). A major theme of this work is the successful struggle of local authorities to resist the centralization of administrative authority.
13 In 1939 these grants were sharply curtailed by the government in the hope, as expressed by

the premier, that the universities would be compelled 'to readjust the whole system of fees and increase the assessment against non-resident pupils.' See E.E. Stewart, 'The Role of the Provincial Government in the Development of Higher Education in Ontario 1795–1964,' doctoral thesis, University of Toronto, 1970, 369.
14 Ontario, Department of Education, *Annual Report* (Toronto, 1945), 1
15 Ibid., 31
16 Ibid., 1949, 6–9
17 Ibid., 1951. 2
18 Ibid., 1952, 2
19 M.C. Urquhart and K.A.H. Buckley, eds., *Historical Statistics of Canada*, 1st ed. (Toronto: Macmillan, 1965), 600
20 W.G. Fleming, *Ontario's Educative Society*, vol. 1 (Toronto: University of Toronto Press, 1971), 158–60
21 *Debates*, 21 Feb. 1963, 915
22 Fleming, *Ontario's Educative Society*, 157
23 The government explained that the complications were necessary because the situation in Ontario was more complex than in the United States. See *Debates*, 21 Feb. 1963, 918–19, and the further elaboration by Mr Davis, *Debates*, 27 Jan. 1964, 217–20.
24 Toronto *Globe and Mail*, 22 Feb. 1963, 1
25 D.M. Cameron, *Schools for Ontario: Policy-Making, Administration and Finance in the 1960's* (Toronto: University of Toronto Press, 1972), 271
26 PAO, D. Allen to T.M. Russell, Taxation and Fiscal Policy Branch, Treasury and Economics, 26, Aug. 1969, Series VIII-1, Box 10, Interdepartmental Committee on Education Grants
27 Ontario, Department of Education, *Living and Learning, The Report of the Provincial Committee on Aims and Objectives of Education in the Schools of Ontario* (Toronto, 1968), 5
28 Ibid., 37
29 See Committee of Presidents of Universities of Ontario, *Post-Secondary Education in Ontario 1962–1970* (Toronto: University of Toronto Press, 1963) and *Debates*, 21 May 1965.
30 E. Glor, 'Formation of the Colleges of Applied Arts and Technology,' Mimeo, unpublished research study prepared for the Commission on Post-Secondary Education in Ontario, Toronto, 1970, 3–4
31 *Debates*, 21 May 1965
32 Canada, *Report of the Royal Commission on National Development in the Arts, Letters and Sciences* (Ottawa: Queen's Printer, 1951), 143
33 See Stewart, 'The Role of the Provincial Government in the Development of Higher Education in Ontario,' 470.
34 See R.S. Harris, *Quiet Evolution: A Study of the Educational System of Ontario* (Toronto: University of Toronto Press 1967), 119.
35 J.A. Corry, 'The University and the Canadian Community,' presidential address to the Association of Universities and Colleges of Canada, 27 Oct. 1965
36 W.G. Davis, 'The Government of Ontario and the Universities of the Province,' mimeo, the Frank Gerstein Lecture, York University, 1966, 34
37 This approach was strongly promoted by Dr Wright, who saw in it a practical way of preserving university autonomy while meeting the requirements of public accountability; D.T. Wright, memorandum to Dr. K.W. Taylor and others, 'Formula Operating Grants,' 4 July 1965, files of the Committee on Post-Secondary Education in Ontario.
38 See P. Axelrod, 'Businessmen and the Building of Canadian Universities: A Case Study,' *The Canadian Historical Review*, 63 (1982), 220–1.
39 The prevailing beliefs about the value of a university education, the government's policies with respect to the creation of new universities, and their financial problems are examined in detail in P. Axelrod, *Scholars and Dollars: Politics, Economics, and the Universities of Ontario 1945–1980* (Toronto: University of Toronto Press, 1982).
40 Ontario, Commission on Post-Secondary Education in Ontario, *Draft Report* (Toronto, 1971)
41 Ontario, Commission on Post-Secondary Education in Ontario, *The Learning Society* (Toronto, 1972)

42 Ontario, Committee on the Healing Arts, *Report*, vol. 1 (Toronto, 1970), table 6.9, 192, and *Ontario Statistics 1977*, table 5.12, 138
43 Data for 1953 to 1966 from Ontario, Committee on the Healing Arts, *Report*, vol. 3, 117; data for later years from *Ontario Statistics 1981*, table 5.12, 136
44 Ontario, Committee on the Healing Arts, *Report*, vol. 1, 156, and *Ontario Statistics 1977*, vol. 1, 130
45 *Ontario Statistics 1981*, table 5.4, 127. About two-thirds of the nurses registered in Ontario were employed as nurses in the province.
46 See Ontario, Committee on the Healing Arts, *Report*, vol. 1, 164.
47 Lang, *The Service State Emerges in Ontario*, table 7, 83
48 Ontario Economic Council, *Issues and Alternatives 1976: Health* (Toronto: OEC, 1976), table 3, 42, and *Ontario Statistics 1981*, table 5.9, 132
49 Ontario, Department of Public Health, *Annual Report 1948*, 105
50 In 1946-7, for example, health expenditures amounted to approximately $20 billion out of a total provincial budget of $183 million.
51 See K. Bryden, 'How Medicare Came to Ontario,' in D.C. MacDonald, ed., *Government and Politics in Ontario*, 35.
52 PAO, M. Phillips, speech at nomination meeting, Orono, Ontario, 24 Oct. 1951, mimeo, RGC3-1-1-a, Box 12, Health #2
53 Ontario, Department of Public Health, *Annual Report 1958*, 63
54 For an account of the development of mental health care facilities in the province during this period see C. Hanley, *Mental Health in Ontario*, a study prepared for the Committee on the Healing Arts (Toronto, 1970); and A. Richman, *Psychiatric Care in Canada: Extent and Results* (Ottawa: Royal Commission on Health Services, 1964).
55 D. Guest, *The Emergence of Social Security in Canada* (Vancouver: University of British Columbia Press, 1980), 100
56 For a detailed account of this and the subsequent negotiations, see M. Taylor, *Health Insurance and Canadian Public Policy* (Montreal: McGill-Queen's University Press, 1978).
57 See Ontario, Committee on the Healing Arts, *Report*, vol. 1, 122-3.
58 See *Debates*, 5 March 1959, 826, and 2 Feb. 1960, 124-5.
59 See Canada, *Report of the Royal Commission on Health Services* (Ottawa: Queen's Printer, 1964) (the 'Hall Report').
60 For a brief account of the events in Saskatchewan in the summer of 1962 see W.P. Thompson, *Medical Care: Programs and Issues* (Toronto: Clarke-Irwin, 1964), chap. 5, 'Saskatchewan's Experience,' 56-89.
61 K. Bryden, 'How Medicare Came to Ontario,' 40
62 See G.R. Weller, 'Health Care and Medicare Policy in Ontario,' in G.B. Doern and V.S. Wilson, eds, *Issues in Canadian Public Policy* (Toronto: Macmillan, 1974), 95.
63 Toronto *Globe and Mail*, 26 April 1963, 1-2
64 See *Debates*, 5 Dec. 1963, 106-8, and Toronto *Globe and Mail*, 25 April 1963, 6.
65 Toronto *Globe and Mail*, 11 June 1966, 6
66 Toronto *Globe and Mail*, 18 June 1969, 6
67 For a detailed account of these developments see M. Taylor, 'The Canadian Health Insurance Program,' *Public Administration Review*, 33 (1973), 31-9; and G.R. Weller, 'Health Care and Medicare Policy in Ontario.'
68 *Debates*, 25 Jan. 1966, 6
69 Ontario, Committee on the Healing Arts, *Report*, vol. 1, 5
70 See J.W. Grove, *Organized Medicine in Ontario*, a study prepared for the Ontario Committee on the Healing Arts (Toronto, 1969).
71 See R.D. Fraser, *Selected Economic Aspects of the Health Care Sector in Ontario*, a study prepared for the Ontario Committee on the Healing Arts (Toronto, 1970).
72 Ontario, Committee on the Healing Arts, *Report*, vol. 1, 129
73 D.K. Foot, *Provincial Public Finance in Ontario: An Empirical Analysis of the Last Twenty-Five Years* (Toronto: OEC, 1977), table 25, 79
74 Ibid., 35
75 See, for example, R.G. Evans, 'Does Canada Have Too Many Doctors? - Why Nobody

Loves an Immigrant Physician,' *Canadian Public Policy*, 2 (1976), 147–60; and A. Blomqvist, *The Health Care Business* (Vancouver: The Fraser Institute, 1979).
76 See *Debates*, 9 March 1976, 180.
77 R.B. Splane, *The Development of Social Welfare in Ontario 1791–1893* (Toronto: University of Toronto Press, 1965)
78 Canadian Intergovernmental Conference Secretariat, *The Income Security System in Canada: Report for the Interprovincial Conference of Ministers Responsible for Social Services* (Ottawa, 1980), 16. The original legislation applied mainly to urban workers and excluded persons employed in farming, fishing, forestry, domestic service, or government. Nurses, teachers, and most workers earning $2,000 a year or more were also excluded.
79 Much of the groundwork had been laid by the Royal Commission on Dominion-Provincial Relations in its report and background studies, notably A.E. Grauer, 'Public Assistance and Social Insurance,' appendix 6, Ottawa, 1939. Subsequently the idea of a comprehensive national social security system was explored in the *Report on Social Security for Canada*, prepared for the federal government by Leonard Marsh in 1942 (reprinted Toronto: University of Toronto Press, 1975); in a report written by Charlotte Whitton (*The Dawn of Ampler Life*) for the national Conservative party in 1943 (Toronto: Macmillan, 1943); and in a book, by H.M. Cassidy, *Social Security and Reconstruction in Canada* (Toronto: Ryerson Press, 1943).
80 Guest, *The Emergence of Social Security in Canada*, 130–1
81 For an analysis of the plan see K. Bryden, *Old Age Pensions and Policy-Making in Canada* (Montreal: McGill-Queen's University Press, 1974).
82 Data after Lang, *The Service State Emerges in Ontario*, table 3, 74–5
83 G. Young, 'Federal-Provincial Grants and Equalization,' *Issues and Alternatives 1977: Intergovernmental Relations* (Toronto: OEC, 1977), 49
84 PAO, Discussion Notes, Hon. T.L. Wells, Federal-Provincial Conference of Welfare Ministers, May 1971, Series VIII-1, Box 311, Welfare and Income Support Programs
85 See R. Simeon, *Federal-Provincial Diplomacy: The Making of Recent Policy in Canada* (Toronto: University of Toronto Press, 1973), 87.
86 Most day-care facilities in the province remained under private ownership but were subject to provincial licensing requirements.
87 R.H. Frank, 'The Distribution of Personal Income in Ontario and the Ten Economic Regions,' *Ontario Economic Review* 4 (1966), 3–9
88 Ontario Economic Council, *Issues and Alternatives 1976: Social Security* (Toronto: OEC, 1976), 11

CHAPTER 7: *Agriculture, Fishing, Fur Production, and Tourism*

1 Ontario, Ministry of Agriculture and Food, *Agricultural Statistics for Ontario 1941–1978* (Toronto, 1979), table 1.4, 6
2 Realized farm net income from Leacy, ed., *Historical Statistics of Canada*, 2nd ed., M50, and deflated by the overall Consumer Price Index.
3 See R.S. Rodd, 'The Crisis of Agricultural Land in the Ontario Countryside,' *Plan Canada*, 16 (1976), 160–70.
4 For purposes of the census, a farm was normally defined as an agricultural holding of one acre or more with sales of agricultural products in the preceding year of $50 or more. In the 1951 and 1956 censuses a farm was defined as an agricultural holding either three acres or more in size or from one to three acres in size and having sales of agricultural products of $250 or more in the preceding year. See Ontario, Ministry of Agriculture and Food, *Agricultural Statistics for Ontario 1941–1978*, 3.
5 R.B. Campbell and R.G.F. Hill, *Trends in Ontario Agriculture* (Toronto: Ontario Ministry of Agriculture and Food, 1973), table 9, 16
6 Ontario Ministry of Agriculture and Food, *Agricultural Statistics for Ontario 1973* (Toronto, 1974), table 12, 11–12
7 Based on current value of farm capital as reported in Leacy, ed., *Historical Statistics of Canada*, 2nd ed., M50, and deflating with machinery and equipment component of GNP implicit price deflator, K181

Notes to pages 136-45   269

8 See Ontario Economic Council, *Ontario: A Society in Transition* (Toronto: OEC, 1972), 46.
9 Based on data in Ontario Ministry of Agriculture and Food, *Agricultural Statistics 1973*, table 13, 14
10 *Debates*, 11 Feb. 1958, 89
11 As reported in Toronto *Globe and Mail*, 15 Feb. 1941, 6
12 See Toronto *Globe and Mail*, 20 Jan. 1941, 6, and Urquhart and Buckley, eds., *Historical Statistics of Canada*, 1st ed., 361.
13 See Toronto *Globe amd Mail*, 2 Dec. 1942, 9.
14 As reported in Toronto *Globe and Mail*, 9 Jan. 1943, 4
15 Toronto *Globe and Mail*, 4 Dec. 1945, 6
16 Ontario, Commission on Agriculture, *Interim Report* (Toronto, 1945), 67
17 J.E. O'Meara, *Ontario's Co-operatives 1946-1947* (Toronto: Ontario Department of Agriculture, 1948), 1-8
18 Ontario, Department of Agriculture and Food, *Ontario's Co-operatives 1971-72* (Toronto, 1973), 6-8
19 A. Contini, *Agricultural Marketing Legislation in Ontario* (Toronto: Ontario Ministry of Agriculture and Food, 1973), n.p. Some of the economic implications are discussed in H. Blum, 'Agricultural Producers' Marketing Boards in Ontario,' mimeo, Ontario Department of Agriculture and Food, 13 June 1969, 2-3.
20 The precise numbers are not available, but in the early 1970s there were more farmers registered under marketing boards than there were census farms in the province. See Contini, *Agricultural Marketing Legislation*.
21 In practice, approval by 66 per cent of those eligible to vote in such a contest was required to obtain implementation of the plan.
22 This was true during the 1940s and until about 1955. See G.F. Perkin, *Marketing Milestones in Ontario 1935-1960* (Toronto: Ontario Department of Agriculture, 1962), 93.
23 H. Blum, *Ontario Farm Products Marketing Board* (Toronto: Ministry of Agriculture and Food, 1972), n.p. The apple marketing board was also unusual because it provided consumer representation.
24 The Ontario Egg and Fowl Marketing Plan was one of the few examples of the purely promotional type of activity until it was reorganized in the early 1970s.
25 Statutes of Ontario, 1934, cap. 30, sec. 3-(1)
26 Toronto *Globe and Mail*, 2 Oct. 1946, 1
27 Ontario, Royal Commission on Milk, Report (Toronto, 1947), 147
28 Ibid., 63
29 Ibid., ii
30 Ontario, Milk Industry Inquiry Committee Report (Toronto, 1965), 2-3
31 Some support for this position was provided by a study of the industry reported in the *Ontario Economic Review* at about the same time. See D. Allan, 'Concentration and Competition in Ontario's Fluid Milk Industry,' *Ontario Economic Review*, 3 (1965), 3-14.
32 Ibid., 44
33 PAO, Memorandum on the Milk Inquiry Report, 27 April 1965, RG16, B-1-1, Box 200, Milk Marketing Plan, 1963-6. The separate Cream Marketing Board was established at the same time.
34 The staggering complexity of this system was examined in Kates, Peat Marwick, *Marketing Industrial Milk in Ontario*, a study prepared for the Economics Branch and the Milk Commission of Ontario (Toronto: Ontario Department of Agriculture and Food, 1972), III-2.
35 Broadwith, Hughes, and Associates, 'The Ontario Milk Marketing Board: An Economic Analysis,' in Ontario Economic Council, *Issues and Alternatives 1978: Government Regulation*, 95
36 Ibid., 99
37 See, for example, D. Lees and J. Lawrence, 'Red Tape Does Not a Fine Cheddar Make,' *Harrowsmith*, 3 (1978), 36-49.
38 PAO, H.C. Pauls, Market Research Specialist to D.E. Williams, Ontario Food Council, 6 Nov. 1967, RG16, F-8-1, Box 7, R.G. Bennett, ADM, General Correspondence, 1967. Also see *Debates*, 16 June 1966.

39 PAO, Frost Files, G. Gathercole to L.M. Frost, 20 Oct. 1958, Box 2, General Correspondence, Department of Agriculture
40 Ontario, Department of Economics, *Submission to the Agricultural Enquiry Committee*, 19 Nov. 1959, 4–17
41 Ontario, Agricultural Marketing Enquiry Committee Report (Toronto, 1961), 137
42 The committee also made some rather vague recommendations about reorganizing marketing boards into a vertically integrated system of interest group organizations that would negotiate prices and terms of sale for farm products as well as support research and foster more understanding of the problems involved. For a lucid analysis of the committee's recommendations see A.W. Wood, 'Agricultural Marketing Enquiry Committee of Ontario Report: A Review Article,' *Canadian Journal of Agricultural Economics*, 10 (1962), 1–9.
43 PAO, W.A. Goodfellow, Minister of Agriculture, to W.M. McIntyre, Secretary of Cabinet, 25 Nov. 1958, RG3, C-4, Box 3, Ontario Federation of Agriculture, 1958
44 PAO, W.A. Goodfellow, Minister of Agriculture, to R.A. Farrell, Department of the Prime Minister, 1 Sept. 1960, Box 2, General Correspondence, Agriculture in Northern Ontario
45 *Debates*, 27 Nov. 1962, 5
46 PAO, Department of Agriculture, Press Release, 4 Nov. 1964, XI-2-3, Box 1, ARDA, Misc. Correspondence
47 PAO, W.G.R. Cameron, Economic Policy Adviser, Policy Planning Division, to D.W. Stevenson, Executive Director, Policy Planning Division, 3 July 1969, Box 1, ARDA, Series IV-1
48 Ontario, Ontario Farm Income Committee, *The Challenge of Abundance* (Toronto, 1969)
49 As quoted in the *Toronto Star*, 7 Jan. 1969
50 W.J. White, 'Farm Income Policy in Ontario: Review and Analysis,' *Canadian Journal of Agricultural Economics*, 17 (1969), 132–40
51 Ontario Farm Income Committee, *The Challenge of Abundance*, 141. According to press reports, this proposal was given 'cautious approval' by OFA and OFU representatives at a meeting of provincial farm leaders, although the OFU representative apparently abstained when the issue was put to a vote. See *Toronto Star*, 20 Jan. 1969, 8.
52 Ontario Royal Commission on the Egg Industry, Report (Toronto, 1972), 10
53 Ibid., 33–5
54 The interdependence of policy at the federal and provincial level was particularly well illustrated in the unsuccessful effort to maintain Ontario's small sugar-beet industry. Despite subsidies that amounted to 55 cents out of every dollar paid for sugar beets produced in Ontario and vigorous efforts on the part of a Sugar Beet Marketing Board to maintain output, acreage planted to sugar beets in Ontario declined steadily in the 1950s and 1960s. When the Tate organization closed its plant at Chatham in 1968 the Ontario government rejected proposals that it take the plant over, and the industry was allowed to disappear. See *London Free Press*, 12 June 1968.
55 See A.H. Lawrie, *Lake Superior: A Case History of the Lake and Its Fisheries*, Technical Report No. 19, (Ann Arbor, MI: Great Lakes Fishery Commission, 1973), 33.
56 Ontario, Ministry of Natural Resources, *Out of the Water: Ontario's Freshwater Fish Industry* (Toronto, n.d.), 49
57 Ibid., 17
58 For an account of these trends as they affected the Lake Erie fishery see F. Prothero, *The Good Years: A History of the Commercial Fishing Industry on Lake Erie* (Belleville: Mika, 1972), 35–6.
59 L. Lambert, *Ontario's Lake Erie Commercial Fishery – A Social and Economic Profile* (Toronto: Ontario, Ministry of Natural Resources, 1975), 10–15
60 See E.S. Rogers, *Ojibwa Fisheries in Northwestern Ontario* (Toronto: Ministry of Natural Resources, 1972), 8–11
61 Canada, Freshwater Fish Marketing Corporation, *Annual Report, 1971–72*, 4
62 Ontario Ministry of Natural Resources, *Out of the Water*, 49
63 For a thoughtful discussion of the implications of this with respect to the native people and northern development policy in Ontario see Rogers, *Ojibwa Fisheries*, Part V, 'Thoughts as to the Future.'

64 H.S. Lambert and P. Pross, *Renewing Nature's Wealth* (Toronto: Ontario, Department of Lands and Forests, 1967), 473-4
65 *Ontario Statistics 1981*, 446
66 For a general treatment of the history and principles of tourism see R.W. McIntosh, *Tourism: Principles, Practices, Philosophies* (Columbus, OH: Grid Publishing, 1980).
67 D.R. Richmond, 'Whither the Tourist Industry,' *Ontario Economic Review*, 1 (1963), n.p.
68 Ibid.
69 Kates, Peat Marwick, *Economic Significance of Travel in Canada* (Toronto: Canadian Tourist Association, 1969), 1-1
70 W.D. Cahill and C.A. Neale, *The Economic Impacts of Recreation and Tourism: A Selective Bibliography* (Monticello, IL: Vance Bibliographies, n.d.) #P 356, 1
71 Ontario, Department of Economics, *Economic Survey of Ontario, 1954* (Toronto, 1955), F-123
72 Ontario, Ministry of Industry and Tourism, Tourism Research Branch, *Tourism Statistical Handbook 1975* (Toronto, 1975), table 10, n.p.
73 Ontario, Ministry of Natural Resources, *Ontario Provincial Parks, Statistical Report 1972* (Toronto, 1973), 4
74 As estimated by Balmer, Crapo and Associates in their study, *Tourism Development in Ontario* (Toronto: Ontario Ministry of Industry and Tourism, 1977), iii
75 Toronto *Financial Post*, 2 Oct. 1965, 74
76 *Monetary Times*, 129 (1961), 89-90
77 For a brief history of the region see Kates, Peat Marwick, *Northwestern Ontario Tourist Industry Study*, a report prepared for the Department of Tourism and Information, Government of Ontario, May 1968, 1-11.
78 The problem of estimating revenues from tourism is discussed below.
79 Data from Kates, Peat Marwick, *Northwestern Ontario Tourist Industry Study*, 15-16
80 One reason for the failure of some attempts to reduce regional inequalities was the tendency for many kinds of expansion in outlying areas to yield at least equal benefits to the more developed central regions. See A.A. Kuburski, J.R. Williams, and P.J. George, 'Sub-Provincial Regional Income Mutlipliers in the Ontario Economy: An Income-Output Approach,' *Canadian Journal of Economics*, 8 (1975), 67-91.
81 See Ontario, Ministry of Industry and Tourism, 'The Economic Impact of Tourism in Ontario and Regions,' Tourism Policy and Research Section, 1978, 3-5.
82 The social costs as well as the economic benefits of tourism to 'host' regions were at this time beginning to claim scholarly attention. See, for example, J.M. Bryden, *Tourism and Development: A Case Study of the Commonwealth Caribbean* (Cambridge: Cambridge University Press, 1973), chap. 5, 'Measuring the Economic and Social Impact of Tourism in Developing Countries.'

CHAPTER 8: *Mines and Forests*

1 Ontario Economic Council, *Issues and Alternatives 1978: Business Investment* (Toronto: OEC, 1978), table A-18, 85
2 McIntyre Porcupine Mines Limited, *Annual Report 1940* (Toronto, 1940)
3 See chapter 5, above.
4 Toronto *Globe and Mail*, 6 March 1940, 1-2.
5 PAO, G.D. Conant, Address to the Women's Canadian Club, Sudbury, 18 Dec. 1942, Conant Files, Box 414, Press Release
6 PAO, M.F. Hepburn to William Simpson, Kirkland Lake Mine and Mill Workers Union, 15 Oct. 1942, Box 327, Department of Mines
7 Pickle Crow Gold Mines, *Annual Report 1942* (Toronto, 1942)
8 PAO, Department of Mines, Minister's Files, G.C. Bateman, Metals Controller, Department of Munitions and Supply, to R. Laurier, Minister of Mines, Ottawa, 1 May 1942, Box 1, Laurier
9 M. Tremblay, 'The Colossus of Superior,' *Monetary Times*, 111 (1943), 72-6

272 Notes to pages 166–83

10 PAO, Drew File, L Frost, Ontario Treasury Department to George Drew, 16 Feb. 1944, Box 466
11 PAO, Frost Files, L. Frost to Michipicoten Iron Mines Limited, 20 Sept. 1944, Box 25, Subject Files, Mines, Iron Ore, Michipicoten
12 W.J. Gorman, 'Steep Rock Iron Mine,' *Canadian Geographical Journal*, 25 (1942), 247–56
13 J. Cowan, *Steep Rock Iron Mines* (Toronto: Northern Miner Press, n.d.), 7
14 Press coverage of the Caland development was favourable, in some cases enthusiastic. See, for example, Toronto *Globe and Mail*, 19 Jan. 1950, 6.
15 *Debates*, 27 Jan. 1965, 70
16 Ontario, Department of Natural Resources, *Ontario Mineral Review 1976–77* (Toronto, 1977), 32
17 For a general account of these developments see D.M. LeBourdais, *Canada and the Atomic Revolution* (Toronto: McClelland and Stewart, 1959), chap. 10–14.
18 *Canada Year Book 1957–58* (Ottawa: DBS, 1959), 502
19 LeBourdais, *Canada and the Atomic Revolution*, 124
20 PAO, IMMSW, Brief to the Select Committee on Mining, 10 Dec. 1964
21 LeBourdais, *Canada and the Atomic Revolution*, 141
22 PAO, R.W. Macaulay, Minister of Energy Resources to Gordon Churchill, Minister of Trade and Commerce, 19 Nov. 1959, RG13, 1-A-6, Box 1, Energy Resources
23 Ibid., Box 45, GC-Elliot Lake Situation III
24 PAO, Energy / Natural Resources, Cabinet Submission, Joint Report, Ontario Uranium Supply and Pricing Policy, 10 July 1975, RG1, AA-1-3, Box 4, Mines
25 Ontario, Royal Commission on Mining Report (Toronto, 1944), 16–17
26 PAO, Frost Files, L. Frost, Memorandum, re Cobalt, 17 July 1944, Subject Files, Cobalt
27 Until then most of the ore mined at Cobalt had been processed at Deloro, Ontario.
28 Production of cobalt, apart from its importance in prolonging the life of the Cobalt mining district, was never an important part of Ontario's total mineral production. The combined yield of cobalt, bismuth, cadmium, calcium, lead, magnesium, selenium, tellurium, and tin, was only 3 per cent of the total value of metallic mineral production in 1975.
29 Ontario, Ministry of Natural Resources, *The Ontario Mining Industry, Present and Future* (Toronto, 1978), 21
30 PAO, A.F. Lawrence, Minister of Mines to A. Carruthers, Chief Government Whip, 8 April 1970, Minister, Box 4, Promotion and Development, Resources Development
31 PAO, A.F. Lawrence, Minister of Mines, to Texasgulf Sulphur Company, April 1969, GG13, A-8-a, Box 21, Texas Gulf
32 PAO, J.P. Robarts to R.L. Kellock, QC 25 June 1969, RG13, A-8-a, Box 1, Mines Tax, 1969. Also see *Debates*, Nov. 1968, 5.
33 H.V. Nelles *The Politics of Development* (Toronto: Macmillan, 1974), 490
34 Ibid., 491
35 See the report of a speech by Leslie Frost, Toronto *Globe and Mail*, 20 Jan. 1944, 16.
36 *Debates*, 15 March 1945, 223ff
37 *Debates*, 9 March 1946, 36–8
38 *Debates*, 1 April 1953, vol. 34, DD12
39 *Debates*, 29 March 1955, 1377
40 *Debates*, 14 March 1961, 2092–3.
41 Rent is a term used in economics to refer to any payment made for the use of a factor of production which, like land, is in fixed supply. Ideally it represents the 'pure' return to such a factor and in practice would be measured by deducting from the value of a product all the labour, capital, and other factor costs incurred in its production.
42 E. Kierans, *Report on Natural Resources Policy in Manitoba*, prepared for the Secretariat for the Planning and Priorities Committee of Cabinet, Government of Manitoba, Winnipeg, Feb. 1973
43 Ontario, Committee on Taxation, *Final Report*, vol. 3 (Toronto, 1967), 32
44 Underlying such recommendations was the recognition that traditional royalties and other kinds of taxes on mining production were inefficient instruments for the appropriation of rents. Mining profits taxes are a superior alternative, because they would be expected to have

Notes to pages 183-92   273

little effect on the allocation of resources. See H.G. Grubel and S.S. Smith, 'The Taxation of Windfall Gains on Stocks of Natural Resources,' *Candian Public Policy*, 1 (1975), 13-30; also H. Campbell, W.D. Gainer, and A. Scott, 'Resource Rents, How Much and for Whom?' in A. Scott, ed., *Natural Resource Revenue: A Test of Federalism* (Vancouver: University of British Columbia Press, 1976), 118-37.

45 See, for example , J. Spence, 'Essential Characteristics of Mining Related to Taxation Policy,' an appendix to a brief prepared by the International Nickel Company of Canada on the Report of the Ontario Committee on Taxation, Feb. 1968.

46 *Debates*, 4 March 1969, 1815

47 See, for example, G. Anders et al., *Investment Effects on the Mineral Industry of Tax and Environmental Policy Changes: A Simulation Model*, Ontario, Ministry of Natural Resources, Mineral Resources Branch, Background Paper No. 5, Toronto, 1978.

48 The Division of Mines in the Ministry of Natural Resources, for example, was concerned about the fact that by the mid-1970s the return on mining investment in the province was no higher than on risk-free bonds. It proposed that taxes should be revised 'to make the expected rate of return obtainable more attractive in comparison with that offered by alternative investment possibilities.' See Ontario, Ministry of Natural Resources, *The Ontario Metal Mining Industry, Present and Future* (Toronto, 1977), 13 and 16.

49 See J.C. Leith, *Exploitation of Ontario Mineral Resources: An Economic Policy Analysis* (Toronto: OEC, 1976), 37, and Ontario Economic Council, *Issues and Alternatives 1978: Business Investment* (Toronto: OEC, 1978), 53

50 H.J. Mcgonigal, 'Trade Liberalization and the Forest Industries,' *Ontario Economic Review*, 6 (1968),3-13

51 Ontario, Department of Natural Resources, *The Forest Industry of Ontario, 1976* (Toronto, 1976), table 27, 52

52 R.S. Lambert and P. Pross, *Renewing Nature's Wealth: A Centennial History of the Public Management of Lands, Forests and Wildlife in Ontario 1763-1957* (Toronto: Ontario, Department of Lands and Forests, 1967), 344

53 PAO, *Proceedings of the Select Committee on Administration of Natural Resources by the Department of Lands and Forests*, 1939

54 Lambert and Pross, *Renewing Nature's Wealth*, 355

55 PAO, F.A. MacDougall Papers, Timber and Administration - Reminiscences, 1971-2, Box 13, dated 13-2-68; also, Letters and Notes, Retirement, 1966, Box 12, dated 19-7-66

56 PAO, F.A. MacDougall Papers, M.F. Hepburn to N.O. Hipel, 8 April 1943, Box 3, Department of Lands and Forests, 1940-6

57 PAO, C.D. Howe to E.E. Johnson, 29 Aug. 1940, Great Lakes Lumber and Shipping Limited, transcript, 204

58 The situation at the Lakehead had been investigated in 1943 by a commission (the Guthrie Commission) which almost resulted in the creation of a permanent 'Lands and Forests Commission' of the kind proposed several years earlier by George Drew. Legislation was passed providing for the establishment of such a body, but no commissioners were appointed and the matter went no further. See Lambert and Pross, *Renewing Nature's Wealth*, 396.

59 PAO, Memorandum to Minister re Pulpwood Exported from Ontario, 6 Feb. 1947, RG1, E-10, Box 19, Timber Management Policy, vol. 1.

60 PAO, Armstrong Forest Co. et al, to C.E. Mapledoram, Minister of Lands and Forests, 9 Aug. 1954, RG1, EA3, Box 1, Export Policy

61 PAO, Frost Files, Address by L.M. Frost, 'Forest Policy of the Government of Ontario,' Box 21, General Correspondence, Canadian Pulp and Paper Industry

62 PAO, RG1, EA3, Box 3, Management, 1952

63 In the case of private lands and forests controlled by conservation authorities and municipalities, the goverment proposed to implement an expanded program of supplying nursery stock for reforestation.

64 PAO, S.W. Tenduf-La, Department of Lands and Forests to D.P. Drysdale, Timber Branch, 2 Feb. 1968, re Interview with Union Officials, RG1, E-10, Box 202, Union of Lumber and Sawmill Workers, vol. 2

CHAPTER 9: *Manufacturing*

1 The classification used here was suggested by D.H. Fullerton and H.A. Hampson in *Canadian Secondary Manufacturing Industry*, a study prepared for the Royal Commission on Canada's Economics Prospects (Ottawa, 1957).
2 The major changes in the concepts and definitions used in the official statistics on manufacturing occurred in 1960 and 1970. The interested reader should consult Leacy, ed., *Historical Statistics of Canada*, 2nd ed., section R.
3 The data are for 'census value added by manufacturing' deflated using the 'manufacturing industry selling price' index. See ibid., R97, R91, and K68.
4 Constant dollar figures. Employment and production data used are on a total manufacturing activity basis.
5 For a discussion of the problems involved see U. Zohar, *Canadian Manufacturing: A Study in Productivity and Technological Change*, vol. 1 (Ottawa: Canadian Institute for Economic Policy, 1982), chap. 2.
6 C.R.A. Kahn, 'The Structure and Concentration of Ontario Manufacturing and Its Relative Position in Canada,' *Ontario Economic Review*, 1 (May 1963–April 1964), n.p.
7 Ontario, Department of Economics, *Ontario: Economic and Social Aspects* (Toronto, 1961), 44
8 Fullerton and Hampson, *Canadian Secondary Manufacturing Industry*, 1957, 440
9 *Ontario Statistics 1975*, 527–9
10 See S. Hymer and R. Rowthorn, 'Multinational Corporations and International Oligopoly: the Non-American Challenge,' in C.P. Kindleberger, ed., *The International Corporation* (Cambridge, MA: MIT Press, 1970).
11 N.C. Field and D.P. Kerr, *Geographical Aspects of Industrial Growth in the Metropolitan Toronto Region* (Toronto: Department of Treasury and Economics, Regional Development Branch, 1968), 4
12 Ibid., 91. There is some doubt as to whether manufacturing in the province was becoming more or less geographically concentrated as a result of such developments. See K.A.J. Hay, 'Trends in the Location of Industry in Ontario 1945–1959,' *Canadian Journal of Economics and Political Science*, 31 (1965), 380.
13 S. Reisman, *The Canadian Automotive Industry: Performance and Proposals for Progress* (Ottawa: Supply and Services Canada, 1978), 91
14 D.A. Wilton, 'An Econometric Model of the Canadian Automotive Manufacturing Industry and the 1965 Automotive Agreement,' *Canadian Journal of Economics*, 5 (1972), 157
15 S. Reisman, *The Canadian Automotive Industry*, 15
16 PAO, L. Frost to R.W. Todgham, Chrysler Corporation, Box 7, General Correspondence – Auto Industry, 1958
17 N. Kristoffy, 'The Canadian Automotive Industry and the 1965 Agreement,' *Ontario Economic Review*, 11 (1973), n.p.
18 Ibid.
19 These concerns were spelled out in two papers produced within TEIGA: 'Performance under the Auto Pact: An Ontario Perspective,' April 1976 and 'Canada's Share of the North American Automotive Industry: An Ontario Perspective,' May 1978.
20 See Kates, Peat Marwick, *Foreign Ownership and the Auto Parts Industry*, a Study Prepared for the Select Committee on Economic and Cultural Nationalism (Toronto, 1973) table 3-13.
21 Ontario TEIGA, 'Canada's Share of the North American Automotive Industry,' 24
22 *Saturday Night*, 24 April 1943, 34–5
23 H.F. Irwin, as quoted in 'Can Textile Men Hold Wartime Gains?' Toronto *Financial Post*, 16 July 1949
24 Statistics Canada, *Cotton Yarn and Cloth Mills* (34-205) and *Wool Yarn and Cloth Mills* (34-209), both annual
25 PAO, Eastern Ontario Associated Boards of Trade, Brief, 2 March 1954, Box 189, GC – Textile Industry in Ontario
26 Toronto *Financial Post*, 23 July 1966

27 The only other large, integrated iron and steel facility was the DOSCO establishment in Nova Scotia, parts of which required extensive rehabilitation before war requirements could be met.
28 W. Kilbourn, *The Elements Combined: A History of the Steel Company of Canada* (Toronto: Clarke-Irwin, 1960), 167–75
29 C.P. Honey, 'The Growth and Development of Primary Iron and Steel in Ontario,' *Ontario Economic Review*, 2 (1964), n.p.
30 R.L. Deily and W.E. Pietrucha, *Steel Industry in Brief: Canada* (Green Brook, NJ: Institute of Iron and Steel Studies, 1975)
31 With the exception of Dofasco which managed to sustain the older type of relations.
32 Kilbourn, *The Elements Combined* , 232
33 Deily and Pietrucha, *Steel Industry in Brief*, 23
34 D.V. Love, 'The Lumber Industry in Ontario,' mimeo, Department of Natural Resources, n.d., 12
35 See V. Bladen, *An Introduction to Political Economy* (Toronto: University of Toronto Press, 1951), chap. 7; and J.A. Guthrie, *An Economic Analysis of the Pulp and Paper Industry*, (Washington State University Press, 1972), and *The Newsprint Paper Industry: An Economic Analysis* (Cambridge, MA: Harvard University Press, 1941).
36 Ontario, Department of Natural Resources, *The Forest Industry in the Economy of Ontario* (Toronto, 1977), 33
37 Ontario Economic Council, *Ontario's Forest-Based Industry* (Toronto: OEC, 1970), 4
38 Kates, Peat Marwick, *Foreign Ownership and Forest-Based Industries*, A Study Prepared for the Select Committee on Economic and Cultural Nationalism (Toronto, 1973), 45
39 A.J. Gillies, 'Municipal Industrial Development with Special Reference to Kitchener,' in D.F. Walker and J.H. Bater, eds., *Industrial Development in Southern Ontario* (Waterloo: Department of Geography, University of Waterloo, 1974), 204
40 *Debates*, 2 April 1947, 84–5
41 *Debates*, 14 March 1958, 861–2
42 *Debates*, 14 March 1958
43 *Debates*, 18 April 1963
44 *Debates*, 18 April 1963
45 The passage quoted reflects the unsophisticated reasoning that continued to characterize the public utterances of provincial government officials on economic issues even at a time when the government was making considerable use of highly trained professionals in the field of economic analysis. The speech quoted appears to draw upon ideas discredited in the nineteenth century, and while much of the modern theory the minister's advisers must have been pressing on him may have been difficult to translate into language suitable for a speech in the legislature, it is notable that a major policy position could still be supported with such forms of argument in the 1960s.
46 *Debates*, 18 April 1963
47 PAO, Frost files, R.A. Farrell to James Duncan, Anglo-Canadian Trade, 12 June 1958, Box 4, GC
48 See A. Breton, *Discretionary Government Policies in Federal Countries* (Montreal: Canadian Trade Committee, 1967), 10.
49 In 1961 the Department of Planning and Development was renamed the Department of Commerce and Development. In 1962 the Department of Commerce and Development was combined with the Department of Economics (created in 1957) to form the Department of Economics and Development. In 1969 the Department of Economics and Development was combined with the Department of Treasury to create the Department of Treasury and Economics. In 1971 the Department of Treasury and Economics was combined with the Department of Municipal Affairs to create the Department of Treasury, Economics and Intergovernmental Affairs (TEIGA). See *Ontario Economic Review* 11 (1973), 3–9.
50 See the analysis in Foot, *Provincial Public Finance in Ontario*.

276 Notes to pages 224–32

CHAPTER 10: *The Economic Role of the Provincial Government*

1 See F.F. Schindeler, *Responsible Government in Ontario* (Toronto: University of Toronto Press, 1969), table 4, 20.
2 Foot, *Provincial Public Finance in Ontario*, table 5, 12
3 Ibid., 15
4 D.R. Richmond, *The Economic Transformation of Ontario 1945–1973* (Toronto: OEC, 1974), table II, 43
5 Ontario Economic Council, *Issues and Alternatives 1976: The Process of Public Decision-Making* (Toronto: OEC, 1977), table 5, 68
6 Schindeler, *Responsible Government in Ontario*, 21
7 Schindeler, *Responsible Government in Ontario*, 24, n. 19
8 Foot, *Provincial Public Finance in Ontario*, 19; also see Ontario Economic Council, *Issues and Alternatives 1976: The Process of Public Decision Making*, 8–9.
9 Foot, *Provincial Public Finance in Ontario*, 190
10 The distinction between current and capital spending was dropped in 1968 when, following recommendations of the Ontario Committee on Taxation, the province's expenditures were reorganized on a consolidated basis and reported as net general or gross general expenditure, with the difference being the amount of the shared-cost grants received by the province from the federal government. See Richmond, *Economic Transformation of Ontario*, 35.
11 *Debates*, 14 Feb 1967, 477
12 *Debates*, 23 March 1968, 661–2
13 *Debates*, 4 March 1969, 1804
14 Ontario, *Tax Reform White Paper* (Toronto: Department of Treasury and Economics, 1969)
15 See Foot, *Provincial Public Finance in Ontario*, 191.
16 T.A. Wilson, 'The Province and Stabilization Policy,' in Ontario Economic Council, *Issues and Alternatives 1977: Intergovernmental Relations* (Toronto: OEC, 1977), 129
17 Ibid., 129
18 On the establishment of Metropolitan Toronto and issues arising subsequently, see Ontario, Royal Commission on Metropolitan Toronto, *Report* (Toronto, 1963).
19 The premier, John Robarts, remarked in 1964 that if 'sound community planning is not carried out satisfactorily within local self-government, we may have to explore other alternatives.' See Ontario Economic Council, *Subject to Approval: A Review of Municipal Planning in Ontario* (Toronto: OEC, 1973), 161.
20 See L.D. Feldman, *Ontario 1945–1973: The Regional Dynamic* (Toronto: OEC, 1974), 22–3. These bodies were initially called 'Regional Development Associations.'
21 T.N. Brewis, *Regional Economic Policies in Canada* (Toronto: Macmillan, 1969), 211–12
22 PAO, Definition of Trade and Industry Branch Policy as it Relates to Regional Development Councils, 21 June 1966, Series XI-2-3, Box 7, Regional Development Council – Correspondence
23 The study yielded three volumes of findings: MTARTS, *Growth and Travel, Past and Present*, vol. 1, 1966; *Choices for a Growing Region*, vol. 2, 1967; *Regional Goals*, vol. 3, 1968; all published by the Community Planning Branch of the Department of Municipal Affairs.
24 PAO, Federal Provincial Rural Rehabilitation and Development Agreement: Background Notes and Comments Regarding the Proposed Agreement, 8 Oct. 1964, RG1, E10, Box 89, ARDA
25 PAO, Department of Economics and Development, White Paper on Regional Development, 8 Dec. 1965, RG19, Series J, Box 21, Regional Development – White Paper
26 Ontario TEIGA, Regional Development Branch, *Design for Development Phase I*, 1966; *Design for Development Phase II*, 1968; *Design for Development, the Toronto-Centered Region*, 1970; *Design for Development Phase III*, 1972
27 See G.R. Weller, 'Hinterland Politics: The Case of Northwestern Ontario,' *Canadian Journal of Political Science*, 10 (1977), 744–5.
28 PAO, H.I. MacDonald, Address, 'Competition for the Use of Land in Ontario,' Ontario Institute of Agrologists, Proceedings of the Tenth Annual Meeting, 21–2 April 1969, RG19, Series J, Box 17, Ontario Instutute of Agrologists – Conference
29 For a useful review of the issues see J.S. Dupré, *Intergovernmental Finance in Ontario: A*

Provincial-Local Perspective, a study prepared for the Ontario Committee on Taxation (Toronto: Queen's Printer, 1967).
30 Feldman, *Ontario 1945–1973*, 22
31 J. Manthorpe, *The Power and the Tories: Ontario Politics 1953 to the Present* (Toronto: Macmillan, 1974), 212
32 *Debates*, 26 April 1971, 863
33 Ibid.
34 *Debates*, 28 March 1972, 699
35 Ontario, Committee on Government Productivity, *Report Number Ten: A Summary*, March 1973, 8
36 See R.M. Novick, 'Social Policy: The Search for a Provincial Framework,' in D.C. MacDonald, *The Government and Politics of Ontario*, rev. ed. (Toronto: Van Nostrand Reinhold, 1980), 382–405.
37 Ontario, Joint Committee on Economic Policy, *Directions for Economic and Social Policy in Ontario* (Toronto, 1974), 24
38 Ontario, Committee on Government Productivity, *Interim Report*, No. 3 (Toronto, 1971), 51–2
39 Ontario Joint Committee on Economic Policy, *Directions for Economic and Social Policy in Ontario* (Toronto, 1974), 25
40 *Debates*, 14 April 1975, 813
41 *Debates* 6 April 1976, 1131
42 Ibid.

CHAPTER 11: *Conclusion*

1 *Ontario Statistics 1981*, table 1.9, 22
2 S.D. Clark, *The Suburban Society* (Toronto: University of Toronto Press, 1966), 244
3 *Gallup Report*, 28 Dec. 1968
4 Ontario, Advisory Task Force on Housing Policy, *Report*, Toronto, Aug. 1973, 36 (The 'Comay Report'). Also see P. Barnard and Associates, *Summary of Recent Trends in Supply, Demand and Need for Housing in Ontario*, report prepared for the Advisory Task Force on Housing Policy (Toronto, 1973).
5 A. Hansen, presidential address, American Economic Association March, 1939, *American Economic Review*, 29, 1–15. These ideas were also discussed in his book, *Full Recovery or Stagnation* (New York: Norton, 1938).
6 R.F. Neill, *A New Theory of Value: The Canadian Economics of H.A. Innis* (Toronto: University of Toronto Press, 1972), 69–70
7 This was particularly evident in the relations between the province and the potentially strongest unit of local government, Metropolitan Toronto.
8 See Ontario, Committee on Government Productivity, Task Force Hydro, *Hydro in Ontario: A Future Role and Place*, Report No. 1 (Toronto, 1972); also Ontario, Select Committee of the Legislature Investigating Ontario Hydro, *A New Policy Direction for Ontario Hydro* (Toronto, 1976).
9 *Debates*, 11 March 1975, 3
10 *Ontario Statistics 1981*, 333

Index

Abitibi Pulp and Paper Company, 187, 189
aggregate demand, 4, 11
Agricultural Marketing Enquiry Committee (Ontario), 145–6
Agricultural Rehabilitation and Development Act (ARDA) (Canada), 147
agricultural settlement, 14
Agricultural Stabilization Act (Canada), 143
agriculture, 19, 134–50; co-operatives, 138–9; dairy industry, 140–5; economic efficiency criteria applied to, 147; employment in, 30; export markets, 145–6; growth of domestic market, 136, 145–6, marketing boards, 19, 139–45; mechanization of, 15, 135–6; in northern Ontario, 60; production quotas in, 140; and rural communities, 150; and rural poverty, 147; during Second World War, 138; size and number of farms, 135; specialization in, 136
Air Canada, 69
air pollution. *See* pollution.
air transport, 67–9; airport facilities, 67–8; introduction of jet aircraft, 68; local air services, 69; municipal airfields, 68; in northern Ontario, 68–9; provincial government policy, 68; regional carriers, 68–9; and tourist industry, 161
Alberta: natural gas supplies, 72–6; oil reserves, 73;
alcohol: licensing and consumption, 243–4
Algoma region, 169
Algoma Steel Corporation, 210
American Federation of Labour (AFL), 36
apartment buildings: construction of and condominium form of ownership in, 50
apprenticeship: Department of Labour (Ontario) programs, 107
asbestos: mining of, 179
Atlantic Acceptance Corporation, 64
Atlantic Charter, 127

Atlas Steel Company, 211
Auto Pact, 205–6
automation: in steel industry, 211
automobile industry, 202–7; imports, 203; productivity, 205–6; specialization, 205; volume of production, 203, 206
Automotive Parts Manufacturers' Association, 204
Automotive Products Agreement (1965), 205–7
aviation. *See* air transport.

balance of payments (Canada), 5, 204, 206, 219
Bancroft, Ontario: uranium mining, 170
bank mergers, 94
Bank of Canada, 4
banks. *See* finance.
basic oxygen furnace, 211
Bassett, John, 79
Bell Telephone Company, 77–8
Bethlehem Steel Company, 167
Beveridge, Sir William, 18
birth rate (Ontario), 27–8
Bladen, V.W., 204–5
Board of Broadcast Governors (BBG), 79
Board of Transport Commmissioners, 58
Brampton Paper Company, 189
branch plants, 202
British connection, 18, 86
British Mortgage and Trust, 95
Bruce Lake, Ontario, 169
Bruce nuclear power station, 55
budget (Ontario): and economic stabilization, 23, 226–9, 234–5, 238; impasse of 1969, 234; highway spending, 51–3; and mining tax, 183; pipeline projects, 75; public works items, 52; public works expenditures, timing of, 55; school board financing, 110; spending on education, 105,

108, 109, 110–15; spending on health care 119–20, 125–6; spending on welfare, 129–33.
budgetary process, 227
building land; supply of, 48–9
building trades, 46
bureaucracy: growth of, 244
business cycle, 6
'Buy Ontario' policy, 86

Cabinet Committee on Policy Development (Ontario), 231
Caland Ore Company, 167
Campbell Soup Company. *See* strikes and lock-outs.
Canada Assistance Plan (1966), 131
Canada Deposit Insurance Corporation, 95
Canada Pension Plan, 128
Canadian Association for Adult Education, 18
Canadian Broadcasting Corporation, 78–9
Canadian Congress of Labour (CLC), 36
Canadian Dairy Commission, 143
Canadian Meat Board, 140
Canadian Medical Association, 120, 122
Canadian Sickness Survey, 118
capital: formation, 43, 102, 245; human, 103–4; markets, *see* finance; resources, 42–55; stock, measurement of, 42
CCF-NDP, 18; and economic role of government, 250; and highway spending, 52; housing policies, 47; and mineral taxation, 182; and public ownership of gas pipelines, 74–5
Central Mortgage and Housing Corporation (CMHC), 47
Central Ontario Lakeshore Urban Complex (COLUC), 30
CFRB (radio station), 78
chain stores, 87–8
charitable organizations, 101
Chevrier Report (1938), 64
chicken and egg marketing 'war,' 149
civil service 16, 20; collective bargaining in, 37–8; size, 224–5
Clark, S.D., 246
Cobalt mining camp, 172–4
Cochrane, Ontario, 61
collective bargaining. *See* industrial relations.
collective conservatism, 248
Colleges of Applied Arts and Technology (CAATS), 112–13
commercial policy, 195
Commission on Post-Secondary Education in Ontario (COPSEO), 114–15
Committee on Government Productivity, 233–6, 251
Committee on the Healing Arts, 124–5

Committee on Taxation (Ontario), 232–3
Committee on University Affairs, 113
Commonwealth Air Training Program, 67
communications, 76–81; educational television broadcasting, 79–80; radio broadcasting, 78; telegraph, 76; telephones, 76–8; television broadcasting, 78–80
communists, 18
concentration, 242, 244–5; in automobile industry, 203–4; in construction industry, 45; in copper mining, 177; in dairy industry, 141–2
conditional grants, 24
condominiums, 50
Congress of Industrial Organizations (CIO), 34–5
conservation. *See* environment, pollution.
conservatism, 234
Consolidated Building Corporation, 49
Consolidated Denison Mines Limited, 170
construction industry, 43–55; branches of, 42; concentration in, 45; contractors' associations in, 46; ease of entry into, 45; inefficiency in, 45; technological change in, 46
consumer spending: regional distribution of within Ontario, 85
Consumers' Gas Limited, 73, 74, 75
co-operative movement, 16; in agriculture, 138–9; in manufacturing, 201
copper mining, 177
Cornwall, Ontario, 54
corporate enterprise: in agriculture, 136
Corry, J.A., 115–16
counter-cyclical budgeting. *See* budget, economic stabilization.
Coyne, James, 4
CP Air, 69
Croll, Senator, 132
Crown Timber Act (Ontario), 191

dairy industry: cheese production, 144–5; competition in 141; concentration in, 142; Ontario Milk Marketing Board, 143–5; quota system, 144.
Davis, D.O., 114
Davis, W.G., 112, 234
day care, 132
death rate (Ontario), 28
Denny, M., 6
dentistry. *See* health care.
Department (Ontario) of: Agriculture, 138; Economics and Regional Development, 231; Education, 79, 110; Energy and Resources, 42; Financial and Commercial Affairs, 99; Labour, 107; Lands and Forests, 186–7, 189–90, 192; Municipal Affairs,

230; Planning and Development, 20–1, 41, 218; Public Welfare, 129; Social and Family Service (subsequently Community and Social Services), 129; Treasury and Economics, 232; Treasury, Economics and Intergovernmental Affairs (TEIGA), 235–6; University Affairs, 113
department stores, 87–91 passim
Depression (of 1930s), 3, 15; and capital stock, 42–3; public spending on health, education and welfare, 101; farm incomes, 137; labour in mining, 164; manufacturing output, 195; social welfare programs, 126
'Design for Development' program, 231, 233
doctors. See health care.
Dominion Foundries and Steel Limited (Dofasco), 62, 169, 210
Dominion-Provincial Conference (1945), 21, 127
Douglas Point, Ontario, 55
Dowie, I.R., 124
Drew, George, 18, 21, 23, 60
Duff Royal Commission (Railways), 58

Eastern Ontario Development Corporation, 221
Eaton, Cyrus, 166
Economic Council of Canada: and returns to investment in education, 32, 103
economic growth, 6–7
economic planning. See planning.
education: administration and finance 105–15; baby boom, effects of, 106; capital spending on, 108; and changing age composition of population, 30; and economic growth, 247; economic returns to, 107; foundation tax scheme, 109–10; goals of, 107–8; government spending on, 105, 108, 109, 110–15; Hall-Dennis Committee, 111–12; and labour supply, 32–3; post-secondary enrolments, 104–5; post-secondary financing, 115; primary and secondary school enrolments, 104; proposals for in '22 Points Declaration,' 19, 106; Roman Catholic school funding, 109; school board amalgamation, 110; teacher training and certification, 106; and unemployment, 112; vocational, 20, 106, 108–9
educational requirements for jobs, 240
educational television, 79–81
Eldorado Mining and Refining (Crown Corporation), 170–1
electric power: construction, 51, 53–5; nuclear, 54–5; rural electrification, 15, 135
Elliot Lake, Ontario, 169–71, 230
Emergency Gold Mining Assistance Act (1948), 164

emigration, 28
employment: in agriculture, 134; in construction, 44–5, 55; in Great Lakes fisheries, 151; in hospitals, 116–17; in manufacturing, 195–6, 197; in services sector, 7–8, 33, 82; in wholesale and retail trade, 91, 93
energy: prices, 6; supplies of from western Canada, 72–6
English River, 54
engineering construction 44, 50–5
entertainment, 92–3
environment, 6, 40–2, 233, 253. See also pollution.
'Essential services,' 37–8
European Common Market, 83, 195
exchange rate, 4–5
exports, 4–5
expressways, 53, 66
'evergreen licences' (forestry), 192

Falconbridge Nickel Mines Limited, 169
family allowances, 127
Farm Products Marketing Act (1946), 139
farming: as basic industry, 15; corporate form of ownership, 136; employment and income in, 134; facilities and amenities, 15; fur, 155–7; mechanization of, 135–6, 243; part-time, 240; rationalization of, 146–7; income, 134; use of electric power in, 135
farmland, 14; conversion of, 245; marginal, 40, 134, 239
farms: capital employed, 136; family 146; income from, 147–8; machinery prices, 136; population, 136; production, 15; size and number, 135. See also farming.
Federal Agricultural Stabilization Program, 148
federal-provincial relations, 226–8, 234, 242, 251
Federal-Provincial Rural Rehabilitation and Development Agreement (1962, 1964), 231
federal-provincial shared-cost programs 129, 131
fee-for-service financing of health care, 119
fertility. See birth rate (Ontario).
finance, 93–100; chartered banking, 93–4; credit unions, 94; foreign ownership of financial institutions, 99–100; insurance companies, 94; mutual funds, 100; regulation of financial institutions, 95–100; resource allocating function of financial markets, 97–8; Toronto Stock Exchange, 96–7; trust and loan companies, 94
Firestone, O.J., 45, 111
fiscal policy, 4
Fisheries Prices Support Board, 152

fishing industry, 151–5; capital, 151–2; employment, 151–3; incomes, 152; inland waters, 153–5; and native people, 154; producer organizations, 152; volume and output, 152
Foot, D.K., 125, 224, 226
forecasting, 227
foreign investment, 86. See also foreign ownership.
foreign ownership, 7, 99–100, 195, 202–3, 214
foreign trade: and Keynesian economic theory, 10
forest industries, 19, 184–92
free enterprise, 238, 245
Free Enterprise Hog Producers' Association, 140
Freshwater Fish Marketing Corporation, 154
Frost, Leslie, 22, 23, 24, 59, 60, 75, 181, 190, 204
fuel supplies, 72
fur farming, 155–7
Fuss, M., 6

Ganaraska River, 41
General Agreement on Tariffs and Trade, 83
General Timber Company, 189
Geological Survey of Canada, 167
Geraldton, Ontario, 177
Glassco Commission, 233
GO commuter service, 66
gold mining, 163–5
government policy (federal): housing, 45; macro-economic management, 11, 13; and manufacturing, 194–5; mining incentives, 174; need for a national economic policy, 238; pipelines, 73; television broadcasting, 78; textile industry, 209
government policy (Ontario): agriculture, 138, 147–8, 149–50; budget priorities, 226–7; export of pulpwood, 190; foreign ownership, 99–100; forest industries, 187–92; fur trapping, 155; mining industries, 166, 180–5; pollution abatement in industry, 217; promotion of manufacturing, 217–22; public service unions, 37–8; regional development, 84; regional planning, 217–19, 230–1; renewable resources, 40; 're-privatization,' 236–7; securities regulation, 94–100; spending, 16, 50–5, 83–4, 101, 133, 223–4, 226, 234, 235, 237, 254; television, 80–1; trade, 86; transportation, 66–7, 72; white paper on forest management, 191
government role in economy: 12, 15, 17, 82, 137–38, 234, 249, 252, 145, 164
Great Bear Lake, N.W.T., 169
Great Lakes: fishing industry, 151–2; hydroelectric power, 53; pollution of, 41
Great Lakes Lumber Company, 188
Gross National Product (GNP), 6, 14
Gross Provincial Product (GPP), 83, 162, 219, 223–4

Haileybury Institute for Mining, 106–7
Hall-Dennis Committee, 109, 11–12
Hansen, Alvin, 11, 249
health care, 115–26; dentists, 117–18; expenditures on, 116, 118–19, 125–6; hospitals, 116–17; insurance, 120–2, 123–4; and labour productivity, 115; nursing services, 117; physicians' services, 117; public health offices, 120; shortage of workers for, 116; standards and costs, 20, 247; tuberculosis, 120
health insurance. See health care.
Hepburn, Mitchell, 16, 35, 164, 188
highways: construction of 50–1; Trans-Canada, 23
'Home Ownership Made Easy' plan, 48
Hope Royal Commission on Education, 107–8
hospital insurance. See health care.
hospitals. See health care.
housing, 19, 24, 45, 46–50, 246
Howe, C.D., 74, 188
human capital, 103–4
Hyde Park Agreements (1942), 163
Hydro-Electric Power Commission, 20. See also Ontario Hydro.
hydroelectric power, 14, 53–5. See also Ontario Hydro.

immigration, 28, 150, 239, 241, 252
imports, 85–6, 212
income distribution, 132
income elasticity of demand, 82
Industrial Disputes Investigation Act, 35
Industrial Milk Production Incentive program, 144
industrial promotion, 218–19, 232
industrial relations, 19, 34–8, 241; compulsory arbitration, 37–8; construction industry, 38, 44, 45, 46; in 'essential services,' 36, 37; health care workers, 37, 126; iron and steel industry, 212; Kirkland Lake strike (1941), 163; legislation, 36; Rand Commission proposals, 37–8; public sector, 38–9; trucking industry, 65
industrial strategy, 217–18
infant mortality, 247

Index 283

inflation, 3, 4, 5, 126, 229, 234, 235, 237, 254
Innis, H.A., 250
innovation. *See* technology.
Input-output analysis, 161
insecticides: aerial spraying of, 191
insider trading, 98
Interdepartmental Advisory Committee on Regional Development, 231-2
interest rates, 5
International Nickel Company (INCO), 42, 168-9, 175-6
Interprovincial Mining Committee, 96
Interprovincial Pipeline Company, 73
Interprovincial Steel and Pipe Company, 212
iron and steel industry, 210-13; automation in, 211; industrial relations, 212; management, 212
iron mining, 165-9
iron ore: and St Lawrence Seaway, 69
Iroquois, Ontario, 54
Investment, 6, 42, 102; and government bond yields, 242. *See also* capital.

James Bay, 53; seaport proposal, 63
Japan, 195
Johnson, E.E., 188

Kalamazoo Vegetable Parchment Company, 41
Kapuskasing, Ontario, 62
Kelly Commission (Inquiry into the Windfall Mines affair), 97-9
Kennedy, H., 189-90
Kennedy tax cut (U.S.), 4
Kenora, Ontario
Keynesian economics, 7, 9, 11, 12, 16, 18, 21, 127, 226-9, 248, 250, 254
Kidd Creek mine, 62, 174, 177; also see Texas Gulf Sulphur
Kierans, E., 182
Kimber, J.R., 97
Kimberly-Clark Paper Company, 189
Kirkland Lake, Ontario, 62, 167
Korean War, 4, 83, 173
Krever, H., 124

labour: court, 35; force, 3, 26-7, 31-4; in forest industries, 186; organization, 16; supply, 32-3, 241; in textile industry, 208
Labour Progressive party, 181
Labour Relations Board, 36
laissez-faire, 11
Lake of the Woods, 160
land resources, 39-42
leisure, 243

life expectancy, 246-7
life styles, 92, 243
local government reorganization, 232
London, Ontario, 41
Lorimer, J., 45
low-cost housing, 47-8
lumber industry, 161, 187, 213-14

Macaulay, R., 219
Macdonald, Sir John A., 18
MacDougall, F.A., 187
McKeough, D., 234
McLaughlin, G., 143
McLuhan, Marshall, 80
Macpherson Royal Commission on Transportation, 58-60
macro-economic theory, 8, 12
Madawaska River, 53-4
Magpie Mine, 166
Malvern subdivision (Toronto), 48
Manitouwadge base-metal mines, 174-5, 177, 230
manpower planning, 33
manufacturing, 6, 13-14, 83; automobile, 202-7; development during Second World War, 198-9; employment, 195-6; foreign investment in 201-2; hours of work in, 32; import competition, 198-200; importance of in provincial economy, 219; iron and steel, 210-13; location of, 201-2; Ontario's pre-eminence in, 194; ownership in, 200-1; post-war adjustment in, 199; productivity of labour in, 196-7; promotion of by provincial government, 217-22; scale of operations, 196-7; technical change in, 196-7; textile, 207-10; twenty leading industries in, 200; defined by type, 193; value added per employee, 196; value of output as percentage of total goods production, 200; value of production, 195; wood-using industries, 213-17
Marathon Paper Company, 189
marginal farmland, 40, 134, 239
maritime provinces, 29
market system, 16, 125, 184, 237, 249
marketing boards, 139-45, 149
Marmora, Ontario, 167
Massey Royal Commission, 78
Mattagami River, 54
mechanization (in forest industries), 186
media, 240
mercury pollution, 152-4
mergers: banking, 94
metal refining: provincial policy, 184-5
Metropolitan Toronto. *See* Toronto.

Michipicoten iron ore range, 166
migration: inter- and intraprovincial, 29
milk. *See* agriculture; dairy industry.
Milk Act (1965), 143
Milk Control Board, 141
Milk Industry Inquiry Committee, 142
Minaki Lodge, 160
mining industry, 19, 162–84, 245; training in, 106–7; value of mineral production, 162. *See also* names of mines and minerals.
mining stocks, 95–6
monetary policy, 4, 5
money supply, 5
Montreal, 14
Moose River, 54
Moosonee: ocean port proposal, 57
mortality rate. *See* death rate (Ontario).
motor transport. *See* road transport.
movie theatres, 93
multinational corporations, 73, 254
multiplier: theory of, 10
municipal reorganizaiton, 232, 237, 242

Nanticoke, 213
National Energy Policy, 73
national income accounting, 12
National Harbours Board, 71
National Housing Act (1944), 47
National Transportation Act (1967), 59
native people: and inland fishery, 153–4; and tourist industry, 161
natural gas, 72
Natural Products Marketing Act (1934), 139
natural resources, 15. *See also* land resources.
Neill, R., 250
Nelles, H.V., 180–1
neo-conservatism. *See* new conservatism.
net migration, 27
net reproduction rate, 252
new conservatism, 235, 237, 238
New Helen iron mine, 167
Niagara Falls, 53
nickel mining, 176–7
nickel-copper mining, 174–7
night shopping, 90
Nipigon River, 54
non-metallic mineral mining, 179
norOntair (crown corporation), 69
North Bay, Ontario, 61
Northern Ontario, 240, 253–4; abandonment of marginal farmland, 134; agricultural development, 40, 147; air transport, 68–9; communications, 77–8; educational facilities, 106; fishing industry, 153–4; fur farming, 155–7; housing programs, 48, hydroelectric power projects, 53; natural gas services, 75–6; Ontario Northland Transportation Commission as development agency, 62–3; population loss, 30; promotion of industrial development in, 221; and social problems of southern Ontario, 60; use of snowmobiles in 154; Temiskaming and Northern Ontario Railway, 60; tourism, 59–61; wild fur production, 155; wild rice harvesting, 154
Northern Ontario Assistance in Housing Program, 48
Northern Ontario Develoment Corporation, 221
Northern Ontario Natural Gas Company, 75
Northern Ontario Pipeline Crown Corporation, 75
nuclear power, 54–5
nurses. *See* health care.
nylon, 209–10

occupational health, 241
Old Age Assistance Program, 128
Oliver, F.R., 137
Ontario Committee on Taxation, 228
Ontario Council of Commercial Fisheries, 152
Ontario Council on Health, 124
Ontario Credit Union League, 94
Ontario Department of Economics, 145
Ontario Department of Mines, 167
Ontario Development Agency, 221
Ontario Economic Council, 65, 132, 184
Ontario Educational Communications Authority (OECA), 80–1
Ontario Farm Income Committee, 148–9
Ontario Farm Products Marketing Act (1937), 139
Ontario Farmers' Union, 148
Ontario Federation of Agriculture, 137, 143, 148
Ontario Food Council, 149
Ontario Forest Resources Commission (proposed), 19
Ontario Guaranteed Mortgage Loan Program, 48
Ontario Health Insurance Act, 124
Ontario Highway Transport Board, 65
Ontario Hog Producers' Association, 140
Ontario Hospital Services Commission, 122, 125
Ontario Hospital Services Plan, 122
Ontario Housing Corporation (OHC), 47–8, 50, 131
Ontario Hydro, 53–5, 70, 77, 154, 187, 253
Ontario Joint Committee on Economic Policy, 236
Ontario Labour Relations Board, 37

Index 285

Ontario Milk Marketing Board, 143–5
Ontario Municipal Board, 64
Ontario Northland Communications (ONC), 77
Ontario Northland Railway (ONR), 61, 62–3, 169, 179
Ontario Northland Transportation Commission (ONTC), 62
Ontario Paper Company, 189
Ontario Prospectors' and Developers' Association, 96
Ontario Public Service Labour Relations Tribunal, 38
Ontario Research Foundation, 218
Ontario Securities Act, 95
Ontario Securities Commission, 95–100
Ontario Telephone Authority, 77
Ontario Trucking Association, 64–5
Ontario Water Resources and Supply Committee, 41
OPEC oil cartel, 5, 184
Order-in-Council PC1003 (Canada), 36
Oshawa, 90
Ottawa River, 53
output: by type of industry, 82

participation rates (labour force), 31–2
personal disposable income, 84–5
Petrochemical industry, 76
Physicians. *See* Health care.
Pickering nuclear power station, 55
pipelines, 72–6
planning, 21, 22, 58–9, 217–19, 229, 233, 237, 245, 250–2
Planning and Development Act (1937), 229
platinum group metal mining, 179
policy. *See* government policy.
Policy and Priorities Board, 235
pollution, 40, 66, 151–4, 217, 221, 246
population, 27–31, 239
Port Credit, Ontario, 73
poverty, 132, 147, 248
prairie provinces, 29
prescription drugs, 132
price controls, 4
price levels. *See* inflation.
price supports: in agriculture, 143
price leadership: in steel industry, 212
productive capacity, 26
productivity, 5, 6, 26, 32, 135, 142, 196–7, 205, 206, 208–9, 216–17, 241
propensity to import, 10–11
Provincial Committee on the Aims and Objectives of Education in the Schools of Ontario. *See* Education: Hall-Dennis Committee.
provincial rights, 18, 20, 21, 100

Provincial School of Textiles, 208
public administration: in 1940s, 15–16
public transport, 65–6
public works, 23, 55, 229
Public Vehicles Act, 65
pulp and paper companies, 187–8, 191
pulp and paper industry, 160, 214–17
pulpwood concessions, 186–8
pulpwood exports, 190
Pulpwood Supply Company, 189
purchasing policies, 220

Quebec, 22, 207
Queen Elizabeth Way, 15

radio. *See* communications: radio broadcasting.
rail transport, 56–63
railroads. *See* rail transport.
railways. *See* rail transport.
Rand, I.C., 37–8
rationing (in Second World War), 4
real income, 83–4, 242
redistribution of income, 132
reforestation, 191–2, 245
regional development, 147, 218, 228–33
regional development councils, 230
regional government, 232, 237
regional growth, 85
regional planning, 229, 230, 231
'Rent Geared to Income' program, 48, 131–2
Rent Supplement program, 132
'Re-privatization,' 236–7
resale price maintenance, 88
research and development, 6
retail sales tax, 229
retail trade, 87–92
Richard L. Hearn generating station, 54
road and highway mileage, 53
road transport, 63–7
Roads to Resources program 186
Robarts, J., 109, 112, 123, 124, 233
Royal Commission on the Automobile Industry (Bladen Commission), 204–5
Royal Commission on Dominion-Provincial Relations (Rowell-Sirois Commission), 137
Royal Commission on Forestry (Kennedy Commission), 40, 189
Royal Commission on Health Services (Hall Commission), 122
Royal Commission on National Development in the Arts, Letters and Sciences (Massey Commission), 113
Royal Commission on Taxation (Carter Commission), 183
Royal Securities Limited, 99
rural community life, 239

286 Index

rural non-farm population, 30
Rural Telephones Act, 77
rural-urban shift of population, 30
Ryerson Institute of Technology, 107

St Laurent, L., 23
St Lawrence River, 53
St Lawrence Seaway, 23, 39, 44, 54, 58, 69–72
St Lawrence Seaway Development Corporation, 70
salt: mining, 179
Sarnia, 73
Saskatchewan: health insurance, 122–3
savings, 241
sawmills, 213
scale: in automobile industry, 204–5; in lumber industry, 214; in textile industry, 207
school taxes. See education.
schools. See education.
Second World War: and agriculture, 140; and automobile industry, 203; and female labour force, 31; and iron and steel industry, 210; labour legislation, 35; and lumber industry, 213; and manufacturing, 195–8; and textile industry, 207–8; and unemployment, 3
securities legislation: and gold mining industry, 163. See also finance.
Select Committee on the Municipal Act and Related Acts (1965), 232
service industries: growing importance of, 7, 14, 240
services sector, 7; See also service industries.
service trades establishments, 92
sewage systems, 15, 49
Sheridan Park Research Community, 221
Sherman iron mine, 169
silver-cobalt mining, 172–4
smelting: zinc, 179
Smooth Rock Falls, 62
social security, 18. See also welfare.
social services, 23–4
social welfare. See welfare.
Spadina Expressway, 53
specialization: in automobile industry, 205
Spruce Falls, 62
staple theory, 12–3
Steel Company of Canada (STELCO), 210, 212–13
steel industry. See iron and steel industry.
Steep Rock Lake iron ore mines, 166–7
Stock Frauds Prevention Act, 95
stockyards, 19
strikes and lock-outs, 35, 36, 38, 163, 212
structural change in the economy, 6

subdivision approval, 230
subsidized housing, 47
suburbs, 48, 50
subway: Toronto, 66
Sudbury, 40, 42, 69, 79, 168, 174
sulphate pulp process, 215
Superior, Wisconsin, 73
synthetic textiles, 209–10

tariff, 193, 204, 207, 209
tax reform, 227–8
taxes, 19, 229, 242; and mining industry, 180–4
tax-rental agreements. See tax-sharing agreements.
tax-sharing agreements, 22, 23–4, 25
Technical and Vocational Training Agreement, 24, 108
technical change. See technology.
technical efficiency, 245
technology, 6, 193, 221, 253; in automobile industry, 203; in construction industry, 46, 214; in dentistry, 118; in forest industries, 186; in iron and steel industry, 168, 210–11; long-distance pipelines, 73; in manufacturing, 196–7; in mining, 163; prospecting, 178; in pulp and paper industry, 214–15
telegraph. See communications.
telephones. See communications.
television, 93, 244. See also communications; broadcasting.
Texas Gulf Sulphur Company, 97, 174–5, 177
textile industry, 207–10
Thompson, Manitoba, 175
Timiskaming and Northern Ontario Railway, 56, 61. See also Ontario Northland Railway.
Timmins, Ontario, 177
tolls: St Lawrence Seaway, 71–2
Toronto, Ontario, 14, 29, 65–6, 71, 76, 202, 208, 230, 239, 242
Toronto Area Transit Authority, 66
Toronto Stock Exchange, 96–9
tourist industry, 157–61
trade, 12, 83, 85–7, 209
'Trade Crusade,' 86, 220–1
trade liberalization, 195
Trades and Labour Congress (TLC), 36
Transair Limited, 69
TransCanada Airlines, 67
TransCanada Highway, 58, 160
TransCanada Pipelines Limited, 75
transportation. See under headings for type of transportation: air transport, rail transport, road transport, water transport.

Index 287

trucking industry. *See* road transport.
Turgeon Royal Commission on Transportation, 58
'22 Points' declaration, 17, 18, 250

Underhill, F., 18
unemployment, 3, 4, 5, 9, 18, 20, 21–2, 33–4, 126, 227, 229, 231, 234, 241, 248
unemployment insurance, 24
Unemployment Insurance Act, 127
Union Gas Limited, 74–5
United Auto Workers, 204
United Co-operatives of Ontario, 139
United States: auto agreement with, 205–7; educational levels, 102; exports to, 10; fuel supplies, 72, 74; imports from, 85–6, 145; influence in forest industries, 187–8; markets for lumber, 188; military programs, 4; nickel-copper and cobalt requirements, 174; and pulp and paper industry, 216–17; television broadcasting, 78–9; trade promotion in, 219; uranium requirements, 169–71
United States Defense Materials Procurement Agency, 174
Universities. *See* education; post-secondary.
uranium, 39, 169–72
urban sprawl, 49
urban transit, 65, 66, 67
Urban Transportation Development Corporation (UTDC), 66–7
urbanization, 243, 252–3
Urquhart, M.C., 124
Urquhart Royal Commission on Mining, 95–6

value added in manufacturing, 196
values: social, 251

vertical integration: forest industries, 185
veterans, 60–1, 107
Viet Nam War, 4, 83
Vocational Training Co-ordination Act (1945), 108

wage and price controls: during Second World War, 4
wages: textile industry, 208
Wartime Housing Limited, 46
water resources, 53
water and sewage systems, 23, 41
water transport, 69–72
welfare, 20, 126–33, 128–9, 132; family allowances, 127; Guaranteed Annual Income Systems (GAINS), 130; Guaranteed Income Supplement, 129; housing benefits, 131–2; old age security, 127–8; prescription drug plans, 132; restructuring of system, 248; spending on, 129–30
welfare state, 127, 244
Wells, D.C., 141–2
White River Air Services Limited, 69
wholesale and retail trade, 86–92
wild rice, 154
Wilson, T.A., 228
Windfall Oils and Mines Limited, 97–8
Winnipeg River, 54
women: in labour force, 31–2; 93
wood-using industries, 213–17
working conditions, 241
World War II. *See* Second World War.
Wright, D.T., 113–14

zinc mining, 177–9

330　　Rea, K. J.
.9713　　The prosperous years
R287

Date